INSPRINT AUTOMATION MASTERY

Elevate Your Agile Testing Game

Partha Sarathi Samal, Suresh Kumar Palus, Behrang Zandi, Sai Kiran Padmam

Made with ❤ on the Notion Press Platform
www.notionpress.com

TABLE OF CONTENTS

Appendix D: References and Further Reading

PREFACE

In the dynamic and fast-paced world of software development, staying ahead of the curve is not just an advantage but a necessity. This book, *"In-Sprint Automation Mastery: Elevate Your Agile Testing Game,"* is designed to equip software professionals—developers, testers, project managers, and Agile practitioners—with the knowledge, strategies, and tools needed to excel in a rapidly evolving industry. By focusing on in-sprint automation, this guide provides a comprehensive approach to mastering Agile testing, enabling teams to achieve both speed and quality without compromise.

Our journey in writing this book has been both challenging and deeply rewarding. Drawing on years of experience, research, and hands-on application, we have distilled our knowledge into a practical guide that offers actionable insights into in-sprint automation. Each chapter is crafted to deliver real-world strategies, complete with tools, frameworks, and examples, allowing readers to integrate these practices directly into their Agile workflows.

WHY WE WROTE THIS BOOK

Our motivation for writing In-Sprint Automation Mastery stems from the shared challenges we have encountered in our respective careers. As the demand for faster delivery cycles and higher software quality continues to grow, in-sprint automation has become a cornerstone for Agile teams. Yet, many organizations struggle to incorporate automation seamlessly within sprints. We aimed to create a resource that addresses these pain points and empowers teams to embrace automation as a core part of their Agile processes.

WHO WILL BENEFIT FROM THIS BOOK

This book is written for a wide audience within the Agile ecosystem, including software testers, automation engineers, developers, project managers, and Agile coaches. Whether you are new to in-sprint automation or looking to refine and deepen your skills, In-Sprint Automation Mastery provides practical guidance that will meet you at your level. Through detailed examples and practical solutions, we aim to help teams and individuals achieve consistent quality and continuous improvement in their Agile workflows.

STRUCTURE OF THE BOOK

We begin with the foundational concepts of Agile testing, outlining the evolution of software testing practices and the critical role that in-sprint automation plays in Agile environments. Each chapter thereafter delves into specific aspects of automation within Agile, covering essential topics like tool selection, UI and API testing, building robust CI/CD pipelines, and continuous feedback mechanisms. Throughout, we address common challenges and offer best practices, illustrated with case studies and real-world scenarios.

- Fundamentals of In-Sprint Automation
- Strategies for Implementing In-Sprint Automation
- UI Automation Testing in Sprints
- API Automation Testing in Sprints
- Continuous Integration and Continuous Deployment in In-Sprint Automation
- Case Studies and Real-World Examples

ACKNOWLEDGMENTS

We owe a debt of gratitude to our colleagues, mentors, friends, and family who have supported and encouraged us throughout the writing of this book. Their insights, feedback, and patience have been invaluable in helping us shape this material. Special thanks to our professional networks, whose challenges and triumphs in implementing Agile practices provided inspiration for many of the concepts covered here.

ABOUT THE AUTHORS

In-Sprint Automation Mastery is the product of a collaborative effort by a diverse team of professionals, each of whom brings unique expertise and experience to the table:

- **Partha Sarathi Samal**, *Author, Quality Engineering Manager Paramount*
- **Suresh Kumar Palus**, *Co-Author Automation Lead Paramount*
- **Behrang Zandi**, *Co-Author Sr Quality Engineer Paramount*
- **Sai Kiran Padmam**, *Co-Author Sr DevOps Engineer Paramount*

Together, we have navigated the complexities of Agile, automation, and software testing across a variety of industries and settings. Our shared goal with this book is to make in-sprint automation accessible, actionable, and impactful for Agile teams everywhere.

A JOURNEY OF CONTINUOUS LEARNING

In-sprint automation is an evolving discipline, shaped by technological advancements and the changing demands of software development. We hope this book serves as a valuable resource, one that you can return to as you continue to refine your skills and adapt to new challenges. Agile and automation are both journeys of continuous improvement, and we invite you to join us in pushing the boundaries of what's possible in software testing.

Thank you for embarking on this journey with us. We hope that *In-Sprint Automation Mastery* not only equips you with the skills to succeed but also inspires you to innovate and elevate your Agile testing game.

Sincerely,

Partha Sarathi Samal

Suresh Kumar Palus

Behrang Zandi

Sai Kiran Padmam

INSPIRATION FOR THE BOOK

Of passion for quality, our journey took flight,
From days filled with code to late hours of night.

Each bug and each fix, a story to tell,
The triumphs and trials we all know so well.

Through hackathons fueled by innovation's spark,
Where ideas soared and goals found their mark.

Our mentors and leaders, our friends by our side,
Guided each chapter with knowledge and pride.

In teamwork's embrace, our skills grew strong,
In moments of struggle, where we all belong.

Each conversation, defect, and each test,
Wove threads of wisdom we're eager to attest.

From laughter and learning, from joy and strain,
We crafted this book through growth and through pain.

A tribute, a guide, to share what we know,
A nugget of wisdom in each word we show.

So may you, the reader, see between these lines,
A legacy that's born of ambitious designs.

A guide to who seeks and to those who strive
for growing together, and truly thrive.

To all those who read, may you carry on,
With purpose and passion, from dusk until dawn.

Inspired by the journey we've taken here,
To build and to share and to, persevere.

And when you close this book, may you truly find,
Your quality champion, awaken, in mind.

A beacon to lead, to innovate, to grow,
To pass it forward, and always to know.

This book is a tribute to those who dared,
Who built with heart, who endlessly cared.

Inspired by teamwork, the highs and the low,
A love letter to learning, may it eternally glow.

To grow with each challenge, to cherish each friend,
A spirit of quality, from beginning to end.

So may these words live, as a guide and a spark,
For those seeking wisdom, for those who embark.

May it inspire, as it inspired us,
With gratitude deep, and dreams robust.

INTRODUCTION TO THE BOOK

"In-Sprint Automation Mastery: Elevate Your Agile Testing Game" offers an in-depth exploration of in-sprint automation within the context of Agile methodologies. This book goes beyond theory, providing practical guidance through real-world examples, case studies, and step-by-step instructions. We cover various topics, from the fundamentals of Agile testing and the principles of Test-Driven Development (TDD) and Behavior-Driven Development (BDD), to advanced strategies for UI, API, and mobile automation.

Each chapter builds upon the previous one, ensuring a comprehensive learning experience. Whether you're new to Agile testing or an experienced professional looking to enhance your skills, this book offers something valuable. We delve into the details of integrating testing tools with CI/CD pipelines, managing test environments, and overcoming common challenges in in-sprint automation. By the end of this book, you'll have a solid understanding of how to implement and manage effective in-sprint automation practices in your projects. This book is meticulously structured to cater to both beginners and experienced professionals. We begin with foundational concepts, gradually moving towards advanced topics, ensuring that readers build a strong understanding before diving into complex strategies. Each chapter ends with a summary and practical exercises to reinforce learning.

The book is rich with real-world examples and case studies. These examples are drawn from various industries, illustrating how in-sprint automation can be effectively implemented in different contexts. By providing these examples, we aim to bridge the gap between theory and practice, showing readers how to apply the concepts in their own projects.

In addition to the textual content, we provide access to online resources, including sample test scripts, templates, and video tutorials. These resources are designed to complement the book and provide hands-on experience with the tools and techniques discussed.

A recurring theme in this book is the importance of continuous improvement. In-sprint automation is not a one-time effort but an ongoing process that evolves with the project. We provide strategies for monitoring and refining automation practices to ensure they remain effective and aligned with project goals.

We emphasize the importance of collaboration between different roles in a software project. From developers to testers to operations teams, everyone plays a crucial role in in-sprint automation. The book provides practical advice on fostering a collaborative culture and leveraging the strengths of each team member.

By the end of this book, readers will have a comprehensive understanding of in-sprint automation and the confidence to implement these practices in their own projects. Whether you are looking to improve your testing processes, enhance team collaboration, or deliver higher quality software faster, this book is your guide to achieving those goals.

Why is In-Sprint Automation Critical?

In-sprint automation is a crucial aspect of modern software development for several reasons:

1. **Speed and Efficiency**: In today's fast-paced development environments, delivering high-quality software quickly is essential. In-sprint automation enables teams to run tests continuously, providing immediate feedback and allowing for faster iterations. This rapid feedback loop is critical in Agile environments where changes are frequent, and time-to-market is short.

2. **Quality and Reliability**: Automated tests help identify bugs and issues early in the development cycle, reducing the risk of defects reaching production. This leads to more reliable and stable software releases. By catching defects early, teams can address them before they become more complex and costly to fix.

3. **Cost-Effectiveness**: By catching defects early and reducing the need for extensive manual testing, in-sprint automation can significantly lower the overall cost of development. Automated tests can be run repeatedly at no additional cost, ensuring that any changes made to the codebase do not introduce new defects.

4. **Team Collaboration**: In-sprint automation fosters a culture of collaboration between developers, testers, and operations teams. It aligns with Agile principles, promoting shared responsibility for quality and encouraging continuous improvement. This collaborative approach ensures that all team members are always aware of the quality and health of the project.

5. **Scalability**: As projects grow in complexity, maintaining high-quality standards becomes more challenging. In-sprint automation provides a scalable solution, ensuring that testing processes can keep pace with development. Automated tests can be easily scaled to cover new features and functionalities as the project evolves.

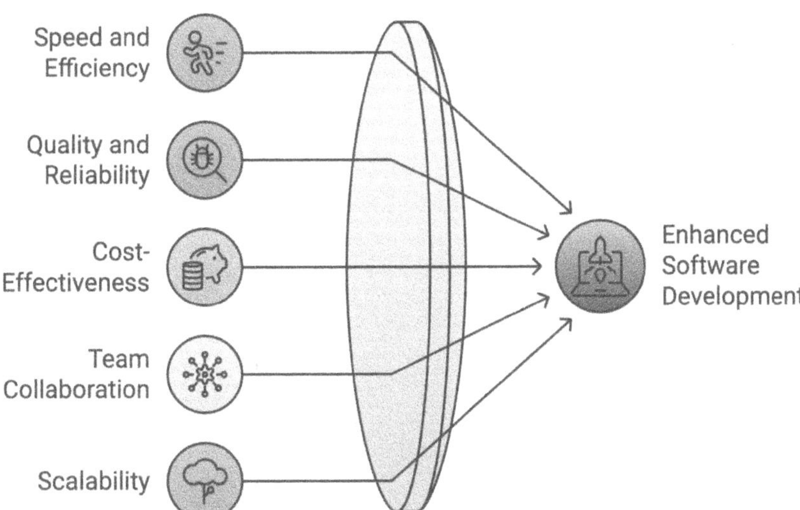

This book emphasizes the importance of in-sprint automation and provides practical guidance on how to implement it effectively, ensuring that your team can deliver high-quality software quickly and efficiently.

The Evolution of Software Testing

Software testing has come a long way since its inception. In the early days, testing was often a separate phase that occurred after development was complete. This waterfall approach had significant drawbacks, including late discovery of defects, extended project timelines, and high costs associated with fixing bugs late in the process.

The advent of Agile methodologies revolutionized software testing by integrating it into the development process. Agile testing emphasizes continuous testing, collaboration, and feedback, allowing teams to identify and address issues early. The principles of TDD and BDD further enhanced this approach, promoting the development of testable code and fostering better communication between stakeholders.

The introduction of automation tools and frameworks has been a game-changer, enabling teams to automate repetitive tasks and focus on more complex testing scenarios. Modern automation tools support a wide range of testing activities, from unit and integration tests to performance and security testing.

As we move into the era of DevOps and continuous delivery, the role of automation in software testing continues to grow. In-sprint automation, with its emphasis on immediate feedback and integration with CI/CD pipelines, represents the next step in this evolution. It ensures that testing keeps pace with development, enabling teams to deliver high-quality software faster and more efficiently.

In this book, we explore the journey of software testing from its early days to the current state of in-sprint automation. We highlight the key milestones and innovations that have shaped the industry, providing context for the strategies and techniques discussed in the subsequent chapters. By understanding the evolution of software testing, readers will appreciate the significance of in-sprint automation and be better equipped to implement it in their projects.

The transition from waterfall to Agile methodologies marked a significant shift in software development. We discuss the limitations of the waterfall model, such as delayed feedback and high costs of late defect detection, and how Agile methodologies addressed these challenges by promoting iterative development, continuous testing, and early feedback.

Automation has played a pivotal role in the evolution of software testing. Initially, automation efforts focused on reducing the manual effort required for repetitive tasks. As tools and frameworks evolved, automation expanded to cover a wide range of testing activities, including unit tests, integration tests, performance tests, and security tests. This chapter delves into the history of automation tools, highlighting key innovations and their impact on testing practices.

The advent of DevOps has further transformed software testing. DevOps emphasizes the integration of development and operations teams, fostering a culture of collaboration and shared responsibility for quality. We explore how automation fits into the DevOps pipeline, enabling continuous integration, continuous delivery, and continuous testing. By integrating automation with CI/CD pipelines, teams can achieve faster feedback, higher quality, and more reliable software releases.

In-sprint automation represents the latest advancement in the evolution of software testing. By integrating testing activities within the development sprint, teams can achieve immediate feedback and ensure that testing keeps pace with development. We discuss the principles of in-sprint automation, its benefits, and how it differs from traditional testing approaches. This chapter sets the stage for the detailed strategies and techniques discussed in the subsequent chapters.

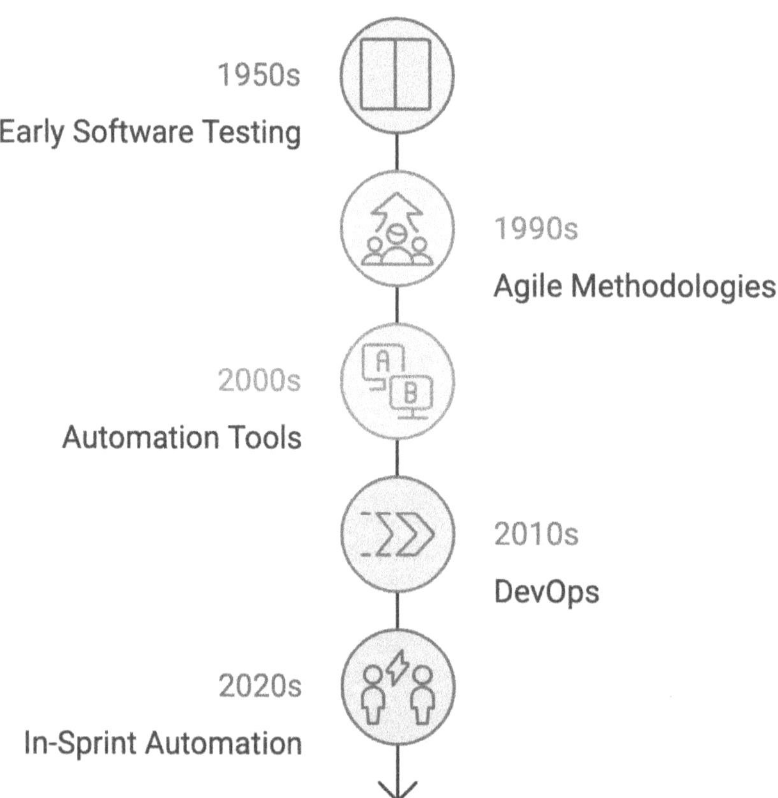

In a Nutshell

The journey of software testing has been marked by continuous innovation and improvement. From the early days of manual testing to the latest advancements in in-sprint automation, the field has evolved to meet the changing needs of software development. By understanding this evolution, readers will appreciate the significance of in-sprint automation and be better equipped to implement these practices in their projects.

This book aims to provide a comprehensive guide to mastering in-sprint automation, making it an invaluable resource for developers, testers, and Agile practitioners. By focusing on practical strategies, real-world examples, and interactive content, we hope to empower readers to achieve excellence in their software projects.

Whether you are new to Agile testing or an experienced professional looking to enhance your skills, **"In-Sprint Automation Mastery: Elevate Your Agile Testing Game"** is your guide to achieving success in the ever-evolving world of software development. We invite you to join us on this journey and explore the transformative potential of in-sprint

## CHAPTER 1

INTRODUCTION TO AGILE TESTING

In today's fast-paced software development landscape, Agile testing has become a cornerstone for delivering high-quality software that meets user needs quickly and efficiently. Unlike traditional testing approaches that often occur after the development phase, Agile testing is integrated throughout the development cycle, ensuring continuous feedback and improvement. This approach not only enhances the quality of the final product but also promotes collaboration, adaptability, and customer satisfaction.

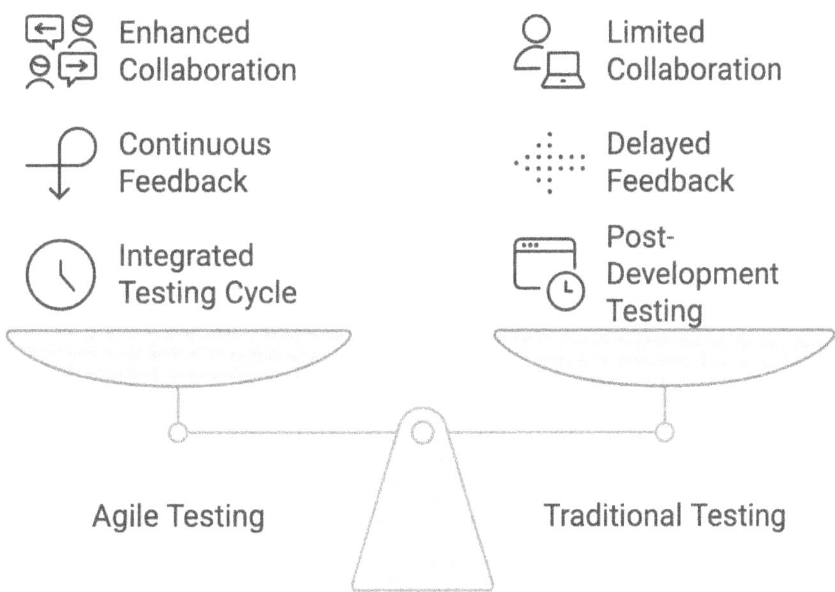

Agile testing vs. traditional testing tradeoffs.

OVERVIEW OF AGILE METHODOLOGIES

Agile methodologies represent a shift from traditional, rigid development processes to a more flexible, collaborative, and iterative approach. These methodologies are built on a foundation of principles and practices that focus on delivering value to customers quickly and efficiently, while maintaining the ability to adapt to changes in requirements or market conditions.

The core idea behind Agile is to break down the development process into smaller, manageable pieces, known as iterations or sprints, allowing for continuous delivery of software that can be tested and reviewed throughout the development cycle. This approach contrasts with traditional methods like Waterfall, where all development is completed before testing begins, often leading to delays and missed deadlines.

Key Principles of Agile

Let's delve into the key principles that define Agile methodologies:

1. *Customer Collaboration Over Contract Negotiation*

In traditional software development models, the relationship between the customer and the development team is often governed by a detailed contract that specifies every aspect of the project. This contract can sometimes lead to conflicts when changes are needed, as the team may be bound by the original terms.

In Agile, the focus shifts from strict adherence to contracts to ongoing collaboration with the customer. This means that instead of rigidly following a predefined plan, the development team works closely with the customer throughout the project, ensuring that their needs and expectations are continually met.

Example:

Imagine you're developing an e-commerce website for a client. In a traditional model, the requirements would be locked down at the beginning, and any changes would require contract amendments. In Agile, however, you might release a basic shopping cart feature early and get feedback from the client. If the client realizes they need a different payment gateway, the team can adapt quickly, ensuring that the final product better meets the client's needs.

2. *Responding to Change Over Following a Plan*

One of the most significant advantages of Agile methodologies is the emphasis on flexibility. In traditional approaches, changes in project requirements can be difficult and costly to implement, often leading to project delays. Agile methodologies embrace change, allowing teams to respond swiftly to new information or shifting market demands.

Agile teams work in short iterations, typically two to four weeks long, and reassess priorities at the end of each iteration. This means they can pivot or adjust their focus as needed, ensuring the final product is relevant and valuable.

Example:

Consider a startup developing a mobile app. Midway through development, the team learns that a competitor has launched a similar app. With Agile, the team can quickly shift focus to unique features that differentiate their app, such as integrating with a popular social media platform, without derailing the entire project.

3. *Working Software Over Comprehensive Documentation*

Traditional software development often involves extensive documentation that outlines every detail of the system being built. While documentation is important, it can sometimes become a burden, especially if it takes precedence over actual development work.

Agile methodologies prioritize working software over comprehensive documentation. This doesn't mean documentation is ignored, but rather that the primary measure of progress is the delivery of functional software. Agile teams create just enough documentation to support the software's development and use, but they focus more on delivering features that work.

Example:

In a traditional project, the team might spend weeks creating detailed design documents before any coding begins. In an Agile project, the team might start coding the core functionality right away, delivering a prototype that the client can interact with. Documentation is created as needed, but the focus is always on delivering something tangible and functional.

4. *Individuals and Interactions Over Processes and Tools*

Agile places a strong emphasis on the people involved in the project and how they interact with each other. While processes and tools are still important, they are considered secondary to the effectiveness of the team's communication and collaboration.

Agile teams are often cross-functional, meaning they include members with different skills and expertise. This setup encourages open communication and allows for quick decision-making, as team members can collaborate directly rather than relying on formal processes.

Example:

In a traditional setting, a tester might have to wait for a developer to finish their work before testing can begin, often leading to delays. In an Agile team, the tester works closely with the developer throughout the iteration, identifying potential issues early and ensuring a smoother development process.

KEY CHALLENGES: BALANCING FLEXIBILITY WITH CONSISTENT DELIVERY

While Agile's flexibility is one of its greatest strengths, it also presents significant challenges, particularly in balancing the need for adaptability with the requirement to deliver consistently. Agile teams must be able to pivot in response to changing customer needs or market conditions without compromising the quality or timeline of their deliverables. However, this flexibility can sometimes lead to issues such as scope creep, where the project's scope expands beyond the original plan, or inconsistent delivery schedules, where teams struggle to meet deadlines due to frequent changes.

1. Challenge: Scope Creep

Scope creep occurs when new features, functions, or requirements are added to a project without corresponding increases in time, resources, or budget. In an Agile environment, where change is expected and welcomed, it can be easy for teams to overextend themselves by continually adding to the scope of work within a sprint or iteration. This can lead to incomplete or poorly executed features, increased pressure on the team, and ultimately, a product that doesn't meet its original goals.

Example:

Imagine a team working on a new feature for an e-commerce platform. Initially, the team plans to implement a basic product filtering system. However, as the sprint progresses, stakeholders request additional filter options, a complex search algorithm, and integration with third-party data sources. Without proper management, these requests can balloon the scope of the sprint, leading to delays and incomplete features.

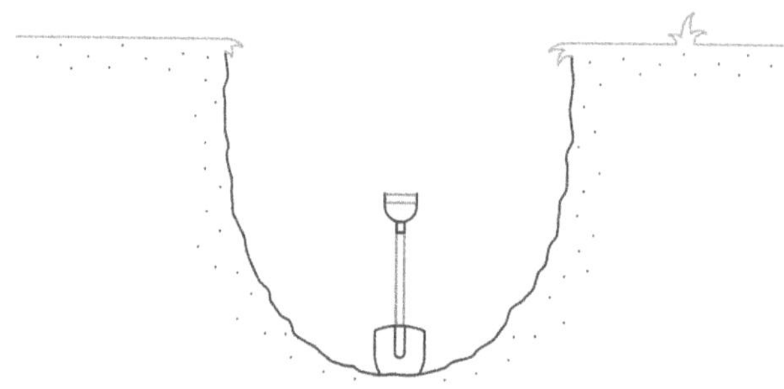

2. Challenge: Inconsistent Delivery

Agile teams are expected to deliver working software at the end of each sprint. However, the flexibility to accommodate changes can sometimes disrupt the team's ability to consistently deliver high-quality increments on time. Frequent changes to requirements or priorities can lead to rework, bottlenecks, and stress on the team, making it difficult to maintain a steady pace of delivery.

Example:

A team working on a mobile application might have a sprint planned to deliver a new user interface (UI) component. Midway through the sprint, a critical bug is discovered in a different part of the application, requiring immediate attention. The team shifts focus to fix the bug, but this disrupts the work on the UI component, leading to delays in its delivery.

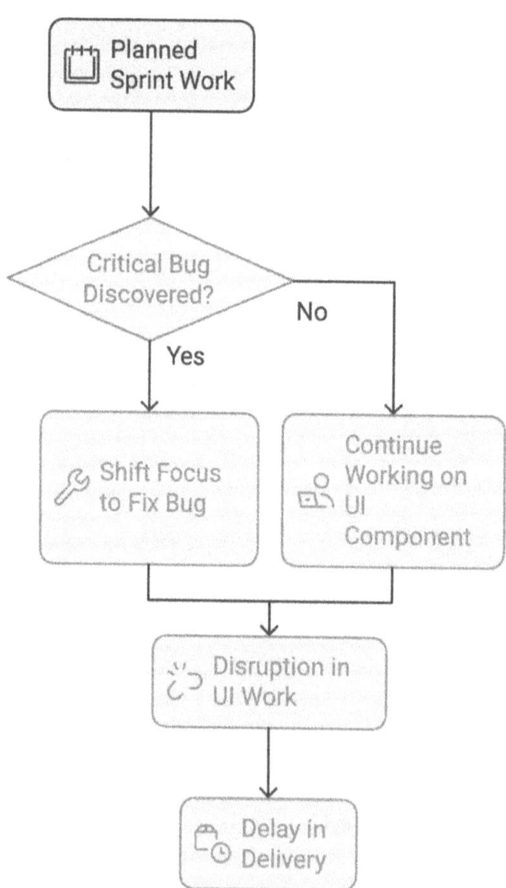

SOLUTIONS: IMPLEMENTING BEST PRACTICES FOR TEAM COMMUNICATION AND INCREMENTAL DELIVERY

To overcome these challenges, Agile teams must adopt best practices that promote effective communication and ensure incremental, consistent delivery of work. These practices help teams stay focused on their goals while remaining flexible enough to adapt to changes without sacrificing quality or delivery timelines.

1. Establish Clear Communication Channels

Effective communication is crucial in Agile teams, as it ensures that everyone is aligned and aware of changes as they occur. Regular, structured communication helps prevent misunderstandings and ensures that the team can adapt quickly to new information without disrupting their workflow.

Best Practices

- **Daily Stand-ups:** Conduct short, focused daily stand-up meetings where team members discuss what they accomplished yesterday, what they plan to do today, and any obstacles they face. This ensures everyone is on the same page and can address issues promptly.
- **Backlog Grooming:** Regularly review and refine the product backlog to ensure that the most critical tasks are prioritized and well understood by the team. This reduces the likelihood of scope creep by ensuring that new requests are properly vetted and incorporated into future sprints if necessary.
- **Clear Documentation:** While Agile emphasizes working software over comprehensive documentation, maintaining clear and concise documentation of requirements, decisions, and changes is essential. This helps ensure that all team members and stakeholders have a shared understanding of the project's direction.

Example:

A team using Scrum holds daily stand-ups to discuss progress and any changes in priorities. If a stakeholder requests a new feature mid-sprint, the team discusses it in the stand-up, assesses its impact, and decides whether to incorporate it immediately or add it to the backlog for a future sprint.

2. Implement Incremental Delivery with Focus on MVP

To maintain consistency in delivery while accommodating changes, Agile teams should focus on delivering **Minimum Viable Products (MVPs)** or small, functional increments of the product that provide value to the customer. By delivering these small increments regularly, teams can gather feedback, adapt to changes, and continue to deliver value without overcommitting.

Best Practices

- **Focus on MVP:** Prioritize delivering the simplest, functional version of a feature that provides value. This allows the team to gather feedback early and iterate based on real-world usage.
- **Time-Boxing:** Stick to the time-boxed nature of sprints or iterations. Even if a feature isn't fully complete, deliver what is done and gather feedback. This keeps the momentum going and ensures that the team is consistently delivering increments of value.
- **Retrospectives:** After each sprint, hold a retrospective meeting to reflect on what went well, what didn't, and how the team can improve. This continuous improvement process helps the team refine their approach to balancing flexibility and consistent delivery.

Example:

In a sprint focused on developing a new payment gateway for an e-commerce site, the team might first deliver an MVP that handles basic transactions. In the next sprint, they could build upon this by adding additional features like multi-currency support and fraud detection. This incremental approach ensures that the team delivers working software regularly while iterating and improving based on feedback.

Delivering Value through Incremental Improvement

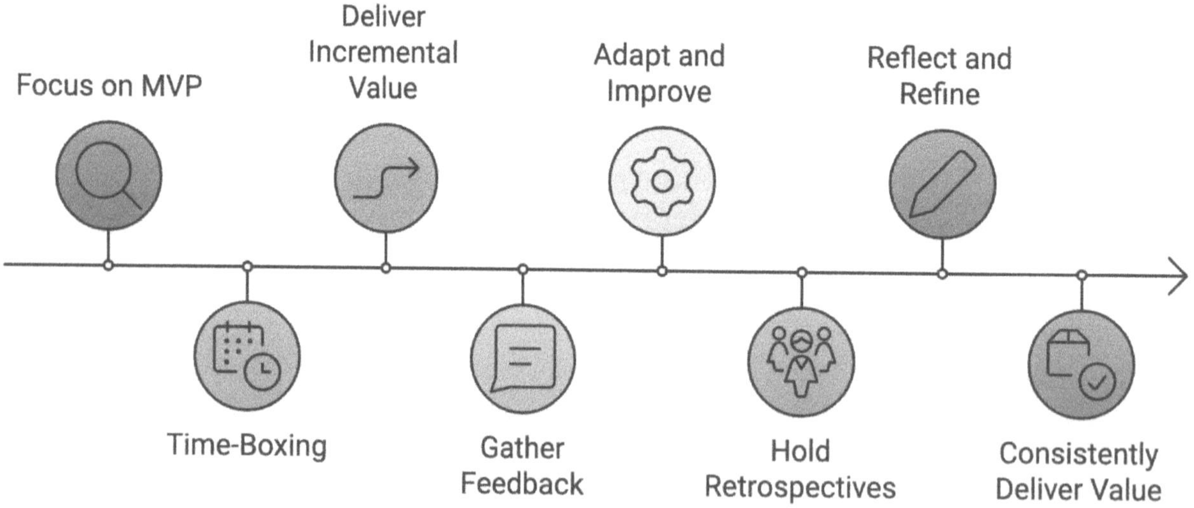

AGILE FRAMEWORKS: SCRUM, KANBAN, AND EXTREME PROGRAMMING (XP)

Agile methodologies encompass a variety of frameworks, each with its approach to implementing Agile principles. The most common ones are Scrum, Kanban, and Extreme Programming (XP). While each has its unique practices, they all share the Agile emphasis on collaboration, flexibility, and iterative development.

1. Scrum

Scrum is one of the most widely used Agile frameworks. It structures work into fixed-length iterations called sprints, usually lasting between two and four weeks. Each sprint begins with a planning meeting, where the team selects the work to be completed during the sprint. Daily stand-up meetings help keep the team on track, and at the end of the sprint, the team holds a review to demonstrate the completed work and a retrospective to reflect on what could be improved.

Example:
A development team working on a new feature for a social media platform might use Scrum to manage their work. They would break the feature down into smaller tasks, select a few of these tasks to complete in the next two-week sprint, and then focus exclusively on those tasks until the sprint ends. After each sprint, they review their progress with the product owner and adjust their approach based on feedback.

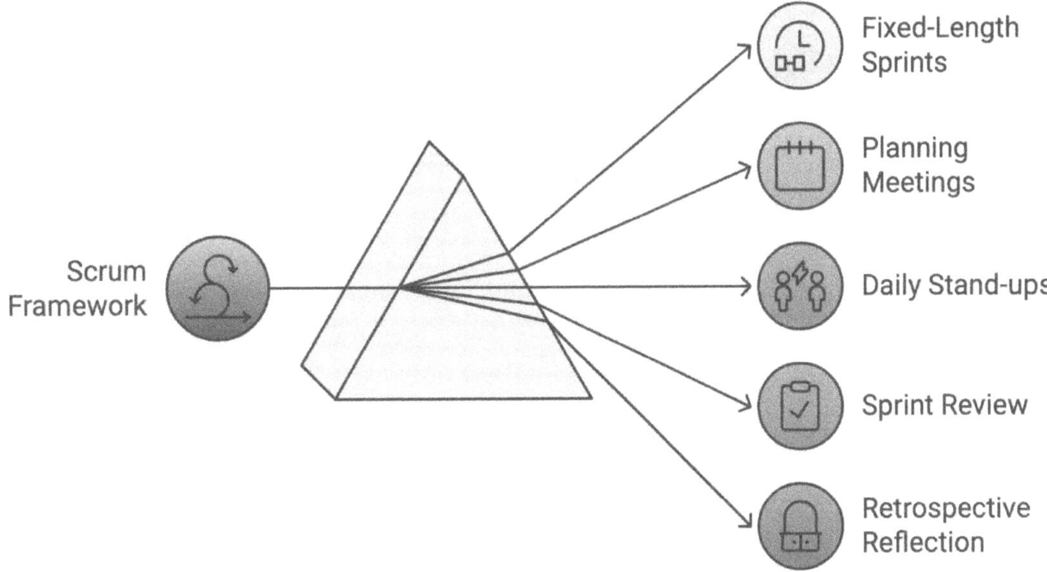

2. Kanban

Kanban focuses on visualizing the workflow and improving the flow of tasks through that workflow. Instead of fixed-length sprints, Kanban allows for continuous delivery, where tasks are completed as they are ready. A Kanban board is typically used to track the progress of tasks, with columns representing different stages of the process (e.g., "To Do," "In Progress," "Done").

Example:
A team responsible for maintaining an existing web application might use Kanban to manage their tasks. New bug reports and feature requests are added to the "To Do" column, and team members pull tasks from this column as they can work on them. This approach ensures that high-priority items are addressed quickly, without the need for planning meetings or fixed sprint durations.

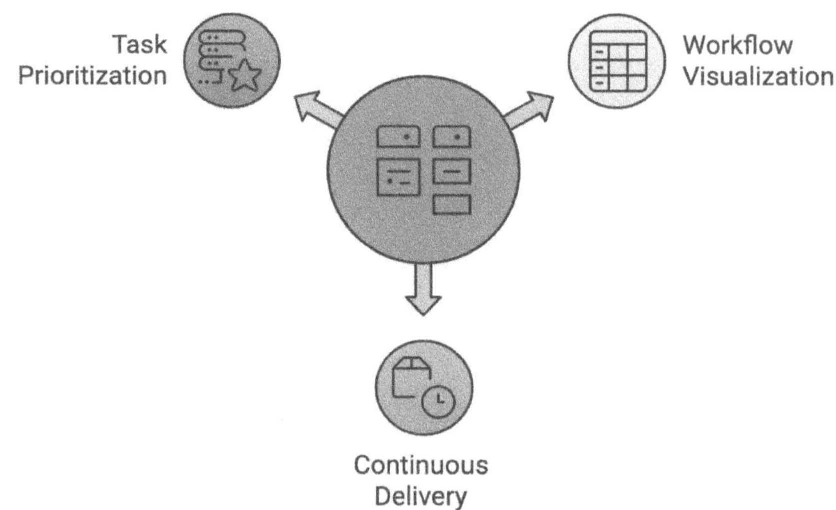

3.   Extreme Programming (XP)

Extreme Programming (XP) is an Agile framework that takes certain Agile practices to their logical extremes. It emphasizes technical excellence through practices like pair programming, test-driven development (TDD), and continuous integration. XP aims to improve software quality and responsiveness to changing customer requirements.

Example:

In an XP team, two developers might work together on a single piece of code, one writing the code while the other reviews each line as it's written (pair programming). They also write tests for their code before writing the code itself (TDD), ensuring that each piece of functionality works as expected before moving on to the next. This rigorous approach helps catch bugs early and ensures that the software remains robust and adaptable to changes.

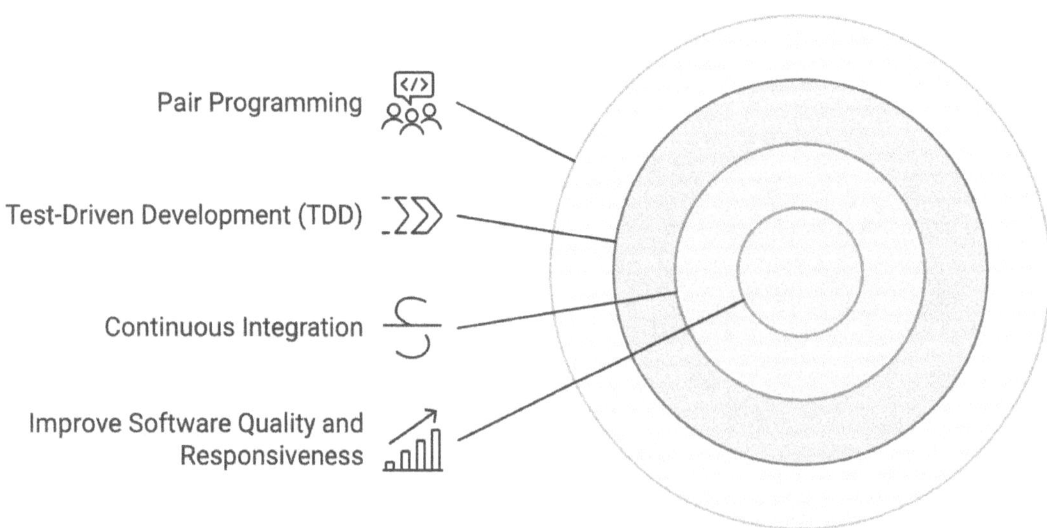

INTRODUCTION TO SAFE (SCALED AGILE FRAMEWORK)

As Agile methodologies have proven successful in small and medium-sized teams, larger organizations with more complex needs have sought ways to scale Agile across multiple teams and departments. The **Scaled Agile Framework (SAFe)** was developed to address this challenge. SAFe provides a structured and systematic approach for applying Agile principles across large enterprises, allowing multiple teams to work in harmony while delivering high-quality products that align with the organization's strategic goals.

Understanding the Need for SAFe

In small Agile teams, managing workflows, communication, and alignment with business objectives is relatively straightforward. However, as organizations grow, with multiple teams working on interconnected parts of a large system, the complexity increases. Without a coordinated approach, teams might develop solutions that don't align with the broader business strategy, leading to inefficiencies and missed opportunities.

SAFe solves this problem by introducing a framework that scales Agile practices across teams, programs, and entire portfolios. It aligns the efforts of all teams with the organization's strategic objectives, ensuring that every piece of work contributes to the broader goals.

Key Components of SAFe

SAFe is structured into four levels, each serving a distinct purpose within the framework. Understanding these levels is crucial to grasping how SAFe enables large organizations to function efficiently while adhering to Agile principles.

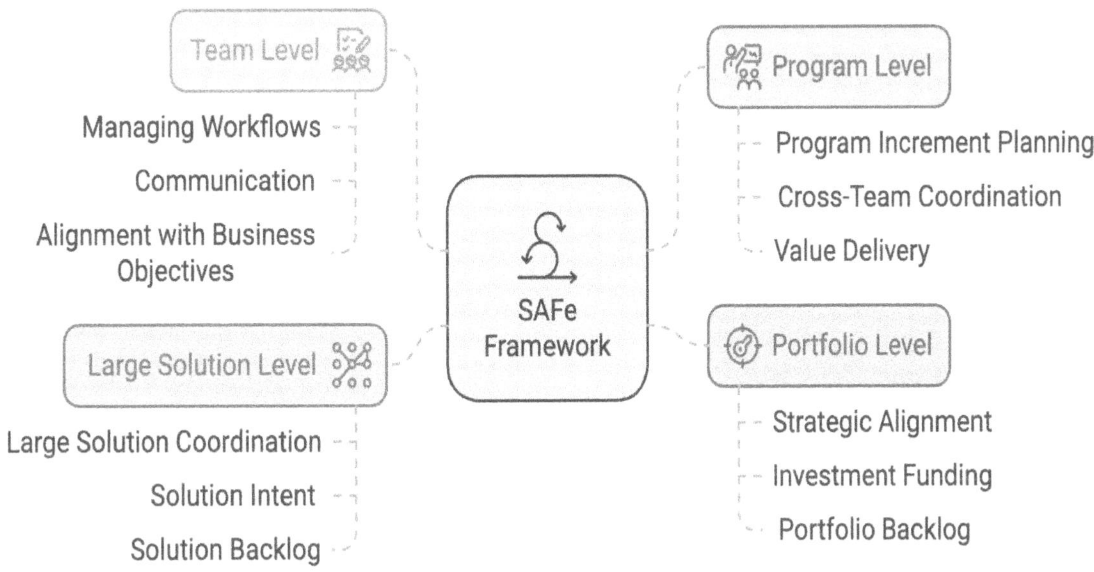

1. *Team Level*

At the **Team Level**, individual Agile teams operate similarly to traditional Agile teams, using frameworks like Scrum or Kanban. These teams are responsible for delivering small, manageable increments of work within a short time frame, typically within 2-week to 4-week sprints.

Each team is cross-functional, meaning it includes all the necessary roles (e.g., developers, testers, product owners) to deliver a complete, working piece of software. The team works on specific features or components of a larger system, with a focus on continuous delivery and improvement.

Example:

Imagine a software company that's developing a new banking app. At the Team Level, one Agile team might be responsible for building the login functionality. They would work in sprints to design, develop, test, and refine the login feature, using daily stand-ups, sprint reviews, and retrospectives to manage their progress.

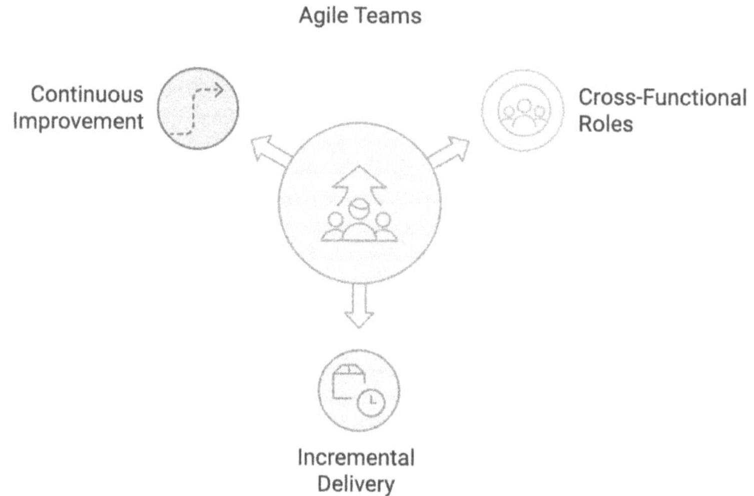

2. *Program Level*

The **Program Level** in SAFe coordinates multiple Agile teams that work together to deliver a larger, integrated product or solution. This level introduces the concept of the **Agile Release Train (ART)**, which is a long-lived team of Agile teams working together on a common mission.

Each ART typically consists of 5 to 12 Agile teams (each at the Team Level), and they operate on a synchronized cadence—usually in Program Increments (PIs) that last about 8 to 12 weeks. The Program Level ensures that all teams are aligned to a shared vision, and their outputs are integrated into a cohesive product.

Example:

Continuing with the banking app example, at the Program Level, the login team, along with teams working on account management, transaction processing, and customer support features, would all be part of the same Agile Release Train. These teams would work in parallel, but their work would be synchronized to ensure that at the end of each Program Increment, the app has all its parts integrated and functioning together.

3. Portfolio Level

At the **Portfolio Level**, SAFe connects the work being done at the Team and Program levels to the organization's broader business strategy. This level manages the portfolio of projects and initiatives that are critical to achieving the organization's strategic goals.

The Portfolio Level is where **Lean Portfolio Management (LPM)** practices come into play. LPM ensures that the organization's resources are allocated efficiently across various programs and initiatives, aligning them with the overall business objectives. This level also includes **Epic Owners** who manage significant business initiatives, known as epics, ensuring that they align with strategic themes and receive the necessary attention and resources.

Example:

For the banking app, the Portfolio Level would involve the senior management and executives who determine the strategic priorities, such as increasing user engagement or enhancing security features. They would oversee the various Agile Release Trains and ensure that the development work aligns with these high-level business goals.

4. Large Solution Level

The **Large Solution Level** in SAFe is specifically designed for very complex systems that require coordination across multiple Agile Release Trains. This level is necessary when the solution being developed is so large and intricate that it involves many teams working together across different programs and ARTs.

At this level, SAFe introduces additional roles and artifacts to manage the complexity, such as Solution Architects, who design and guide the overall architecture, and Solution Management, who ensures that the solution meets the needs of the end-users and stakeholders.

Example:

If the banking app is part of a larger system that also includes desktop applications, backend services, and third-party integrations, the Large Solution Level would manage the coordination across all these components. The focus here is on ensuring that the entire ecosystem works seamlessly together, even though different parts may be developed by different teams or vendors.

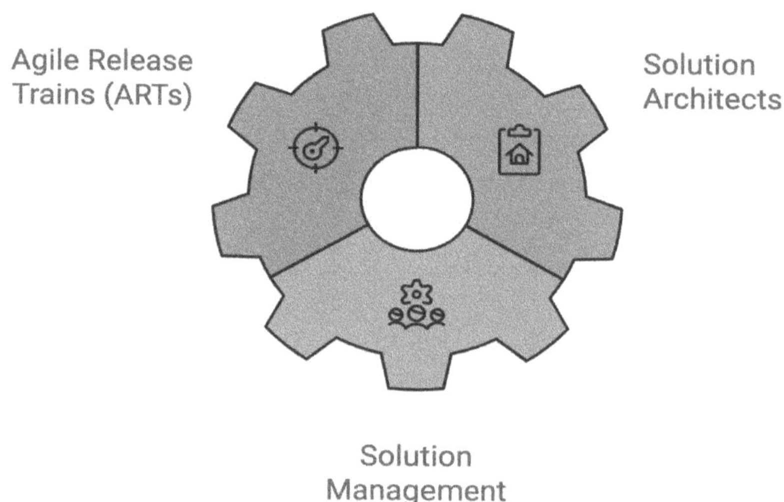

HOW SAFE SUPPORTS LARGE ORGANIZATIONS

SAFe is specifically designed to support large organizations by providing a framework that scales Agile practices without sacrificing the principles that make Agile effective. By dividing work into manageable levels—Team, Program, Portfolio, and Large Solution—SAFe ensures that everyone in the organization, from developers to executives, is aligned and working towards the same goals.

SAFe also emphasizes the importance of leadership in creating a culture of continuous improvement. It encourages organizations to adopt Lean-Agile principles at all levels, fostering a mindset that prioritizes delivering value, improving quality, and responding quickly to change.

Key Challenges: Scaling Agile Across Multiple Teams Without Losing Efficiency

Scaling Agile across multiple teams within a large organization presents several significant challenges. While individual teams might function effectively using frameworks like Scrum or Kanban, coordinating the efforts of multiple teams working on interrelated projects can lead to inefficiencies, communication breakdowns, and misalignment with business goals. Here are some of the key challenges:

1. *Challenge: Maintaining Alignment Across Teams*

In large organizations, different teams often work on various aspects of a complex product or system. Without a unified framework, these teams might drift out of sync, leading to inconsistencies, duplicated efforts, and features that do not integrate well. Maintaining alignment between teams is critical to ensure that all components of the product work together seamlessly and that the teams' efforts contribute to the overall business objectives.

Example:

Imagine an enterprise software company with multiple teams working on different modules of a customer relationship management (CRM) system. One team might be developing the sales module, while another works on the customer support module. Without proper alignment, these teams might develop features that are inconsistent in terms of user experience or data handling, leading to integration challenges and a disjointed final product.

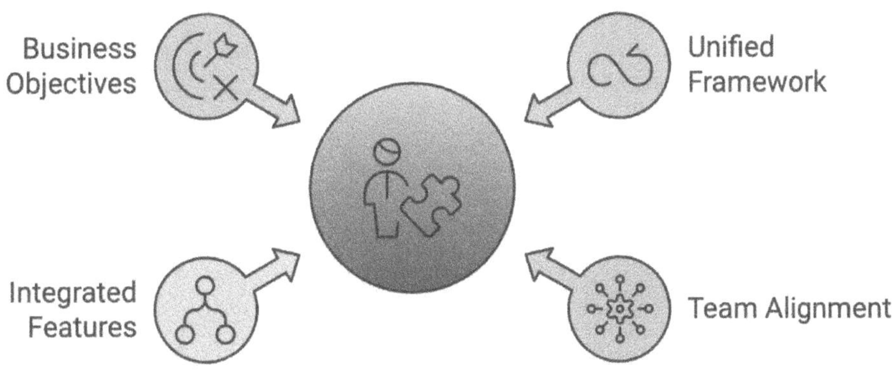

2. *Challenge: Coordinating Dependencies Between Teams*

As multiple Agile teams work concurrently on different parts of a product, dependencies between these teams can become a significant bottleneck. For example, one team might rely on the completion of a specific API by another team before they can proceed with their own work. Managing these dependencies without causing delays or reducing productivity is a major challenge in scaling Agile.

Example:

In the same CRM system example, the team working on the sales module might need an API developed by the customer support team to access customer data. If the API is delayed, the sales team's progress is stalled, potentially pushing back their delivery timelines and causing a ripple effect on the overall project schedule.

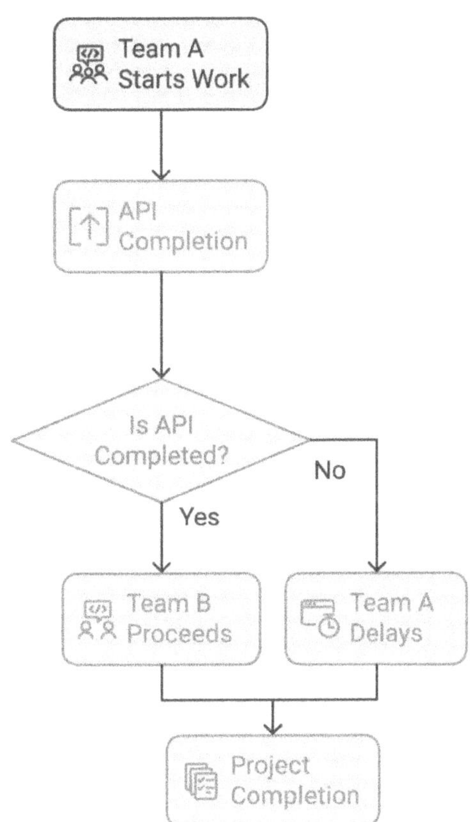

3.   *Challenge: Balancing Local Autonomy with Centralized Control*

Agile promotes autonomy and self-organization within teams, which is crucial for maintaining speed and flexibility. However, as organizations scale, there is a need for some level of centralized control to ensure that teams are aligned with the broader business strategy. Balancing this autonomy with the necessary oversight and coordination is a delicate task.

Example:

If each Agile team in a large organization has complete autonomy over their work, they might make decisions that optimize for their local objectives but are suboptimal for the overall business. For instance, a team might choose a specific technology stack that works best for their module but creates integration challenges when other teams are using different technologies. Centralized guidelines and coordination are needed to avoid such conflicts.

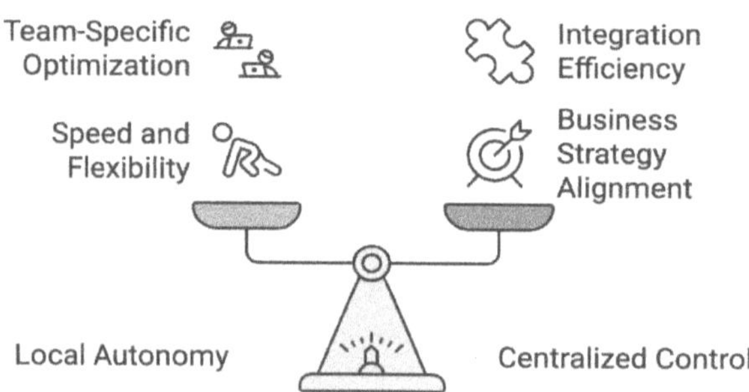

Balancing autonomy and control in Agile teams.

Solutions: Utilizing SAFe's Structured Approach and Regular Synchronization

SAFe provides a structured framework that addresses these challenges by offering a clear, scalable approach to implementing Agile practices across large organizations. Here's how SAFe helps overcome the key challenges of scaling Agile:

1.   *Establishing a Clear Hierarchy with Defined Roles and Responsibilities*

SAFe's structure is designed to maintain alignment and coordination across all levels of the organization. By defining clear roles and responsibilities at each level—Team, Program, Portfolio, and Large Solution—SAFe ensures that everyone understands their part in the broader context of the organization's goals.

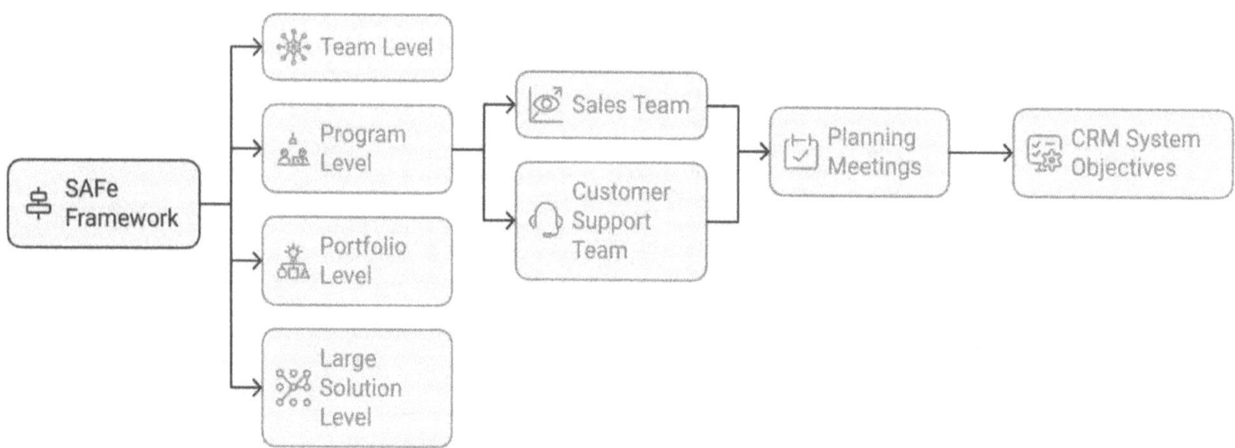

- **Team Level:** Individual Agile teams function similarly to how they would in Scrum or Kanban, focusing on delivering small, functional increments of work. However, they operate within a larger context where their work is aligned with the goals set at higher levels.
- **Program Level:** At this level, multiple teams working on related features or components are grouped into an Agile Release Train (ART). The ART provides a structure for aligning these teams towards a shared vision and managing dependencies between them.
- **Portfolio Level:** This level connects the work of the Agile Release Trains to the organization's strategic objectives, ensuring that the work being done aligns with business goals. Lean Portfolio Management practices are used to prioritize and fund work at this level, balancing local team autonomy with centralized oversight.
- **Large Solution Level:** For very complex products or systems, the Large Solution Level helps coordinate multiple Agile Release Trains, ensuring that all parts of the solution work together seamlessly.

Example:
In the CRM system scenario, the sales and customer support teams would be part of the same Agile Release Train at the Program Level. They would have regular planning and synchronization meetings to ensure that their work aligns and dependencies are managed. At the Portfolio Level, the broader objectives for the CRM system are set, ensuring that all teams contribute towards a cohesive, integrated product.

2. *Regular Synchronization and Cadence*

SAFe promotes regular synchronization and cadence through events such as Program Increment (PI) Planning, Iteration Planning, and System Demos. These events help ensure that all teams are aligned, dependencies are identified and managed, and progress is tracked regularly.

- **Program Increment (PI) Planning:** This event occurs at the start of each PI, typically every 8 to 12 weeks. During PI Planning, all teams in the Agile Release Train come together to plan their work for the next increment. This ensures that all teams are aligned, their dependencies are managed, and they have a shared understanding of the goals for the PI.
- **Iteration Planning:** Similar to sprint planning in Scrum, Iteration Planning happens at the start of each iteration (usually every 2 weeks) within the PI. Teams plan their work for the iteration, ensuring that they remain aligned with the overall goals set during PI Planning.
- **System Demos:** At the end of each iteration, teams demonstrate the working software they have developed. This regular cadence of demos helps stakeholders and other teams see the progress being made and provide feedback, ensuring that the product evolves in line with business needs.

Example:
In our CRM system example, during PI Planning, the sales and customer support teams would identify and plan for any dependencies, such as the API development. They would set goals that align with the overall CRM product strategy. Regular system demos would then allow stakeholders to see the integrated progress, providing an opportunity to catch and correct any issues early.

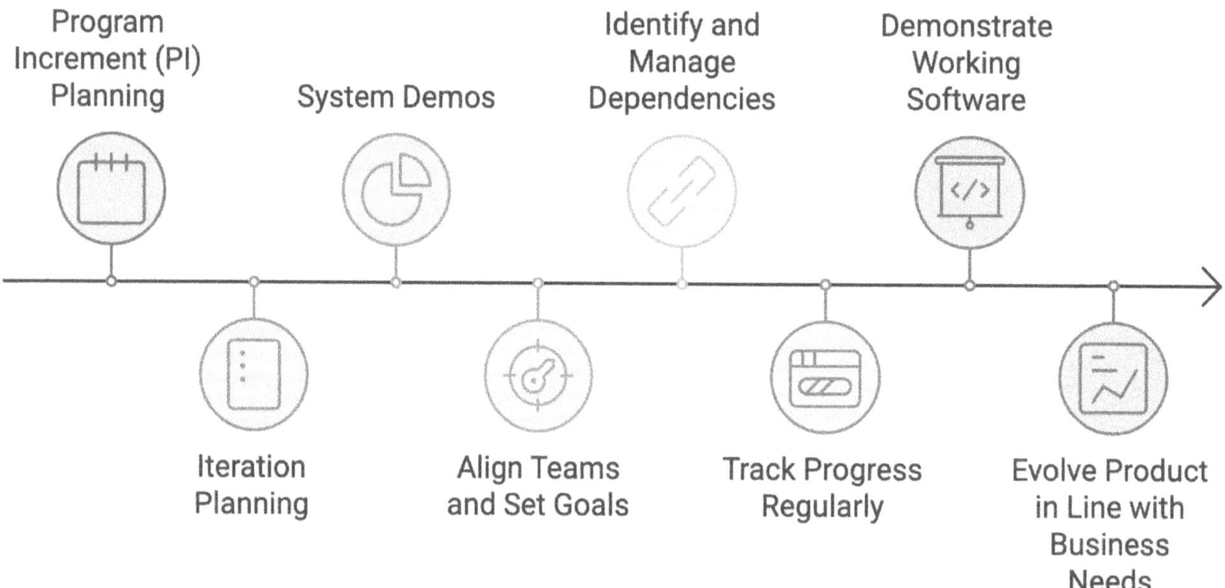

3. *Balancing Autonomy and Alignment with Lean Portfolio Management*

SAFe allows teams to maintain their autonomy while ensuring that their work aligns with the organization's strategic objectives through Lean Portfolio Management (LPM). LPM enables organizations to allocate resources efficiently, prioritize work that delivers the most value, and make informed decisions about investments in different projects or programs.

- **Strategic Themes:** At the Portfolio Level, SAFe introduces strategic themes that guide the decision-making process across the entire portfolio. These themes ensure that the work being done at the team and program levels is aligned with the long-term goals of the organization.
- **Guardrails and Governance:** While teams have the autonomy to decide how they achieve their objectives, SAFe provides guardrails and governance to ensure consistency and alignment across the organization. This includes standardized practices for budgeting, road mapping, and performance tracking, which help balance local decision-making with organizational alignment.

Example:

In a large enterprise implementing multiple modules of a CRM system, Lean Portfolio Management would ensure that the work done by various teams aligns with the strategic goal of increasing customer satisfaction. The strategic themes might include enhancing customer support capabilities and improving sales automation. Teams working on different modules would align their work with these themes, ensuring that every feature delivered contributes to these broader objectives.

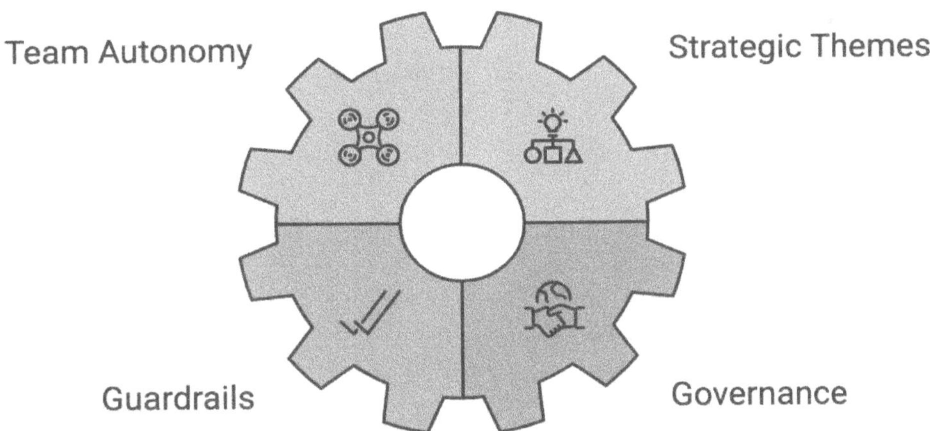

THE ROLE OF SPRINTS IN AGILE

In Agile development, sprints are the heartbeat of the process. Particularly within the Scrum framework, sprints are essential for organizing work, maintaining focus, and ensuring continuous delivery of valuable software. A sprint is a short, time-boxed period—usually lasting between 1 to 4 weeks—during which a specific set of tasks, known as user stories, are completed and made ready for potential release. The sprint structure allows teams to deliver incremental product improvements regularly, enabling frequent feedback and adaptation.

Key Aspects of Sprints

Sprints are composed of several key activities that ensure the team remains aligned, focused, and productive throughout the development cycle. Each of these activities plays a critical role in the success of the sprint and the overall Agile process.

1. *Sprint Planning*

Sprint Planning is the event that kicks off each sprint. Before the sprint begins, the team holds a Sprint Planning meeting to decide which items from the product backlog—known as user stories—will be completed during the sprint. This meeting typically involves the entire team, including developers, testers, and the Product Owner.

The goal of Sprint Planning is to create a clear, actionable plan for the sprint. The team discusses each user story, estimates the effort required, and determines what can realistically be achieved within the sprint timeframe. By the end of the meeting, the team should have a sprint backlog, which is a list of the user stories that they commit to completing.

Example:
Imagine a development team working on a mobile banking app. During Sprint Planning, the team might decide to focus on user stories related to account management, such as creating and editing user profiles. They estimate the time needed to develop, test, and integrate these features and agree to complete them within the next two-week sprint.

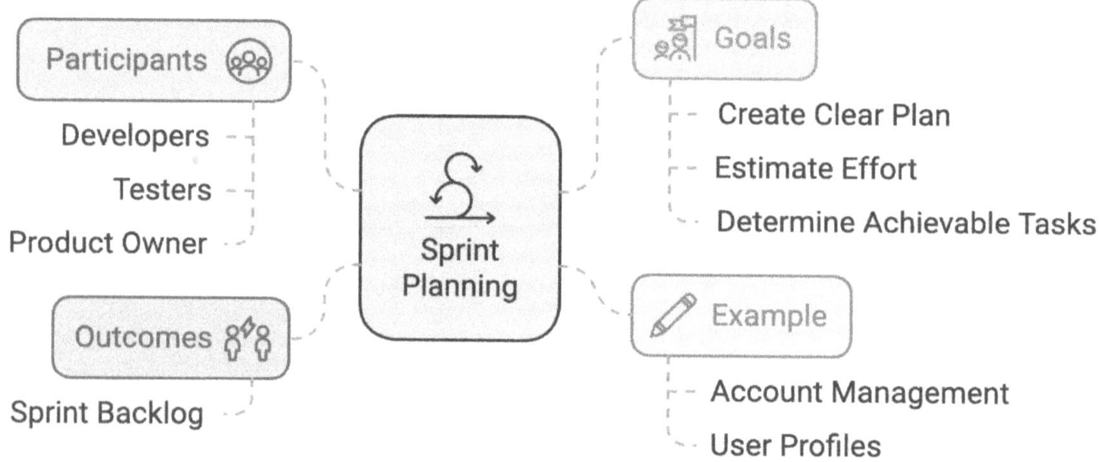

2. *Daily Stand-ups*

Daily Stand-ups, also known as Daily Scrums, are short, time-boxed meetings held every day during the sprint. These meetings are typically 15 minutes long and are designed to keep the team aligned and aware of each other's progress. Each team member answers three questions:

- What did I do yesterday?
- What will I do today?
- Are there any obstacles in my way?

The Daily Stand-up fosters transparency and collaboration, allowing the team to quickly identify and address any issues that might impede progress.

Example:

During a Daily Stand-up, a developer might mention that they are struggling with a bug in the login feature that they worked on yesterday. This prompts another team member, who has experience with similar issues, to help, ensuring that the problem is resolved quickly without delaying the sprint.

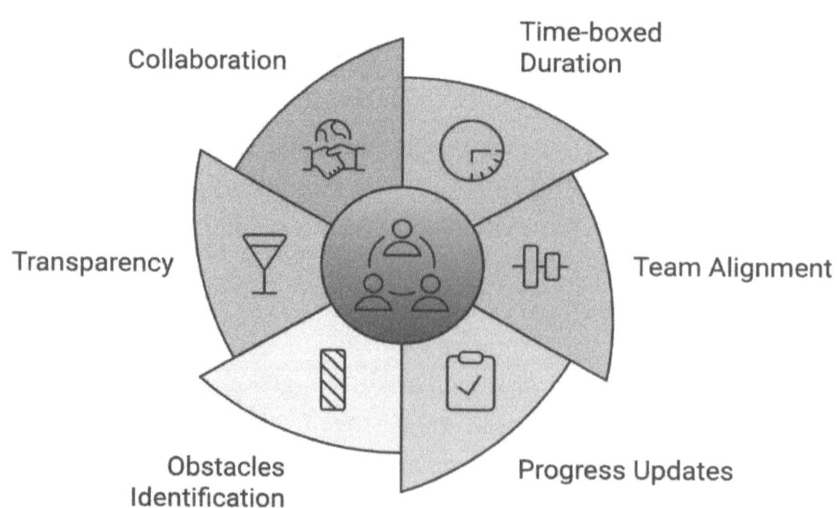

3. Sprint Execution

Sprint Execution is where the bulk of the work happens. During this phase, the team collaborates closely to complete the user stories selected during Sprint Planning. The focus during execution is on maintaining high quality, meeting the sprint goals, and ensuring that the work is progressing as planned.

Throughout Sprint Execution, team members might pair up to solve problems, share knowledge, and ensure that the code they produce is robust and meets the definition of done (DoD) for each user story. Continuous integration and testing are key practices during this phase to catch issues early and ensure that the product increment is of high quality.

Example:

In the context of the mobile banking app, Sprint Execution might involve developers writing code for the account management features, while testers create and run automated tests to ensure the new functionality works as intended. The team continuously integrates their work, testing the app on various devices to ensure compatibility and performance.

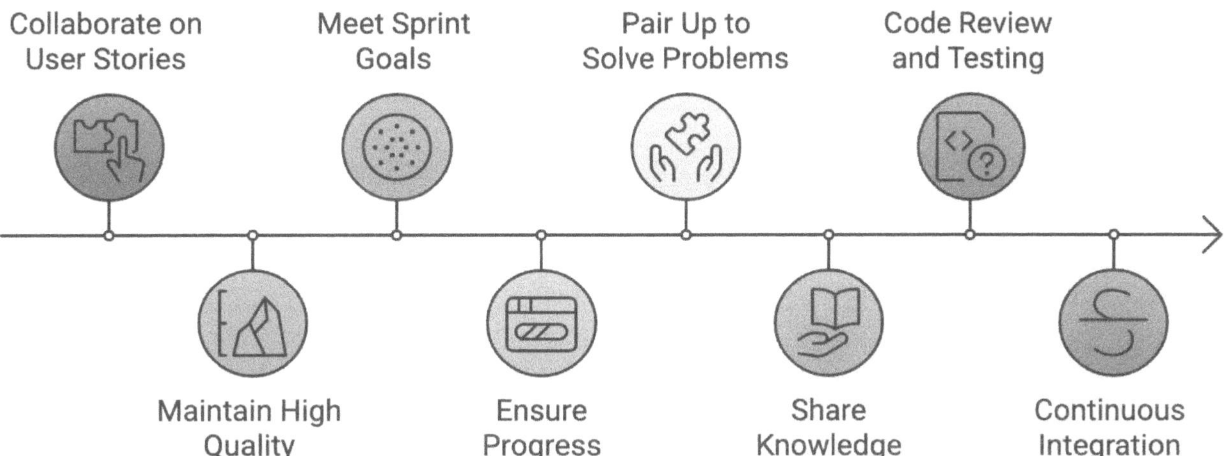

4. Sprint Review

At the end of the sprint, the team holds a Sprint Review meeting to present the work they have completed to the Product Owner and other stakeholders. This meeting is an opportunity to demonstrate the product increment—typically a working piece of software that includes the features developed during the sprint.

The Sprint Review allows stakeholders to see the progress firsthand, provide feedback, and suggest adjustments or new priorities for future sprints. It ensures that the team is delivering value to the business and that the product is evolving in the right direction.

Example:

For the mobile banking app, the Sprint Review might involve the team demonstrating the new account management features. The Product Owner might interact with the app, testing the new functionality, and providing feedback that will inform the planning of the next sprint.

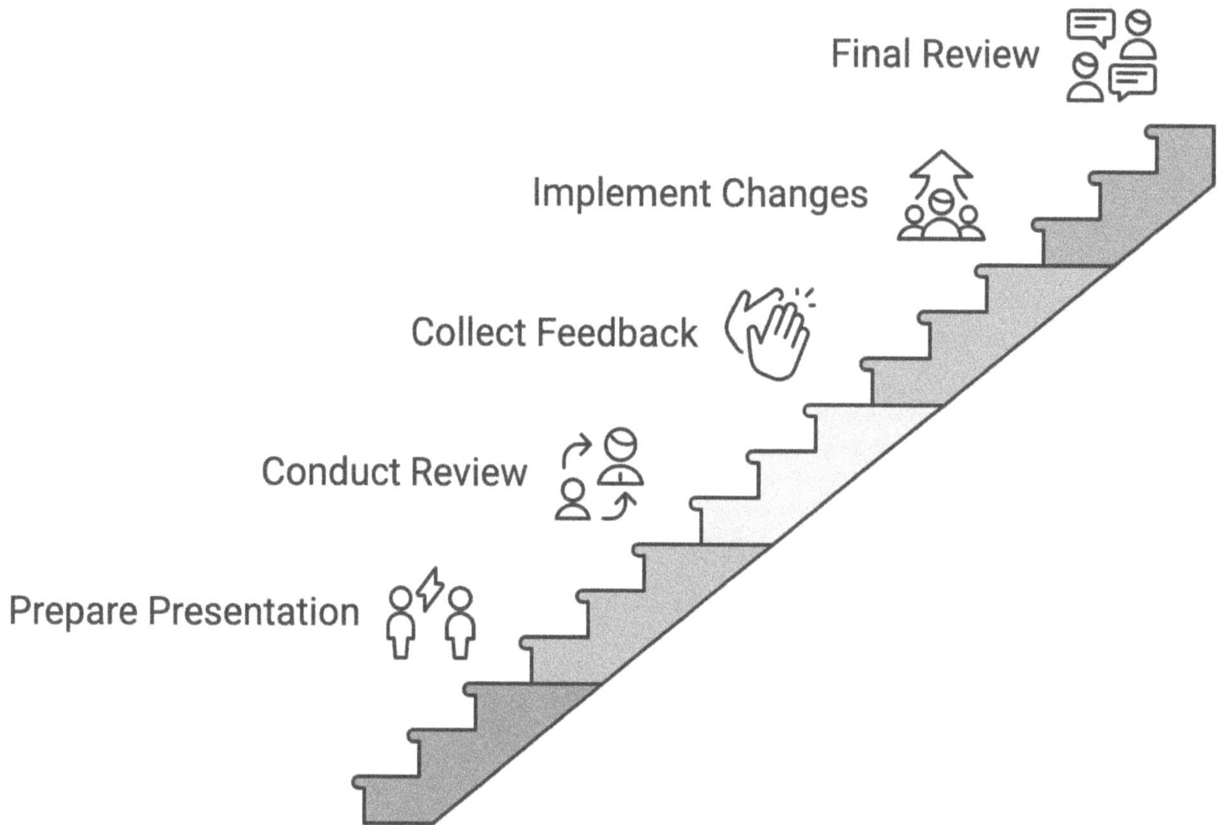

5. *Sprint Retrospective*

The Sprint Retrospective is the final meeting of the sprint. It's a time for the team to reflect on the sprint that just ended, discussing what went well, what didn't go as planned, and how processes can be improved for the next sprint. The goal of the retrospective is to foster continuous improvement by identifying actionable steps that the team can take to enhance their performance.

During the retrospective, the team might identify process improvements, like better ways to handle code reviews or more effective communication strategies. The insights gained during this meeting are crucial for improving future sprints and ensuring that the team continues to evolve and improve over time.

Example:

In the mobile banking app project, the team might reflect on challenges faced during the Sprint Execution, such as delays in testing due to insufficient test cases. As a result, they might decide to create more comprehensive test cases during the next sprint's planning phase to avoid similar delays.

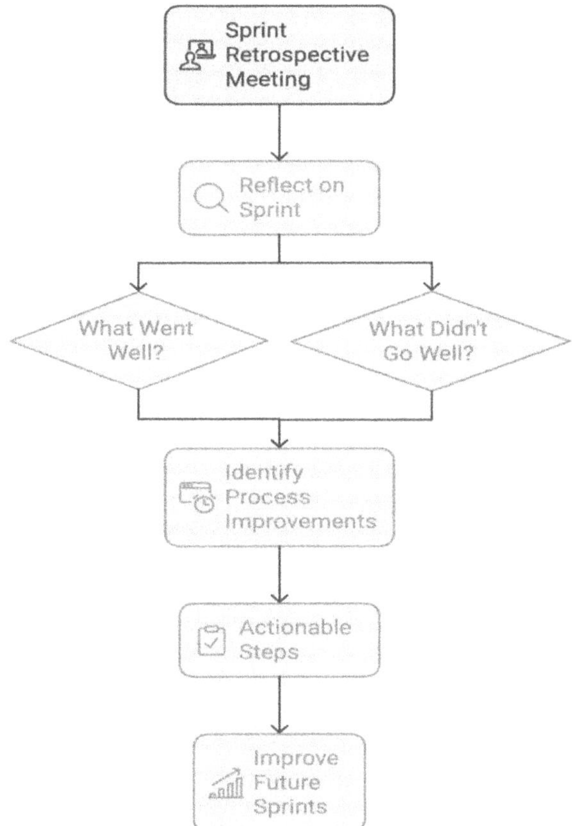

THE CONTINUOUS CYCLE OF SPRINTS

Sprints are central to the Agile approach because they allow for regular, iterative progress. Each sprint produces a potentially shippable product increment that can be reviewed and adjusted based on stakeholder feedback. This iterative cycle ensures that the product evolves in line with user needs and market demands, while also enabling the team to learn and improve with each sprint.

Key Challenges: Ensuring Clarity and Consistency in User Stories and Definitions

While these Agile concepts are fundamental to the process, teams often face challenges in maintaining clarity and consistency, particularly with user stories and the definition of done. Ambiguities in these areas can lead to misunderstandings, misaligned expectations, and incomplete or subpar work.

1. *Challenge: Writing Clear and Effective User Stories*

User stories are short, simple descriptions of a feature or function from the end-user's perspective. They are intended to communicate what needs to be built and why, in a way that is understandable to both technical and non-technical stakeholders. However, writing user stories that are both clear and detailed enough to guide development can be challenging.

Example:

A vague user story like "As a user, I want to be able to manage my account" can leave too much room for interpretation. What does "manage my account" mean? Does it involve updating personal details, changing the password, or managing payment methods? Without clear details, the development team might misunderstand the requirements, leading to incomplete or incorrect implementation.

2.   *Challenge: Defining and Adhering to the Definition of Done*

The definition of done (DoD) is a shared understanding of what it means for a task or user story to be considered complete. It typically includes criteria such as passing all tests, code review approval, and deployment to a staging environment. A poorly defined or inconsistently applied DoD can lead to quality issues, where work is marked as done even though it is not fully ready for release.

Example:

If the DoD for a user story includes "code is written and tested," but there's no clear requirement for documentation or performance testing, the team might deliver code that works technically but is not maintainable or scalable. This can lead to problems later in the project when the incomplete work must be revisited.

Solutions: Continuous Refinement and Collaborative Discussions During Sprint Planning

To overcome these challenges, Agile teams should focus on continuous refinement of user stories and definitions, combined with collaborative discussions during sprint planning. This ensures that everyone has a clear understanding of what needs to be done and how success will be measured.

1.   *Continuous Refinement of User Stories*

Refining user stories is an ongoing process that helps ensure that stories are clear, actionable, and aligned with the team's capabilities and the project's goals.

Best Practices

- **Start with the User's Perspective:** Write user stories from the end-user's perspective, focusing on the value the feature provides. Include specific details to avoid ambiguity.
- **INVEST Criteria:** Use the INVEST acronym to guide user story refinement:
  - **Independent:** The story should be self-contained, with no dependencies on other stories.
  - **Negotiable:** The details can be discussed and adjusted as needed.
  - **Valuable:** The story should deliver value to the end user.
  - **Estimable:** The team should be able to estimate the effort required to complete the story.
  - **Small:** The story should be small enough to complete within a sprint.
  - **Testable:** There should be clear acceptance criteria to verify that the story is done.
- **Collaborate with Stakeholders:** Regularly involve stakeholders in refining user stories to ensure that their needs and expectations are understood and clearly communicated.

Example:

Instead of the vague story "As a user, I want to be able to manage my account," a refined story might read: "As a user, I want to update my personal details (name, address, phone number) so that my account information is accurate and up to date." This provides clear guidance to the development team and can be further broken down into smaller tasks if needed.

2. *Collaborative Discussions During Sprint Planning*

Sprint planning is the ideal time to ensure that everyone on the team understands the user stories, the definition of done, and the goals for the sprint. Collaborative discussions during sprint planning help align the team and set clear expectations for the work to be completed.

Best Practices

- **Clarify User Stories:** During sprint planning, take the time to discuss each user story in detail. Ensure that all team members understand what is required and what the acceptance criteria are.
- **Review the Definition of Done:** Revisit the DoD during sprint planning to ensure that it is up to date and applicable to the current sprint's work. Make sure that the DoD is comprehensive and includes all necessary quality checks.
- **Estimate Effort Together:** Involve the entire team in estimating the effort required for each user story. This helps ensure that estimates are realistic and that the team is committed to the sprint goals.

Example:

In a sprint planning meeting, the team discusses a user story for adding a password recovery feature to the app. The team reviews the acceptance criteria, which include a functional recovery flow, user notifications, and security checks. They also agree on the DoD, which requires not only that the feature works but also that it passes security testing and is documented. By the end of the meeting, everyone is clear on what needs to be done and what "done" means for this feature.

CONCLUDING REMARKS

As we conclude this chapter, we've explored the foundational elements of Agile testing, delving into the methodologies, frameworks, and key concepts that are essential for successful Agile practices. We've discussed the challenges that teams face in maintaining focus during sprints, avoiding scope creep, and ensuring clarity and consistency in user stories and definitions.

Through practical strategies like regular backlog grooming, strict adherence to sprint goals, and continuous refinement of user stories, we've seen how these challenges can be overcome to achieve a balanced, efficient, and effective Agile process.

But this is just the beginning.

In the next chapter, we will dive deeper into the world of **In-Sprint Automation**—a game-changer in Agile development. We'll explore how integrating automation into your sprints can supercharge your testing processes, improve quality, and accelerate delivery times. You'll discover the critical roles that Test-Driven Development (TDD) and Behavior-Driven Development (BDD) play in creating a seamless, automated workflow, and how these practices can be integrated into your sprints for maximum impact.

Get ready to take your Agile practices to the next level as we unlock the secrets to mastering In-Sprint Automation. The journey ahead promises to be both challenging and rewarding, and by the end of it, you'll be equipped with the tools and knowledge to transform your Agile teams into powerhouses of efficiency and quality.

Are you ready to automate your way to excellence? Let's dive in.

## CHAPTER 2

FUNDAMENTALS OF IN-SPRINT AUTOMATION

WHAT IS IN-SPRINT AUTOMATION?

In-Sprint Automation refers to the practice of incorporating automated testing and other automation activities directly within the same sprint (a short, defined period of work, typically 1 to 4 weeks) in which the software development occurs. The goal of in-sprint automation is to ensure that by the end of each sprint, not only is the new functionality developed, but it is also thoroughly tested and ready for potential release without the need for additional testing cycles.

In traditional software development models, testing (especially automated testing) often occurs after the development phase is complete. This can lead to delays, as issues discovered during testing might require developers to go back and fix problems, sometimes long after the code was originally written. In contrast, in-sprint automation aligns the development and testing processes, enabling continuous integration of quality checks throughout the sprint. This results in faster feedback, quicker identification of bugs, and a smoother path to delivering high-quality software incrementally.

Nuances of In-Sprint Automation

Understanding in-sprint automation involves breaking down its key components and how they interact within the Agile development process:

1. **Automation Within the Sprint:**
   - The primary idea behind in-sprint automation is that every user story (a small, individual task or requirement) completed during a sprint should be accompanied by automated tests that verify the functionality of that story. This means that as new features are developed, tests are simultaneously written and executed to ensure that the new code works correctly and doesn't break existing functionality.
   - For example, if the sprint goal is to add a new login feature to an app, in-sprint automation ensures that by the end of the sprint, the feature is not only coded but also has automated tests verifying that users can log in successfully under various conditions.

2. **Test Automation Frameworks:**
   - Implementing in-sprint automation requires using test automation frameworks—software tools that allow testers and developers to write scripts that automatically execute tests. These tests can include unit tests (which check individual components of the software), integration tests (which check how different parts of the software work together), and UI tests (which simulate user interactions with the software).

- For instance, frameworks like Selenium (for UI automation) or JUnit (for unit testing) are commonly used in Agile teams to facilitate in-sprint automation.

3. Continuous Integration (CI) Integration:

- In-sprint automation is closely tied to Continuous Integration (CI), a practice where developers frequently merge their code changes into a shared repository. Automated tests are run as part of the CI process to ensure that the new code integrates smoothly with the existing codebase and that no new bugs are introduced.
- A typical CI pipeline might include steps like code compilation, running automated tests, and deploying the software to a staging environment. If any automated tests fail during this process, the team is immediately notified, allowing them to address the issue within the same sprint.

4. Collaboration Between Developers and Testers:

- In-sprint automation necessitates close collaboration between developers and testers. Rather than working in silos, where developers write code and then pass it off to testers after the fact, in-sprint automation involves both roles working together from the start. Testers might work with developers to define test cases before coding even begins, ensuring that tests are aligned with the development process.
- This collaboration helps to ensure that tests are written and executed as part of the development workflow, leading to faster feedback and more reliable software.

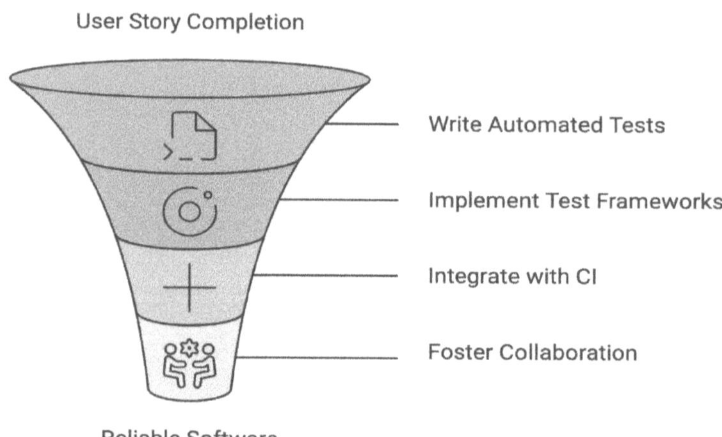

KEY CHALLENGES: INTEGRATING AUTOMATION WITHIN TIGHT SPRINT TIMELINES

While in-sprint automation offers many benefits, it also presents several challenges, particularly when it comes to integrating automation activities within the tight timelines of a sprint. Here's a closer look at these challenges and how they can impact teams:

1. Challenge: Limited Time for Test Development:

Explanation: Sprints are short, typically lasting between 1 to 4 weeks. This limited timeframe can make it challenging to write and execute all the necessary automated tests, especially when the team is also focused on developing new features.

Impact: If there isn't enough time to create thorough automated tests, there's a risk that testing will be rushed or incomplete, leading to undetected bugs and potential issues down the line. Moreover, if the testing phase isn't fully automated, manual testing might need to fill the gaps, which can slow down the process and negate some of the benefits of in-sprint automation.

2. Challenge: Complexity of Automation Tasks:

Explanation: Automation tasks can be complex, particularly when dealing with intricate user interfaces, legacy systems, or multiple dependencies. Developing and maintaining automated test scripts requires a certain level of expertise, which not all team members might possess.

Impact: Teams might struggle to keep up with the demands of in-sprint automation, especially if the automation tools and frameworks are not user-friendly or if team members lack the necessary skills. This can lead to delays and incomplete automation, making it harder to achieve the desired level of quality within the sprint.

3. Challenge: Flaky Tests and Maintenance:

Explanation: Automated tests, particularly those that interact with the user interface, can sometimes be unreliable, known as "flaky tests." These are tests that might pass sometimes and fail at other times, often due to factors like timing issues or environmental dependencies.

Impact: Flaky tests can erode confidence in the automation process. If tests are unreliable, teams may spend more time investigating false failures, which can slow down the sprint and lead to frustration. Additionally, maintaining and updating automated tests as the codebase evolves can be time-consuming, further complicating in-sprint automation.

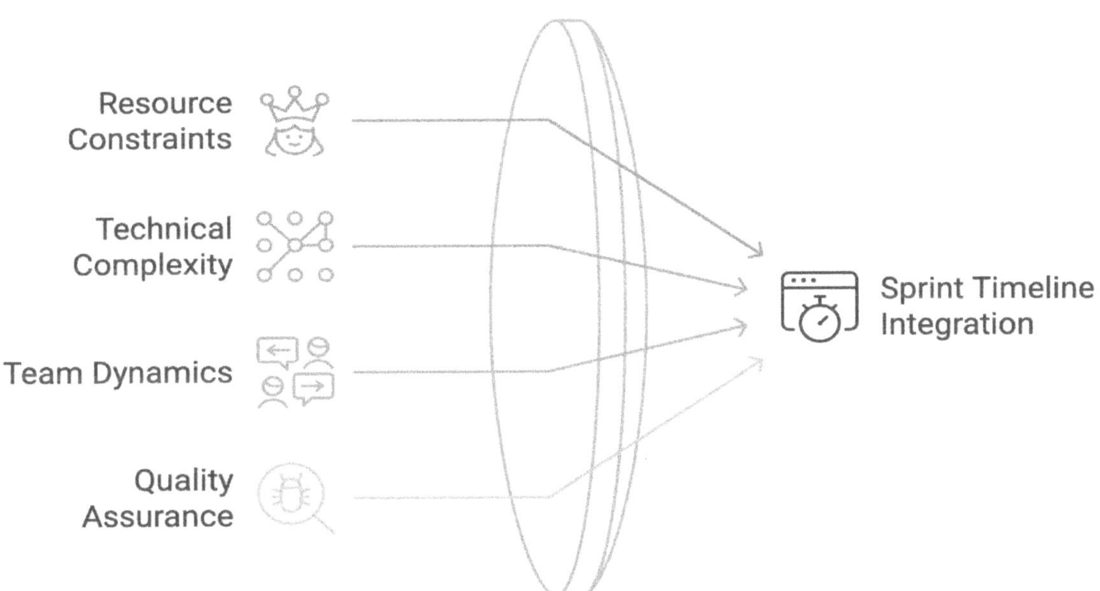

SOLUTIONS: PRIORITIZING HIGH-IMPACT AREAS FOR AUTOMATION AND INCREMENTAL INTEGRATION

To successfully integrate automation within sprint timelines, teams can adopt the following strategies:

Focus on High-Impact Areas:

Explanation: Not all features or tasks within a sprint carry the same level of risk or importance. By prioritizing high-impact areas for automation, teams can ensure that the most critical parts of the application are thoroughly tested, even if time is limited.

Approach: Identify the most important features or those that are most likely to break and focus on automating tests for these areas first. For example, core functionalities like login processes, payment gateways, or critical API integrations should be automated before less critical features. This ensures that the most valuable parts of the application are always covered by automated tests, even if time runs short.

Adopt Incremental Integration of Automation:

Explanation: Rather than trying to automate everything from the start, teams can adopt an incremental approach to automation. This means starting with basic automation and gradually building up more comprehensive test coverage as the project progresses.

Approach: Begin by automating the simplest and most straightforward tests, such as unit tests for new code. Over time, as the team becomes more comfortable with the tools and processes, more complex tests (like integration tests or UI tests) can be added. This incremental approach allows the team to gain confidence in automation without overwhelming them with complexity all at once.

Leverage Automation Tools and Frameworks Efficiently:

Explanation: The choice of tools and frameworks can significantly impact the success of in-sprint automation. Using tools that integrate well with the existing development environment and that are easy for team members to use can streamline the process.

Approach: Select automation tools that are user-friendly and offer strong support for Continuous Integration (CI). Tools like Selenium for UI testing, JUnit for unit testing, or Cucumber for BDD can be integrated into the CI pipeline to ensure that automated tests are run consistently and efficiently. Additionally, using tools that support parallel test execution can help reduce the time required for testing, making it easier to stay within sprint timelines.

Foster Collaboration and Knowledge Sharing:

Explanation: Successful in-sprint automation requires collaboration between developers, testers, and other team members. Sharing knowledge and best practices within the team can help ensure that everyone is on the same page and that automation tasks are completed efficiently.

Approach: Encourage developers and testers to work together from the start of each sprint. For example, pair programming sessions between developers and testers can help ensure that test cases are well-defined and aligned with the code being developed. Additionally, holding regular knowledge-sharing sessions or workshops can help team members improve their automation skills and stay up-to-date with the latest best practices.

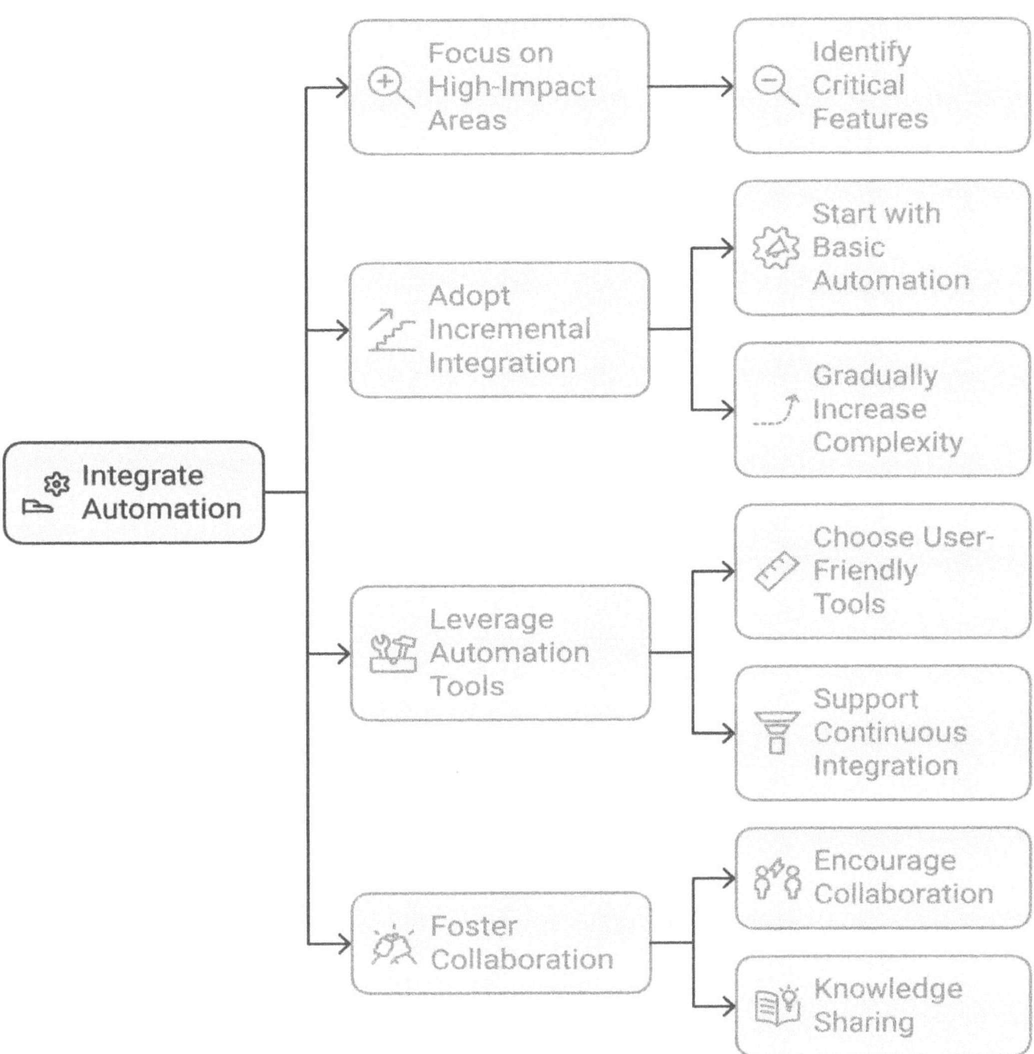

In-sprint automation is a powerful approach that can significantly enhance the efficiency and quality of Agile development. However, integrating automation within tight sprint timelines presents challenges that require careful planning and execution. By prioritizing high-impact areas for automation, adopting an incremental approach, leveraging the right tools, and fostering collaboration, teams can overcome these challenges and fully realize the benefits of in-sprint automation.

As you continue to explore the fundamentals of in-sprint automation, remember that this practice is not just about writing automated tests—it's about integrating testing into the very fabric of the development process, ensuring that quality is built into the product from the ground up. This holistic approach will set the stage for more advanced topics in automation, such as Test-Driven Development (TDD) and Behavior-Driven Development (BDD), which we'll explore in the following sections.

AUTOMATION TOOL SELECTION CRITERIA

When implementing in-sprint automation, one of the most critical decisions is selecting the right automation tools. The tools you choose can significantly impact the efficiency, effectiveness, and overall success of your automation efforts. With a wide variety of tools available, each with its strengths and weaknesses, making the right choice requires careful consideration of several key factors. The goal is to choose tools that not only fit your current needs but also scale with your project and integrate smoothly into your existing workflows.

Checklist for Automation Tool Selection

Before diving into the details, here's a checklist to guide your automation tool selection process:

1. **Compatibility with Existing Technology Stack***:*
   - Does the tool integrate well with your current programming languages, frameworks, and platforms?
   - Is it compatible with your development environment (e.g., IDEs, build systems)?

2. **Ease of Integration with CI/CD Pipelines***:*
   - Can the tool be easily integrated into your Continuous Integration (CI) and Continuous Deployment (CD) pipelines?
   - Does it support automated triggering of tests during builds?

3. **Support for TDD/BDD***:*
   - Does the tool support Test-Driven Development (TDD) or Behavior-Driven Development (BDD) practices?
   - Are there built-in features or plugins that facilitate TDD/BDD workflows?

4. **Learning Curve and Usability***:*
   - Is the tool user-friendly, with an intuitive interface and easy setup?
   - How steep is the learning curve for team members who are not familiar with the tool?

5. **Scalability and Flexibility***:*
   - Can the tool scale with your project as it grows?
   - Is it flexible enough to handle different types of tests (unit, integration, UI)?

6. **Community Support and Documentation***:*
   - Is there a strong community around the tool, providing regular updates, plugins, and troubleshooting help?
   - Does the tool have comprehensive documentation and tutorials?

7. **Cost and Licensing***:*
   - What are the costs associated with the tool (e.g., licenses, subscriptions)?
   - Are there free or open-source alternatives that meet your needs?

8. **Cross-Platform and Cross-Browser Testing***:*
   - Does the tool support testing across different platforms (e.g., Windows, macOS, Linux) and browsers?
   - Can it simulate different devices for mobile testing?

9. **Test Maintenance and Reporting***:*
   - How easy is it to maintain tests over time as the codebase evolves?
   - Does the tool provide detailed reports that help in diagnosing failures and understanding test results?

10. **Security and Compliance***:*
    - Does the tool meet your organization's security requirements?
    - Is it compliant with industry standards and regulations?

Automation Tool Selection Criteria detailed

Let's break down these criteria in more detail to understand their importance and how they impact your automation strategy.

1. *Compatibility with Existing Technology Stack*

When choosing an automation tool, it must integrate well with the technologies you're already using. This includes your programming languages, frameworks, and platforms. For example, if your application is built using JavaScript frameworks like React or Angular, you should choose a tool that supports JavaScript for writing tests, such as Jest or Cypress.

Strategic Note: Ensure that the automation tool is compatible with your existing tech stack to avoid unnecessary workarounds or the need to introduce new technologies just to support testing.

2. *Ease of Integration with CI/CD Pipelines*

Automation tools should integrate seamlessly into your Continuous Integration (CI) and Continuous Deployment (CD) pipelines. This allows for automated tests to be triggered during each build, ensuring that every code change is tested before it's merged into the main codebase. Tools like Jenkins, CircleCI, or GitHub Actions often have plugins or direct support for popular testing frameworks, making this integration easier.

Strategic Note: The ability to integrate with CI/CD pipelines is critical for maintaining the efficiency of in-sprint automation, ensuring tests are run frequently and providing fast feedback to the development team.

3. *Support for TDD/BDD*

Test-Driven Development (TDD) and Behavior-Driven Development (BDD) are key practices in Agile testing. TDD focuses on writing tests before the actual code, guiding the development process, while BDD emphasizes collaboration between developers, testers, and business stakeholders by writing tests in a natural language format. Tools like JUnit, NUnit, or Jasmine are excellent for TDD, while Cucumber or SpecFlow are popular for BDD.

Strategic Note: If your team practices TDD or BDD, ensure the tool supports these methodologies effectively, including the ability to write, manage, and execute tests in line with these practices.

4. *Learning Curve and Usability*

The ease of use of an automation tool can make or break its adoption by the team. A tool with a steep learning curve can slow down the process, especially if team members are new to automation. It's essential to choose a tool that team members can pick up quickly and that offers a smooth setup and intuitive interface.

Strategic Note: Consider the learning curve and usability of the tool to ensure that it doesn't become a bottleneck in your automation process. Training and onboarding resources can also play a significant role here.

5. *Scalability and Flexibility*

As your project grows, so will the need for more extensive and complex testing. The tool you choose should be able to scale with your project, handling an increasing number of tests and more complicated test scenarios. It should also be flexible enough to support different types of tests, from unit tests to integration and UI tests.

Strategic Note: Opt for a tool that not only meets your current needs but can also grow with your project, handling more complex tests and larger codebases.

6. Community Support and Documentation

A strong community around an automation tool can be invaluable. It provides access to plugins, troubleshooting tips, and regular updates that keep the tool relevant and effective. Additionally, comprehensive documentation and tutorials help your team get up to speed quickly and resolve any issues that arise.

Strategic Note: A tool with a robust community and thorough documentation ensures long-term support and continuous improvement, which is critical for keeping up with the fast pace of Agile development.

7. Cost and Licensing

While free tools are appealing, sometimes investing in a paid tool can offer better support, more features, or integrations that save time and improve efficiency. However, it's essential to balance cost with the benefits provided, ensuring that the tool fits within your budget while meeting your needs.

Strategic Note: Evaluate the cost-benefit ratio of the tool, considering both immediate needs and long-term value. Don't overlook free or open-sourcetools, but weigh them against commercial options to see which offers the best value.

8. Cross-Platform and Cross-Browser Testing

If your application needs to run on various platforms and browsers, your automation tool must support cross-platform and cross-browser testing. Tools like Selenium or BrowserStack are designed for such scenarios, allowing you to test how your application performs in different environments.

Strategic Note: Ensure the tool can handle the complexity of cross-platform and cross-browser testing to provide comprehensive test coverage across all the environments your application supports.

9. Test Maintenance and Reporting

As your tests grow in number, maintaining them becomes a challenge. A good automation tool should make it easy to update and maintain tests, as well as provide detailed reports that help you quickly identify and fix issues. Look for tools that offer clear, actionable reports and features that simplify test maintenance, such as modular test designs or version control integration.

Strategic Note: Prioritize tools that offer strong support for test maintenance and reporting to keep your automation suite efficient and effective as it scales.

10. Security and Compliance

In today's environment, ensuring that your automation tools meet security and compliance standards is vital, especially if you're working in regulated industries like finance or healthcare. The tool should offer features that help maintain compliance, such as secure data handling and audit trails.

Strategic Note: Don't overlook security and compliance requirements when selecting an automation tool, particularly if your application deals with sensitive data or is subject to regulatory standards.

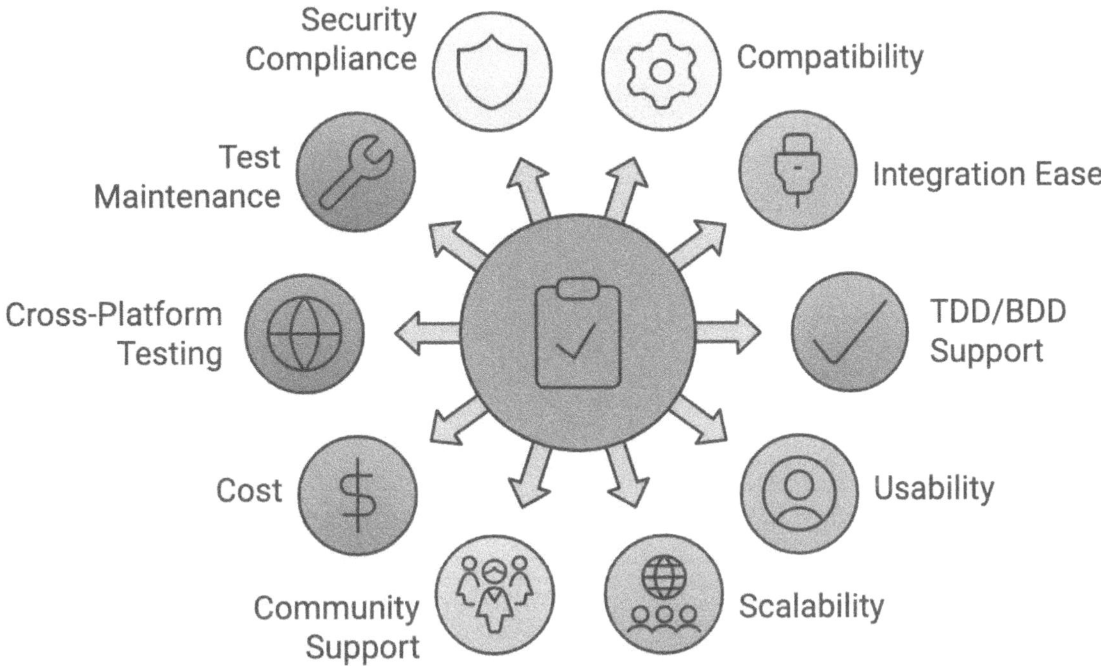

Key Challenges: Choosing Tools That Integrate Well with Existing Workflows and That Can Be Easily Adopted by the Team

Selecting the right automation tool is not without its challenges. Two of the most significant hurdles are ensuring the tool integrates well with your existing workflows and that it can be easily adopted by the team.

1. Challenge: Ensuring Smooth Integration with Existing Workflows

Integrating a new tool into an established workflow can be challenging, especially if your team is already accustomed to certain processes and tools. Introducing a new tool that doesn't mesh well with existing systems can lead to inefficiencies, confusion, and resistance from team members.

Impact: Poor integration can disrupt the development process, leading to delays, errors, or incomplete test coverage. It can also create additional work, as team members may need to find workarounds or manually bridge gaps between tools.

2. Challenge: Adoption by the Team

Even if a tool is technically the best fit, it can fail if the team is reluctant to adopt it. This reluctance can stem from a lack of familiarity with the tool, a steep learning curve, or simply resistance to change. If the tool is difficult to use or requires significant retraining, team members may stick to old habits or avoid using the tool altogether.

Impact: Without full team adoption, the benefits of automation are lost, and the tool may become a costly investment with little return. Incomplete adoption can also lead to inconsistent testing practices, reducing the effectiveness of your automation strategy.

Solutions: Outline Key Factors to Consider, Such as Ease of Integration, Support for TDD/BDD, Learning Curve, and Community Support

To overcome these challenges, it's essential to take a strategic approach to selecting automation tools. Here's how you can address the key challenges of integration and adoption:

1. Prioritize Ease of Integration

To ensure that the new tool integrates smoothly with your existing workflows, consider the following factors:

- **Compatibility with Existing Tools**: Choose an automation tool that works well with your current CI/CD pipelines, development environments, and other software tools. For instance, if you are using Jenkins for CI, ensure the tool has a well-supported Jenkins plugin or API that allows for easy integration.
- **API and Webhooks**: Tools with robust APIs and support for webhooks can be integrated more easily into custom workflows. This flexibility allows you to tailor the tool to fit seamlessly into your processes, reducing the need for manual interventions.
- **Automated Triggering**: Look for tools that can automatically trigger tests based on events in your CI/CD pipeline, such as code commits or builds. This ensures that testing becomes a natural part of the development process rather than an afterthought.

    Actionable Tip: Run a pilot integration with the tool in a small, controlled environment to identify any potential issues before rolling it out across the entire team. This allows you to address integration challenges early and adjust your approach as needed.

2. Ensure the Tool Supports TDD/BDD Practices

If your team follows Test-Driven Development (TDD) or Behavior-Driven Development (BDD), the tool you select should support these methodologies. Here's how to ensure compatibility:

- **Built-in Support for TDD**: The tool should allow for the easy creation and execution of unit tests that guide the development process. This might include support for test-first development and features that integrate testing seamlessly into the coding workflow.
- **BDD Compatibility**: For teams practicing BDD, the tool should support natural language test writing (e.g., using Gherkin syntax) and offer strong integration with BDD frameworks like Cucumber or SpecFlow. This ensures that tests are aligned with business requirements and are understandable by non-technical stakeholders.

Actionable Tip: Evaluate the tool's documentation and community resources for examples of TDD/BDD usage. This can give you a clear idea of how well the tool supports these practices in real-world scenarios.

3. Consider the Learning Curve and Provide Training

To ensure that the tool is adopted effectively by the team, it's important to assess its usability and provide the necessary training:

- **User-Friendliness**: Opt for tools with intuitive interfaces and well-organized documentation. A tool that is easy to navigate reduces the learning curve and allows team members to become proficient more quickly.
- **Training Resources**: Check whether the tool offers tutorials, webinars, or training sessions. These resources can help onboard team members more efficiently and reduce the time it takes for them to start using the tool effectively.
- **Pair Programming and Mentorship**: Encourage experienced team members to pair up with those who are less familiar with the tool. This peer-to-peer learning approach can help spread knowledge and increase overall team competence with the tool.

Actionable Tip: Organize an internal workshop or lunch-and-learn session focused on the new tool. This gives the team a chance to explore the tool together, ask questions, and build confidence in using it.

4. *Leverage Community Support and Documentation*

A strong community and good documentation are vital for overcoming challenges related to tool adoption and troubleshooting:

- **Active Community**: A tool with an active user community can be a valuable resource for finding solutions to common problems, discovering best practices, and staying informed about updates or new features. Look for tools that have active forums, GitHub repositories, or Slack groups where users share knowledge.
- **Comprehensive Documentation**: Ensure that the tool has detailed, up-to-date documentation. This should include clear instructions for setup, usage, integration, and troubleshooting. Comprehensive documentation minimizes the time spent on trial and error and helps resolve issues quickly.

Actionable Tip: Before committing to a tool, explore its community forums or support channels to see how responsive and helpful the community is. This can give you an idea of the level of support you can expect.

5. *Pilot the Tool in a Controlled Environment*

Before fully integrating a new automation tool into your entire workflow, it's wise to pilot it in a controlled environment. This allows you to test its compatibility, usability, and effectiveness on a smaller scale, reducing the risk of disruption.

- **Start Small**: Use the tool on a smaller project or a single sprint to evaluate its performance and integration capabilities. This approach allows you to identify any issues and address them without impacting your entire development process.
- **Gather Feedback**: Collect feedback from the team during the pilot phase to understand their experience with the tool. This feedback is crucial for making informed decisions about whether to proceed with full adoption or to explore other options.

Actionable Tip: Document the pilot phase, noting any challenges encountered and how they were resolved. This documentation can serve as a guide when rolling out the tool to the rest of the team.

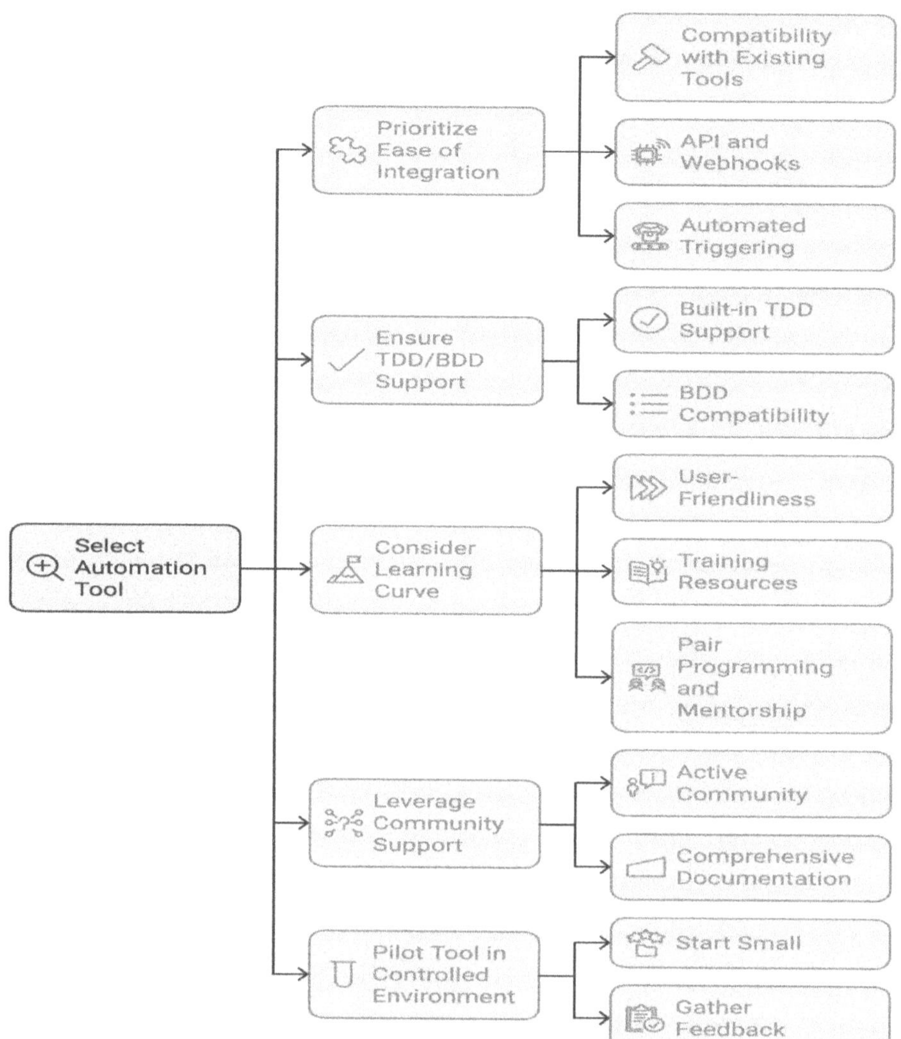

Selecting the right automation tool is a crucial step in implementing effective in-sprint automation. By carefully considering factors such as compatibility, integration, usability, and community support, you can choose a tool that not only fits your current needs but also scales with your project and team.

Addressing the challenges of integration and adoption requires a strategic approach. By prioritizing ease of integration, supporting TDD/BDD practices, minimizing the learning curve, and leveraging community resources, you can overcome these challenges and ensure that the tool enhances your automation efforts rather than hindering them.

As you move forward with in-sprint automation, remember that the right tools, combined with thoughtful implementation and continuous learning, are key to achieving efficient, reliable, and scalable testing processes. With the right foundation in place, you'll be well-prepared to tackle the complexities of Agile development and deliver high-quality software with confidence.

IMPORTANCE OF TEST-DRIVEN DEVELOPMENT (TDD)

Test-Driven Development (TDD) is a software development practice where developers write tests for a specific functionality before writing the code that implements that functionality. This approach is integral to Agile methodologies because it helps ensure that the code is thoroughly tested, reliable, and maintainable from the outset. TDD not only improves the quality of the code but also guides the development process, leading to more focused and efficient coding practices.

How TDD Works

The TDD process follows a simple, iterative cycle known as "Red-Green-Refactor":

1. **Red**: Write a test for the next piece of functionality you want to add. Initially, this test will fail because the functionality doesn't exist yet—hence, the "red" phase.
2. **Green**: Write the minimal amount of code necessary to make the test pass. This phase is called "green" because the test suite should now pass, indicating that the code works as intended.
3. **Refactor**: Clean up the code you've just written, improving its structure and readability without changing its behavior. The test suite should still pass after refactoring.

This cycle repeats for every new feature or functionality, ensuring that each piece of code is covered by tests before it's fully developed. The discipline of TDD promotes better design, reduces the chances of introducing bugs, and makes the code easier to maintain.

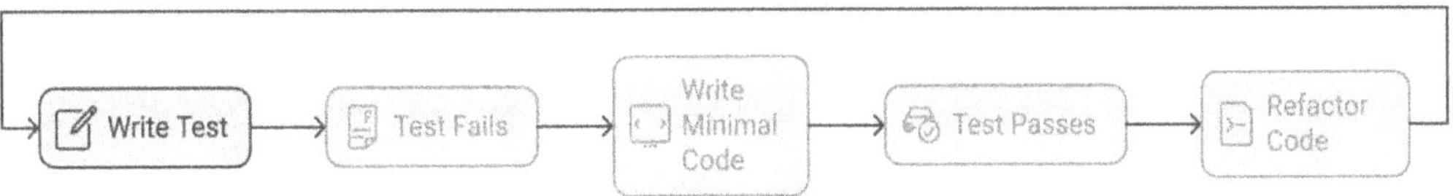

Benefits of TDD

1. **Higher Code Quality*:***
   - Since tests are written before the code, TDD encourages developers to think about the design and requirements before diving into implementation. This often leads to cleaner, more modular code with fewer bugs.

2. **Immediate Feedback*:***
   - TDD provides instant feedback on whether the new code works correctly and whether it breaks any existing functionality. This reduces the time spent debugging and allows developers to identify and fix issues as they arise.

3. **Better Documentation*:***
   - The tests themselves serve as a form of documentation, providing a clear, executable specification of what the code is supposed to do. This makes it easier for new developers to understand the codebase and for existing developers to revisit their work later.

4. **Facilitates Refactoring*:***
   - With a comprehensive suite of tests in place, developers can refactor code with confidence, knowing that any changes that break functionality will be immediately caught by the tests.

5. **Encourages Simple Design*:***
   - TDD promotes the writing of only the necessary code to pass the tests, which often results in simpler, more maintainable designs. This helps avoid over-engineering and keeps the codebase manageable.

6. **Improved Collaboration*:***
   - TDD can improve collaboration between developers and testers by ensuring that both parties have a clear understanding of the requirements and the criteria for success. It also helps bridge the gap between development and quality assurance by making testing an integral part of the development process.

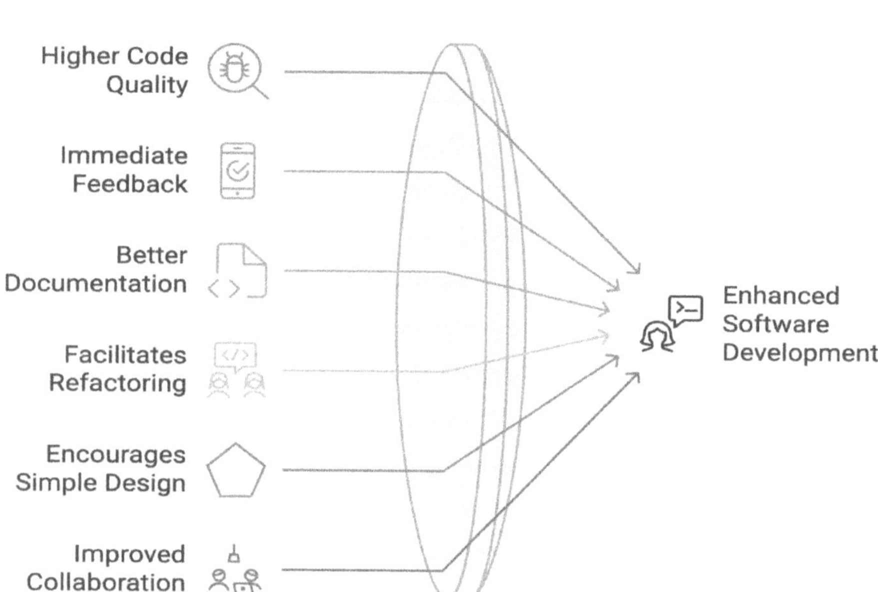

Key Challenges: Ensuring All Team Members Are Proficient in TDD Practices

While TDD offers significant benefits, implementing it across a team can be challenging, particularly if team members are not already familiar with TDD practices. Here are some of the key challenges that teams may face:

1. Challenge: Lack of Familiarity with TDD

Explanation: Not all developers are familiar with the TDD process, and those who are new to it may find it difficult to adjust to writing tests before writing code. This can be especially true for developers who are accustomed to traditional development approaches where testing is often done after the code is written.

Impact: Without a solid understanding of TDD, developers may struggle to write effective tests or may skip the process altogether, undermining the benefits of TDD. This can lead to inconsistent test coverage, missed bugs, and lower overall code quality.

2. Challenge: Resistance to Change

Explanation: Implementing TDD often requires a cultural shift within the development team. Developers who are used to working in a certain way may resist adopting TDD, either because they don't see the value in it or because they find it difficult to change their habits.

Impact: Resistance to TDD can lead to incomplete or inconsistent adoption, where some team members embrace TDD while others do not. This can create friction within the team and result in a fragmented approach to testing and development.

3. Challenge: Time Constraints

Explanation: TDD can initially seem time-consuming, especially when developers are under tight deadlines. Writing tests before code can feel like it slows down the development process, and teams may be tempted to skip the TDD process to save time.

Impact: Skipping TDD to save time often results in lower-quality code that requires more debugging and refactoring later, ultimately increasing the overall development time and cost.

Solutions: Providing Regular Training and Mentoring on TDD Techniques

To successfully implement TDD across a team, it's crucial to provide regular training and mentoring. This helps ensure that all team members are proficient in TDD practices and can apply them effectively in their work.

1. Organize TDD Workshops and Training Sessions

Explanation: Regular workshops and training sessions can help team members understand the principles and practices of TDD. These sessions should cover the basics of TDD, including the Red-Green-Refactor cycle, writing effective tests, and integrating TDD into daily development workflows.

Critical Insight: Hands-on workshops where developers practice writing tests and implementing TDD in a controlled environment can be particularly effective. This allows them to experiment with TDD in a low-pressure setting before applying it to real projects.

2. Provide Access to TDD Resources

Explanation: Ensure that team members have access to a wealth of resources on TDD, including books, online courses, and tutorials. These resources can provide additional learning opportunities and reinforce the concepts covered in training sessions.

Critical Insight: Curate a list of recommended resources, such as "Test-Driven Development by Example" by Kent Beck, or online platforms like Pluralsight and Udemy that offer courses on TDD. Encourage team members to explore these resources at their own pace.

3. Implement Pair Programming and Mentorship

Explanation: Pair programming, where two developers work together on the same piece of code, can be a valuable way to spread TDD knowledge. Pair a developer who is experienced with TDD with one who is less familiar, allowing for real-time learning and mentorship.

Critical Insight: Mentorship programs can help foster a culture of continuous learning and support. Assign TDD mentors within the team who can provide guidance and answer questions as developers work to integrate TDD into their workflows.

4. Integrate TDD into the Development Process Gradually

Explanation: Instead of enforcing TDD across the entire team all at once, consider a gradual approach. Start by applying TDD to new projects or specific parts of the codebase. This allows developers to get comfortable with TDD without feeling overwhelmed.

Critical Insight: Track the progress of TDD adoption and celebrate successes, such as improved code quality or reduced bug counts. This positive reinforcement can help build momentum and encourage further adoption.

5. *Address Time Management Concerns*

Explanation: To alleviate concerns about the time commitment required for TDD, emphasize the long-term benefits, such as reduced debugging time and fewer regressions. Provide examples of how TDD can ultimately speed up the development process by preventing issues before they arise.

Critical Insight: Use metrics to demonstrate the impact of TDD, such as reduced bug rates or faster release cycles. This data can help convince skeptics that the initial time investment in TDD pays off in the long run.

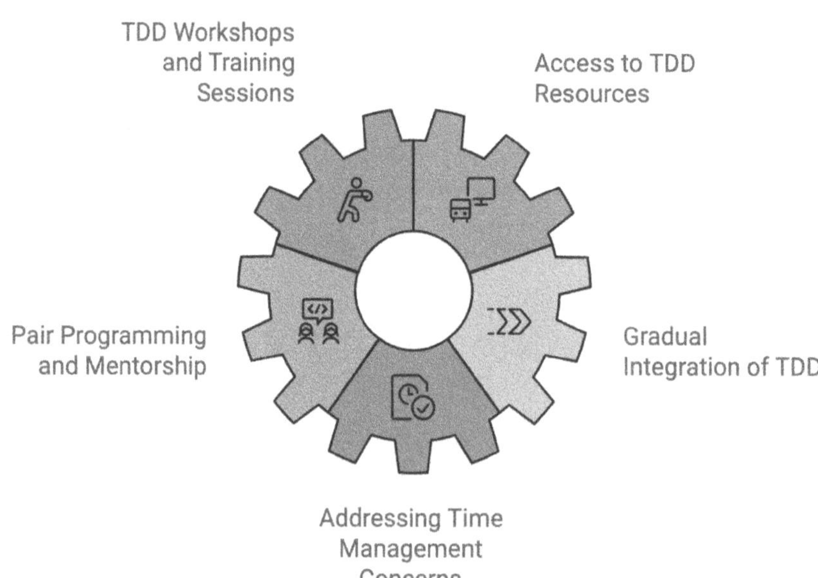

In a Nutshell

Test-driven development (TDD) is a powerful practice that can significantly improve code quality, facilitate collaboration, and enhance the overall development process. However, successfully implementing TDD across a team requires overcoming challenges related to familiarity, resistance to change, and time management. By providing regular training, fostering a culture of mentorship, and integrating TDD gradually, teams can ensure that all members become proficient in TDD and can leverage its benefits effectively.

As you continue to explore the fundamentals of in-sprint automation, keep in mind that TDD is not just a technique but a mindset that prioritizes quality, clarity, and continuous improvement. With the right support and resources, your team can make TDD an integral part of its development process, leading to more reliable and maintainable software.

IMPORTANCE OF BEHAVIOR-DRIVEN DEVELOPMENT (BDD)

Behavior-Driven Development (BDD) is an Agile software development methodology that extends the principles of Test-Driven Development (TDD) by focusing on the behavior of the application from the perspective of its stakeholders. BDD aims to improve communication between developers, testers, and non-technical stakeholders, ensuring that the software being developed meets the actual business requirements. The core idea behind BDD is to describe the behavior of a feature in a language that all parties can understand, typically using a structured format known as Gherkin.

How BDD Works

BDD involves writing test scenarios in a natural language format that describes the desired behavior of the system in terms of user actions and outcomes. These scenarios are often written collaboratively by developers, testers, and business stakeholders, ensuring that everyone has a shared understanding of the feature being developed. The scenarios are then automated and used as acceptance criteria for the feature.

The typical structure of a BDD scenario uses the "Given-When-Then" format:
1. **Given**: Describes the initial context or preconditions.
2. **When**: Specifies the action or event that triggers the behavior.
3. **Then**: Describes the expected outcome or result.

Example:
> *Feature: User login*
> *Scenario: Successful login with valid credentials*
> *Given the user is on the login page*
> *When the user enters valid credentials*
> *Then the user should be redirected to the dashboard*

In this example, the scenario describes a feature (user login) in a way that is easy for both technical and non-technical team members to understand. Once this scenario is written, it can be automated using BDD tools like Cucumber, which allows the scenario to be run as an automated test.

Benefits of BDD

1. Enhanced Collaboration:
- BDD fosters collaboration between developers, testers, and business stakeholders. By involving all relevant parties in the creation of test scenarios, BDD ensures that the entire team is aligned on what needs to be built and why.

2. Improved Requirements Clarity:
- BDD helps bridge the gap between business goals and technical implementation by providing a clear, shared language for discussing requirements. This reduces misunderstandings and ensures that the development team builds exactly what the business needs.

3. Living Documentation:
- BDD scenarios serve as living documentation for the system. As the scenarios are written in a structured, human-readable format, they remain relevant throughout the lifecycle of the project and can be easily updated as requirements evolve.

4. Early Detection of Issues:
- By defining and agreeing on the expected behavior before development begins, BDD helps identify potential issues or misunderstandings early in the process. This reduces the risk of rework and ensures that the software meets business expectations from the outset.

5. Better Test Coverage:
- BDD promotes comprehensive test coverage by focusing on the different behaviors the system should exhibit. This ensures that all relevant user scenarios are considered and tested, leading to a more robust and reliable system.

6. Facilitates Continuous Feedback:

- ○ BDD encourages continuous feedback from stakeholders throughout the development process. As scenarios are automated and run frequently, stakeholders can see the progress and provide feedback in real-time, allowing for course corrections if necessary.

Key Benefits of BDD

Key Challenges: Aligning BDD Practices with Business Goals and Technical Implementation

While BDD offers significant advantages, aligning its practices with both business goals and technical implementation can be challenging. Here are some of the key challenges that teams may face:

1. Challenge: Ensuring Stakeholder Engagement

Explanation: BDD relies heavily on the active participation of business stakeholders in writing and reviewing scenarios. However, getting stakeholders to commit the time and effort required for effective BDD can be difficult, especially if they are not familiar with the process or do not see its immediate value.

Impact: Without active stakeholder engagement, BDD scenarios may not accurately reflect business goals, leading to a disconnect between the software being developed and the needs of the business. This can result in wasted effort and features that do not deliver the expected value.

2. Challenge: Bridging the Gap Between Business Language and Technical Implementation

Explanation: BDD scenarios are written in natural language, which can sometimes be too abstract or high-level for developers to implement directly. Translating these scenarios into executable code that accurately reflects the intended behavior can be challenging, especially when dealing with complex business logic.

Impact: If the BDD scenarios are not sufficiently detailed or if there is a lack of clear communication between stakeholders and developers, the resulting implementation may not align with the original business intent. This can lead to misunderstandings, bugs, and ultimately, software that fails to meet user expectations.

3. Challenge: Maintaining BDD Scenarios as the Project Evolves

Explanation: As a project progresses and requirements change, it's essential to keep BDD scenarios up to date. However, maintaining and updating these scenarios can be time-consuming, especially if the project is large or complex.

Impact: If BDD scenarios are not regularly updated to reflect changes in requirements, they can become outdated and lose their value as living documentation. This can lead to scenarios that no longer match the current state of the software, reducing their effectiveness as tests and as a communication tool.

Solutions: Involving Business Stakeholders in the BDD Process to Ensure Alignment

To effectively align BDD practices with business goals and technical implementation, it's crucial to involve business stakeholders throughout the process. Here's how you can address the challenges:

1. Foster Stakeholder Engagement Early and Continuously

Explanation: To ensure that business stakeholders are actively involved in the BDD process, it's important to engage them early and keep them involved throughout the project. This can be done by clearly communicating the benefits of BDD and how it directly impacts the quality and relevance of the final product.

Essential Point: Schedule regular BDD workshops or collaborative sessions where stakeholders, developers, and testers come together to discuss and write scenarios. By making these sessions a routine part of the development process, stakeholders are more likely to stay engaged and see the value in their contributions.

Example: In a project to develop a new e-commerce platform, the product owner and other business stakeholders could participate in bi-weekly BDD sessions where they help define and review scenarios for key features like the checkout process or user account management. This involvement ensures that the scenarios accurately capture the business requirements.

2. Provide Training and Resources on BDD

Explanation: To bridge the gap between business language and technical implementation, it's essential to provide training for both stakeholders and developers on how to write effective BDD scenarios. This training should cover the basics of BDD, the structure of Gherkin syntax, and best practices for translating scenarios into executable tests.

Essential Point: Develop clear guidelines and templates for writing BDD scenarios, making it easier for stakeholders and developers to create scenarios that are both understandable and actionable. Additionally, consider using tools that integrate BDD with your existing development environment, such as Cucumber for Java or SpecFlow for .NET.

Example: Organize a training session where stakeholders learn how to write Gherkin scenarios and developers learn how to implement them in the codebase. Providing examples of well-written scenarios and common pitfalls can help both groups improve their BDD skills.

3. Establish Clear Communication Channels

Explanation: Effective communication is key to ensuring that BDD scenarios accurately reflect business goals and are correctly implemented by the development team. Establishing clear communication channels between stakeholders, developers, and testers can help ensure that everyone is on the same page.

Essential Point: Use collaboration tools like Confluence, JIRA, or Slack to facilitate ongoing communication and ensure that scenarios are regularly reviewed and updated as the project evolves. Regular stand-up meetings or sprint reviews can also be used to discuss the progress of BDD scenarios and address any issues.

Example: Set up a dedicated Slack channel where stakeholders can ask questions and provide feedback on BDD scenarios. Developers can use this channel to clarify requirements or discuss technical challenges, ensuring that everyone has a shared understanding of the goals.

4. Regularly Review and Update BDD Scenarios

Explanation: As requirements change, it's essential to keep BDD scenarios up to date. This requires regular reviews and updates to ensure that the scenarios continue to reflect the current state of the project and the latest business priorities.

Essential Point: Schedule regular scenario review sessions where the team revisits existing BDD scenarios and makes any necessary updates. This can be done at the end of each sprint or iteration, ensuring that the scenarios remain relevant and useful throughout the project lifecycle.

Example: At the end of each sprint, the team could review all BDD scenarios related to the features developed during that sprint. Any changes to the requirements or behavior of the system should be reflected in the updated scenarios, ensuring that they remain accurate and useful as tests.

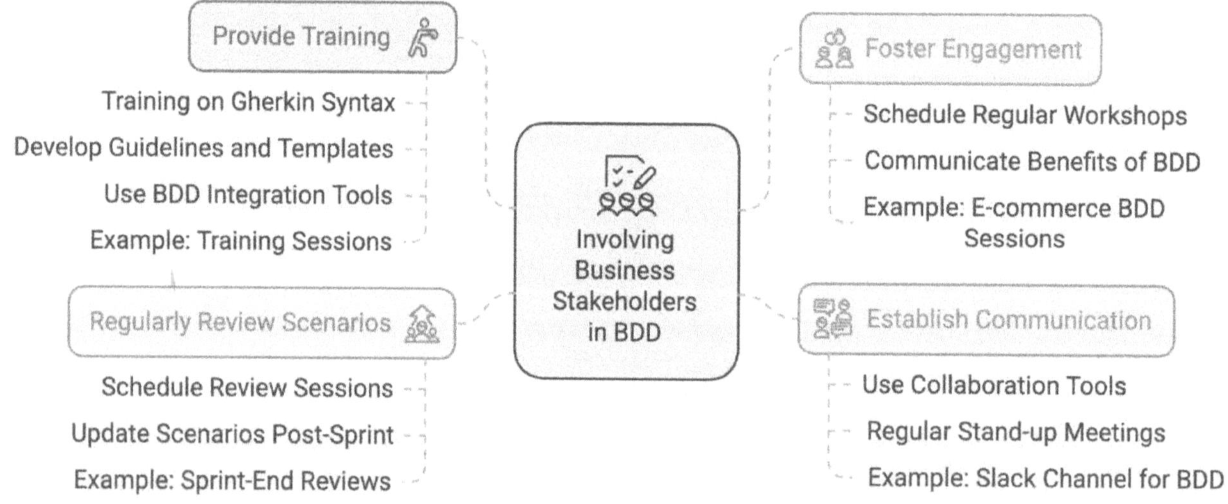

In a Nutshell

Behavior-driven development (BDD) is a powerful methodology that bridges the gap between business goals and technical implementation by encouraging collaboration and clear communication among all project stakeholders. While implementing BDD can be challenging, especially in aligning it with business goals and ensuring its correct implementation, these challenges can be overcome by involving stakeholders throughout the process, providing training and resources, establishing clear communication channels, and regularly reviewing and updating scenarios.

By making BDD an integral part of your development process, you can ensure that the software you build not only meets technical standards but also delivers real value to the business and its users. As you continue to explore the fundamentals of in-sprint automation, keep in mind that BDD is not just about writing tests—it's about fostering a shared understanding of what success looks like for your project. With the right approach, BDD can help your team create software that truly aligns with business goals and meets user needs. This alignment between business objectives and technical implementation is crucial for delivering high-quality software that satisfies stakeholders and end-users alike.

INTEGRATION OF TDD AND BDD IN IN-SPRINT AUTOMATION

Test-Driven Development (TDD) and Behavior-Driven Development (BDD) are both integral to the Agile methodology, but they serve different purposes within the development lifecycle. TDD focuses on ensuring that the code functions correctly by writing tests before the code itself, while BDD emphasizes defining the behavior of the application in a language that is understandable to both technical and non-technical stakeholders. When integrated effectively in in-sprint automation, TDD and BDD can significantly enhance the quality and alignment of the software with business requirements.

How TDD and BDD Work Together

In a typical Agile sprint, TDD and BDD can be used in tandem to ensure that both the technical correctness and the business relevance of the code are maintained. Here's how they complement each other:

1. **Starting with BDD:**
   - The process usually begins with BDD, where scenarios are written to define the desired behavior of a feature. These scenarios are written in a structured language (like Gherkin) that describes how the system should behave from the user's perspective. The scenarios serve as acceptance criteria that the feature must meet to be considered complete.

2. **Transitioning to TDD:**
   - Once the BDD scenarios are defined, the development process moves to TDD. Here, developers write unit tests based on the specific functionality needed to fulfill the BDD scenarios. These tests are written before the actual code, ensuring that the code is developed with a clear focus on passing these tests.

3. **Development and Continuous Integration:**
   - The developer then writes the minimal code necessary to pass the unit tests, ensuring that the code meets the requirements outlined in the BDD scenarios. As each piece of functionality is completed and passes the unit tests, it is integrated into the main codebase through continuous integration (CI) pipelines.

4. **Automated Testing and Feedback:**
   - As part of in-sprint automation, the BDD scenarios are automated and run as acceptance tests in the CI pipeline. These automated tests validate that the code behaves as expected from the user's perspective. If any of these tests fail, the developer is immediately notified, allowing for quick resolution of issues within the same sprint.

5. Refactoring*:*

- ○ With both the BDD acceptance tests and the TDD unit tests in place, developers can confidently refactor the code to improve its structure and efficiency, knowing that any changes that break functionality will be caught by the tests.

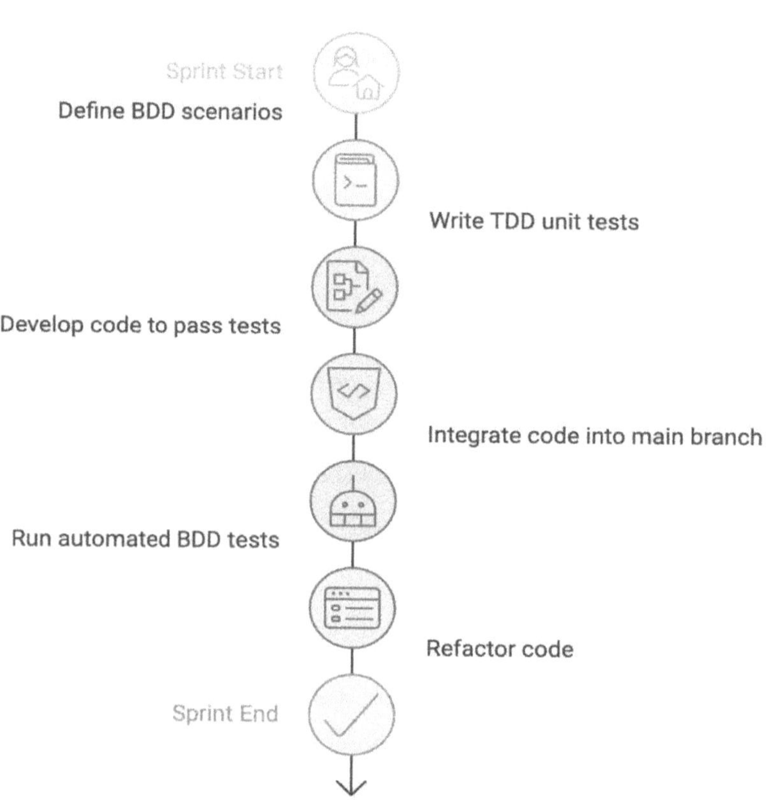

Benefits of Integrating TDD and BDD in In-Sprint Automation

1. Alignment Between Business Goals and Technical Implementation*:*

- ○ The combination of BDD and TDD ensures that the software being developed aligns with both business goals and technical requirements. BDD focuses on defining the desired behavior, while TDD ensures that the code meets these expectations through rigorous testing.

2. Comprehensive Test Coverage*:*

- ○ Integrating TDD and BDD results in comprehensive test coverage, addressing both the low-level functionality (via TDD) and the high-level user behaviors (via BDD). This reduces the likelihood of bugs and ensures that the software behaves correctly under various conditions.

3. Improved Communication*:*

- ○ BDD facilitates communication between developers, testers, and business stakeholders by using a common language to describe features. TDD complements this by providing a technical assurance that the code meets these descriptions.

4. Faster Feedback Loops:
- With automated tests running as part of the CI pipeline, developers receive immediate feedback on whether their code meets both the technical and business requirements. This allows for faster iteration and quicker delivery of high-quality software within each sprint.

5. Reduced Risk of Rework:
- By validating both the functionality and the behavior of the software throughout the development process, the integration of TDD and BDD reduces the risk of costly rework. This proactive approach helps catch issues early, before they become more complex and time-consuming to fix.

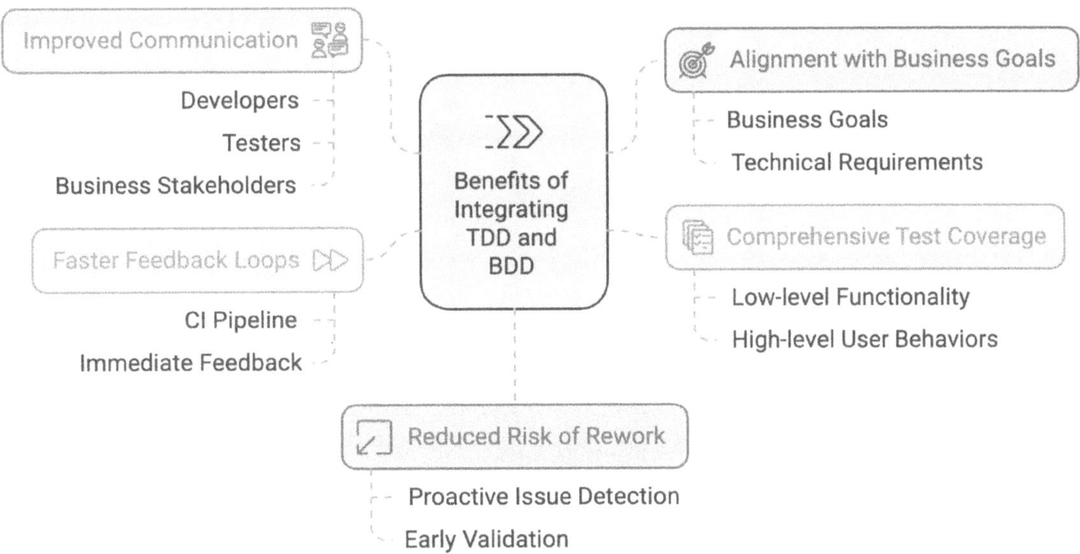

Key Challenges: Combining TDD and BDD Without Slowing Down the Development Process

While the integration of TDD and BDD offers significant benefits, it also presents certain challenges, particularly in the context of maintaining sprint velocity and avoiding delays. Here are the key challenges:

1. Challenge: Managing the Increased Workload

Explanation: Both TDD and BDD involve writing tests before the code is developed. This can initially seem like an additional workload, as it requires more time and effort upfront to create both the unit tests for TDD and the acceptance tests for BDD.

Impact: The increased workload can lead to slower progress, especially if the team is not familiar with TDD and BDD practices. This may result in delays within the sprint, potentially jeopardizing the timely delivery of features.

2. Challenge: Ensuring Consistent Integration

Explanation: Integrating TDD and BDD into the same sprint can be challenging, as it requires seamless collaboration between developers, testers, and business stakeholders. Without consistent integration, there can be gaps in coverage, leading to misalignment between the code and the defined behavior.

Impact: Inconsistent integration can cause delays in feedback, leading to potential issues being discovered late in the sprint. This can result in rework or incomplete features, ultimately affecting the quality and reliability of the software.

3.   Challenge: Tool Compatibility and Integration

Explanation: Using separate tools for TDD and BDD can complicate the development process, especially if the tools do not integrate well with each other or with the CI pipeline. This can lead to fragmented workflows and inefficiencies.

Impact: Poor tool integration can slow down the development process, as developers may need to manually coordinate between different tools or handle compatibility issues. This can hinder the smooth execution of in-sprint automation.

Solutions: Using Tools That Support Both Practices and Facilitate Smooth Integration

To effectively integrate TDD and BDD in in-sprint automation without slowing down the development process, it's essential to use tools and practices that support both methodologies and facilitate their integration. Here's how to achieve this:

1.   Choose Integrated Tools

Explanation: Select tools that are designed to work well together, allowing for seamless integration of TDD and BDD practices. Some tools, such as Cucumber (for BDD) and JUnit (for TDD), have strong support for integration with CI pipelines and other development tools.

Critical Insight: Look for tools that offer plugins or extensions to support both TDD and BDD in a single environment. For example, Cucumber and JUnit can be integrated with Jenkins to automate the execution of both unit and acceptance tests as part of the CI pipeline.

Example: A team could use Cucumber for writing BDD scenarios in Gherkin and JUnit for TDD unit tests, both of which are executed automatically in a Jenkins pipeline. This ensures that all tests are run consistently and provides immediate feedback on the code.

2.   Prioritize Test Writing Within the Sprint

Explanation: To avoid bottlenecks, prioritize the writing of TDD and BDD tests early in the sprint. This allows the team to identify potential issues before they become critical and ensures that the development process remains aligned with the defined behavior.

Critical Insight: Encourage the team to adopt a test-first mindset, where tests are considered an integral part of the development process rather than an afterthought. This approach helps maintain momentum and prevents delays later in the sprint.

Example: During sprint planning, the team could allocate specific time for writing BDD scenarios and TDD tests for each user story. This ensures that both types of tests are prioritized and completed before the feature is developed.

3. *Foster Collaboration Among Team Members*

Explanation: Effective integration of TDD and BDD requires close collaboration between developers, testers, and business stakeholders. Establishing regular communication and collaboration sessions can help ensure that everyone is aligned and working towards the same goals.

Critical Insight: Use daily stand-ups, sprint reviews, and retrospective meetings to discuss the progress of TDD and BDD integration, address any challenges, and make necessary adjustments. This continuous collaboration helps maintain alignment and ensures that the development process remains efficient.

Example: In a daily stand-up, the team could discuss the status of TDD and BDD tests, identify any blockers, and collaborate on solutions. Regular check-ins ensure that the tests are integrated smoothly and that the team remains on track.

4. *Automate Testing and Reporting*

Explanation: Automate the execution of TDD and BDD tests as part of the CI pipeline to ensure that tests are run consistently and without manual intervention. Automated reporting tools can also provide immediate feedback on test results, helping the team quickly identify and resolve issues.

Critical Insight: Use tools like Jenkins or GitHub Actions to automate the testing process and generate reports that highlight any test failures or discrepancies between the TDD and BDD tests. This automation reduces the risk of human error and speeds up the feedback loop.

Example: Configure Jenkins to automatically run both TDD unit tests and BDD acceptance tests after each code commit. The results are then compiled into a report that is shared with the team, allowing for quick identification and resolution of any issues.

Integrating TDD and BDD in In-Sprint Automation

In a Nutshell

The integration of Test-Driven Development (TDD) and Behavior-Driven Development (BDD) in in-sprint automation can significantly enhance the quality and alignment of software with business requirements. By using tools that support both practices, prioritizing test writing within the sprint, fostering collaboration, and automating the testing process, teams can overcome the challenges of combining TDD and BDD without slowing down development.

In-sprint automation, when combined with TDD and BDD, ensures that the software not only functions correctly but also meet the expectations of both technical and non-technical stakeholders. As you continue to refine your Agile practices, remember that the integration of TDD and BDD is not just about testing—it's about building a shared understanding of what success looks like and working together to achieve it.

CREATING A SUSTAINABLE AUTOMATION STRATEGY

In the fast-paced world of Agile development, having an automation strategy is crucial for ensuring that software is thoroughly tested and delivered with high quality. However, it's not just about automating tests—it's about creating a sustainable automation strategy that can evolve and remain effective as the project grows and changes over time. A sustainable automation strategy is one that can be maintained, adapted, and scaled as needed, without becoming a burden on the development team.

Key Elements of a Sustainable Automation Strategy

1. **Comprehensive Coverage and Prioritization:**
   - Your automation strategy should start with identifying what to automate. Not every test case needs to be automated, and trying to automate everything can lead to wasted effort and maintenance headaches. Focus on automating the most critical and repetitive tasks, such as regression tests, smoke tests, and high-risk areas of the application.
   - **Prioritization**: Prioritize test cases that provide the most value in terms of reducing manual testing time and catching critical issues early. This includes tests that cover core functionalities, integrations, and user flows that are prone to breaking.

2. **Modular and Scalable Test Design:**
   - Designing your automated tests in a modular and scalable way is key to sustainability. This means breaking down tests into smaller, reusable components that can be easily updated and maintained as the project evolves.
   - **Scalability**: As the project grows, so does the codebase and the number of test cases. A scalable test design ensures that adding new tests or updating existing ones does not exponentially increase the maintenance effort.

3. **Integration with CI/CD Pipelines:**
   - A sustainable automation strategy must include integration with Continuous Integration and Continuous Deployment (CI/CD) pipelines. Automated tests should be executed as part of the CI process, ensuring that every change to the codebase is validated by running relevant tests.
   - **Continuous Feedback**: This integration provides immediate feedback to developers about the impact of their changes, enabling them to catch and fix issues early, before they become bigger problems.

4. **Regular Maintenance and Refactoring:**
   - Automated tests, like any other part of the codebase, require regular maintenance. As the software evolves, tests may need to be updated, refactored, or even discarded if they are no longer relevant. Regular maintenance ensures that the test suite remains effective and efficient over time.
   - **Refactoring**: Refactoring tests helps to improve their readability, performance, and reliability. It also involves removing duplicate code and restructuring tests to make them easier to maintain.

5. **Handling Flaky Tests:**
   - Flaky tests are tests that sometimes pass and sometimes fail, often due to factors like timing issues or dependencies on external systems. These tests can undermine the reliability of your automation strategy, leading to false positives or negatives.
   - **Addressing Flakiness**: Identifying and addressing flaky tests is critical for maintaining trust in your test suite. This might involve stabilizing the test environment, increasing timeouts, or redesigning tests to eliminate flakiness.

6. **Documentation and Knowledge Sharing:**
   - Documenting the automation strategy, including how tests are organized, how they are executed, and how they should be maintained, is essential for ensuring that the strategy can be sustained over time, even as team members change.
   - **Knowledge Sharing**: Regularly share knowledge about the automation strategy with the team. This includes holding workshops, code reviews, and training sessions to ensure that everyone understands how to contribute to and maintain the test suite.

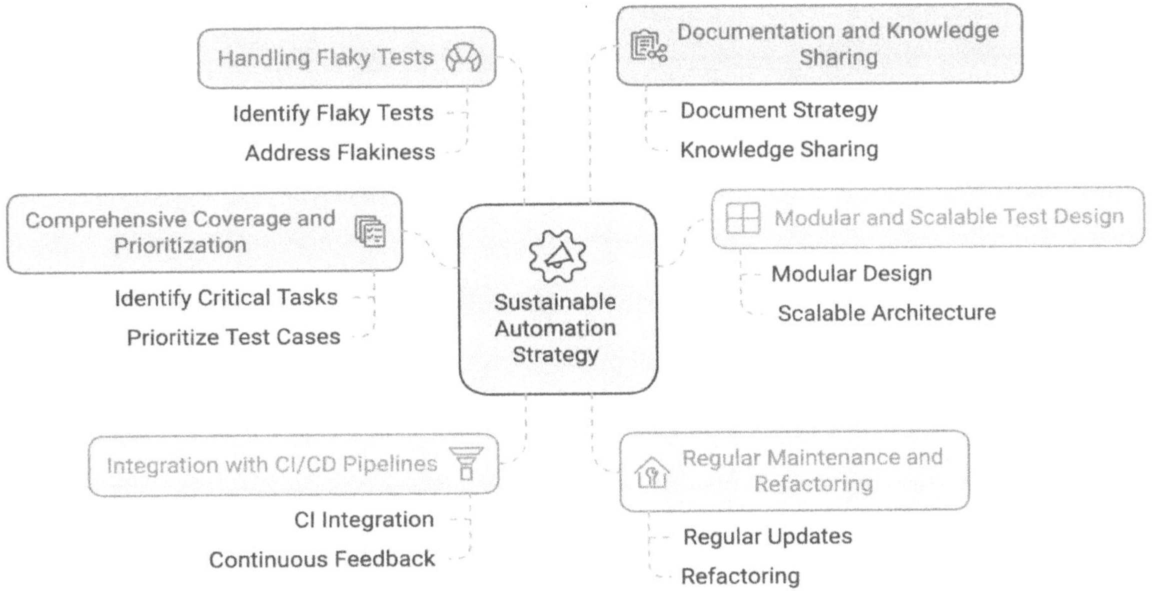

Key Challenges: Maintaining Automated Tests and Ensuring They Remain Effective as the Project Evolves

While creating a sustainable automation strategy offers many benefits, maintaining that strategy as the project evolves presents several challenges:

1. Challenge: Keeping Up with Code Changes

Explanation: As the project evolves, the codebase changes, sometimes rapidly. New features are added, existing features are modified, and bugs are fixed. These changes can cause automated tests to break or become outdated, leading to a loss of confidence in the test suite.

Impact: If automated tests are not regularly updated to reflect changes in the codebase, they can become ineffective, leading to missed bugs or false positives. This can slow down development as developers spend more time investigating and fixing test failures.

2. Challenge: Managing Test Maintenance Overhead

Explanation: Automated tests require ongoing maintenance to ensure they continue to run efficiently and accurately. As the number of tests grows, so does the maintenance overhead. Without proper management, this can become a significant burden on the development team.

Impact: High maintenance overhead can lead to neglected test suites, with tests becoming outdated or redundant. This reduces the overall effectiveness of the automation strategy and can lead to critical issues slipping through the cracks.

3. Challenge: Dealing with Flaky Tests

Explanation: Flaky tests, which are tests that pass or fail inconsistently, are a common problem in automated test suites. They can be caused by issues such as network instability, timing dependencies, or poorly written tests.

Impact: Flaky tests can erode confidence in the test suite, as developers may start to ignore test failures, assuming they are due to test flakiness rather than actual issues in the code. This can result in real bugs going unnoticed and making their way into production.

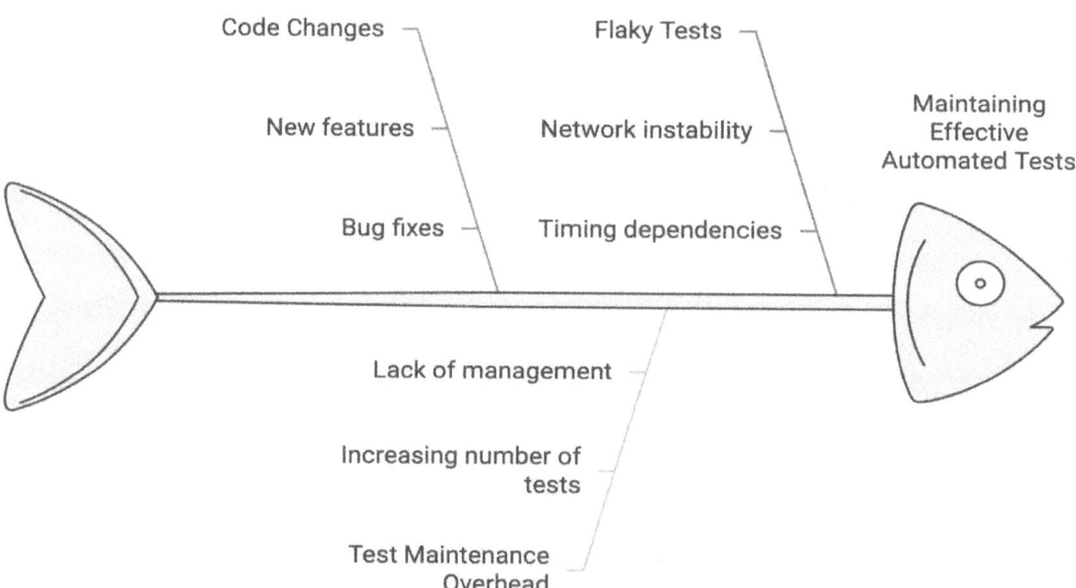

Solutions: Emphasize the Importance of Creating a Long-Term Plan for Test Maintenance, Refactoring, and Dealing with Flaky Tests

To overcome these challenges and ensure that your automation strategy remains sustainable, it's essential to develop a long-term plan that includes regular maintenance, refactoring, and strategies for dealing with flaky tests. Here's how to do it:

1. Implement a Regular Maintenance Schedule

Explanation: Just as the codebase needs regular maintenance, so too does the test suite. Implement a schedule for reviewing and updating automated tests to ensure they remain relevant and effective. This might include tasks such as updating tests to reflect changes in the code, removing obsolete tests, and optimizing slow tests.

Critical Insight: Assign dedicated time during each sprint for test maintenance. This ensures that maintaining the test suite becomes a regular part of the development process, rather than something that is only done when issues arise.

Example: Set aside one day at the end of each sprint for the team to review and update automated tests. This includes checking for any tests that failed during the sprint, analyzing the root cause of the failures, and making necessary updates.

2. Prioritize Refactoring of Tests

Explanation: Refactoring is an essential practice for keeping the test suite clean, efficient, and easy to maintain. Regularly refactor tests to improve their structure, remove duplication, and enhance readability. This makes it easier to update tests as the project evolves and reduces the likelihood of introducing errors.

Critical Insight: Incorporate test refactoring into the development process, treating it with the same importance as code refactoring. This helps ensure that the test suite remains maintainable and effective over time.

Example: During code reviews, include a review of the corresponding tests. Look for opportunities to refactor tests alongside the code, ensuring that both the codebase and the test suite remain clean and well-organized.

3. Actively Manage and Eliminate Flaky Tests

Explanation: Flaky tests are a significant challenge to maintaining a reliable test suite. Actively identify and address flaky tests to prevent them from undermining the effectiveness of your automation strategy. This might involve stabilizing the test environment, redesigning tests to remove dependencies on external systems, or increasing timeouts.

Critical Insight: Establish a process for tracking flaky tests and assigning them to developers for resolution. This ensures that flaky tests are not ignored and that the test suite remains trustworthy.

Example: Use a tool or tracking system to flag flaky tests. Assign these tests to a specific team member each sprint to investigate and fix, ensuring that flaky tests are addressed promptly and do not accumulate.

4. *Foster a Culture of Test Ownership and Continuous Improvement*

Explanation: A sustainable automation strategy requires a team that takes ownership of the test suite and is committed to continuously improving it. Encourage team members to take responsibility for the quality of the tests they write and to contribute to the ongoing improvement of the automation strategy.

Critical Insight: Promote a culture where maintaining and improving the test suite is seen as a shared responsibility. Regularly hold workshops, training sessions, and retrospectives focused on testing practices to encourage continuous learning and improvement.

Example: Organize monthly workshops where team members can share tips and best practices for maintaining and improving the test suite. Use these sessions to discuss common challenges, such as dealing with flaky tests, and to brainstorm solutions.

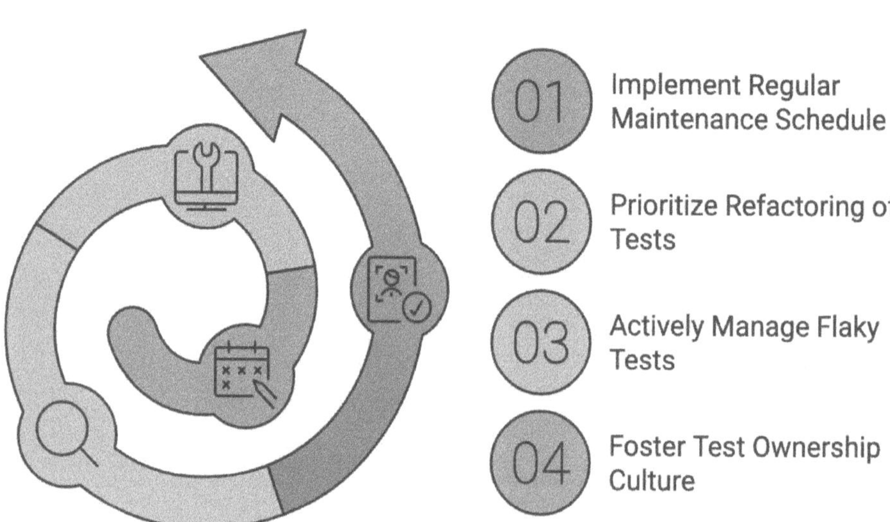

In a Nutshell

Creating a sustainable automation strategy is essential for ensuring that your automated tests continue to deliver value as the project evolves. By implementing regular maintenance, prioritizing refactoring, actively managing flaky tests, and fostering a culture of ownership and continuous improvement, you can overcome the challenges associated with maintaining a large and effective test suite.

In the context of in-sprint automation, a sustainable strategy not only helps maintain the quality of the software but also supports the fast-paced, iterative nature of Agile development. By ensuring that your tests remain effective and relevant over time, you can deliver high-quality software consistently, sprint after sprint.

COLLABORATION BETWEEN DEVELOPERS AND TESTERS

In Agile development, the collaboration between developers and testers is critical to the success of the project. Unlike traditional software development models, where testing often occurs after the development phase, Agile emphasizes the continuous involvement of testers throughout the development process. This close collaboration ensures that quality is built into the software from the very beginning, rather than being tested for later.

In an Agile environment, developers and testers work together to define requirements, write tests, and ensure that the software meets the desired quality standards. This collaboration is particularly important in the context of in-sprint automation, where testing is integrated into each sprint, and the feedback loop between development and testing is fast and continuous.

How Collaboration Between Developers and Testers Works

Shared Understanding of Requirements

Developers and testers work together to ensure a shared understanding of the requirements and user stories. This often involves collaborative discussions during sprint planning meetings, where both parties contribute to defining the acceptance criteria for each feature.

Example: Before starting development on a new feature, developers and testers might review the user story together, discussing potential edge cases and how they will be tested. This collaboration ensures that both parties are aligned on what needs to be built and how it will be validated.

Test-Driven Development (TDD) and Behavior-Driven Development (BDD)

In **TDD**, developers write tests before writing the code, ensuring that the code is developed with testing in mind from the outset. Testers can contribute by helping to define these tests and ensuring that they cover all necessary scenarios.

In **BDD**, testers, developers, and business stakeholders collaborate to write scenarios that describe the desired behavior of the software. These scenarios are then automated and used to validate that the software meets the business requirements.

Example: During a BDD session, testers might work with developers and product owners to write Gherkin scenarios that describe how a new feature should behave. These scenarios are then used by developers to guide the implementation and by testers to automate the acceptance tests.

Continuous Integration and Continuous Testing

Collaboration between developers and testers is essential for maintaining a continuous integration (CI) pipeline. As developers commit code, automated tests are run to ensure that the new code does not introduce any regressions or bugs. Testers and developers must work closely to ensure that these tests are comprehensive and reliable.

Example: Developers might work with testers to ensure that the automated tests in the CI pipeline cover all critical paths. If a test fails, the developer and tester can collaborate to diagnose and fix the issue quickly.

Joint Ownership of Quality

In Agile, quality is a shared responsibility. Developers and testers both take ownership of the quality of the software, working together to identify and fix issues as early as possible. This collaboration reduces the chances of defects making it to production and ensures that the final product meets user expectations.

Example: Instead of waiting for testers to find bugs after the development is complete, developers proactively seek feedback from testers throughout the development process. This might involve pairing sessions where developers and testers work together to test new features as they are being developed.

Regular Communication and Feedback Loops

Effective collaboration requires regular communication between developers and testers. Daily stand-up meetings, sprint reviews, and retrospectives provide opportunities for both groups to share updates, discuss challenges, and provide feedback.

Example: In daily stand-up meetings, testers might raise issues they encountered during testing, allowing developers to address them promptly. In sprint retrospectives, both developers and testers can discuss what went well and what could be improved in their collaboration.

Collaboration Between Developers and Testers

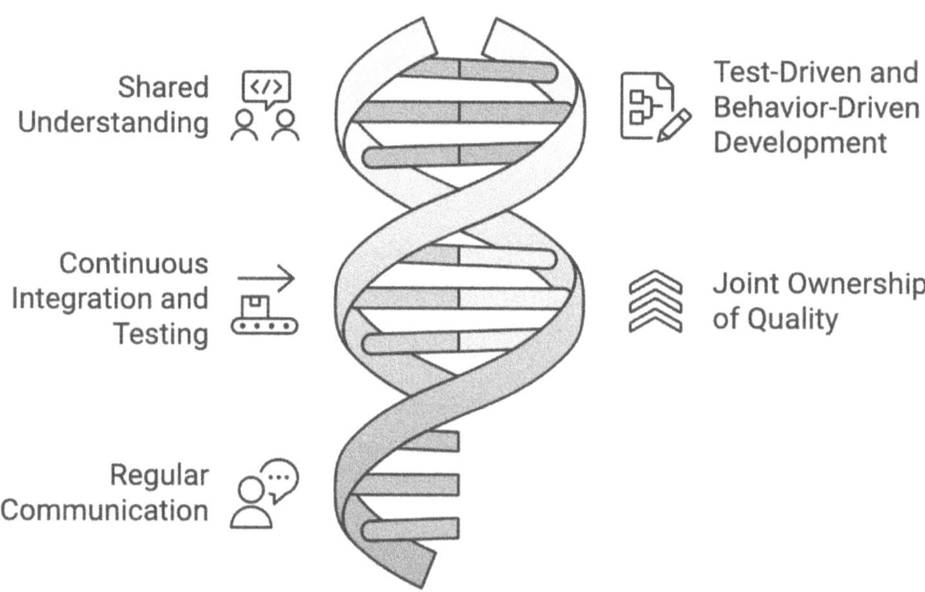

Key Challenges: Ensuring Smooth Communication and Collaboration Between Developers and Testers, Especially in Distributed Teams

While collaboration between developers and testers is critical, it can be challenging to maintain smooth communication and effective collaboration, particularly in distributed teams. Here are some of the key challenges:

1. *Challenge: Communication Barriers*

Explanation: In distributed teams, where developers and testers may be working from different locations, communication can be a significant challenge. Time zone differences, language barriers, and the lack of face-to-face interaction can lead to misunderstandings and delays.

Impact: Poor communication can result in misaligned expectations, overlooked bugs, and slower progress. If developers and testers are not on the same page, it can lead to rework and decreased efficiency.

2. *Challenge: Lack of Shared Tools and Processes*

Explanation: Without shared tools and processes, collaboration between developers and testers can become disjointed. If developers and testers use different tools or follow different workflows, it can create gaps in communication and make it difficult to track progress or share information.

Impact: Disconnected tools and processes can lead to inefficiencies, with team members spending extra time and effort trying to coordinate their work. This can result in slower feedback loops and delayed releases.

3.   *Challenge: Cultural and Organizational Differences*

Explanation: In distributed teams, cultural and organizational differences can impact how developers and testers work together. Different attitudes towards communication, decision-making, and problem-solving can create friction and make collaboration more difficult.

Impact: Cultural and organizational differences can lead to misunderstandings, reduced trust, and lower morale. If team members do not feel comfortable communicating openly or if their contributions are not valued, it can negatively affect the overall quality of the software.

Solutions: Foster a Collaborative Culture and Use Tools That Facilitate Communication

To overcome these challenges and ensure smooth communication and collaboration between developers and testers, it's essential to foster a collaborative culture and use tools that facilitate communication. Here's how to achieve this:

1.   *Foster a Collaborative Culture*

Explanation: Building a collaborative culture where developers and testers see themselves as part of the same team is crucial. This involves encouraging open communication, mutual respect, and shared responsibility for quality.

Critical Insight: Encourage developers and testers to work together on tasks, share knowledge, and support each other in achieving common goals. Promote a culture where quality is everyone's responsibility, not just the testers.

Example: Implement pair programming or test-driven development (TDD) sessions where developers and testers work together on writing and testing code. This hands-on collaboration helps build trust and ensures that both parties are aligned on the project's goals.

2.   *Use Collaborative Tools*

Explanation: Leverage tools that facilitate real-time communication, collaboration, and information sharing between developers and testers. These tools should integrate well with the team's existing workflows and support both synchronous and asynchronous communication.

Critical Insight: Tools like Slack, Microsoft Teams, and Zoom can be used for real-time communication, while tools like JIRA, Confluence, and GitHub facilitate collaboration on tasks and documentation. Ensure that all team members are trained on these tools and use them consistently.

Example: Set up dedicated channels in Slack or Microsoft Teams for each project or feature, where developers and testers can discuss issues, share updates, and collaborate on solutions. Use JIRA to track bugs and test cases, ensuring that everyone has visibility into the status of each task.

3.   *Implement Regular Check-Ins and Feedback Loops*

Explanation: Regular check-ins and feedback loops are essential for maintaining alignment and ensuring that any issues are addressed promptly. Daily stand-ups, sprint reviews, and retrospectives provide opportunities for developers and testers to communicate and collaborate effectively.

Critical Insight: Use these meetings to discuss progress, identify blockers, and plan the next steps. Encourage open communication and create a safe environment where team members feel comfortable sharing their thoughts and concerns.

Example: In daily stand-ups, developers and testers can update each other on their progress and any challenges they are facing. In sprint retrospectives, both groups can reflect on what went well and what could be improved in their collaboration.

4.   *Bridge Cultural and Organizational Differences*

Explanation: Acknowledge and respect cultural and organizational differences within the team. Encourage team members to learn about each other's backgrounds and working styles to build mutual understanding and trust.

Critical Insight: Provide training on cultural awareness and communication skills to help team members navigate differences and work together more effectively. Foster an inclusive environment where diverse perspectives are valued and integrated into the project.

Example: Organize team-building activities or virtual social events where developers and testers from different locations can get to know each other on a personal level. This helps break down barriers and fosters a sense of camaraderie and collaboration.

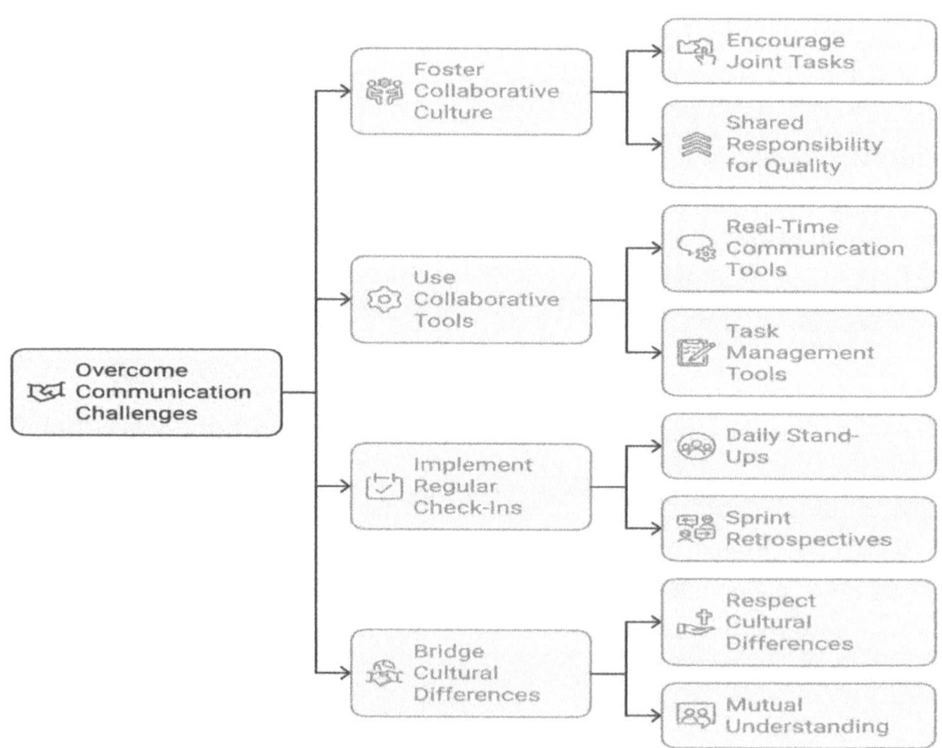

In a Nutshell

Effective collaboration between developers and testers is essential for delivering high-quality software in an Agile environment. By fostering a collaborative culture, using the right tools, implementing regular check-ins, and bridging cultural differences, teams can overcome the challenges of distributed work and ensure smooth communication and collaboration.

In the context of in-sprint automation, strong collaboration between developers and testers ensures that quality is built into the software from the start. This collaboration not only improves the efficiency and effectiveness of the development process but also leads to better outcomes for the end users. As you continue to refine your Agile practices, remember that collaboration is key to success—by working together, developers and testers can achieve more than they could alone.

HANDLING LEGACY CODE IN IN-SPRINT AUTOMATION

Legacy code refers to any code that is inherited from previous versions of the software or developed by previous teams, often without proper documentation or automated tests. This code can be stable and functional but may also be difficult to modify or extend due to its age, complexity, or lack of test coverage. In the context of in-sprint automation, working with legacy code presents unique challenges, particularly when trying to introduce automated tests without disrupting the ongoing development process.

Understanding the Nature of Legacy Code

Legacy code is often characterized by the following traits:

- **Lack of Automated Tests**: Most legacy code lacks automated test coverage, making it risky to change. This is because developers cannot easily verify that their changes haven't broken existing functionality.
- **Complexity and Entanglement**: Legacy code can be highly complex, with tightly coupled components and dependencies that make it hard to isolate parts of the code for testing.
- **Unclear Documentation**: Often, the documentation for legacy code is outdated or nonexistent, making it difficult for current developers to understand how the code works or why certain decisions were made.
- **Risk of Introducing Bugs**: Modifying legacy code without tests is risky because there's no immediate way to verify that the changes haven't introduced new bugs.

Why Addressing Legacy Code Matters

In an Agile environment, where rapid iteration and continuous improvement are key, legacy code can become a bottleneck. It can slow down the development process, increase the risk of introducing bugs, and make it harder to implement new features or refactor existing ones. By bringing legacy code into the fold of in-sprint automation, teams can gradually improve the maintainability and reliability of their codebase, making it easier to work with over time.

Key Challenges: Writing Tests for Legacy Code Without Slowing Down the Sprint

Introducing automated tests into a legacy codebase presents several challenges, especially when trying to maintain the pace of Agile sprints:

1. *Challenge: Limited Time and Resources*

Explanation: In a typical sprint, the development team is already focused on delivering new features and fixing bugs. Finding the time and resources to write tests for existing legacy code can be difficult, especially if the code is complex and not well-understood.

Impact: Without automated tests, developers may be reluctant to modify legacy code, leading to technical debt and a slower pace of development. However, diverting too much time to writing tests for legacy code can slow down the sprint and delay the delivery of new features.

2.   Challenge: Difficulty in Isolating Code for Testing

Explanation: Legacy code is often tightly coupled, meaning that different parts of the code depend on each other in ways that are difficult to untangle. This makes it challenging to isolate specific functions or modules for testing without affecting other parts of the system.

Impact: The lack of modularity in legacy code can make it difficult to write effective tests. Developers may need to refactor the code to make it testable, which can be time-consuming and risky, especially if the code is not well-understood.

3.   Challenge: Fear of Breaking Existing Functionality

Explanation: Without automated tests, any change to legacy code carries the risk of breaking existing functionality. Developers may be hesitant to make changes or introduce tests because they cannot easily verify that the code still works as intended.

Impact: This fear of breaking the code can lead to a reluctance to refactor or improve the legacy codebase, resulting in ongoing technical debt and a codebase that becomes increasingly difficult to maintain over time.

Solutions: Incrementally Introduce Automation into Legacy Codebases

To address these challenges and successfully introduce automation into legacy codebases without slowing down the sprint, teams can adopt the following strategies:

1.   Start with High-Risk and High-Value Areas

Explanation: Not all legacy code needs to be tested or refactored immediately. Start by identifying the parts of the legacy codebase that are most critical to the application's functionality or that are most likely to be modified in future sprints. These areas are often the best candidates for introducing automated tests because they represent the highest risk if something goes wrong.

Simple Explanation: Focus first on testing the parts of the legacy code that are most important and that you're likely to change soon. This helps you avoid introducing bugs in critical areas while keeping the process manageable.

Example: If you're working on an e-commerce application, the payment processing module might be a high-risk area that warrants early attention. Start by writing automated tests for this module to ensure it continues to function correctly even as you make changes.

2.   Use Characterization Tests to Understand Legacy Code

Explanation: Before making any changes to legacy code, write characterization tests. These are tests that describe the current behavior of the code, even if that behavior is not well-understood or documented. Characterization tests help you establish a baseline for how the code currently works, so you can identify any unintended changes when you start refactoring.

Simple Explanation: Write tests that show how the legacy code works right now, even if you're not sure what it's supposed to do. This way, you can tell if your changes cause any problems.

Example: For a legacy login system, you might write characterization tests that verify how the system handles different user credentials, even if the code itself is complex and poorly documented. These tests help you ensure that your changes don't break the login functionality.

3. *Refactor Incrementally*

Explanation: Rather than trying to refactor large sections of legacy code all at once, break down the work into smaller, manageable pieces. Start by refactoring the most critical or most frequently modified parts of the codebase, and gradually work your way through the rest of the code. Each small refactoring should be followed by adding automated tests to ensure the changes don't introduce new bugs.

Simple Explanation: Make small, safe changes to the legacy code, one step at a time. After each change, add tests to make sure everything still works.

Example: If you're refactoring a legacy function that calculates tax, start by simplifying just one part of the function and writing tests to cover that change. Once you're confident that the tests pass and the function still works as expected, move on to the next part.

4. *Introduce Tests During Bug Fixes*

Explanation: When you need to fix a bug in legacy code, use this opportunity to introduce automated tests. Start by writing a test that replicates the bug, ensuring that the test fails. Then, fix the bug and verify that the test passes. This approach not only helps you fix the immediate issue but also adds to your suite of automated tests, improving the codebase over time.

Simple Explanation: Whenever you fix a bug in the legacy code, write a test that shows the bug is fixed. This way, you build up your test coverage gradually.

Example: Suppose there's a bug in the way discounts are applied in a shopping cart. First, write a test that demonstrates the bug (e.g., by showing that the discount is calculated incorrectly). Then, fix the bug and run the test again to make sure it now passes.

5. *Use Mocks and Stubs to Isolate Tests*

Explanation: When dealing with tightly coupled legacy code, it can be difficult to isolate individual components for testing. In these cases, use mocks and stubs to simulate the behavior of dependent components. This allows you to test specific parts of the code without having to deal with the entire system.

Simple Explanation: If the legacy code is too tangled to test easily, use mock versions of the code's dependencies to focus on just the part you're interested in.

Example: If you're testing a legacy method that relies on an external database, you can use a mock database to simulate the data without having to set up a full database environment. This makes it easier to write and run tests.

6. *Integrate Legacy Code Testing into the Sprint Workflow*

Explanation: Integrating legacy code testing into the sprint workflow helps ensure that progress is made consistently. Allocate a small portion of each sprint to focus on legacy code—whether it's writing new tests, refactoring, or addressing technical debt. This approach ensures that legacy code is gradually improved without overwhelming the team or slowing down the sprint.

Simple Explanation: Dedicate a bit of time in each sprint to improve and test the legacy code. This way, you're always making progress without slowing down the main work.

Example: During sprint planning, allocate time for legacy code tasks, such as writing characterization tests or refactoring a specific module. Over time, these small efforts will significantly improve the overall quality of the legacy codebase.

Improve Legacy Code with Automated Testing and Refactoring

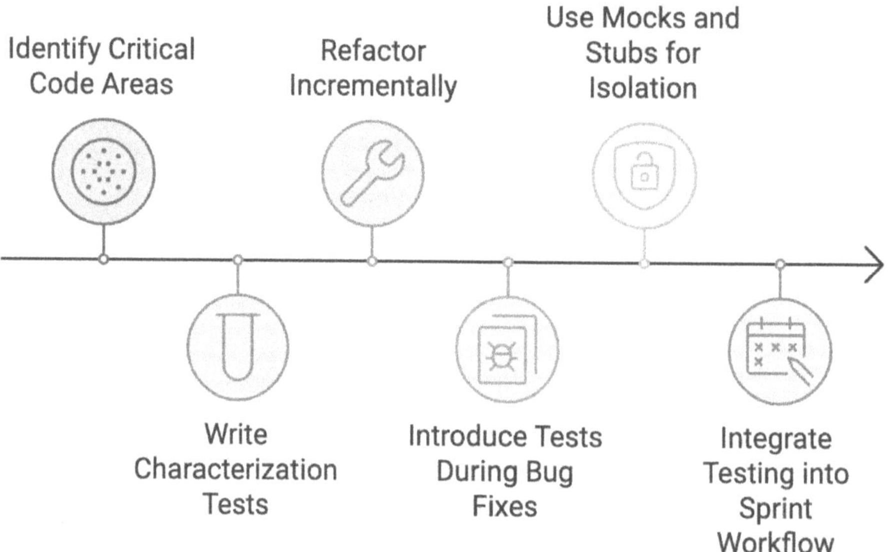

In a Nutshell

Handling legacy code in the context of in-sprint automation is a challenging but essential task. Legacy code often lacks the automated test coverage that modern code enjoys, making it risky to change and difficult to maintain. However, by incrementally introducing automation into the legacy codebase, focusing on high-risk areas, using characterization tests, refactoring gradually, and integrating this work into the sprint workflow, teams can improve the quality and maintainability of legacy code without slowing down the sprint.

By taking a strategic and incremental approach, teams can gradually bring legacy code up to modern standards, reducing technical debt and making the codebase easier to work with. This not only improves the reliability of the software but also empowers the development team to innovate and extend the system with greater confidence.

## CHAPTER 3

IMPLEMENTING IN-SPRINT AUTOMATION

In-sprint automation is a critical practice in Agile development, enabling teams to maintain high quality and speed as they deliver new features within short development cycles. Effective in-sprint automation relies heavily on well-crafted user stories that are not only clear and concise but also incorporate automation requirements from the start. This approach ensures that automated testing is integrated seamlessly into the development process, helping to catch defects early and reduce rework.

CRAFTING EFFECTIVE USER STORIES

User stories are the foundation of Agile development, describing the desired functionality from the user's perspective. They guide the development process and serve as the basis for planning, coding, and testing. Crafting effective user stories involves more than just outlining what a feature should do; it also involves defining how that feature will be tested, particularly through automation.

Incorporating Automation Requirements into User Stories

Why Automation Requirements Matter

Incorporating automation requirements directly into user stories ensures that testing is considered from the very beginning of the development process. This approach helps prevent situations where a feature is developed without a clear plan for how it will be tested, leading to potential delays or incomplete testing. By embedding automation criteria within the user stories, teams can align their development and testing efforts, ensuring that both are completed within the sprint.

Automation requirements in user stories typically define what needs to be automated, such as specific scenarios, edge cases, and the expected outcomes. These requirements guide the development of automated tests, ensuring they are aligned with the functionality.

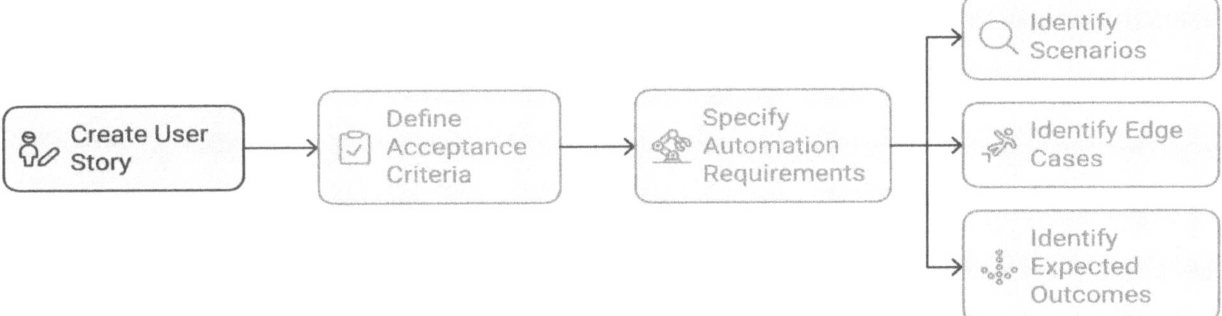

Example of an Enhanced User Story

A basic user story might look like this:

"As a user, I want to reset my password so that I can regain access to my account if I forget my password."

An enhanced version with automation requirements might include:

Acceptance Criteria:

1. The user must receive an email with a password reset link.
2. The reset link should be valid for 24 hours.
3. Automated test criteria:
   - Verify that the email is sent within 5 minutes.
   - Test various scenarios, such as invalid email formats and expired links.
   - Ensure that the user is redirected to a confirmation page after resetting the password.

Key Challenge: Ensuring That User Stories Not Only Describe the Feature but Also Include Clear Criteria for What Needs to Be Automated

The Challenge

One of the main challenges in Agile development is ensuring that user stories are comprehensive enough to guide both development and testing. While it's essential to describe the functionality, it's equally important to specify how that functionality will be tested, particularly through automation. Without clear automation criteria, teams may struggle to develop relevant tests, leading to gaps in test coverage or misunderstandings about what needs to be validated.

Another challenge is balancing the detail in user stories. They need to be detailed enough to guide development and testing but not so complex that they become unwieldy or difficult to understand. Striking this balance requires collaboration between developers, testers, and product owners.

Solutions: Work Closely with Testers to Integrate Automation Requirements into the User Stories, Ensuring They Are Clear and Actionable

Collaborative Approach

The best way to overcome this challenge is through close collaboration between developers, testers, and product owners during the creation of user stories. This collaborative approach ensures that everyone involved in the development process has a shared understanding of what needs to be built and how it will be tested.

Steps to Integrate Automation Requirements

Involve Testers Early

Involve testers in the early stages of user story creation. Their input is valuable in identifying potential test scenarios and automation opportunities. This collaboration helps ensure that automation requirements are considered from the outset.

Example: During the sprint planning meeting, developers, testers, and product owners can work together to review user stories and discuss the necessary automated tests.

Define Clear Acceptance Criteria

Each user story should include clear and specific acceptance criteria that outline what needs to be tested. This includes functional tests, edge cases, and any non-functional requirements like performance or security tests. These criteria should be written in a way that is easy to translate into automated tests.

Example: For a feature that allows users to upload files, acceptance criteria might include tests for file size limits, supported formats, and handling of corrupted files.

Use Automation-Friendly Language

Write user stories and acceptance criteria in a way that is easy to automate. This means avoiding ambiguous language and focusing on measurable outcomes. The goal is to make it straightforward for testers to develop automated tests that match the criteria.

Example: Instead of saying, "The page should load quickly," specify "The page should load within 2 seconds under normal conditions."

Regularly Review and Refine

As the project progresses, regularly review and refine user stories and their associated automation requirements. This ongoing review process helps ensure that the user stories remain relevant and that the automated tests continue to provide value.

Example: At the end of each sprint, hold a retrospective to discuss the effectiveness of the automated tests and identify any gaps in the user stories that need to be addressed in the next iteration.

Document Automation Requirements

Keep a record of the automation requirements as part of the user story documentation. This documentation serves as a reference for future sprints and helps maintain consistency in how automation is handled across the project.

Example: Use a shared document or project management tool like JIRA to document user stories, including their automation criteria, so that all team members can easily access and review them.

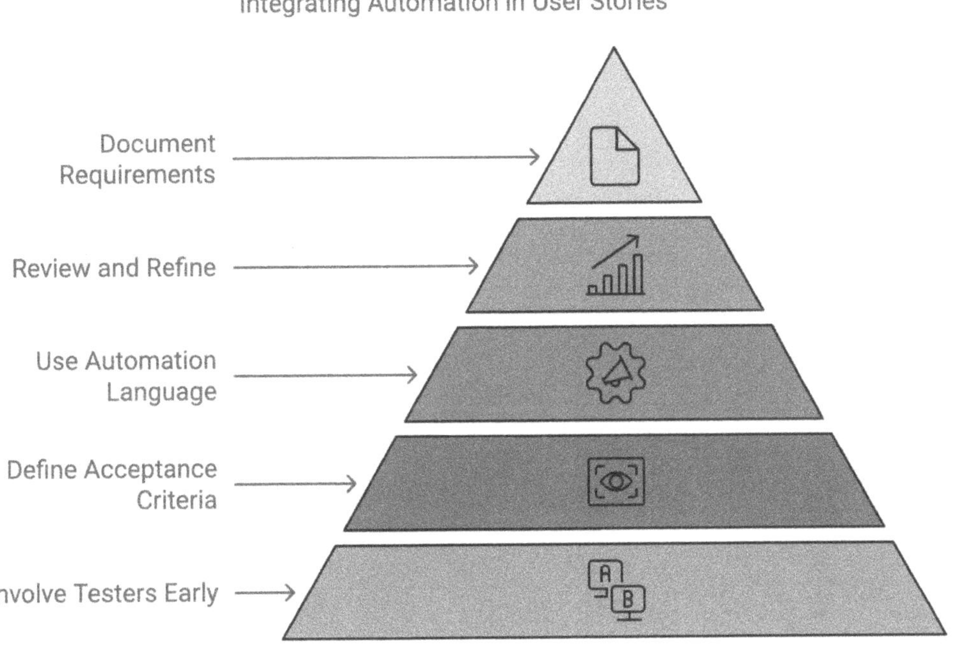

Benefits of This Approach

By integrating automation requirements into user stories from the start, teams can ensure that testing is an integral part of the development process rather than an afterthought. This approach leads to higher-quality software, as potential issues are identified and addressed early in the sprint. It also improves efficiency, as developers and testers have a clear roadmap for what needs to be built and tested, reducing the likelihood of rework.

Moreover, this collaborative approach fosters better communication between developers, testers, and product owners, leading to a more cohesive team and a smoother development process. It helps ensure that everyone is aligned on the goals of the sprint and that the final product meets both technical and business requirements.

In a Nutshell

Crafting effective user stories with integrated automation requirements is a crucial strategy for successful in-sprint automation. By working closely with testers and defining clear, actionable criteria, teams can ensure that their user stories guide both development and testing efforts, leading to higher-quality outcomes and more efficient sprints. This approach not only improves the robustness of the software but also enhances team collaboration and alignment, ultimately contributing to the overall success of the Agile process.

ENSURING USER STORIES MEET THE DEFINITION OF DONE

The Definition of Done (DoD) is a critical concept in Agile development, serving as a shared understanding among team members about what it means for a user story to be considered complete. It sets the standard for quality and ensures that all necessary work is completed before a feature is marked as "done." This includes everything from coding and testing to documentation and deployment readiness. To ensure that software quality is maintained throughout the development process, it is essential to integrate automation into the Definition of Done.

Automation as a Part of the Definition of Done (DoD)

Why Automation Should Be Included in the DoD?

Incorporating automation into the Definition of Done is vital because it ensures that the software is not only feature-complete but also tested and validated through automated processes. This approach guarantees that the software works as intended and that any changes made during the sprint do not introduce new bugs or regressions.

When automation is part of the DoD, it sets a clear expectation that every user story will have corresponding automated tests that must pass before the story is considered done. This reduces the risk of defects slipping through to later stages of development or production, where they are more costly and time-consuming to fix.

Example of an Updated Definition of Done

A basic Definition of Done might include criteria like:

- Code is written and reviewed.
- Functional testing is complete.
- Documentation is updated.

An enhanced DoD that includes automation might add:

- Automated unit tests are written and pass.
- Automated integration tests are executed and pass.
- Automated acceptance tests are completed and validate the user story.

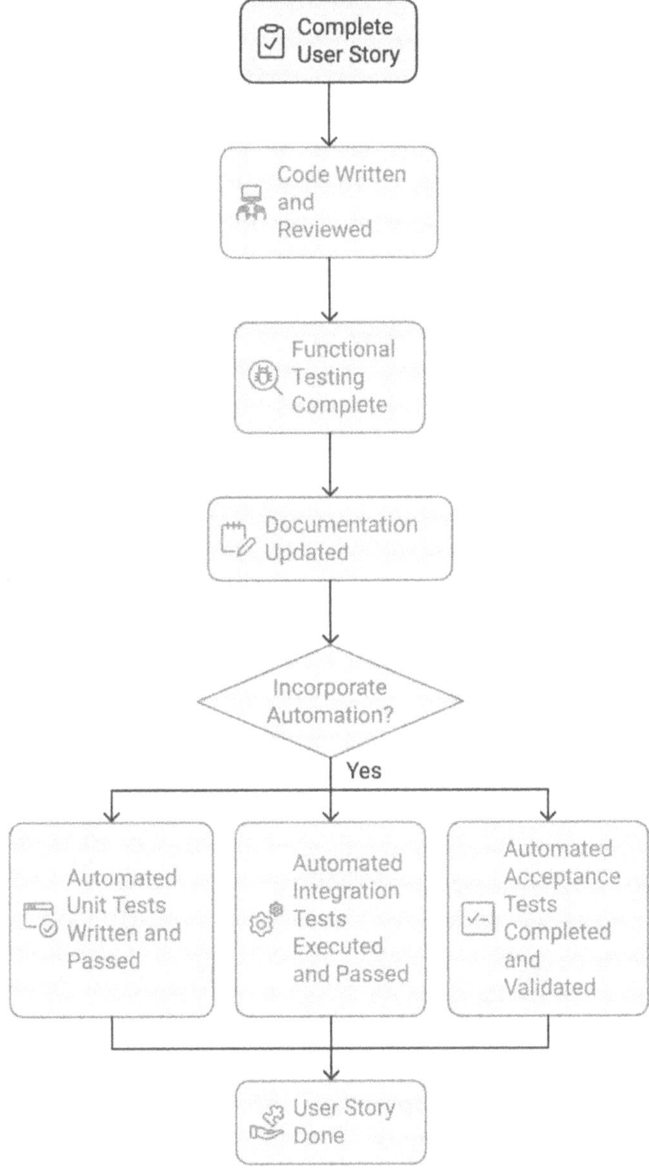

Key Challenge: Aligning the Definition of Done to Include Both Feature Completion and the Corresponding Automated Tests

The Challenge

One of the key challenges in Agile development is aligning the team's understanding and application of the Definition of Done, especially when it includes automated testing. Teams often struggle with consistently applying the DoD across different user stories and sprints, particularly when automation is not traditionally part of their workflow. Additionally, there might be resistance to updating the DoD to include automation due to concerns about the time and effort required to implement and maintain automated tests.

Another challenge is ensuring that the automated tests are thorough and relevant to the feature being developed. If the automated tests are not well-aligned with the user story, they may not provide the intended value, potentially leaving critical aspects of the feature untested.

Solutions: Update the Definition of Done Checklist to Explicitly State the Requirement for Passing Automated Tests as Part of the Completion Criteria

Steps to Integrate Automation into the DoD

Collaborate on Defining the Updated DoD

Engage the entire team, including developers, testers, and product owners, in the process of updating the Definition of Done. This ensures that everyone has a shared understanding of what is required and buys into the process. By including all stakeholders in the discussion, you can address any concerns and ensure that the updated DoD reflects the team's commitment to quality.

Example: During a sprint retrospective, the team can discuss the current DoD and identify gaps where automation could be incorporated. Together, they can agree on specific automated tests that should be included as part of the DoD.

Explicitly Include Automated Testing in the DoD Checklist

The updated DoD should explicitly state that a user story is not considered done until all relevant automated tests have been written and successfully executed. This might include unit tests, integration tests, and acceptance tests, depending on the complexity of the feature.

Example: Update the DoD checklist in your project management tool (like JIRA) to include items such as "Automated unit tests pass" and "Automated integration tests complete," ensuring these tasks are tracked and completed before the story is closed.

Make Automated Testing a Standard Practice

To align with the updated DoD, make automated testing a standard part of the development process. This means that developers should write tests as they code, and testers should focus on creating automated acceptance tests as part of their work. The goal is to ensure that automation is not seen as an add-on but as an integral part of delivering a complete user story.

Example: Establish a rule that no code can be merged into the main branch until all automated tests associated with that code pass. This practice reinforces the importance of automated testing and ensures that it is consistently applied.

Provide Training and Resources

If the team is not yet familiar with automated testing, provide training and resources to help them integrate it into their workflow. This might involve workshops on how to write effective automated tests, how to use specific testing frameworks, or how to interpret test results.

Example: Organize a series of training sessions on writing automated tests using a specific framework like Selenium for UI tests or JUnit for unit tests. Providing these resources helps the team build confidence in their ability to meet the updated DoD.

Monitor and Enforce the Updated DoD

After updating the DoD, it's important to monitor its application and ensure that it is consistently enforced. This can be done through regular reviews and audits of completed user stories to verify that all automated tests have been written and passed.

Example: During sprint reviews, the Scrum Master or another team member could verify that each user story meets the updated DoD, including the successful execution of all automated tests. If any criteria are not met, the story should be sent back to the development team for completion.

Iterate and improve the DoD

The Definition of Done should not be static; it should evolve as the team improves its processes and as new challenges arise. Regularly review and refine the DoD to ensure it continues to serve the team's needs and supports the delivery of high-quality software.

Example: At the end of each release cycle, hold a retrospective focused specifically on the DoD. Discuss what worked well, what didn't, and how the DoD can be further refined to support the team's goals.

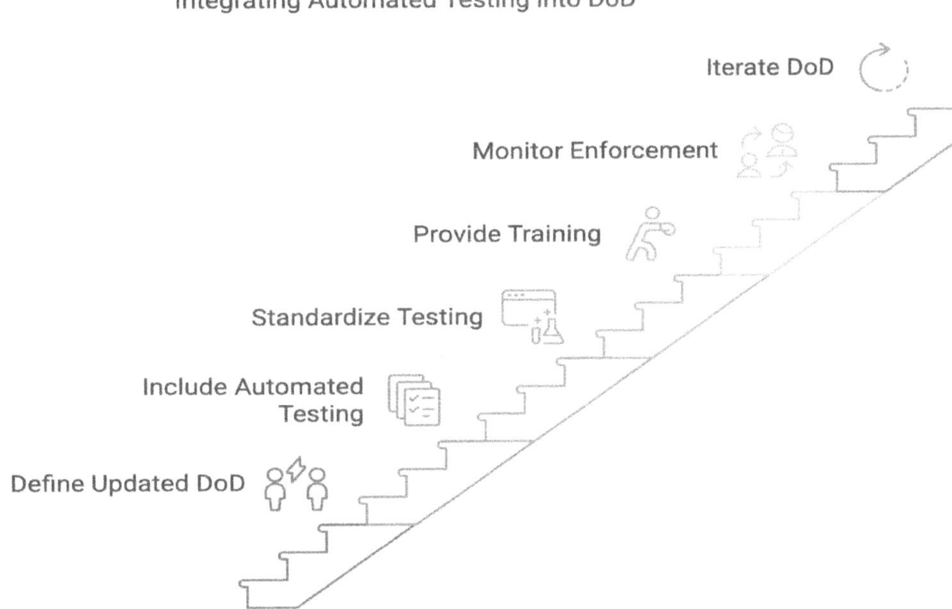

Benefits of Including Automation in the DoD

By including automation in the Definition of Done, teams can ensure that quality is built into the development process from the start. This approach reduces the risk of defects making it into production, shortens the feedback loop, and increases confidence in the software being delivered. It also fosters a culture of continuous improvement, where the team is always looking for ways to enhance their processes and deliver better results.

Moreover, a DoD that includes automation helps standardize expectations across the team, ensuring that everyone is working towards the same goals and understands what is required to consider a user story truly "done." This alignment leads to more efficient sprints, higher-quality software, and greater satisfaction among stakeholders.

In a Nutshell

Ensuring that user stories meet a comprehensive Definition of Done that includes automation is a crucial strategy for maintaining high-quality standards in Agile development. By updating the DoD to explicitly require passing automated tests and making this practice a standard part of the development process, teams can align their efforts more effectively, reduce the risk of defects, and deliver more reliable software. This approach not only strengthens the development process but also enhances collaboration, accountability, and the overall success of Agile projects.

IMPLEMENTING FUNCTIONAL TESTING IN SPRINTS

Functional testing is a crucial aspect of ensuring that the software behaves as expected and meets the defined requirements. In the context of Agile development, functional testing must be integrated into each sprint to validate that new features and changes work correctly before they are released. This involves writing and executing tests that verify the functionality of the application, typically focusing on what the system should do from the user's perspective.

In an Agile environment, where development cycles are short and iterative, it is essential to implement functional testing in a way that aligns with the pace of the sprint. This means that testing must be efficient, automated where possible, and integrated seamlessly into the development process. The goal is to catch and address issues early, reducing the risk of defects and ensuring that the software is ready for release at the end of each sprint.

Integration of Non-Functional Testing within Sprints

Why Non-Functional Testing Matters

While functional testing focuses on verifying that the software does what it is supposed to do, non-functional testing assesses how the software performs under certain conditions. This includes tests for performance, security, usability, reliability, and scalability. Non-functional testing is critical because it ensures that the software not only functions correctly but also meets performance and quality standards that are crucial for user satisfaction and business success.

In traditional development models, non-functional testing is often conducted late in the development cycle, sometimes even after the software has been fully developed. However, in Agile, waiting until the end to perform non-functional testing can be risky and counterproductive. Issues discovered late in the process are often more difficult and costly to fix. Therefore, it is important to integrate non-functional testing within sprints, alongside functional testing, to identify and address potential problems early.

Key Challenge: Balancing the Execution of Functional and Non-Functional Tests Within the Sprint Timeline

The Challenge

One of the primary challenges in Agile development is balancing the execution of both functional and non-functional tests within the tight timelines of a sprint. Sprints are typically short, often lasting just two weeks, and teams are under constant pressure to deliver new features and improvements. This can make it difficult to find time to perform thorough non-functional testing without compromising the sprint's objectives.

Functional tests, which validate the core functionality of the application, are often prioritized because they directly relate to the user stories being developed. However, neglecting non-functional testing can lead to performance issues, security vulnerabilities, and other problems that might not be apparent until the software is in production. Therefore, teams must find a way to integrate both types of testing into the sprint without overwhelming their workflow or missing deadlines.

Solutions: Prioritize Critical Non-Functional Tests and Automate Them to Run Alongside Functional Tests, Integrating Them into the CI/CD Pipeline for Continuous Validation

Strategic Integration of Testing

To effectively balance functional and non-functional testing within the sprint, it is essential to prioritize and automate critical non-functional tests. This approach allows teams to validate the software's performance, security, and other key attributes without significantly increasing the testing burden or extending the sprint timeline.

Steps to Integrate Non-Functional Testing with Functional Testing
Identify Critical Non-Functional Tests Early

At the beginning of each sprint, identify the critical non-functional tests that need to be performed. These are the tests that address the most important quality attributes for the current features, such as performance under load, security vulnerabilities, or compliance with accessibility standards.

Example: If the sprint includes features related to user login and authentication, critical non-functional tests might include security tests for SQL injection vulnerabilities and performance tests for login response times under heavy load.

Automate Where Possible

Automation is key to integrating non-functional testing into the sprint without adding excessive manual work. Many non-functional tests, such as performance, load, and security tests, can be automated using tools designed specifically for these purposes. By automating these tests, they can be run regularly and with minimal effort, allowing the team to quickly validate that the software meets non-functional requirements.

Example: Use tools like JMeter for performance testing and OWASP ZAP for automated security testing. These tools can be configured to run specific non-functional tests as part of the CI/CD pipeline, ensuring that they are executed consistently.

Integrate Non-Functional Tests into the CI/CD Pipeline

Integrating non-functional tests into the CI/CD pipeline ensures that they are executed continuously throughout the development process. This integration allows teams to detect and address issues as soon as they arise, rather than waiting until the end of the sprint or release cycle.

Example: Configure the CI/CD pipeline to trigger non-functional tests after each code commit or nightly build. This way, performance, and security tests run automatically, and any failures are immediately reported to the team for quick resolution.

Prioritize Based on Impact and Risk

Given the time constraints of a sprint, it may not be feasible to run all possible non-functional tests. Prioritize the tests that address the highest-impact areas or the greatest risks to the application. This prioritization ensures that the most critical aspects of the software are validated first, reducing the likelihood of significant issues in production.

Example: If the application handles sensitive user data, prioritize security testing to ensure that vulnerabilities are caught early. If the application is expected to handle a large number of users, focus on performance and scalability tests.

Review and Adjust Testing Strategies Regularly

Regularly review the effectiveness of your testing strategies, including the balance between functional and non-functional testing. Use sprint retrospectives to discuss what worked well and what could be improved.

Adjust your approach as needed to ensure that both functional and non-functional requirements are adequately tested within the sprint.

Example: After each sprint, hold a retrospective focused on testing. Discuss whether the critical non-functional tests were effectively integrated and whether they provided valuable insights. Adjust the testing strategy based on the team's feedback and any issues encountered.

Communicate the Importance of Non-Functional Testing

Ensure that all team members, including developers, testers, and product owners, understand the importance of non-functional testing. This understanding helps build a culture where quality is prioritized across all aspects of the software, not just its functionality.

Example: During sprint planning, discuss the non-functional requirements alongside the functional ones. Ensure that everyone understands how these requirements contribute to the overall quality of the product and the user experience.

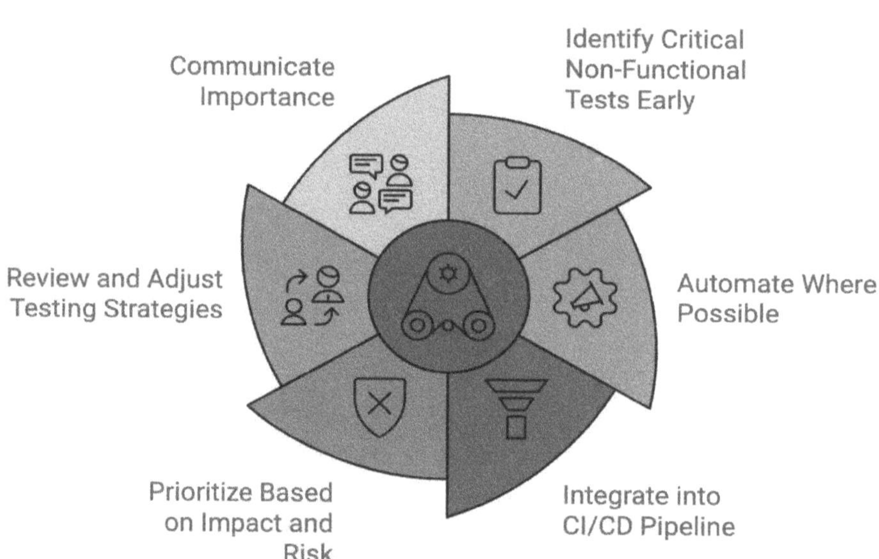

Benefits of Balancing Functional and Non-Functional Testing

By effectively balancing the execution of functional and non-functional tests within the sprint, teams can deliver software that not only meets the functional requirements but also performs well under expected conditions and is secure, reliable, and user-friendly. This approach leads to a more comprehensive validation process, reducing the risk of post-release issues and improving the overall quality of the software.

Integrating non-functional testing into the sprint also helps identify potential bottlenecks, security vulnerabilities, and performance issues early, when they are easier and less costly to fix. This proactive approach enhances the team's ability to deliver high-quality software on time and within budget, while also meeting the expectations of end-users and stakeholders.

In a Nutshell

Implementing functional testing in sprints is essential for validating the core functionality of the software, but it is equally important to integrate non-functional testing to ensure the software meets broader quality standards. By prioritizing critical non-functional tests, automating them, and integrating them into the CI/CD pipeline, teams can balance the demands of both types of testing within the sprint timeline. This approach not only improves the efficiency of the testing process but also enhances the overall quality of the software, leading to more successful Agile development outcomes.

CONDUCTING SPRINT REVIEWS AND DEMOS TO PO AND STAKEHOLDERS

Sprint reviews and demos are an essential part of the Agile process, providing an opportunity for the team to showcase the work completed during the sprint. These sessions allow product owners (PO) and stakeholders to see the progress made, provide feedback, and ensure that the development is aligned with business goals. The effectiveness of these reviews is crucial for maintaining stakeholder engagement and ensuring that the project stays on track.

Including Automated Test Results in Sprint Reviews

Why Include Automated Test Results?

Incorporating automated test results into sprint reviews adds transparency to the development process, demonstrating that the features not only work as expected but have also been thoroughly tested. By including these results, the team can assure that the software meets quality standards, reducing the risk of defects and increasing confidence in the product.

Automated test results show that the software has been validated against predefined criteria, which is particularly important for ensuring that the features are ready for release. Presenting these results during the sprint review helps to highlight the quality of the work completed and the effectiveness of the testing processes.

Key Challenge: Presenting Automated Test Results in a Way That Is Understandable to Non-Technical Stakeholders Without Overwhelming Them with Details

The Challenge

One of the main challenges in sprint reviews is communicating technical details, such as automated test results, clear and accessible to non-technical stakeholders. While developers and testers may understand the intricacies of test execution, product owners and business stakeholders may not have the same level of technical knowledge. Therefore, it's important to present the results in a way that provides meaningful insights without overwhelming them with technical jargon or excessive details.

If the presentation of automated test results is too technical or detailed, it can lead to confusion, disengagement, or misinterpretation of the software's quality. On the other hand, if the results are too simplified, stakeholders might not fully appreciate the thoroughness of the testing that has been conducted.

Solutions: Develop a Standard Format for Reporting Test Results During Demos, Focusing on Pass/Fail Outcomes and Overall Test Coverage Rather Than the Specifics of Each Test

Steps to Simplify and Standardize the Presentation of Automated Test Results

Use a High-Level Summary Approach

Start by providing a high-level summary of the test results, focusing on the overall outcomes rather than the specifics of each individual test. This might include the number of tests executed, the percentage of tests that passed, and any critical issues that were identified and resolved.

Example: Present a simple dashboard showing that 95% of the automated tests passed, with only a few minor issues identified and fixed. This gives stakeholders a clear picture of the software's quality without diving into the technical details.

Focus on Pass/Fail Outcomes

When presenting test results, focus on the pass/fail status of the tests rather than the detailed execution of each one. Highlight the success rate and mention any failed tests that were critical and how they were addressed.

Example: Use a visual representation, like a green/red bar chart, to show the pass/fail outcomes. For instance, "Out of 100 automated tests, 95 passed, and 5 failed, all of which were resolved within the sprint."

Highlight Test Coverage

Emphasize the overall test coverage to show how well the software has been tested. Test coverage indicates the proportion of the code or features that have been tested, providing assurance that the testing is thorough.

Example: Include a statement like, "Our automated tests covered 85% of the new feature's functionality, ensuring that the critical aspects were thoroughly tested."

Use Visual Aid

Utilize visual aid like charts, graphs, and dashboards to make the test results more engaging and easier to understand. Visual representations can quickly convey the key points without requiring stakeholders to interpret complex data.

Example: Show a pie chart that illustrates the distribution of test coverage across different features or a bar graph that compares test results from different sprints to show progress over time.

Explain the Impact

Briefly explain the significance of the test results in terms of product quality and readiness. This helps stakeholders understand why the test outcomes matter and how they contribute to the overall success of the project.

Example: "The high pass rate of our automated tests indicates that the new feature is stable and ready for deployment, with minimal risk of bugs impacting the user experience."

Keep It Concise

While it's important to provide meaningful insights, keep the presentation concise. Stick to the most critical information and avoid going into technical details unless specifically asked. The goal is to give stakeholders the confidence that the product has been well-tested without overwhelming them with information.

Example: Summarize the automated testing efforts in a few key bullet points, followed by a brief Q&A session where stakeholders can ask for more details if needed.

Prepare a Detailed Report for Technical Stakeholders

If there are stakeholders who are interested in more detailed technical information, prepare a separate, more detailed report that can be reviewed outside of the main sprint review. This report can include specifics about the test cases, logs, and any technical challenges encountered.

Example: Provide a detailed PDF report or a link to a JIRA dashboard for technical stakeholders who want to delve deeper into the automated test results.

Benefits of a Standardized, Simplified Approach

By developing a standard format for reporting automated test results during sprint reviews, teams can ensure that the information is communicated effectively to all stakeholders, regardless of their technical background. This approach helps maintain stakeholder engagement, builds trust in the development process, and provides assurance that the software is of high quality.

A simplified and consistent presentation of test results also makes it easier to compare progress across different sprints and identify trends in the software's quality over time. This allows both the team and stakeholders to make informed decisions about the next steps and priorities for upcoming sprints.

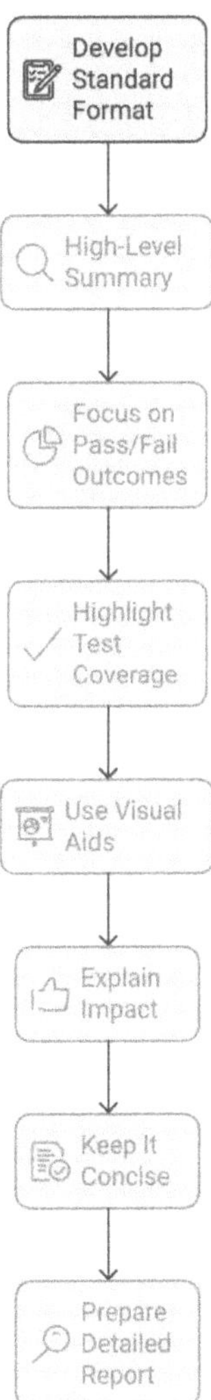

In a Nutshell

Conducting effective sprint reviews and demos is crucial for keeping stakeholders informed and engaged in the Agile process. Including automated test results in these reviews adds transparency and demonstrates the quality of the work completed. By developing a standard, simplified format for presenting these results—focusing on pass/fail outcomes, test coverage, and the overall impact—teams can communicate technical details in a way that is accessible and meaningful to all stakeholders. This approach not only enhances the clarity and effectiveness of sprint reviews but also strengthens the overall development process, leading to better outcomes and higher stakeholder satisfaction.

INCORPORATING CONTINUOUS FEEDBACK LOOPS

Continuous feedback loops are a vital part of Agile development, ensuring that information flows constantly between different stages of the development process. This feedback helps teams quickly identify issues, adjust their approach, and improve the quality of the software they are building. In the context of in-sprint automation, continuous feedback loops are especially important because they enable developers to catch and fix issues early, keeping the development process on track and maintaining high standards of quality.

Why Continuous Feedback from Automated Tests Matters?

Automated tests are designed to run frequently—often after every code change or build—to ensure that new changes do not introduce bugs or regressions. Continuous feedback from these automated tests provides developers with immediate insights into the state of the codebase, allowing them to quickly address any problems that arise. This rapid feedback is crucial in Agile development, where short sprints and quick iterations mean that any delay in identifying issues can have a significant impact on the project's timeline and quality.

Continuous feedback helps maintain the flow of the development process by ensuring that developers are constantly informed about the quality of their code. It also reduces the risk of accumulating technical debt, as issues are addressed as soon as they are identified, rather than being deferred to a later stage.

Key Challenge: Integrating Automated Test Feedback into the Development Process Without Causing Distractions

The Challenge

While continuous feedback is essential, one of the key challenges is ensuring that this feedback is integrated into the development process without causing distractions. If developers are constantly interrupted by alerts or notifications, it can disrupt their focus and productivity. On the other hand, if the feedback is too infrequent or delayed, important issues might be missed, leading to bigger problems down the line.

Balancing the need for timely feedback with the need to maintain a productive workflow is critical. The goal is to provide developers with the information they need to fix issues quickly, without overwhelming them with constant interruptions or noise.

Solutions: Set Up Notifications or Dashboards That Alert Developers of Test Failures Without Interrupting Their Workflow, Allowing Them to Address Issues as They Arise

Steps to Integrate Continuous Feedback Effectively
Use Non-Intrusive Notifications

Implement a system that provides notifications about test failures in a way that is informative but not disruptive. For example, instead of using pop-up alerts that can break a developer's concentration, consider using less intrusive notifications like updates in a designated Slack channel, email summaries, or notifications on a development dashboard.

Example: Set up a Slack bot that posts test failure notifications in a specific channel dedicated to test results. Developers can check these notifications at their convenience without being interrupted during their coding sessions.

Create a Centralized Dashboard

Develop a centralized dashboard that aggregates all automated test results and provides an at-a-glance view of the current state of the codebase. This dashboard should highlight any test failures, as well as key metrics like the percentage of passing tests, the number of critical issues, and trends over time. By having a single place to monitor the health of the project, developers can stay informed without needing to sift through individual notifications.

Example: Use tools like Jenkins, CircleCI, or GitLab to create a dashboard that displays the status of all automated tests in real-time. Developers can access this dashboard whenever they need to review the test results.

Set Priorities for Notifications

Not all test failures are equally urgent. Configure the notification system to prioritize critical issues, ensuring that developers are alerted to the most important problems first. Less critical issues can be summarized in a daily or weekly report, allowing developers to address them as part of their regular workflow without being interrupted.

Example: Configure the CI/CD system to send immediate notifications for test failures related to security vulnerabilities or critical functionality, while less urgent issues, such as minor UI glitches, are included in a daily summary report.

Schedule Regular Check-Ins

Encourage developers to regularly check the test results as part of their routine, such as during daily stand-ups or at the end of a coding session. This practice ensures that feedback is reviewed and acted upon without the need for constant real-time alerts.

Example: Integrate a quick review of the dashboard into the daily stand-up meeting, where the team discusses any critical test failures and assigns responsibility for fixing them.

Use Visual Indicators for Immediate Insight

Incorporate visual indicators like color-coded statuses (e.g., green for all tests passing, red for failures) into the dashboard or notifications. This helps developers quickly assess the situation and decide if immediate action is needed.

Example: Implement a traffic light system on the dashboard—green indicates all tests are passing, yellow indicates some warnings or non-critical failures, and red indicates critical failures that need immediate attention.

Automate Follow-Up Actions

Set up automated workflows that trigger follow-up actions based on the test results. For example, if a critical test fails, the system could automatically create a JIRA ticket and assign it to a developer. This reduces the manual effort required to track and manage issues, allowing developers to focus on fixing problems rather than managing their workflow.

Example: If an automated security test fails, the CI/CD system could automatically generate a high-priority ticket in JIRA, assign it to the security team, and link it to the relevant part of the codebase for quick reference.

Benefits of an Effective Continuous Feedback Loop

By integrating continuous feedback from automated tests in a way that is informative but non-intrusive, teams can maintain a steady flow of information without disrupting their work. This approach helps developers stay on top of issues as they arise, reducing the risk of defects and improving the overall quality of the software. It also enhances productivity, as developers can focus on coding without being constantly interrupted by alerts.

A well-implemented feedback loop ensures that the development process remains agile and responsive, with issues being addressed quickly and efficiently. This not only leads to better software but also fosters a more collaborative and proactive development environment.

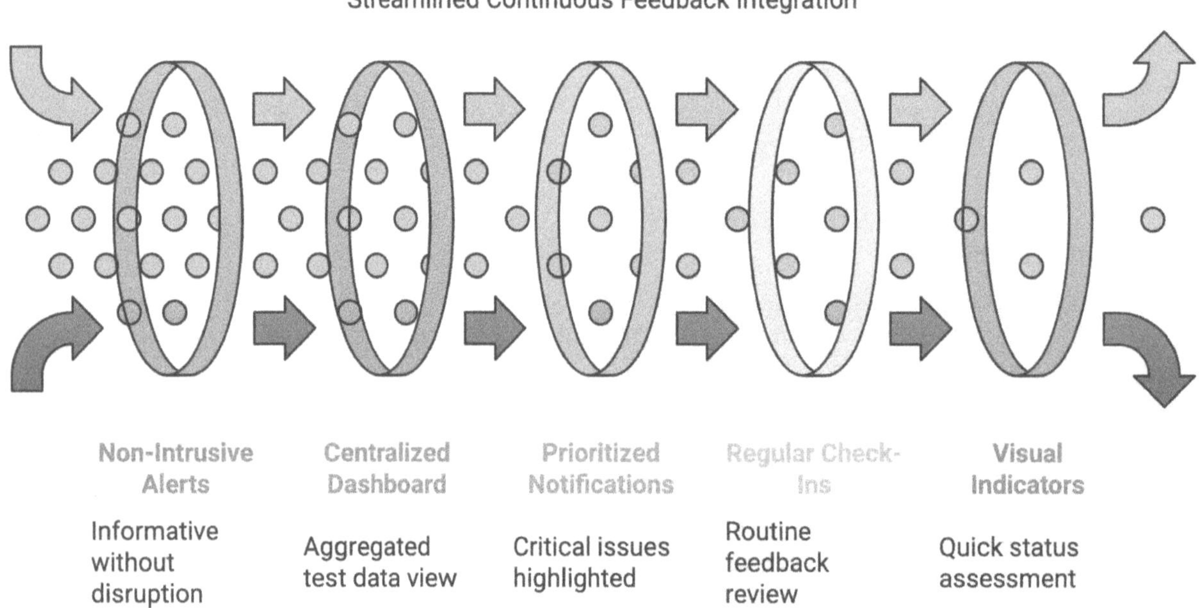

In a Nutshell

Incorporating continuous feedback loops into the development process is essential for maintaining quality and agility in Agile development. By setting up non-intrusive notifications, using centralized dashboards, and prioritizing critical issues, teams can integrate automated test feedback in a way that enhances productivity without causing distractions. This approach ensures that developers have the information they need to address issues quickly, leading to more reliable software and a smoother, more efficient development process.

MANAGING TEST DATA AND ENVIRONMENTS FOR IN-SPRINT AUTOMATION

In-sprint automation is a crucial practice in Agile development, allowing teams to test new features and changes as they are developed. However, for in-sprint automation to be effective, it's essential to manage test data and environments properly. These elements form the backbone of the testing process, ensuring that automated tests run smoothly and yield reliable results. Poor management of test data and environments can lead to inconsistencies, false positives or negatives, and a lack of trust in the testing process, ultimately slowing down the development cycle and reducing the quality of the software.

Effective Management of Test Data and Environments

Why Test Data and Environments Matter?

Test data refers to the input data used during testing to validate whether the software behaves as expected. This data needs to be realistic and comprehensive, covering a wide range of scenarios to ensure that all aspects of the application are tested. On the other hand, test environments are the systems and settings where the tests are executed, simulating real-world conditions as closely as possible. These environments must be stable, consistent, and isolated from other systems to provide accurate test results.

Managing test data and environments effectively is critical because:

- **Consistency**: Consistent test data and environments ensure that test results are reliable and repeatable, which is crucial for identifying real issues rather than noise caused by environmental factors.
- **Realism**: Realistic test data and environments help uncover potential issues that users might face in production, ensuring that the software is robust and user-friendly.
- **Efficiency**: Proper management reduces the time spent troubleshooting false failures caused by bad data or unstable environments, allowing the team to focus on actual issues.

Key Challenge: Ensuring That Test Environments and Data Are Available and Consistent Throughout the Sprint

The Challenge

In a fast-paced Agile environment, where sprints are often just a few weeks long, maintaining consistent and reliable test environments and data can be challenging. Several factors contribute to this challenge:

1. **Environment Drift**: Over time, test environments can drift from the original configuration, leading to inconsistencies between tests. These inconsistencies can cause tests to fail for reasons unrelated to the code changes, such as differences in software versions, network configurations, or database states.
2. **Data Contamination**: Test data can become contaminated over the course of testing, especially when tests modify the data. For example, if a test case modifies a user record, subsequent tests using the same data might produce different results, leading to unreliable testing.
3. **Availability**: Ensuring that the necessary test environments and data are available when needed can be difficult, especially if the same resources are shared across multiple teams or projects. Delays in setting up environments or generating data can slow down the entire testing process, leading to missed deadlines and lower productivity.
4. **Scalability**: As the project grows, the complexity of managing test environments and data increases. This includes handling large volumes of data, ensuring environments scale appropriately, and managing dependencies between different components of the system.

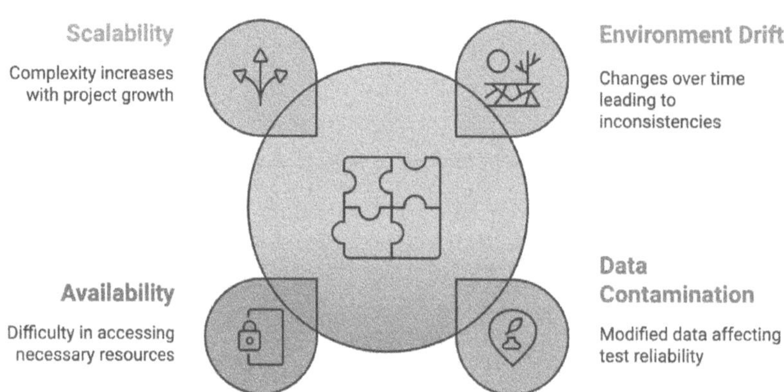

Solutions: Automate the Provisioning of Test Environments and Data, Ensuring They Are Reset Before Each Test Cycle to Avoid Contamination and Inconsistencies

Steps to Manage Test Data and Environments Effectively
Automate Environment Provisioning

Automate the setup and configuration of test environments using tools like Infrastructure as Code (IaC). IaC allows you to define your environment configurations in code, ensuring that they can be easily recreated and modified as needed. By automating this process, you can quickly spin up environments that are consistent and reliable, reducing the risk of environment drift.

Example: Use tools like Terraform or AWS CloudFormation to automate the provisioning of test environments. This ensures that every time a new environment is created, it is identical to the others, with no manual configuration required.

Use Containerization

Containerization tools like Docker can be used to create lightweight, consistent test environments. Containers package the application and its dependencies together, ensuring that the environment is the same wherever the container is deployed. This consistency helps eliminate environment-related issues in testing.

Example: Create Docker containers for your application and its dependencies, ensuring that every test environment is identical regardless of where or when it's deployed.

Automate Data Provisioning and Reset

Automate the creation and reset of test data to ensure that it is consistent and uncontaminated before each test cycle. This can be done using scripts or database snapshots that restore the data to a known good state before each test run. By automating this process, you can eliminate the risk of data contamination and ensure that all tests start with the same baseline.

Example: Implement a script that resets the test database to a known state before each test cycle. This script can be triggered automatically as part of the CI/CD pipeline, ensuring that every test starts with the same data.

Use Synthetic Data Generation

For tests that require large or varied datasets, consider using synthetic data generation tools. These tools can generate realistic test data on demand, tailored to the specific needs of the tests. This approach reduces the reliance on manually created datasets and ensures that tests can cover a wide range of scenarios.

Example: Use a tool like Mockaroo or Faker to generate synthetic test data that mimics real-world data, allowing you to test edge cases and scenarios that might be difficult to replicate with static datasets.

Implement Environment Management Tools

Use environment management tools that allow you to track, configure, and manage multiple test environments simultaneously. These tools can help ensure that environments are properly configured, available when needed, and consistent across the board.

Example: Tools like Ansible or Puppet can be used to manage configurations across multiple environments, ensuring consistency and reducing the manual effort required to maintain them.

Integrate with the CI/CD Pipeline

Integrate the provisioning and management of test environments and data with the CI/CD pipeline. This ensures that environments and data are set up automatically as part of the build process, reducing delays and ensuring that tests are run in consistent conditions.

Example: As part of the CI/CD pipeline, trigger scripts that provision a fresh environment and reset test data before the automated tests run. This integration ensures that every build is tested in a clean, controlled environment.

Monitor and Log Environment and Data Issues

Implement monitoring and logging for test environments and data to quickly identify and resolve issues. By tracking environment stability and data integrity, you can catch problems early and prevent them from affecting the test results.

Example: Use monitoring tools to track the health and status of test environments and set up alerts for any anomalies or failures. Logging can help you trace back any issues to their root cause, whether it's an environment misconfiguration or data inconsistency.

Benefits of Effective Test Data and Environment Management

By automating the provisioning of test environments and data, teams can ensure that tests are run consistently, with reliable and repeatable results. This approach reduces the time spent troubleshooting environment-related issues, allowing the team to focus on actual code problems rather than false positives caused by unstable environments or contaminated data.

Effective management also improves the scalability of the testing process, enabling teams to handle larger and more complex projects without compromising on quality. Automated environment and data management free up resources, reduce manual errors, and provide the flexibility needed to adapt to changing project requirements.

Ultimately, managing test data and environments effectively leads to higher quality software, fewer defects in production, and a smoother, more efficient development process. It fosters a culture of reliability and precision, where testing is seen as an integral part of the development cycle rather than a separate, disconnected activity.

In a Nutshell

Managing test data and environments is a critical aspect of in-sprint automation, directly impacting the reliability and effectiveness of automated tests. By automating the provisioning and reset of test environments and data, teams can overcome the challenges of consistency, availability, and scalability. This approach ensures that tests are run in stable, predictable conditions, yielding trustworthy results and supporting the overall goal of delivering high-quality software on time. Integrating these practices into the CI/CD pipeline further enhances the efficiency and effectiveness of the testing process, leading to better outcomes and a more robust Agile development workflow.

AUTOMATING ACCEPTANCE CRITERIA VERIFICATION

Acceptance criteria are the conditions that a software product must satisfy to be accepted by the end-users, stakeholders, or the product owner. In Agile development, these criteria are typically defined as part of each user story and serve as a key measure of whether a feature is complete and ready for release. Automating the verification of acceptance criteria is essential in ensuring that the software meets the required standards consistently and efficiently, particularly in fast-paced development environments where manual verification can be time-consuming and error-prone.

Why Automating Acceptance Criteria Verification Is Important?

Automating the verification of acceptance criteria provides several significant benefits:

- **Consistency**: Automated tests run the same way every time, ensuring that the acceptance criteria are checked consistently across different builds and environments.
- **Speed**: Automation allows for rapid verification of acceptance criteria, enabling quick feedback loops and faster iterations within sprints.
- **Scalability**: As the codebase grows, manual testing of acceptance criteria becomes impractical. Automated tests can scale with the project, covering a wide range of scenarios without requiring proportional increases in manual effort.
- **Early Detection of Issues**: Automated verification helps catch issues early in the development process, reducing the cost and time associated with fixing bugs found later in the cycle.

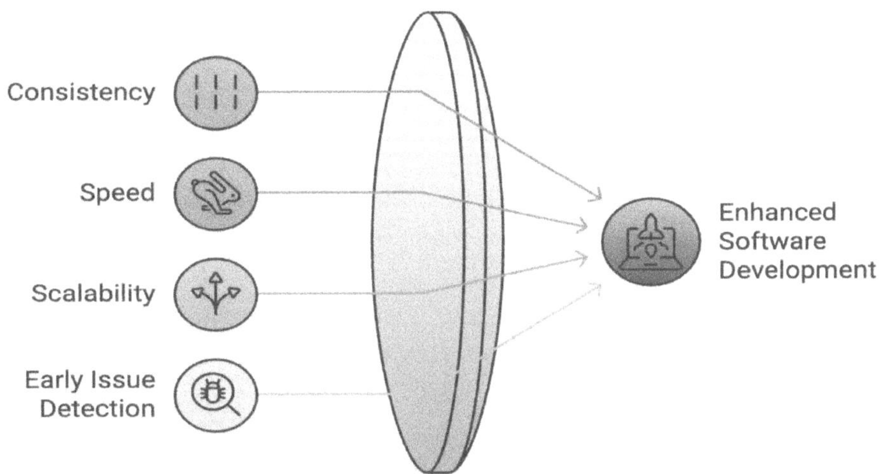

Key Challenge: Writing Automated Tests That Accurately Verify All Acceptance Criteria Without Introducing False Positives or Negatives

The Challenge

One of the main challenges in automating the verification of acceptance criteria is ensuring that the automated tests accurately reflect the criteria without introducing false positives or negatives. A false positive occurs when a test incorrectly passes even though the acceptance criteria have not been met, while a false negative occurs when a test fails despite the criteria being satisfied. Both scenarios can undermine the reliability of the tests, leading to wasted time, missed bugs, and a potential loss of confidence in the testing process.

Several factors contribute to this challenge:

1. Ambiguity in Acceptance Criteria: If the acceptance criteria are not clearly defined, it becomes difficult to translate them into automated tests. Ambiguous criteria can lead to tests that do not fully capture the intended functionality, increasing the risk of false results.
2. Complexity of the Test Scenarios: Complex criteria that involve multiple steps, conditions, or dependencies can be challenging to automate accurately. The more complex the scenario, the higher the likelihood of errors in the test automation.
3. Maintenance of Automated Tests: As the application evolves, the acceptance criteria and the corresponding automated tests may need to be updated. Keeping the tests aligned with the latest criteria while avoiding false results requires careful maintenance and regular reviews.

Solutions: Collaborate with Product Owners and Testers to Define Precise, Measurable Acceptance Criteria That Can Be Effectively Automated

Steps to Effectively Automate Acceptance Criteria Verification
Collaborate Early and Often with Product Owners and Testers

The process of defining acceptance criteria should involve close collaboration between product owners, testers, and developers. By working together from the beginning, the team can ensure that the criteria are both precise and aligned with the intended functionality. This collaboration helps avoid ambiguity and ensures that everyone has a shared understanding of what needs to be tested.

Example: During sprint planning, involve the product owner in discussions about the acceptance criteria. Together with testers and developers, review the criteria to ensure they are clear, measurable, and testable. For example, instead of a vague criterion like "The page should load quickly," define it as "The page should load within 2 seconds under normal network conditions."

Define Precise and Measurable Acceptance Criteria

Acceptance criteria should be specific, unambiguous, and measurable. This means that the criteria should be written in a way that leaves no room for interpretation and can be directly translated into automated test cases. Measurable criteria are easier to test because they provide a clear pass/fail condition.

Example: For a user authentication feature, a precise acceptance criterion might be, "The system should lock the user out after three consecutive failed login attempts, and the lockout should last for 15 minutes." This criterion is clear, specific, and provides measurable conditions that can be tested.

Use Behavior-Driven Development (BDD) to Write Test Scenarios

Behavior-Driven Development (BDD) is an approach that helps bridge the gap between business requirements and technical implementation. BDD uses a common language, typically Gherkin syntax, to write scenarios that describe the expected behavior of the application. These scenarios can then be directly automated, ensuring that the tests align with the acceptance criteria.

Example: Using BDD, the acceptance criterion for the login lockout feature could be written as:
> *Scenario: User is locked out after multiple failed login attempts*
> *Given the user is on the login page*
> *When the user enters incorrect credentials three times*
> *Then the user should be locked out for 15 minutes*

This scenario is easy to automate and directly reflects the acceptance criteria.

Prioritize Critical Acceptance Criteria for Automation

Not all acceptance criteria may need to be automated immediately. Prioritize automation for the most critical criteria—those that have the highest impact on the functionality and user experience. This ensures that the most important aspects of the application are consistently verified without overwhelming the automation efforts.

Example: In an e-commerce application, prioritize automating the acceptance criteria for the checkout process, such as validating payment processing and order confirmation. These are critical to the user experience and should be tested thoroughly.

Regularly Review and Update Automated Tests

As the application evolves, acceptance criteria may change, and new criteria may be introduced. It's essential to regularly review and update automated tests to ensure they remain aligned with the current criteria. This practice helps avoid false positives and negatives, ensuring the tests remain reliable over time.

Example: Schedule regular test maintenance sessions at the end of each sprint to review the automated tests. During these sessions, update the tests to reflect any changes in the acceptance criteria, and remove any outdated tests that no longer apply.

Implement Comprehensive Test Coverage

Ensure that the automated tests cover all possible scenarios, including edge cases and potential failure points. Comprehensive test coverage reduces the likelihood of false positives by ensuring that the tests account for all possible outcomes and conditions.

Example: For the login lockout feature, in addition to testing the standard lockout scenario, create automated tests for edge cases such as:
- The user entering correct credentials after two failed attempts (should not trigger lockout).
- The user attempting to reset the password after being locked out (should prompt password reset but maintain lockout).

Use Continuous Integration (CI) for Automated Test Execution

Integrate automated tests into a continuous integration (CI) pipeline to ensure they are run frequently, ideally after every code commit. This integration provides immediate feedback on whether the acceptance criteria are being met, allowing developers to address issues as soon as they arise.

Example: Set up a CI/CD pipeline in Jenkins, GitLab, or a similar tool, where automated tests for acceptance criteria are executed automatically after every commit. This setup ensures that any failures are caught early, and developers are notified immediately.

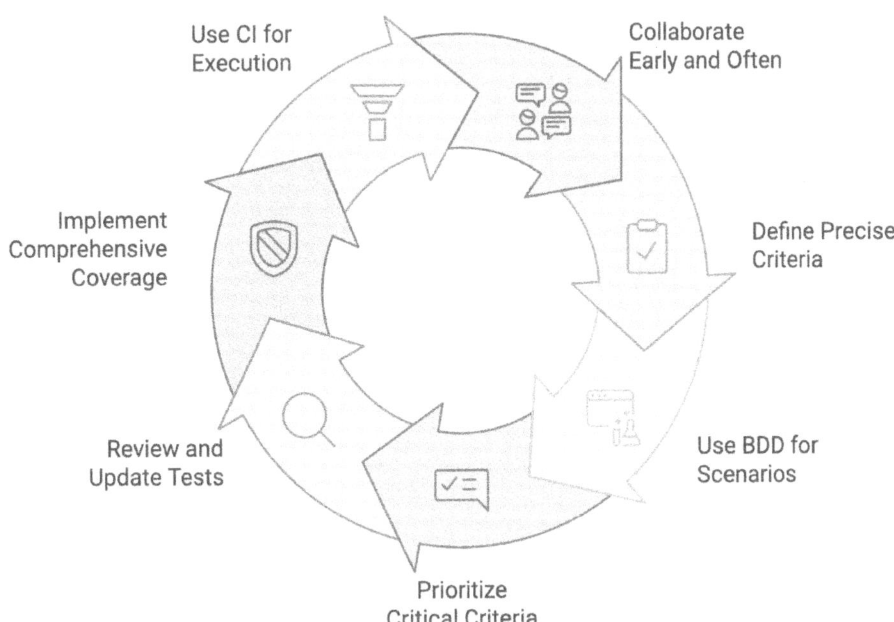

Benefits of Automating Acceptance Criteria Verification

Automating the verification of acceptance criteria offers several key benefits:
- **Reliability**: Automated tests ensure that acceptance criteria are verified consistently across different environments and iterations, reducing the risk of human error.
- **Efficiency**: Automated verification allows for rapid feedback, enabling teams to identify and address issues quickly without the need for time-consuming manual testing.

- **Scalability**: As projects grow, the number of acceptance criteria and the complexity of the application increase. Automation allows the testing process to scale with the project, maintaining high standards of quality without requiring a proportional increase in manual effort.
- **Confidence**: By automating the verification of acceptance criteria, teams can be more confident that the software meets the required standards, leading to fewer issues in production and greater satisfaction among stakeholders.

In a Nutshell

Automating the verification of acceptance criteria is a critical strategy for ensuring that software meets the required standards consistently and efficiently in Agile development. By collaborating closely with product owners and testers, defining precise and measurable acceptance criteria, and prioritizing automation for critical criteria, teams can overcome the challenges of false positives and negatives. This approach not only improves the reliability and efficiency of the testing process but also enhances the overall quality of the software, leading to better outcomes and higher stakeholder satisfaction.

## CHAPTER 4

UI AUTOMATION TESTING IN SPRINTS

UI Automation Testing in sprints is a critical part of ensuring that the software being developed meets the required user experience and functionality standards. In an Agile environment, where development cycles are short and iterative, UI automation allows for continuous validation of the user interface as new features are developed and integrated. By automating these tests, teams can ensure that the UI remains consistent and functional across multiple devices and browsers, which is increasingly important in today's multi-platform world.

INTRODUCTION TO UI TESTING

UI (User Interface) testing is the process of verifying that the user interface of an application behaves as expected. This involves checking that all UI elements, such as buttons, text fields, and menus, are working correctly and that the application responds to user inputs in the intended way. UI testing ensures that users can interact with the application without encountering issues, and that the visual appearance is consistent with the design specifications.

In the context of web applications, UI testing involves testing the application across different web browsers and devices (like desktops, tablets, and smartphones) to ensure it delivers a consistent user experience. This is particularly important because users today access applications on a wide range of devices with varying screen sizes, operating systems, and browser configurations.

Why UI Testing is Important?

1. **User Experience:** The user interface is the first thing users interact with, and it heavily influences their experience with the application. A well-tested UI ensures that users can navigate the application smoothly and that all functionalities work as expected, leading to higher user satisfaction.
2. **Cross-Platform Consistency:** Given the variety of devices and browsers available, ensuring that your application behaves consistently across all platforms is critical. UI testing helps catch inconsistencies and bugs that may only appear on certain devices or browsers.
3. **Early Bug Detection:** By integrating UI testing into the development process, especially in Agile sprints, teams can detect and fix UI-related bugs early in the development cycle, reducing the cost and effort required to fix them later.
4. **Regression Testing:** As the application evolves, UI testing ensures that new features or changes do not break existing functionality. Automated UI tests can be re-run with every code change to identify regressions quickly.

Benefits of UI Automation Testing in Sprints

UI automation testing during sprints brings numerous advantages to the software development process, especially within the Agile framework. By integrating automated testing directly into the sprint cycles, teams can ensure high-quality, consistent product delivery while maintaining rapid development cycles. Here's a detailed look at the benefits:

1.   Ensures Correct Functionality

UI automation testing validates the end-user experience by ensuring that all user interactions (such as clicking buttons, filling out forms, navigating through pages) are functioning as expected. As tests are automated and run frequently throughout the sprint, developers can quickly identify any functionality that isn't working as expected.

Example: If a form on the website stops working due to a recent change, the automation script will catch the issue immediately during the sprint and notify the team.

2.   Meets Quality Standards

By continuously running automated tests during each sprint, teams can ensure that the software meets the required quality standards. Automated tests help detect edge cases or regression issues earlier, which might otherwise be missed in manual testing.

Example: Automated tests can ensure that UI elements, such as buttons and links, work as expected across different browsers and devices, ensuring quality consistency for all users.

3.   Quick Issue Identification

In-sprint UI automation enables rapid identification of defects. Automated tests run after every code commit (as part of Continuous Integration), immediately flagging any issues. This allows developers to fix bugs early, reducing the likelihood of issues being carried into later stages of the project.

Example: A broken UI button due to CSS changes can be detected immediately, rather than being discovered at the end of the sprint or in production.

4.   Efficient Development Cycles

By automating repetitive UI tests, teams save significant time compared to manual testing. Automated tests can be run quickly, frequently, and across different environments without human intervention. This boosts the efficiency of each sprint cycle by allowing developers to focus more on building new features while automated tests handle regression and functionality testing.

Example: A regression suite with hundreds of UI tests can be executed in minutes rather than hours, giving the development team faster feedback on the code's stability.

5.   Enhances Reliability

Manual UI testing is prone to human error, especially when repeatedly testing the same features. Automation scripts, however, perform the same actions with accuracy every time, ensuring that all test cases are executed reliably and consistently.

Example: UI automation scripts can reliably verify that UI elements, such as form validation or dropdown functionality, behave consistently across different releases.

6. *Faster Feedback*

In Agile development, speed is crucial, and automated UI tests provide instant feedback. By running tests frequently within the sprint, developers receive immediate feedback on the state of the application, allowing them to address issues as soon as they arise. This accelerates the development process by reducing bottlenecks caused by waiting for manual testing feedback.

Example: Continuous Integration tools like Jenkins can trigger automated tests after each commit, providing instant results that help teams identify and fix issues without waiting for the end of the sprint.

7. *Continuous Improvement*

UI automation testing encourages a continuous improvement process. Since automated tests run with each build, bugs and issues are addressed immediately. This cycle of rapid detection and resolution ensures the product becomes more stable and resilient over time, allowing for progressive improvements with each sprint.

Example: As new features are added, automated tests ensure that existing functionality is unaffected, allowing teams to build on a stable foundation continuously.

8. *Better Product Delivery*

Automation testing allows teams to deliver higher-quality products to end users. Since issues are caught early and the software is continuously tested, fewer bugs make it to production. This results in a more reliable, stable product with a better user experience. Automated testing also enables teams to meet delivery deadlines with more confidence.

Example: UI automation ensures that critical user flows (like login, checkout, or search functionality) work flawlessly before releasing the product to customers, leading to fewer post-release issues.

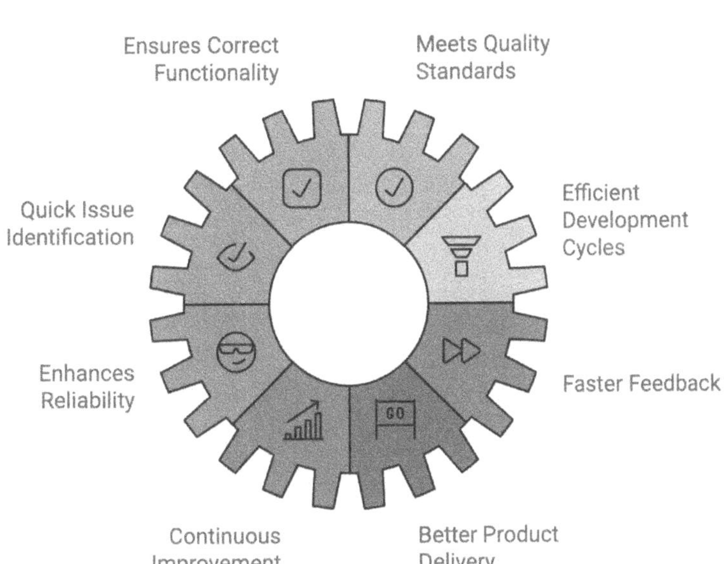

In a Nutshell

UI automation testing in sprints provides numerous benefits, from ensuring functionality and quality to accelerating development cycles and improving product reliability. By leveraging automation, teams can deliver higher-quality products with faster feedback loops and continuous improvement, all while maintaining the pace of Agile development. This results in a more efficient process, reduced risk of human error, and ultimately better product delivery.

Key Challenges: Testing UI Across Multiple Devices and Browsers within the constraints of a Sprint

The Challenge

Testing an application's user interface (UI) across multiple devices, browsers, and operating systems can be time-consuming, especially within the tight deadlines of a sprint. Different browsers and devices often behave inconsistently, meaning that what works on one platform may not work on another. This issue becomes more complex when dealing with modern, responsive applications that need to be verified on various screen sizes and resolutions, including desktop, mobile, and tablet devices. Testing on a wide range of environments manually or even automating tests across these different platforms can stretch the time limits of a sprint and lead to incomplete or inefficient test coverage.

Impact

- **Time Constraints**: Manually testing across multiple platforms can take too long, making it impossible to meet sprint deadlines.
- **Incomplete Test Coverage**: Without proper cross-browser and cross-device testing, bugs may slip through in some environments while passing in others.
- **Delays in Feedback**: Running automated tests sequentially on different devices or browsers increases the total time needed for testing, delaying feedback to developers.
- **Increased Maintenance**: The challenge of keeping up with changing device/browser versions, combined with inconsistent test results, can add extra maintenance overhead for automation scripts.

Solutions:

1. Using Cross-Platform Testing Tools supporting parallel execution

- To address the challenge of testing UI across multiple devices and browsers, teams can use cross-platform testing tools that automate the process of running tests on different environments. These tools allow teams to define test cases once and run them across various browsers and devices, ensuring consistent behavior and appearance.

Examples of Cross-Platform Testing Tools

Selenium Grid

What It Is: Selenium Grid is a tool that allows you to run Selenium tests in parallel across different browsers and machines. It uses a hub and node architecture where the hub manages multiple nodes that execute the tests. Each node can be configured to run on different browsers and operating systems.

How It Helps:
- **Parallel Execution**: Selenium Grid enables the execution of tests in parallel, significantly reducing the time required to test across multiple environments.
- **Custom Configuration**: You can configure nodes to represent different browser and operating system combinations, ensuring comprehensive coverage.

The primary benefit of using Selenium Grid is that it allows tests to be distributed across multiple machines, significantly reducing the time required for testing across various environments.

SELENIUM GRID SETUP – RUNNING NODE AND HUB

In Selenium Grid, the **hub** is the central server that receives all the test execution requests, and the **nodes** are the machines where the tests are executed. These nodes can be configured to run different browsers and versions of browsers, on various operating systems, allowing for parallel and cross-browser testing.

STEP 1: SETTING UP THE HUB

1. **Download Selenium Server**: Download the latest Selenium Server standalone JAR file from Selenium's official website.
2. **Start the Hub**: Open a terminal or command prompt, navigate to the directory where the Selenium JAR file is located, and run the following command to start the hub:

```
java -jar selenium-server-<version>.jar hub
```

This command will start the Selenium Grid hub on your machine, and it will listen on port 4444 by default. You can access the Grid console by navigating to http://localhost:4444/grid/console in your browser. This console will show the status of the hub and the connected nodes.

STEP 2: SETTING UP THE NODE

Once the hub is up and running, you can register nodes that will execute the test cases.

1. **Register a Node**: Open another terminal or command prompt, and register a node to the hub by running the following command:

```
java -jar selenium-server-<version>.jar node --hub http://localhost:4444/grid/
register
```

This command tells the Selenium node to register itself with the hub at localhost:4444. By default, this node will run on the same machine, but you can configure it to run on other machines by specifying their IP addresses.

2. **Specify Browser Configurations**: To specify the browser types, versions, and maximum instances for the node, you can pass additional arguments:

```
java -jar selenium-server-<version>.jar node --hub http://localhost:4444/grid/
register --port 5555 --max-sessions 5 --browser browserName=chrome,maxInstances=5
--browser browserName=firefox,maxInstances=5
```

This configuration allows the node to run up to 5 instances of both Chrome and Firefox browsers.

STEP 3: CONNECTING MULTIPLE NODES

You can repeat the process above to register multiple nodes, each with its own browser configurations. These nodes can be on different machines, allowing you to distribute the test execution load.

RUNNING SELENIUM TESTS VIA SELENIUM GRID ON CHROME BROWSERS

To run tests on Selenium Grid, you need to modify your test scripts to connect to the remote WebDriver running on the hub, instead of a local WebDriver instance. Here's how to run a Selenium test using Selenium Grid on a Chrome browser:

1. **Set Up Desired Capabilities**: In your test script, specify the browser and version you want to run the tests on by setting up **DesiredCapabilities**.
2. **Use RemoteWebDriver**: Connect to the hub using RemoteWebDriver and pass the hub URL.

SAMPLE CODE TO RUN TEST ON CHROME VIA SELENIUM GRID

```java
import org.openqa.selenium.WebDriver;
import org.openqa.selenium.remote.DesiredCapabilities;
import org.openqa.selenium.remote.RemoteWebDriver;

import java.net.MalformedURLException;
import java.net.URL;

public class SeleniumGridTest {
    public static void main(String[] args) throws MalformedURLException {
        // Set desired capabilities for Chrome
        DesiredCapabilities capabilities = DesiredCapabilities.chrome();

        // Connect to the Selenium Grid Hub
        WebDriver driver = new RemoteWebDriver(new URL("http://localhost:4444/
wd/hub"), capabilities);

        // Open a website
        driver.get("https://www.example.com");

        // Print the title of the page
        System.out.println("Page title is: " + driver.getTitle());

        // Close the browser
        driver.quit();
    }
}
```

This code will execute the test on a Chrome browser running on a node connected to the hub.

RUNNING SELENIUM TESTS VIA SELENIUM GRID ON MULTIPLE BROWSERS

To run tests on multiple browsers using Selenium Grid, you need to configure each browser's capabilities in your test script and then execute the test in parallel.

Sample Code for Running on Chrome and Firefox:

```java
import org.openqa.selenium.WebDriver;
import org.openqa.selenium.remote.DesiredCapabilities;
```

```java
import org.openqa.selenium.remote.RemoteWebDriver;

import java.net.MalformedURLException;
import java.net.URL;

public class SeleniumGridMultiBrowserTest {

    public static void main(String[] args) throws MalformedURLException {
        // Running test on Chrome
        DesiredCapabilities chromeCapabilities = DesiredCapabilities.chrome();
        WebDriver chromeDriver = new RemoteWebDriver(new URL("http://localhost:4444/
wd/hub"), chromeCapabilities);
        chromeDriver.get("https://www.example.com");
        System.out.println("Chrome Browser Title: " + chromeDriver.getTitle());
        chromeDriver.quit();

        // Running test on Firefox
        DesiredCapabilities firefoxCapabilities = DesiredCapabilities.firefox();
        WebDriver firefoxDriver = new RemoteWebDriver(new URL("http://
localhost:4444/wd/hub"), firefoxCapabilities);
        firefoxDriver.get("https://www.example.com");
        System.out.println("Firefox Browser Title: " + firefoxDriver.getTitle());
        firefoxDriver.quit();
    }
}
```

This code will run the same test on both Chrome and Firefox browsers by defining the respective browser capabilities.

SELENIUM GRID CONFIGURATION USING JSON FILE

Selenium Grid allows nodes to be configured using JSON files, which simplifies the process of setting up nodes, especially when dealing with complex configurations.

SAMPLE JSON CONFIGURATION FILE FOR A NODE

```json
{
  "capabilities": [
    {
      "browserName": "chrome",
      "maxInstances": 5,
      "platform": "WINDOWS"
    },
    {
      "browserName": "firefox",
      "maxInstances": 5,
      "platform": "WINDOWS"
    }
```

```json
  ],
  "configuration": {
    "port": 5555,
    "hub": "http://localhost:4444/grid/register",
    "maxSession": 5,
    "register": true,
    "registerCycle": 5000
  }
}
```

USING THE JSON FILE TO START THE NODE

To start a node using a JSON file, run the following command:

```
java -jar selenium-server-<version>.jar node --config node-config.json
```

This command will register the node to the hub using the configuration provided in the JSON file.

RUNNING SELENIUM TESTS PARALLELLY ON MULTIPLE BROWSERS VIA SELENIUM GRID DRIVEN BY TESTNG.XML

To run tests in parallel on multiple browsers using Selenium Grid and TestNG, you can configure your test suite using the testng.xml file.

SAMPLE TESTNG.XML CONFIGURATION

```xml
<!DOCTYPE suite SYSTEM "http://testng.org/testng-1.0.dtd">
<suite name="Parallel Browser Suite" parallel="tests" thread-count="2">

    <test name="Test on Chrome">
        <parameter name="browser" value="chrome"/>
        <classes>
            <class name="com.example.tests.SeleniumGridParallelTest"/>
        </classes>
    </test>

    <test name="Test on Firefox">
        <parameter name="browser" value="firefox"/>
        <classes>
            <class name="com.example.tests.SeleniumGridParallelTest"/>
        </classes>
    </test>

</suite>
```

SAMPLE TESTNG TEST CLASS

```java
import org.openqa.selenium.WebDriver;
import org.openqa.selenium.remote.DesiredCapabilities;
import org.openqa.selenium.remote.RemoteWebDriver;
import org.testng.annotations.Parameters;
```

```java
import org.testng.annotations.Test;

import java.net.MalformedURLException;
import java.net.URL;

public class SeleniumGridParallelTest {

    @Test
    @Parameters("browser")
    public void runTest(String browser) throws MalformedURLException {
        DesiredCapabilities capabilities = null;

        if (browser.equals("chrome")) {
            capabilities = DesiredCapabilities.chrome();
        } else if (browser.equals("firefox")) {
            capabilities = DesiredCapabilities.firefox();
        }

        WebDriver driver = new RemoteWebDriver(new URL("http://localhost:4444/
wd/hub"), capabilities);
        driver.get("https://www.example.com");
        System.out.println("Title: " + driver.getTitle() + " on " + browser);
        driver.quit();
    }
}
```

Explanation:
- **testng.xml**: Configures the tests to run in parallel on two browsers (Chrome and Firefox). The parallel="tests" attribute allows TestNG to run the tests on separate threads.
- **SeleniumGridParallelTest**: The runTest method takes the browser name as a parameter and runs the tests on the specified browser.

Selenium Grid is a powerful tool for running parallel and cross-browser tests, which helps reduce the overall test execution time. By configuring nodes and hubs, setting up JSON configurations, and leveraging parallel execution with TestNG, you can significantly improve the efficiency of your UI automation testing, ensuring that your web application performs well across different browsers and environments.

Other Cloud providers

1. BrowserStack
What It Is: BrowserStack is a cloud-based testing platform that provides access to a wide range of real devices and browsers for testing. It allows you to run automated tests on a massive scale without the need for an in-house device lab.

How It Helps:

1. **Real Device Testing**: Unlike emulators, BrowserStack offers real devices, ensuring that tests reflect actual user conditions.
2. **Scalability**: You can scale your testing efforts easily by running tests in parallel across multiple devices and browsers.

Example: If you need to test a responsive design across multiple smartphones, tablets, and desktops, BrowserStack allows you to run your Selenium or Appium tests on these devices simultaneously, providing screenshots, video recordings, and logs for each test run.

Sample Code:

```
DesiredCapabilities caps = new DesiredCapabilities();
caps.setCapability("browser", "Chrome");
caps.setCapability("browser_version", "90.0");
caps.setCapability("os", "Windows");
caps.setCapability("os_version", "10");
caps.setCapability("name", "Login Test");

WebDriver driver = new RemoteWebDriver(new URL("https://username:accessKey@
hub-cloud.browserstack.com/wd/hub"), caps);
driver.get("https://example.com/login");
// Run test
driver.quit();
```

2. *Sauce Labs*

What It Is: Sauce Labs is another cloud-based testing service that supports cross-browser testing on real devices. It integrates with popular CI/CD tools, making it easy to incorporate UI testing into your development workflow.

How It Helps:

1. **Comprehensive Device Coverage**: Sauce Labs offers thousands of real devices and browser combinations.
2. **Integration**: It integrates well with CI/CD pipelines, allowing for continuous testing as part of your build process.

Example: To ensure that your web application's checkout process works seamlessly across all major browsers and devices, you can use Sauce Labs to run your automation tests across the required configurations, automatically triggered by your CI/CD pipeline.

Sample Code:
```
DesiredCapabilities caps = new DesiredCapabilities();
caps.setCapability("platform", "Windows 10");
caps.setCapability("browserName", "Chrome");
caps.setCapability("version", "91.0");
caps.setCapability("name", "Checkout Test");
```

```
WebDriver driver = new RemoteWebDriver(new URL("https://username:accessKey@
ondemand.saucelabs.com:443/wd/hub"), caps);
    driver.get("https://example.com/checkout");
    // Run test
    driver.quit();
```

3. *LambdaTest*

What It Is: LambdaTest is a cloud-based cross-browser testing platform that allows you to run automated Selenium scripts on a scalable cloud grid. It offers support for a wide range of browsers, operating systems, and devices, making it easy to test your application across multiple environments.

How It Helps*:*
1. **Scalable Testing**: LambdaTest allows you to execute tests in parallel across multiple browsers and devices, significantly reducing the time required to validate your UI.
2. **Seamless Integration**: LambdaTest integrates with various CI/CD tools, bug tracking systems, and collaboration platforms, making it easy to integrate into your existing workflow.
3. **Real-Time Testing**: You can perform live interactive testing on real browsers and operating systems, which helps in catching UI issues that might not be detected through automated scripts alone.

Example: If you need to ensure your application's compatibility across various versions of Chrome, Firefox, and Edge on different Windows and macOS environments, LambdaTest can run your Selenium scripts across these combinations in parallel, providing comprehensive reports and logs.

Sample Code:
```
    DesiredCapabilities capabilities = new DesiredCapabilities();
    capabilities.setCapability("browserName", "Chrome");
    capabilities.setCapability("version", "91.0");
    capabilities.setCapability("platform", "Windows 10");
    capabilities.setCapability("name", "LambdaTest Parallel Test");

    WebDriver driver = new RemoteWebDriver(new URL("https://username:accessKey@
hub.lambdatest.com/wd/hub"), capabilities);
    driver.get("https://example.com");
    // Run test
    driver.quit();
```

Benefits of Using Cross-Platform Testing Tools for In-Sprint Automation
- **Efficiency:** Cross-platform testing tools enable the simultaneous execution of automated tests across multiple browsers and devices, significantly speeding up the process and ensuring that testing fits within sprint timelines.
- **Scalability:** As your application grows, these tools allow you to easily scale testing efforts by adding more devices and browsers without additional setup, ensuring that in-sprint automation keeps pace with development.
- **Realistic Testing:** Cloud-based services like BrowserStack, Sauce Labs, and LambdaTest offer testing on real devices and environments, providing more accurate results compared to emulators or simulators, ensuring high-quality feedback during the sprint.

- **Early Detection of Issues:** By integrating cross-platform testing into your CI/CD pipeline, you can identify cross-browser or device-specific issues early in the sprint. This minimizes the time and cost required to resolve defects later, keeping the sprint on track.

In a Nutshell

UI testing across multiple devices and browsers is a challenging but crucial aspect of delivering a seamless and high-quality user experience. For in-sprint automation, leveraging cross-platform testing tools like **Selenium Grid, BrowserStack, Sauce Labs**, and **LambdaTest** enables teams to automate this process efficiently within the sprint timeframe.

These tools not only reduce testing time but also offer the scalability needed to ensure modern web applications perform consistently across various platforms. Integrating these tools into Agile sprints ensures that UI testing progresses alongside rapid development, helping to deliver reliable, user-friendly software within each sprint cycle.

2. *Headless Browsers for In-Sprint Automation*

In in-sprint automation, headless browsers allow for faster execution of UI tests without the overhead of rendering the entire browser UI. This is particularly useful when focusing on functional testing, as it enables tests to run quickly and efficiently in Continuous Integration/Continuous Deployment (CI/CD) environments.   Below, we will explore how headless browsers can be used in popular frameworks like **Selenium** and **TestNG**, along with code examples to demonstrate the implementation.

Using Headless Browsers with Selenium

Headless browsers like **Chrome** and **Firefox** in headless mode are frequently used for automated UI testing in CI/CD pipelines. Here's how you can set up and use headless browsers in Selenium for in-sprint automation.

Example 1: Headless Chrome with Selenium

In this example, we will set up **Chrome** in headless mode using Selenium WebDriver to perform a simple login test.

```java
import org.openqa.selenium.WebDriver;
import org.openqa.selenium.chrome.ChromeDriver;
import org.openqa.selenium.chrome.ChromeOptions;
import org.openqa.selenium.By;
import org.testng.Assert;
import org.testng.annotations.AfterMethod;
import org.testng.annotations.BeforeMethod;
import org.testng.annotations.Test;

public class HeadlessChromeTest {
    WebDriver driver;

    @BeforeMethod
    public void setup() {
        // Set the ChromeDriver path
        System.setProperty("webdriver.chrome.driver", "path/to/chromedriver");
```

```java
        // Configure Chrome options for headless mode
        ChromeOptions options = new ChromeOptions();
        options.addArguments("--headless");
      options.addArguments("--disable-gpu");  // Optional: For older hardware
        options.addArguments("--window-size=1920,1080"); // Set window size

        // Initialize Chrome WebDriver in headless mode
        driver = new ChromeDriver(options);
    }


    @Test
    public void loginTest() {
        // Navigate to the login page
        driver.get("https://example.com/login");

        // Perform login actions
        driver.findElement(By.id("username")).sendKeys("testUser");
        driver.findElement(By.id("password")).sendKeys("testPassword");
        driver.findElement(By.id("loginButton")).click();

        // Validate successful login by checking URL or page content
        Assert.assertTrue(driver.getCurrentUrl().contains("dashboard"));
    }


    @AfterMethod
    public void tearDown() {
        if (driver != null) {
            driver.quit();
        }
    }
  }
```

Explanation:
- **Headless Mode Setup**: The Chrome browser is initialized with the --headless option, meaning that it will not display the UI but will still interact with web elements.
- **Efficient Execution**: By running in headless mode, this test can execute faster and is well-suited for CI environments where GUI access is not needed.
- **Window Size**: Setting the window size (--window-size=1920,1080) is important for ensuring elements are laid out as expected during functional tests.

Example 2: Headless Firefox with Selenium
Here's how you can set up **Firefox** in headless mode using Selenium to run the same login test.

```java
import org.openqa.selenium.WebDriver;
import org.openqa.selenium.firefox.FirefoxDriver;
import org.openqa.selenium.firefox.FirefoxOptions;
import org.openqa.selenium.By;
```

```java
import org.testng.Assert;
import org.testng.annotations.AfterMethod;
import org.testng.annotations.BeforeMethod;
import org.testng.annotations.Test;

public class HeadlessFirefoxTest {
    WebDriver driver;

    @BeforeMethod
    public void setup() {
        // Set the GeckoDriver path for Firefox
        System.setProperty("webdriver.gecko.driver", "path/to/geckodriver");

        // Configure Firefox options for headless mode
        FirefoxOptions options = new FirefoxOptions();
        options.setHeadless(true);

        // Initialize Firefox WebDriver in headless mode
        driver = new FirefoxDriver(options);
    }

    @Test
    public void loginTest() {
        // Navigate to the login page
        driver.get("https://example.com/login");

        // Perform login actions
        driver.findElement(By.id("username")).sendKeys("testUser");
        driver.findElement(By.id("password")).sendKeys("testPassword");
        driver.findElement(By.id("loginButton")).click();

        // Validate successful login by checking URL or page content
        Assert.assertTrue(driver.getCurrentUrl().contains("dashboard"));
    }

    @AfterMethod
    public void tearDown() {
        if (driver != null) {
            driver.quit();
        }
    }
}
```

Explanation:

- **Firefox Headless Mode:** Firefox is initialized with the setHeadless(true) option, allowing it to run tests without rendering the UI.

- **Fast Feedback**: This headless setup ensures faster execution, providing immediate feedback within the sprint cycle without resource-heavy UI rendering.

Using Headless Browsers with TestNG and Parallel Execution

In-sprint automation often requires running multiple tests in parallel to meet tight deadlines. TestNG allows you to execute tests concurrently, even when using headless browsers. Below is an example of how to configure parallel execution of headless browser tests using TestNG.

TestNG Parallel Execution with Headless Chrome and Firefox

Test Class Example (LoginTest.java):

```java
import org.openqa.selenium.WebDriver;
import org.openqa.selenium.chrome.ChromeDriver;
import org.openqa.selenium.chrome.ChromeOptions;
import org.openqa.selenium.firefox.FirefoxDriver;
import org.openqa.selenium.firefox.FirefoxOptions;
import org.testng.annotations.BeforeMethod;
import org.testng.annotations.Parameters;
import org.testng.annotations.Test;

public class LoginTest {
    WebDriver driver;

    @BeforeMethod
    @Parameters("browser")
    public void setup(String browser) {
        if (browser.equalsIgnoreCase("chrome")) {
        System.setProperty("webdriver.chrome.driver", "path/to/chromedriver");
            ChromeOptions options = new ChromeOptions();
            options.addArguments("--headless");
            driver = new ChromeDriver(options);
        } else if (browser.equalsIgnoreCase("firefox")) {
          System.setProperty("webdriver.gecko.driver", "path/to/geckodriver");
            FirefoxOptions options = new FirefoxOptions();
            options.setHeadless(true);
            driver = new FirefoxDriver(options);
        }
    }

    @Test
    public void loginTest() {
        driver.get("https://example.com/login");
        driver.findElement(By.id("username")).sendKeys("testUser");
        driver.findElement(By.id("password")).sendKeys("testPassword");
        driver.findElement(By.id("loginButton")).click();
        Assert.assertTrue(driver.getCurrentUrl().contains("dashboard"));
    }
```

```java
@AfterMethod
public void tearDown() {
    if (driver != null) {
        driver.quit();
    }
}
```

TestNG XML Configuration for Parallel Execution (testng.xml):

```xml
<!DOCTYPE suite SYSTEM "http://testng.org/testng-1.0.dtd" >
<suite name="Parallel Tests" parallel="tests" thread-count="2">
    <test name="Chrome Test">
        <parameter name="browser" value="chrome" />
        <classes>
            <class name="LoginTest" />
        </classes>
    </test>

    <test name="Firefox Test">
        <parameter name="browser" value="firefox" />
        <classes>
            <class name="LoginTest" />
        </classes>
    </test>
</suite>
```

Explanation:
- **Parallel Execution**: In the TestNG suite, the parallel="tests" attribute runs both the Chrome and Firefox headless tests concurrently, reducing the total test execution time within the sprint.
- **Parameterization**: The @Parameters annotation is used to pass browser names (chrome or firefox) to the test methods, allowing you to control which browser is used for each test instance.

Using Headless Browsers in CI/CD Pipelines

Headless browsers are particularly useful for running tests in CI/CD environments, where UI rendering is unnecessary, and test speed is critical. Below is an example of how to configure Jenkins to run headless Chrome tests automatically after a build.

Jenkins Pipeline Configuration (groovy)

```groovy
pipeline {
    agent any
    stages {
        stage('Checkout') {
            steps {
                // Checkout code from version control
                git 'https://github.com/your-repository.git'
            }
        }
```

```
        stage('Build') {
            steps {
                // Build the project (if needed)
                sh './gradlew build'
            }
        }
        stage('Test') {
            steps {
                // Run headless tests
                sh 'mvn test -Dbrowser=chrome'
            }
        }
    }
    post {
        always {
            // Publish test results
            junit '**/target/surefire-reports/*.xml'
        }
    }
}
```

Explanation*:*
- **Headless Test Execution**: The mvn test -Dbrowser=chrome command triggers the Maven build and runs the tests with headless Chrome.
- **Continuous Feedback**: The tests are integrated into the Jenkins pipeline, providing continuous feedback after every build, ensuring that any issues are identified and addressed within the sprint.

Best Practices for Using Headless Browsers in In-Sprint Automation

1. **Parallel Execution**: Always configure parallel execution when using headless browsers to take full advantage of their speed. This ensures that your test suite completes within the sprint cycle, giving you faster feedback.
2. **Smart Wait Strategies**: Headless browsers execute tests faster than standard browsers, which may cause tests to fail if elements are not yet fully loaded or interactable. To prevent this, use **Explicit Waits** or **Fluent Waits** to wait until elements are visible or clickable before performing actions.

Example of Explicit Wait:

```
WebDriverWait wait = new WebDriverWait(driver, 10);
WebElement loginButton = wait.until(ExpectedConditions.elementToBeClickable(By.
id("loginButton")));
loginButton.click();
```

Example of Fluent Wait:

```
Wait<WebDriver> fluentWait = new FluentWait<>(driver)
        .withTimeout(Duration.ofSeconds(30))
        .pollingEvery(Duration.ofSeconds(5))
        .ignoring(NoSuchElementException.class);
```

```
WebElement    element    =    fluentWait.until(driver   ->   driver.findElement(By.
id("elementId")));
    element.click();
```

Explanation: These waits ensure that your tests don't fail because of timing issues or slow-loading elements. In fast execution environments, smart waits are essential to avoid flaky tests.

3. **Headless Browser Testing in CI/CD Pipelines**: Ensure that all your automated UI tests are integrated into the CI/CD pipeline using headless browsers. Headless browsers, especially in CI environments, offer significant performance benefits and can be run on any machine, even those without a graphical user interface (GUI).

CI Tools: Use CI tools like **Jenkins, GitLab CI**, or **CircleCI** to automatically trigger headless browser tests after every code commit or build.

Automation Flow: Implement headless browser tests early in the sprint and integrate them into your CI/CD pipeline to provide immediate feedback to developers, ensuring that newly developed features are continuously tested and validated.

4. **Use for Functional Testing, Not Visual Validation**: While headless browsers are excellent for functional and backend tests, they are not suitable for visual validation. If UI appearance and layout need to be verified, complement headless browser tests with visual tests using full browsers or specialized tools like **Applitools.**

Strategy: Use headless browsers for functional tests (e.g., login, form submission, navigation) and integrate a smaller subset of visual validation tests using full browsers for layout and appearance verification.

5. **Optimize Resources by Running Headless in Parallel**: Leverage parallel execution to run multiple headless browser instances simultaneously across different test cases. Parallel execution optimizes resource utilization, shortens test durations, and ensures that testing is completed within the sprint window.

Example (TestNG parallel execution):

```xml
<suite name="Parallel Suite" parallel="tests" thread-count="4">
    <test name="Chrome Test">
        <parameter name="browser" value="chrome"/>
        <classes>
            <class name="com.example.tests.LoginTest"/>
        </classes>
    </test>

    <test name="Firefox Test">
        <parameter name="browser" value="firefox"/>
        <classes>
            <class name="com.example.tests.LoginTest"/>
        </classes>
    </test>
</suite>
```

In a Nutshell

Headless browsers are an invaluable tool for achieving efficient in-sprint automation. By eliminating the need to render the UI, they speed up test execution, making it easier to run many tests in a short timeframe. Integrated into CI/CD pipelines, headless browsers provide continuous feedback without consuming excessive resources. By following best practices such as parallel execution, using smart waits, and optimizing resource usage, teams can ensure that UI automation fits seamlessly into Agile sprints while maintaining high test coverage and minimizing execution time.

TOOLS AND FRAMEWORKS FOR UI TESTING

Selecting the right tools and frameworks for UI automation is a critical decision that can significantly impact the success of your testing efforts. The tools you choose will determine how easily tests can be written, maintained, and integrated into your development workflow. They will also influence the scalability and effectiveness of your testing strategy.

Key Challenge: Choosing the Right Tools for In-Sprint Automation

Selecting the right tools for in-sprint UI automation testing can be daunting due to the wide range of available options. Each tool has distinct features, advantages, and limitations, and the specific needs of your sprint cycle add complexity. These factors include the technology stack, the type of application being tested (web, mobile, or desktop), the team's skill level, and the need for seamless integration with CI/CD pipelines.

Choosing the wrong tool can lead to inefficiencies, increased test maintenance, and a steep learning curve for the team, which may hinder progress within the sprint. If the selected tool does not align with your project's needs, it can cause gaps in test coverage and make it difficult to achieve automation goals within the sprint timeframe.

Solutions: Evaluating Tools Based on Sprint Requirements and Team Expertise

To select the right tools for in-sprint automation, systematically evaluate them based on your project's sprint-specific requirements and your team's expertise. Below is a checklist that guides the tool selection process, with a focus on the demands of in-sprint automation.

Tool Selection Checklist

1. **Project Requirements**
   - **Type of Application**: Determine whether you are testing a web application, mobile application, desktop application, or a combination. Some tools specialize in certain types of applications.
     - **Example**: Selenium is excellent for web applications, while Appium is better suited for mobile apps.
   - **Technology Stack**: Consider the technologies used in your project (e.g., Java, .NET, React, Angular). Ensure that the tool supports the languages and frameworks your application is built on.
     - **Example**: For a React-based application, tools like Cypress offer built-in support for modern JavaScript frameworks.
   - **Cross-Platform Testing**: If your application needs to be tested across multiple browsers, devices, or operating systems, look for tools that offer robust cross-platform support.
     - **Example**: Tools like BrowserStack, Sauce Labs, and LambdaTest provide cross-browser and cross-device testing capabilities.

2. **Ease of Use and Learning Curve**
   - ○ **Team Expertise:** Assess the technical expertise of your team. If the team is new to automation, choosing a tool with a simpler setup and user-friendly interface may be more effective.
     - **Example:** Cypress is known for its easy setup and use, making it ideal for teams new to automation.
   - ○ **Documentation and Community Support:** Check whether the tool has comprehensive documentation, tutorials, and an active community that can provide support.
     - **Example:** Selenium has extensive documentation and a large community, making it easier to find solutions to common problems.

3. **Integration with CI/CD**
   - ○ **CI/CD Compatibility:** Ensure that the tool integrates well with your CI/CD pipeline, allowing automated tests to run seamlessly as part of the build process.
     - **Example:** Jenkins, GitLab CI, and CircleCI integrate well with most UI automation tools, allowing tests to be triggered automatically on code commits.
   - ○ **Test Reporting:** Look for tools that offer robust reporting features or integrate with reporting tools to track and analyze test results over time.
     - **Example:** Tools like Allure or ExtentReports can be integrated with most automation frameworks to provide detailed test reports.

4. **Scalability**
   - ○ **Parallel Execution:** Choose a tool that supports parallel test execution, especially if you need to run many tests across multiple environments.
     - **Example:** Selenium Grid, BrowserStack, and Sauce Labs allow for parallel test execution, reducing the time required to complete testing.
   - ○ **Handling Large Test Suites:** Consider whether the tool can efficiently manage large test suites without significant performance degradation.
     - **Example:** Test frameworks like TestNG and JUnit, when used with Selenium, allow for structured test suite management and efficient execution.

5. **Cost**
   - ○ **Licensing:** Evaluate the cost of the tool, including licensing fees, and determine whether it fits within your project's budget.
     - **Example:** Open-source tools like Selenium and Cypress are free, but may require additional infrastructure investment for things like cross-browser testing.
   - ○ **Infrastructure Costs:** Consider the cost of the infrastructure needed to support the tool, such as servers for running tests or cloud services for cross-browser testing.
     - **Example:** Cloud-based services like LambdaTest and BrowserStack have subscription fees but may reduce the need for in-house infrastructure.

6. **Maintenance and Support**
   - ○ **Tool Maintenance:** Consider how often the tool is updated and whether it is actively maintained. An outdated tool might lack support for newer technologies or browser versions.
     - **Example:** Selenium is regularly updated to support new browser versions and features, making it a reliable choice for web testing.

○ **Vendor Support**: If you choose a commercial tool, check the level of support provided by the vendor, including response times and available support channels.
  - **Example**: Tools like LambdaTest offer dedicated support, which can be valuable for resolving issues quickly.

Evaluating Tools Based on Project Requirements and Team Expertise

Now that you have a checklist, let's explore how to use it to evaluate different tools for your project.

Step 1: Define Your Project Requirements

Start by listing all the specific requirements of your project. Consider the type of application you are testing, the technology stack, the environments in which the application will run, and the specific features you need to test. For example, suppose you are testing a web application that must run on Chrome, Firefox, and Safari across Windows and macOS. In that case, you will need a tool that supports cross-browser testing and can be integrated into your CI/CD pipeline.

Step 2: Assess Your Team's Expertise

Evaluate the technical skills of your team. If your team is already proficient in a particular programming language or framework, choose tools that leverage that expertise. For instance, if your team is skilled in JavaScript, tools like Cypress or Puppeteer might be a better fit than tools that require knowledge of other languages.

Step 3: Research and Compare Tools

Research tools that match your project requirements and team expertise. Use the checklist to compare the tools on key factors such as ease of use, integration capabilities, scalability, and cost. Create a comparison matrix to visualize the pros and cons of each tool.

Example Comparison Matrix

Feature	Selenium Grid	BrowserStack	Sauce Labs	LambdaTest
Ease of Use	Moderate: Requires manual setup and configuration (hub and nodes).	High: Cloud-based, easy to use with no infrastructure setup.	High: Cloud-based with simple setup, good documentation.	High: Cloud-based, intuitive interface with detailed tutorials.
Cross-Platform Testing	High: Supports various browsers and OS combinations but requires manual setup for each node.	High: Supports 2000+ browsers and real devices for cross-browser testing.	High: Supports thousands of browser and OS combinations with real devices.	High: Supports 2000+ browsers and real devices for testing across platforms.
CI/CD Integration	High: Can be integrated with Jenkins, GitLab, and other CI/CD tools, but requires manual configuration.	High: Seamless integration with CI/CD tools like Jenkins, CircleCI, TravisCI, and GitLab.	High: Integrates with most popular CI/CD tools and provides APIs for custom workflows.	High: Provides seamless integration with Jenkins, CircleCI, GitLab, and other CI/CD tools.
Parallel Execution	High: Supports parallel execution but requires configuration.	High: Supports parallel testing across devices and browsers with easy setup.	High: Extensive support for parallel execution, allowing large-scale parallel test runs.	High: Offers scalable parallel testing with concurrency limits based on subscription plans.
Real Device Testing	Low: Selenium Grid requires physical or virtual devices set up manually.	High: Provides access to real devices and browsers through the cloud.	High: Offers a wide range of real devices and browsers for accurate testing.	High: Provides real device cloud for accurate testing of mobile and web applications.

Scalability	Moderate: Requires manual scaling with additional nodes for larger test suites.	High: Scalable as it's cloud-based and automatically handles scaling for large test suites.	High: Cloud-based platform that automatically scales to handle large-scale parallel tests.	High: Scalable cloud-based infrastructure, ideal for parallel execution and high concurrency.
Cost	Free: Open source, but you need to maintain your own infrastructure.	Subscription: Paid plans based on usage, offers free trials but becomes costly with high concurrency and device usage.	Subscription: Offers various pricing tiers based on concurrency and usage. Enterprise plans available.	Subscription: Paid plans based on the number of parallel sessions and device access, offers affordable pricing with a free tier.
Infrastructure Maintenance	High: Requires manual maintenance of nodes and infrastructure (e.g., VMs, cloud instances, etc.).	Low: Cloud-based, so no need for infrastructure maintenance.	Low: Fully managed cloud-based platform with no need for manual maintenance.	Low: Fully cloud-managed infrastructure with minimal maintenance required.
Browser/OS Support	High: Supports any combination but needs manual configuration for each.	High: Supports a wide range of browser/OS combinations and real devices, including mobile.	High: Offers thousands of browser/OS combinations, including mobile and tablet support.	High: Provides extensive browser/OS coverage with real device support, including mobile browsers.
Community Support	High: Strong community support, as it is open-sourcewith numerous tutorials and forums.	High: Strong support with comprehensive documentation, active forums, and dedicated support.	High: Strong support with excellent documentation, webinars, and a responsive support team.	High: Growing community support with detailed documentation, an active forum, and 24/7 support.
Reporting & Analytics	Low: Basic, requires third-party tools like Allure or custom integrations for detailed reports.	High: Built-in reporting with visual logs, screenshots, and video recordings of test runs.	High: Advanced reporting with screenshots, video recordings, and comprehensive logs.	High: Built-in reporting with screenshots, video recordings, and detailed session logs.
Speed	Moderate: Speed depends on the infrastructure setup, could be slower if not optimized.	High: Cloud infrastructure is optimized for fast execution and parallelization.	High: Optimized for speed with high concurrency support and parallel execution.	High: Fast parallel execution with cloud optimization for quicker feedback loops.

Summary of Key Factors Ease of Use: BrowserStack, Sauce Labs, and LambdaTest are cloud-based and provide a much easier setup compared to Selenium Grid, which requires manual configuration.

- **Cross-Platform Testing:** All tools provide robust cross-platform testing, but BrowserStack, Sauce Labs, and LambdaTest offer real devices and out-of-the-box multi-browser testing.
- **CI/CD Integration:** All tools provide strong CI/CD integration capabilities, but cloud-based tools like BrowserStack, Sauce Labs, and LambdaTest provide simpler integration with minimal setup.
- **Scalability:** Cloud-based tools like BrowserStack, Sauce Labs, and LambdaTest scale automatically, while Selenium Grid requires manual setup and scaling by adding nodes.
- **Cost:** Selenium Grid is free and open-sourcebut requires infrastructure investment. BrowserStack, Sauce Labs, and LambdaTest are subscription-based, with pricing that scales based on concurrency and usage.
- **Maintenance:** Cloud-based solutions (BrowserStack, Sauce Labs, and LambdaTest) eliminate the need for infrastructure maintenance, unlike Selenium Grid, which requires significant manual effort to maintain.
- **Reporting:** Cloud-based tools provide extensive built-in reporting features, while Selenium Grid requires third-party tools for detailed reporting.

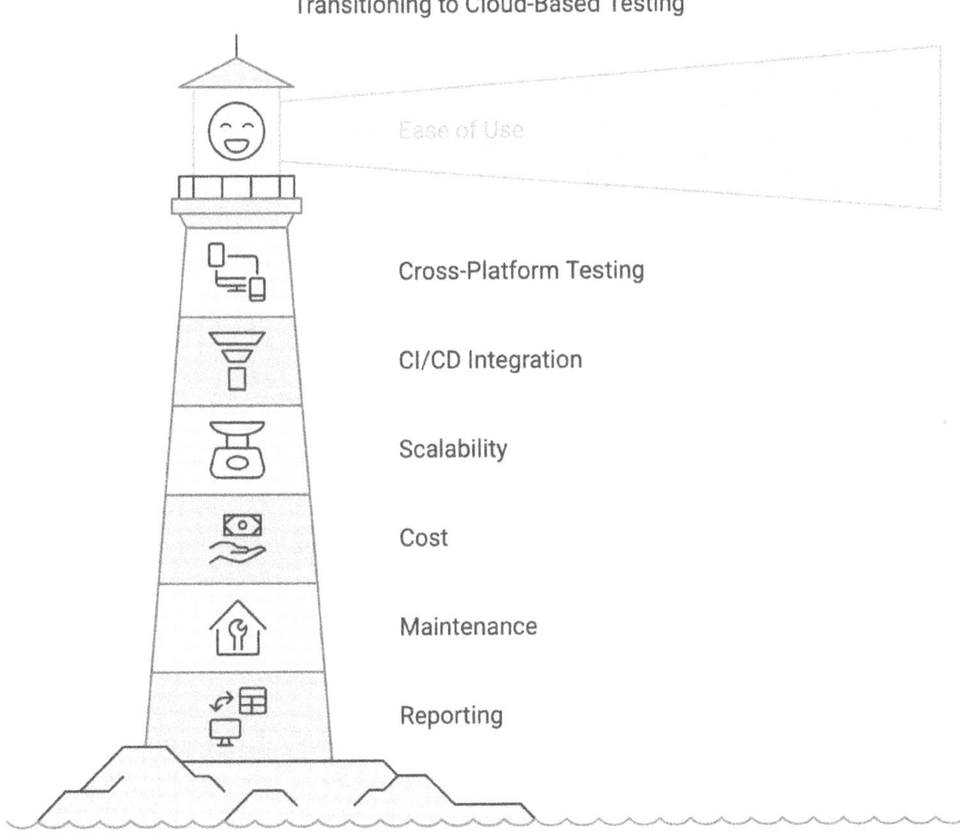

Recommendation based on above factors:

- Selenium Grid is best suited for teams that have the infrastructure and technical expertise to manage nodes and hubs, especially if they are looking for an open-source, cost-effective solution.
- BrowserStack, Sauce Labs, and LambdaTest are ideal for teams that want a fully managed, scalable, cloud-based solution that eliminates the need for maintaining infrastructure. These tools are especially beneficial for projects requiring cross-browser and real-device testing, with strong support for parallel execution and easy CI/CD integration.

Step 4: Conduct a Pilot Test

Before fully committing to a tool, conduct a pilot test by automating a few key test cases using each shortlisted tool. This hands-on experience will give you insights into how well the tool integrates with your existing processes, how easy it is to use, and how well it meets your project's specific needs.

Example: If you are testing a login functionality, automate this test case with Selenium, Cypress, and LambdaTest. Evaluate the ease of writing the tests, the time required to execute them across multiple browsers, and the quality of the test reports generated.

Step 5: Decide

After completing the pilot tests, gather feedback from the team on their experiences with each tool. Consider the results of the pilot tests, along with your initial comparison, to make an informed decision. Choose the tool that best meets your project's requirements, is easy for your team to use, and offers the necessary features for your testing strategy.

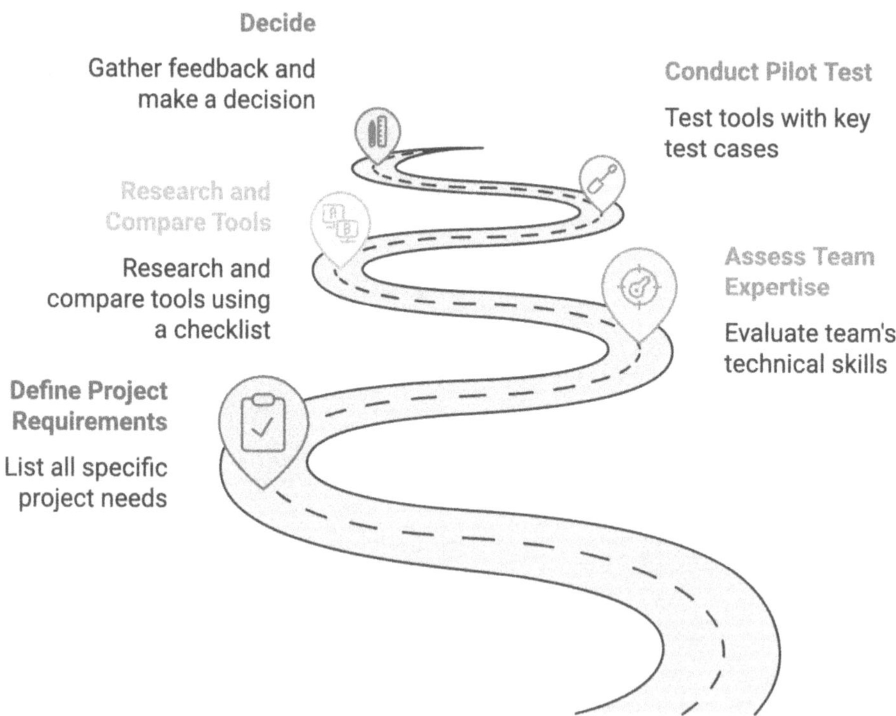

In a Nutshell

Choosing the right tools and frameworks for UI automation testing is a critical step that requires careful consideration of your project's needs and your team's expertise. By using a structured checklist to evaluate tools and conducting pilot tests, you can ensure that you select a tool that not only fits your current requirements but also scales with your project as it grows. The right tool will streamline your testing efforts, integrate smoothly with your development workflow, and help you deliver high-quality software efficiently.

UI AUTOMATION WITH CUCUMBER AND SELENIUM FOR IN-SPRINT AUTOMATION

In-sprint UI automation with **Cucumber** and **Selenium** is a powerful approach for testing web applications. This combination allows teams to use the **Behavior-Driven Development (BDD)** methodology through Cucumber, where test scenarios are written in plain English, and leverage Selenium's robust browser automation capabilities to execute those scenarios in real browsers. This integration enhances collaboration across development, testing, and business teams, ensuring that the behavior of the application aligns with the expected outcomes.

However, implementing UI automation in the context of in-sprint automation presents several challenges. Before addressing these challenges, it is important to follow best practices for using locators in Selenium to ensure that the automation is efficient and maintainable.

Best Practices for Locators in Selenium for In-Sprint Automation

Choosing the right locators in Selenium is crucial for ensuring that the automation is stable and easy to maintain within sprint cycles. When building an in-sprint automation framework, following best practices for locators helps reduce flakiness and makes scripts more reliable

1. *Id, Name, Classname, and Tagname Locators*

These are the simplest and most efficient locators to use when they are available:

- **Id:**
  - o **Best Practice**: Always prefer using the id locator if the element has a unique id attribute. It is the fastest locator and provides the most reliable way to find elements.

```
driver.findElement(By.id("username")).sendKeys("testUser");
```

- **Name:**
  - o **Best Practice**: Use name if no id is available. However, ensure that the name attribute is unique on the page.

```
driver.findElement(By.name("email")).sendKeys("user@example.com");
```

- **Classname:**
  - o **Best Practice**: Use this when the class name is unique and not shared by multiple elements. This is effective for identifying elements with shared characteristics, like buttons or form fields.

```
driver.findElement(By.className("submit-button")).click();
```

- **Tagname:**
  - o **Best Practice**: Useful for working with groups of elements (like forms or tables). Combine it with other locators for more precision.

```
List<WebElement> inputs = driver.findElements(By.tagName("input"));
```

2. *LinkText and PartialLinkText Locators*

These locators are specifically for hyperlinks and are most useful when locating links by their text:

- **LinkText:**
  - o **Best Practice**: Use when the exact link text is known and static. Avoid using this if the link text is dynamically generated or contains special characters.

```
driver.findElement(By.linkText("Forgot Password?")).click();
```

- **PartialLinkText:**
  - o **Best Practice**: Use when only part of the link text is stable or known. Ideal for cases where the entire link text might change but a key part remains the same.

```
driver.findElement(By.partialLinkText("Forgot")).click();
```

3. *Absolute vs. Relative XPaths*

XPath locators are powerful, but they need to be used carefully to avoid brittleness.

- **Absolute XPath:**
  - o **Best Practice**: Avoid using absolute XPaths (/html/body/...) as they rely on the complete structure of the page. Even minor changes in the HTML structure will break the locator.

```
// Avoid this:
driver.findElement(By.xpath("/html/body/div[2]/div[1]/input")).
sendKeys("testUser");
```

- **Relative XPath:**
  - o **Best Practice**: Use relative XPaths that depend on stable attributes like id, name, or text values. This makes the locator more reliable across minor UI changes.

```
// Use this: driver.findElement(By.xpath("//input[@name='username']")).
sendKeys("testUser");
```

4. XPath Operators, Methods, and Axes

XPath allows for precise element selection based on various criteria:

- **Operators**:
  - ○ **Best Practice**: Use logical operators like and or or to narrow down selections based on multiple attributes.

  ```
  driver.findElement(By.xpath("//input[@name='email'  and  @type='text']")).
  sendKeys("user@example.com");
  ```

- **Methods (contains, starts-with)**:
  - ○ **Best Practice**: Use methods like contains() or starts-with() to handle dynamic attribute values or partial matches. This is especially useful for dynamic UIs where attributes might vary slightly.

  ```
  driver.findElement(By.xpath("//button[contains(text(),'Login')]")).click();
  ```

- **Axes**:
  - ○ **Best Practice**: Use axes (following-sibling, parent, ancestor, etc.) to traverse the DOM relative to a stable element.

  ```
  driver.findElement(By.xpath("//label[text()='Password']/following-
  sibling::input")).sendKeys("password123");
  ```

5. CSS Selector Strategies

CSS Selectors are generally faster and more efficient than XPath locators.

- **By Id**:
  - ○ **Best Practice**: If an element has an id, use the #id CSS selector for the fastest access.

  ```
  driver.findElement(By.cssSelector("#username")).sendKeys("testUser");
  ```

- **By Class**:
  - ○ **Best Practice**: Use .className to locate elements by their class. Use caution if multiple elements share the same class name.

  ```
  driver.findElement(By.cssSelector(".submit-button")).click();
  ```

- **By Attribute**:
  - ○ **Best Practice**: Use [attribute=value] to locate elements with specific attributes. This is highly efficient for locating form fields or buttons.

  ```
  driver.findElement(By.cssSelector("input[name='email']")).sendKeys("user@
  example.com");
  ```

- **Hierarchical Selection**:
  - ○ **Best Practice**: Use CSS hierarchical selectors to locate elements nested inside containers.

  ```
  driver.findElement(By.cssSelector("div.container > input[name='email']")).
  sendKeys("user@example.com");
  ```

Implementing UI Automation with Cucumber and Selenium

The **Behavior-Driven Development (BDD)** approach with **Cucumber** and **Selenium** is highly effective for in-sprint automation because it allows teams to write tests in plain English using feature files. This enables better collaboration between developers, testers, and non-technical stakeholders. The tests (written as user stories in Gherkin syntax) can then be automated using Selenium WebDriver, ensuring that functionality aligns with the requirements throughout the sprint.

Below is a step-by-step approach to implementing UI automation with Cucumber and Selenium for in-sprint automation.

Pre-requisites

Before starting with the implementation, ensure the following:

1. **Install Java**: Selenium requires Java, so make sure you have the latest version of the JDK installed.

```
// Check Java version:
java -version
```

2. **Install Maven**: Maven will be used for managing dependencies.

```
// Check Maven version:
mvn -version
```

3. **Set up an IDE**: Use **IntelliJ IDEA** or **Eclipse** with Cucumber and Maven support.

4. **Add Maven Dependencies**: Update the pom.xml file to include the latest versions of **Selenium**, **Cucumber**, **JUnit**, and **TestNG**.

```xml
<dependencies>
    <!-- Selenium WebDriver -->
    <dependency>
        <groupId>org.seleniumhq.selenium</groupId>
        <artifactId>selenium-java</artifactId>
        <version>4.13.0</version>
    </dependency>

    <!-- Cucumber for BDD -->
    <dependency>
        <groupId>io.cucumber</groupId>
        <artifactId>cucumber-java</artifactId>
        <version>7.12.0</version>
    </dependency>

    <!-- Cucumber TestNG Integration -->
    <dependency>
        <groupId>io.cucumber</groupId>
        <artifactId>cucumber-testng</artifactId>
        <version>7.12.0</version>
    </dependency>

    <!-- TestNG -->
    <dependency>
        <groupId>org.testng</groupId>
        <artifactId>testng</artifactId>
        <version>7.9.1</version>
    </dependency>

    <!-- Cucumber JUnit Integration (optional) -->
    <dependency>
        <groupId>io.cucumber</groupId>
```

```xml
            <artifactId>cucumber-junit</artifactId>
            <version>7.12.0</version>
        </dependency>

        <!-- Allure Reporting -->
        <dependency>
            <groupId>io.qameta.allure</groupId>
            <artifactId>allure-cucumber7-jvm</artifactId>
            <version>2.21.0</version>
        </dependency>
    </dependencies>
```

Step 1: Setting Up Directory Structure

Organize your project with a clean directory structure to separate test logic, page objects, configuration files, and feature files for better maintainability.

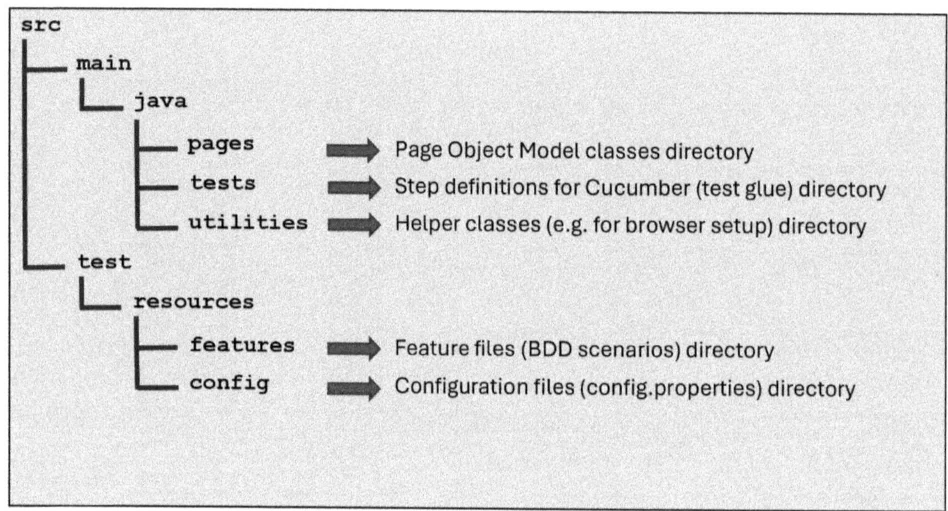

Step 2: Writing Feature Files

Feature files in BDD are written using Gherkin syntax and describe the behavior of the application in plain English. Each feature file contains one or more scenarios that map to specific tests.

Example Feature File: login.feature

```gherkin
Feature: Login to the application
   As a user, I want to be able to log in to the application so that I can access
my account.


   Scenario: Successful login with valid credentials
      Given the user is on the login page
      When the user enters valid credentials
      And clicks the login button
      Then the user is navigated to the dashboard
```

Feature: Describes the overall behavior.
- **Scenario:** Specifies the step-by-step interaction of the user with the application.
- **Gherkin Syntax:** Uses **Given, When, Then** to define the flow of the test.

Step 3: Implementing Step Definitions

The **Step Definitions** are Java methods that map the Gherkin steps to Selenium WebDriver actions. For every step in the feature file, you create a corresponding method in the step definition file.

Example Step Definition for login.feature

```java
import org.openqa.selenium.WebDriver;
import org.openqa.selenium.By;
import org.openqa.selenium.WebElement;
import io.cucumber.java.en.*;

public class LoginSteps {
    WebDriver driver = BrowserFactory.getDriver();

    @Given("the user is on the login page")
    public void theUserIsOnTheLoginPage() {
        driver.get("https://example.com/login");
    }

    @When("the user enters valid credentials")
    public void theUserEntersValidCredentials() {
        WebElement username = driver.findElement(By.id("username"));
        WebElement password = driver.findElement(By.id("password"));
        username.sendKeys("validUser");
        password.sendKeys("validPassword");
    }

    @When("clicks the login button")
    public void clicksTheLoginButton() {
        driver.findElement(By.id("loginButton")).click();
    }

    @Then("the user is navigated to the dashboard")
    public void theUserIsNavigatedToTheDashboard() {
        String expectedTitle = "Dashboard";
        String actualTitle = driver.getTitle();
        Assert.assertTrue(actualTitle.contains(expectedTitle));
    }
}
```

- **Gherkin Steps Mapping**: Each Gherkin step from the feature file is implemented as a method in Java using Cucumber's @Given, @When, and @Then annotations.
- **WebDriver Actions**: Selenium WebDriver is used to interact with the web elements during the test (e.g., entering text and clicking buttons).

Step 4: Implementing Page Object Model (POM)

The **Page Object Model (POM)** separates the test logic from the UI interaction logic, making it easier to maintain tests as the UI changes. Create a separate class for each page of your application.

Example Login Page Object

```java
import org.openqa.selenium.WebDriver;
import org.openqa.selenium.WebElement;
import org.openqa.selenium.support.FindBy;
import org.openqa.selenium.support.PageFactory;

public class LoginPage {
    WebDriver driver;

    @FindBy(id = "username")
    WebElement usernameField;

    @FindBy(id = "password")
    WebElement passwordField;

    @FindBy(id = "loginButton")
    WebElement loginButton;

    public LoginPage(WebDriver driver) {
        this.driver = driver;
        PageFactory.initElements(driver, this);
    }

    public void enterCredentials(String username, String password) {
        usernameField.sendKeys(username);
        passwordField.sendKeys(password);
    }

    public void clickLogin() {
        loginButton.click();
    }
}
```

- **Page Factory**: Helps in initializing web elements using @FindBy annotations.
- **Reusability**: The POM ensures that the interaction logic is reusable across multiple tests.

Step 5: Configuring Cucumber Runner

To execute the Cucumber tests, a **Cucumber TestNG runner** is required. This is where you specify the location of feature files and step definitions.

Example Cucumber TestNG Runner

```java
import io.cucumber.testng.AbstractTestNGCucumberTests;
import io.cucumber.testng.CucumberOptions;
import org.testng.annotations.Test;

@CucumberOptions(
    features = "src/test/resources/features",
```

```
        glue = "com.example.tests",
        plugin = {"pretty", "html:target/cucumber-reports.html", "io.qameta.allure.
cucumber7jvm.AllureCucumber7Jvm"}
    )
    @Test
    public class TestRunner extends AbstractTestNGCucumberTests {
    }
```

- **CucumberOptions**: Specifies the location of the feature files and step definitions (glue).
- **Plugins**: Plugins like **Allure** are used to generate detailed reports.

Step 6: Running Tests in Parallel Using TestNG

For in-sprint automation, running tests in parallel is crucial for reducing execution time. In the testng.xml file, configure parallel execution.

TestNG XML for Parallel Execution

```
<suite name="Cucumber Suite" parallel="methods" thread-count="4">
    <test name="Cucumber Test">
        <classes>
            <class name="com.example.runner.TestRunner"/>
        </classes>
    </test>
</suite>
```

Step 7: Reporting with Allure

Allure reports provide comprehensive and visually appealing reports for test results, which are essential for tracking in-sprint progress and outcomes.

- **Allure Plugin Configuration**: As seen in the runner, add the Allure plugin to generate reports:
  ```
  plugin = {"io.qameta.allure.cucumber7jvm.AllureCucumber7Jvm"}
  ```
- **Generate Reports**: After running the tests, generate the Allure report using Maven:
  ```
  mvn allure:serve
  ```

Step 8: Continuous Integration with Jenkins

For in-sprint automation, it's crucial to integrate tests into your CI pipeline. In Jenkins, configure the job to run the Cucumber tests as part of the build process.

1. Add a **Maven build step** in Jenkins with the following command:
   ```
   mvn test
   ```
2. Use **Allure** to publish test reports by adding the **Allure Jenkins Plugin**.

How BDD Aids In-Sprint Automation

- **Collaboration**: BDD encourages collaboration between developers, testers, and business stakeholders by writing tests in a language that everyone understands (Gherkin).
- **Early Feedback**: Feature files describe behavior upfront, allowing the team to get early feedback on whether the development is meeting requirements.
- **Faster Execution**: With TestNG's parallel execution and headless browsers, BDD tests can be executed quickly, fitting easily into the sprint.

- **Maintainability**: Using POM with Cucumber ensures that tests are maintainable, even as the UI changes, reducing the burden on testers.

Key Challenges in Implementing UI Automation with Cucumber and Selenium for In-Sprint Automation

1.   Challenge: Integrating Cucumber and Selenium into the CI/CD Pipeline

Integrating Cucumber and Selenium with a CI/CD pipeline is essential for in-sprint automation, as tests must run automatically after each build or code commit. However, test execution time, reliability, and timely feedback are critical concerns. Failing tests should provide immediate feedback without blocking development progress, while ensuring that they fit within the sprint cycle.

Solution

- **Automated Triggers**: Use CI/CD tools like **Jenkins**, **GitLab CI**, or **CircleCI** to automatically trigger Cucumber and Selenium tests after every code commit or build. Set up the tests to run in isolated environments like **Docker containers** to ensure consistency across different development machines.

Example: Use Docker to create an isolated test environment:

```
docker run -d -v $(pwd):/usr/src/app -w /usr/src/app selenium/standalone-chrome
```

- **Parallel Execution**: To reduce execution time, enable parallel execution of tests across multiple browsers or environments using tools like **Selenium Grid**, **LambdaTest**, or **BrowserStack**. These tools can distribute tests across different environments simultaneously.

   Example: Configure TestNG for parallel execution in the testng.xml:

```xml
<suite name="Parallel Suite" parallel="tests" thread-count="4">
    <test name="Chrome Test">
        <parameter name="browser" value="chrome" />
        <classes>
            <class name="com.example.tests.LoginTest" />
        </classes>
    </test>
    <test name="Firefox Test">
        <parameter name="browser" value="firefox" />
        <classes>
            <class name="com.example.tests.LoginTest" />
        </classes>
    </test>
</suite>
```

- **Test Isolation**: Ensure that each test is independent, with no shared state between tests. This avoids conflicts when running tests in parallel.
- **Headless Browsers**: Use **headless browsers** like Chrome or Firefox to speed up execution by eliminating the need for UI rendering. This reduces test runtime in CI environments.

Example:

```java
ChromeOptions options = new ChromeOptions();
options.addArguments("--headless");
WebDriver driver = new ChromeDriver(options);
```

2. Challenge: Test Maintenance

As the application's UI evolves during sprints, maintaining UI automation tests becomes challenging. Changes in web elements such as IDs, class names, or dynamic elements may break test locators, causing false failures and consuming valuable time to fix.

Solution

- **Page Object Model (POM)**: Implement the **Page Object Model (POM)** to separate UI locators from test logic. When a UI element changes, only the page object needs updating, reducing the effort required to maintain test scripts.

Example:

```java
public class LoginPage {
    @FindBy(id = "username")
    WebElement usernameField;

    @FindBy(id = "password")
    WebElement passwordField;

    public void login(String username, String password) {
        usernameField.sendKeys(username);
        passwordField.sendKeys(password);
    }
}
```

- **CSS Selectors over XPaths**: Use **CSS selectors** rather than complex XPaths, as they are faster, more stable, and easier to maintain. Avoid using absolute XPaths, which are prone to breaking with minor DOM changes.
- **Version Control**: Store your test scripts and configuration files in a **version control system** like Git. This allows tracking of changes and makes it easy to revert if issues arise.

3. Challenge: Handling Dynamic Web Elements

Modern web applications often involve dynamic elements that load asynchronously (e.g., via AJAX), or have attributes that change based on user interactions. Static locators may fail when interacting with these elements, leading to test instability.

Solution

- **Explicit Waits**: Use **Explicit Waits** (e.g., WebDriverWait) to ensure that elements are present and interactable before Selenium attempts to interact with them. This avoids issues where tests fail because elements are not yet available.

Example:

```java
WebDriverWait wait = new WebDriverWait(driver, 10);
WebElement element = wait.until(ExpectedConditions.elementToBeClickable(By.id("loginButton")));
element.click();
```

- **Fluent Waits**: For unpredictable load times, use **Fluent Waits**, which poll the DOM at regular intervals, allowing more flexibility in dealing with dynamic content.

Example:

```
Wait<WebDriver> wait = new FluentWait<>(driver)
    .withTimeout(Duration.ofSeconds(30))
    .pollingEvery(Duration.ofSeconds(5))
    .ignoring(NoSuchElementException.class);
WebElement    element    =    wait.until(driver    ->    driver.findElement(By.
id("dynamicElement")));
```

4. Challenge: Cross-Browser Compatibility

Ensuring that tests behave consistently across different browsers (e.g., Chrome, Firefox, Safari) is crucial but can be challenging. Certain browsers may handle HTML/CSS/JS differently, leading to inconsistent results during automation testing.

Solution

- **Selenium Grid**: Use **Selenium Grid** to run tests in parallel across different browsers and operating systems. This ensures that the application's behavior is tested across multiple environments without requiring separate tests for each.

Example:

```
DesiredCapabilities capabilities = new DesiredCapabilities();
capabilities.setBrowserName("firefox");
WebDriver driver = new RemoteWebDriver(new URL("http://localhost:4444/wd/hub"),
capabilities);
```

- **Cloud-Based Cross-Browser Tools**: Use services like **BrowserStack**, **LambdaTest**, or **Sauce Labs** to run cross-browser tests in real environments. These platforms offer a variety of browsers and devices, and they integrate well with CI pipelines.
- **CSS and JS Polyfills**: If needed, use polyfills to address browser compatibility issues with CSS or JavaScript features. Ensure that tests account for differences in UI rendering across browsers.

5. Challenge: Speed and Scalability

As test suites grow, running tests sequentially becomes time-consuming, slowing down feedback loops and impacting the ability to maintain fast-paced development cycles within sprints.

Solution

- **Parallel Test Execution**: Use **TestNG** or **JUnit** to run tests in parallel. This allows tests to be executed simultaneously across different threads or environments, reducing the overall execution time and ensuring timely feedback within the sprint.

Example (TestNG parallel execution):

```
<suite name="Parallel Test Suite" parallel="tests" thread-count="4">
    <test name="Chrome Test">
        <parameter name="browser" value="chrome" />
        <classes>
            <class name="com.example.TestClass" />
        </classes>
    </test>
```

```
<test name="Firefox Test">
    <parameter name="browser" value="firefox" />
    <classes>
        <class name="com.example.TestClass" />
    </classes>
</test>
</suite>
```

- **Headless Browsers**: Use **headless browsers** (e.g., Chrome headless) to reduce execution time by eliminating UI rendering. This is especially effective in CI/CD pipelines where visual browser interactions aren't necessary.

Example:

```
ChromeOptions options = new ChromeOptions();
options.addArguments("--headless");
WebDriver driver = new ChromeDriver(options);
```

- **Prioritize Critical Tests**: Focus automation efforts on critical user flows (e.g., login, checkout) that require the most coverage. This ensures fast feedback for the most important features, allowing developers to fix critical issues early in the sprint.

Implementing UI Automation with Cucumber and Selenium

- Integrate Cucumber and Selenium
- Use Automated Triggers
- Enable Parallel Execution
- Ensure Test Isolation
- Use Headless Browsers
- Implement Page Object Model
- Use CSS Selectors
- Use Selenium Grid

In a Nutshell

Implementing UI automation with Cucumber and Selenium for in-sprint automation introduces challenges such as CI integration, test maintenance, handling dynamic elements, and cross-browser compatibility. By using strategies like **parallel execution**, **POM**, and **robust locator techniques**, teams can create scalable, maintainable, and efficient test automation frameworks that keep pace with the rapid development cycles of Agile sprints.

BUILDING A TEST AUTOMATION FRAMEWORK USING SELENIUM AND TESTNG FOR IN-SPRINT AUTOMATION

In-sprint automation requires a well-structured and maintainable test automation framework that integrates seamlessly with the fast-paced cycles of Agile development. Using **Selenium** for browser automation and **TestNG** for test management allows teams to implement **Test-Driven Development (TDD)** practices. This means writing tests for new features within the sprint cycle, ensuring that automated tests are developed in parallel with the application code. Below, we'll cover how to build a robust test automation framework with Selenium and TestNG, focusing on efficient test creation, execution, and maintainability within the sprint.

Pre-requisites for Setting Up the Framework

Before diving into the structure and implementation, ensure the following prerequisites are in place:

1. **Install Java**: Selenium and TestNG run on Java, so ensure you have Java Development Kit (JDK) installed.

```
// Command to check Java version:
java -version
```

2. **Install Maven**: Maven is used for managing dependencies and building the project. Ensure Maven is installed.

```
// Command to check Maven version:
mvn -version
```

3. **Install IDE**: Use an IDE like **IntelliJ IDEA** or **Eclipse** to manage and write your project code.

4. **Add Dependencies**: Use Maven's pom.xml to manage dependencies like Selenium, TestNG, and Allure.

```xml
<dependencies>
    <!-- Selenium WebDriver -->
    <dependency>
        <groupId>org.seleniumhq.selenium</groupId>
        <artifactId>selenium-java</artifactId>
        <version>4.13.0</version> <!-- Latest version as of 2024 -->
    </dependency>

    <!-- TestNG -->
    <dependency>
        <groupId>org.testng</groupId>
        <artifactId>testng</artifactId>
        <version>7.9.1</version> <!-- Latest version as of 2024 -->
    </dependency>

    <!-- Allure Reporting -->
    <dependency>
        <groupId>io.qameta.allure</groupId>
        <artifactId>allure-testng</artifactId>
        <version>2.21.0</version> <!-- Latest version as of 2024 -->
    </dependency>
</dependencies>
```

Framework Structure

A clear and organized directory structure is crucial for maintaining and scaling in-sprint automation. The structure should ensure the separation of concerns, allowing different layers (test, automation, application) to evolve independently.

Suggested Directory Structure

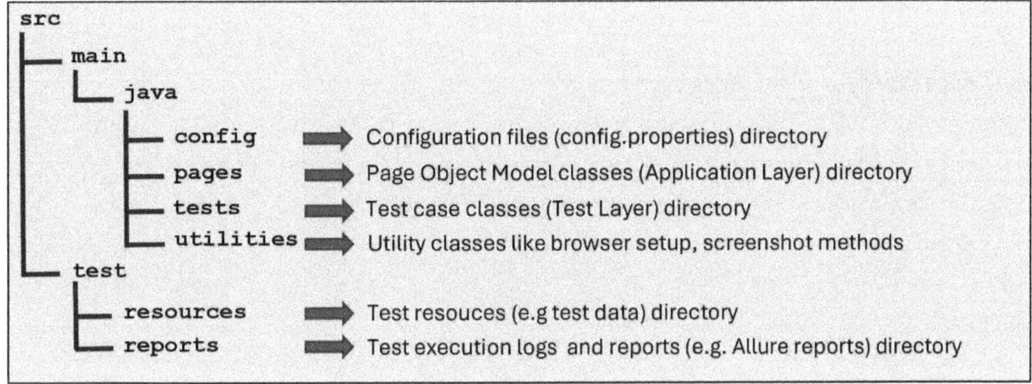

Automation Layer

The **Automation Layer** contains the fundamental methods required for browser automation and navigating through the application. This layer ensures that all repetitive tasks like launching browsers, clicking buttons, and navigating URLs are abstracted into reusable methods.

1.   Creating Methods to Launch Browsers and Navigate to URLs

Create a utility class to handle browser initialization and navigation.

```java
public class BrowserFactory {
    public static WebDriver driver;

    // Method to initialize browser
    public static WebDriver startBrowser(String browser, String url) {
        if (browser.equalsIgnoreCase("chrome")) {
        System.setProperty("webdriver.chrome.driver", "path/to/chromedriver");
            ChromeOptions options = new ChromeOptions();
                options.addArguments("--headless"); // Headless mode for faster
execution
            driver = new ChromeDriver(options);
        } else if (browser.equalsIgnoreCase("firefox")) {
          System.setProperty("webdriver.gecko.driver", "path/to/geckodriver");
            FirefoxOptions options = new FirefoxOptions();
            options.setHeadless(true);
            driver = new FirefoxDriver(options);
        }
        driver.manage().window().maximize();
        driver.get(url);
```

```
        return driver;
    }


    // Method to close the browser
    public static void closeBrowser() {
        driver.quit();
    }
}
```

2. *Wrapper Methods for User Actions*

Abstract common user actions like clicking buttons, entering text, etc., into reusable methods.

```
    public class ActionHelper {
        public static void clickElement(WebDriver driver, By locator) {
            driver.findElement(locator).click();
        }


        public static void enterText(WebDriver driver, By locator, String text) {
            driver.findElement(locator).sendKeys(text);
        }


        public static String getElementText(WebDriver driver, By locator) {
            return driver.findElement(locator).getText();
        }
    }
```

Application Layer

The **Application Layer** is where the **Page Object Model (POM)** comes into play. It contains classes representing different pages of the application, encapsulating UI elements and the logic specific to each page.

1. *Use Page Object Model (POM) or Page Factory*

POM improves test maintainability by centralizing the representation of web elements for each page of the application.

```
    public class LoginPage {
        WebDriver driver;


        // Locators for elements on the login page
        @FindBy(id = "username")
        WebElement usernameField;


        @FindBy(id = "password")
        WebElement passwordField;


        @FindBy(id = "loginButton")
        WebElement loginButton;
```

```java
    // Constructor
    public LoginPage(WebDriver driver) {
        this.driver = driver;
        PageFactory.initElements(driver, this);
    }


    // Actions on the login page
    public void login(String username, String password) {
        usernameField.sendKeys(username);
        passwordField.sendKeys(password);
        loginButton.click();
    }
}
```

Test Layer

The **Test Layer** contains the actual test cases, written using TestNG. These test cases interact with the page objects (from the Application Layer) and contain assertions to validate the behavior of the application.

1. Writing and Managing Test Cases in the Test Layer

A sample test case that tests the login functionality using the LoginPage class.

```java
    public class LoginTest {

        WebDriver driver;

    @BeforeMethod
        public void setUp() {
            driver = BrowserFactory.startBrowser("chrome", "https://example.com/login");
        }

        @Test
        public void testValidLogin() {
            LoginPage loginPage = new LoginPage(driver);
            loginPage.login("testUser", "testPassword");

            // Assert that the login was successful
            Assert.assertTrue(driver.getTitle().contains("Dashboard"));
        }

        @AfterMethod
        public void tearDown() {
            BrowserFactory.closeBrowser();
        }
}
```

Execution Layer

The **Execution Layer** handles how tests are executed using **TestNG XML**, loading configurations from property files, and generating reports.

1. *Running Test Cases Using TestNG XML*

Create a TestNG XML file to define the suite of test cases to be executed.

```xml
<!DOCTYPE suite SYSTEM "http://testng.org/testng-1.0.dtd" >
<suite name="Login Test Suite" parallel="tests" thread-count="2">
    <test name="Login Test">
        <classes>
            <class name="com.example.tests.LoginTest" />
        </classes>
    </test>
</suite>
```

2. *Loading Configurations from config.properties*

Create a config.properties file to store environment-specific data, such as URLs and browser configurations.

```properties
properties
browser=chrome
url=https://example.com/login
```

In your test or browser factory, load configurations like so:

```java
public class ConfigLoader {
    public static Properties loadConfig() {
        Properties prop = new Properties();
        try (InputStream input = new FileInputStream("src/main/resources/config.
properties")) {
            prop.load(input);
        } catch (IOException ex) {
            ex.printStackTrace();
        }
        return prop;
    }
}
```

3. *Generate Logs and Detailed Reports with Allure*

Add Allure annotations to your test cases to generate detailed reports. This helps in providing clear feedback during the sprint.

```java
@Epic("Login Functionality")
@Feature("Valid Login")
@Test(description = "Login with valid credentials")
public void testValidLogin() {
    LoginPage loginPage = new LoginPage(driver);
    loginPage.login("testUser", "testPassword");

    // Log steps and assertions
    Allure.step("Check the page title for dashboard");
```

```java
    Assert.assertTrue(driver.getTitle().contains("Dashboard"));
}
```

4. *Attach Screenshots to Failed Tests*

In the event of a failed test, capture screenshots for debugging and attach them to reports.

```java
@AfterMethod
public void tearDown(ITestResult result) {
    if (ITestResult.FAILURE == result.getStatus()) {
       File screenshot = ((TakesScreenshot) driver).getScreenshotAs(OutputType.
FILE);
        // Save screenshot
        Allure.addAttachment("Screenshot", new FileInputStream(screenshot));
    }
    BrowserFactory.closeBrowser();
}
```

Advanced TestNG Features

TestNG offers a variety of advanced features that can be leveraged for automating UI tests with Selenium in parallel, grouping tests, managing dependencies, and performing data-driven testing—all of which are critical for in-sprint automation. Below, we will cover the **Advanced TestNG Features** in detail, including code examples and best practices.

1. *Execute Test Cases Using TestNG XML Files*

TestNG XML files allow you to organize and execute test cases in a flexible way. By using a TestNG XML file, you can specify which test classes to run, configure parallel execution, and group test cases.

Example: TestNG XML Configuration The following XML file defines a suite of tests and executes them:

```xml
<!DOCTYPE suite SYSTEM "http://testng.org/testng-1.0.dtd" >
<suite name="Suite1">
    <test name="LoginTest">
        <classes>
            <class name="com.example.tests.LoginTest"/>
            <class name="com.example.tests.DashboardTest"/>
        </classes>
    </test>
</suite>
```

- The <suite> tag defines the suite name.
- The <test> tag includes a set of classes, and the <class> tag lists the fully qualified class names for execution.

Running the XML file:
- Use the TestNG runner in your IDE or execute it through the Maven command:

```
mvn test -DsuiteXmlFile=testng.xml
```

2. *Use Methods that Run Before and After Test Executions or Entire Test Suites*

TestNG provides **@BeforeMethod**, **@AfterMethod**, **@BeforeSuite**, and **@AfterSuite** annotations to manage the setup and teardown of resources before and after tests.

Example: Using @BeforeMethod and @AfterMethod

```java
public class LoginTest {
    WebDriver driver;

    @BeforeMethod
    public void setUp() {
        // Set up the browser before each test
        driver = new ChromeDriver();
        driver.get("https://example.com/login");
    }

    @Test
    public void validLoginTest() {
        // Test login functionality
        driver.findElement(By.id("username")).sendKeys("testUser");
        driver.findElement(By.id("password")).sendKeys("testPassword");
        driver.findElement(By.id("loginButton")).click();
        Assert.assertTrue(driver.getTitle().contains("Dashboard"));
    }

    @AfterMethod
    public void tearDown() {
        // Close the browser after each test
        driver.quit();
    }
}
```

- **@BeforeMethod** runs before each test method, typically to set up test data or initialize resources.
- **@AfterMethod** runs after each test method, usually for cleanup (e.g., closing the browser).

3. *Run Test Cases from Multiple Classes or Packages Using a Single XML File*

TestNG XML files can be configured to run test cases from multiple classes or packages. This allows for better test organization and efficient execution of related tests in a single test run.

Example: Running Tests from Multiple Classes and Packages

```xml
<suite name="Suite2">
    <test name="Functional Tests">
        <packages>
            <package name="com.example.tests.functional"/>
            <package name="com.example.tests.integration"/>
        </packages>
    </test>
</suite>
```

In this XML configuration:

- The <package> tag is used to specify which package of test classes to run. All test classes in the specified package will be executed.

4. Group Related Test Cases and Run Them Together via XML

Grouping allows you to categorize test methods and run specific groups based on the requirements of the sprint.

Example: Grouping Test Methods

```java
public class PaymentTest {
    @Test(groups = {"sanity"})
    public void testCreditCardPayment() {
        // Test credit card payment
    }

    @Test(groups = {"regression"})
    public void testPaypalPayment() {
        // Test PayPal payment
    }
}
```

TestNG XML to Run Groups

```xml
<suite name="Suite3">
    <test name="Sanity Tests">
        <groups>
            <run>
                <include name="sanity"/>
            </run>
        </groups>
        <classes>
            <class name="com.example.tests.PaymentTest"/>
        </classes>
    </test>
</suite>
```

- The <groups> tag is used to specify which groups of tests to include.

5. Parameterize Tests Using the @Parameters Annotation

TestNG allows parameterization through the @Parameters annotation. This is useful when you need to pass different sets of data to the same test, like URLs or login credentials.

Example: Using @Parameters in TestNG

```java
public class LoginTest {

    WebDriver driver;

    @BeforeMethod
    @Parameters({"browser", "url"})
    public void setUp(String browser, String url) {
```

```java
            if (browser.equalsIgnoreCase("chrome")) {
                driver = new ChromeDriver();
            } else if (browser.equalsIgnoreCase("firefox")) {
                driver = new FirefoxDriver();
            }
            driver.get(url);
        }


        @Test
        @Parameters({"username", "password"})
        public void loginTest(String username, String password) {
            driver.findElement(By.id("username")).sendKeys(username);
            driver.findElement(By.id("password")).sendKeys(password);
            driver.findElement(By.id("loginButton")).click();
            Assert.assertTrue(driver.getTitle().contains("Dashboard"));
        }


        @AfterMethod
        public void tearDown() {
            driver.quit();
        }
    }
```

TestNG XML Configuration for Parameters

```xml
    <suite name="Parameterized Suite">
      <test name="Login Test">
        <parameter name="browser" value="chrome"/>
        <parameter name="url" value="https://example.com/login"/>
        <parameter name="username" value="testUser"/>
        <parameter name="password" value="testPassword"/>
        <classes>
          <class name="com.example.tests.LoginTest"/>
        </classes>
      </test>
    </suite>
```

6. *Execute Test Cases in Parallel Across Different Browsers*

Parallel execution is crucial in in-sprint automation to ensure that tests run faster and can validate application behavior on multiple browsers simultaneously.

TestNG XML for Parallel Execution

```xml
    <suite name="Parallel Suite" parallel="tests" thread-count="2">
        <test name="Chrome Test">
            <parameter name="browser" value="chrome"/>
            <classes>
                <class name="com.example.tests.LoginTest"/>
```

```
                </classes>
            </test>

        <test name="Firefox Test">
            <parameter name="browser" value="firefox"/>
            <classes>
                <class name="com.example.tests.LoginTest"/>
            </classes>
        </test>
    </suite>
```

- The parallel="tests" attribute specifies that tests should run in parallel, and thread-count="2" defines how many tests will run simultaneously.

7. *Perform Data-Driven Testing with the @DataProvider Annotation (Database and Spreadsheet)*

Data-driven testing allows tests to be run with multiple sets of data. TestNG provides the @DataProvider annotation to handle this, and you can fetch data from databases or spreadsheets (e.g., Excel).

Example: Data-Driven Test Using @DataProvider

```
public class LoginTest {

        @DataProvider(name = "loginData")
        public Object[][] loginDataProvider() {
            return new Object[][] {
                {"testUser1", "password1"},
                {"testUser2", "password2"},
                {"testUser3", "password3"}
            };
        }

        @Test(dataProvider = "loginData")
        public void loginTest(String username, String password) {
            // Login logic
            driver.findElement(By.id("username")).sendKeys(username);
            driver.findElement(By.id("password")).sendKeys(password);
            driver.findElement(By.id("loginButton")).click();
            Assert.assertTrue(driver.getTitle().contains("Dashboard"));
        }
    }
```

Data-Driven Testing with Excel (Spreadsheet)

You can also retrieve data from Excel files using Apache POI.

```
    @DataProvider(name = "excelData")
    public Object[][] getDataFromExcel() throws IOException {
        FileInputStream file = new FileInputStream(new File("data.xlsx"));
        Workbook workbook = new XSSFWorkbook(file);
```

```java
Sheet sheet = workbook.getSheetAt(0);

int rowCount = sheet.getPhysicalNumberOfRows();
    Object[][] data = new Object[rowCount][2]; // Assuming two columns:
username, password

    for (int i = 0; i < rowCount; i++) {
        Row row = sheet.getRow(i);
        data[i][0] = row.getCell(0).getStringCellValue(); // Username
        data[i][1] = row.getCell(1).getStringCellValue(); // Password
    }
    return data;
}
```

Data-Driven Testing with Database

```java
// To fetch data from a database:
    @DataProvider(name = "dbData")
    public Object[][] getDataFromDatabase() throws SQLException {
        Connection conn = DriverManager.getConnection("jdbc:mysql://localhost:3306/
mydb", "user", "password");
        Statement stmt = conn.createStatement();
        ResultSet rs = stmt.executeQuery("SELECT username, password FROM users");

        List<Object[]> data = new ArrayList<>();
        while (rs.next()) {
        data.add(new Object[]{rs.getString("username"), rs.getString("password")});
        }

        return data.toArray(new Object[0][]);
    }
```

Key Challenges and Solutions

1.   Challenge: Managing Test Creation Within Sprint Cycles

In-sprint automation requires automated tests to be written and executed within the same sprint cycle as the feature development. This creates pressure on test creation, as developers and testers must ensure that tests are created in parallel with the evolving application features, all while meeting sprint deadlines. Test creation must be quick but also maintain high quality, to avoid rushing through implementation and introducing errors or incomplete coverage.

Solutions

- **Implement TDD Practices**: Test-driven development (TDD) helps teams stay ahead by writing test cases before or alongside feature development. This ensures that both feature development and testing progress simultaneously, keeping in-sprint coverage high. By defining the behavior of the feature first in the form of tests, developers are guided to build only what is necessary to pass the tests. TDD also reduces the back-and-forth between developers and testers during sprints and ensures that features are built with testing in mind from the outset.

TDD Workflow:
1. Write a test for the new feature (failing initially).
2. Write code to pass the test.
3. Refactor both test and code as necessary.

Example: For a login feature, first create the test case:

```
@Test
public void testLoginWithValidCredentials() {
    LoginPage loginPage = new LoginPage(driver);
    loginPage.login("validUser", "validPassword");
    Assert.assertTrue(loginPage.isLoginSuccessful());
}
```

Then, build the feature code that satisfies this test case.

- **Parallel Execution with TestNG**: TestNG supports parallel test execution, allowing multiple tests to run simultaneously across different threads or environments. This drastically reduces overall test execution time, ensuring that a larger number of test cases can be executed within the sprint cycle.

Benefit: Running tests in parallel reduces execution time, which is crucial for fitting comprehensive test coverage into short sprint timelines.

2. Challenge: Maintaining Automated Tests as the Application Evolves

In fast-paced sprints, the application's UI and functionality may undergo continuous changes, which can cause automated test scripts to break frequently. Maintaining these tests becomes a burden because elements on the page might change (e.g., IDs, class names, or locations in the DOM). If tests are tightly coupled to specific UI elements, they can fail, even if the underlying functionality remains correct. This makes test maintenance a time-consuming task, which can distract from creating new tests and meeting sprint goals.

Solutions

- **Use Page Object Model (POM)**: The **Page Object Model (POM)** is a design pattern that abstracts the UI elements into separate page classes. Each page class represents a single page of the application and contains methods that interact with UI elements. By implementing POM, changes to UI elements can be made in one place (the page class), rather than updating each individual test case. This reduces the maintenance burden when the UI evolves during sprints.

Benefit: Implementing POM reduces duplication in test scripts and allows for easier maintenance when UI changes occur.

- **Regular Refactoring**: Refactor your test code periodically to remove duplication, improve readability, and ensure that your test cases are resilient to change. Regular refactoring also helps in managing technical debt within the test code and ensures that the automation framework evolves along with the application. Establishing a refactoring cycle within sprints ensures that test scripts stay clean, efficient, and maintainable.

3. Challenge: Ensuring Stability and Speed in Automation

Automated tests need to be stable and execute quickly to fit within sprint cycles. Unstable tests that fail intermittently (flaky tests) can cause false negatives, resulting in wasted time on debugging issues that are not real. Additionally, tests that run too slowly can prevent timely feedback to developers, hindering the sprint's progress. These problems are exacerbated in large test suites, where even minor delays or instabilities can add up to significant productivity losses.

Solutions

- **Use Headless Browsers**: Headless browsers, such as **Chrome Headless** and **Firefox Headless**, enable tests to run faster by skipping the UI rendering process. Headless browsers execute commands just like standard browsers but do not display the user interface. This allows tests to execute faster, making it ideal for continuous integration environments where quick feedback is critical. For in-sprint automation, running tests in headless mode ensures that test execution times are minimized while maintaining test coverage.

Benefit: Headless browsers allow tests to execute more quickly, ensuring that they fit within the tight timelines of sprint cycles.

- **Smart Waits**: Use **Explicit Waits** (e.g., WebDriverWait) to ensure that dynamic elements are fully loaded or interactable before performing actions. This helps reduce test flakiness caused by tests attempting to interact with elements that haven't yet appeared on the page. Additionally, using **Fluent Waits** can handle scenarios where the loading time is unpredictable, further improving test stability.

Example of Explicit Wait:

```
WebDriverWait wait = new WebDriverWait(driver, 10);
WebElement loginButton = wait.until(ExpectedConditions.elementToBeClickable(By.
id("loginButton")));
loginButton.click();
```

Benefit: Smart waits improve test stability by ensuring that tests only interact with elements when they are fully ready, reducing false failures.

In a Nutshell

Building an efficient test automation framework using **Selenium** and **TestNG** within the sprint cycle requires a well-structured, maintainable, and scalable approach. By following best practices such as implementing the **Page Object Model (POM)**, leveraging **parallel execution** for faster test runs, and generating detailed reports using tools like **Allure**, teams can ensure that in-sprint automation aligns with the fast pace of Agile development.

TestNG's advanced features, such as parameterization with @Parameters, data-driven testing with @ DataProvider, and parallel execution using **TestNG XML** files, enable efficient management of large test suites. Grouping related tests and setting up before-and-after methods help maintain test stability and structure, ensuring that automation tests evolve alongside the application in a **Test-Driven Development (TDD)** environment.

By integrating TestNG into **CI/CD pipelines** and using headless browsers for execution, teams can achieve continuous feedback, ensure comprehensive test coverage, and manage cross-browser testing efficiently within sprints. These practices ensure that **in-sprint automation** is both sustainable and capable of adapting to evolving application needs, supporting the goal of delivering high-quality software at the speed demanded by Agile methodologies.

## CHAPTER 5

API AUTOMATION TESTING IN SPRINTS

INTRODUCTION TO API TESTING AND SENDING A GET REQUEST

API (Application Programming Interface) testing plays a critical role in the overall software development lifecycle, especially within **agile sprints** where quick iterations and rapid feedback are essential. By testing APIs directly, teams can validate the functionality, performance, security, and reliability of services without the need for a complete front-end, allowing for faster development and defect detection.

This section will cover the fundamentals of **API testing** and demonstrate how to send a **GET request** using popular tools like **Rest Assured**, a Java-based library that simplifies API testing by allowing testers to easily interact with RESTful services. Understanding how to send API requests is the foundation of API testing, and mastering this will help testers to move quickly when developing automated tests within a sprint.

Importance of API Testing in Agile Sprints

In agile development, where teams work in **sprints** (short, iterative cycles), testing must be integrated into the development process. API testing is particularly crucial in this context for several reasons:

1. **Early Detection of Issues**: API testing allows teams to identify issues early in the development cycle. Since APIs serve as the backbone of software, their validation ensures that backend services function correctly, even before the UI is fully developed.
2. **Faster Feedback Loop**: Testing at the API layer reduces the feedback loop. Instead of waiting for the user interface to be ready, testers can directly test the business logic, data models, and service layers, providing immediate insights to developers.
3. **Supports Continuous Integration (CI)**: With automated API tests, teams can run tests at each stage of development, enabling continuous integration and continuous delivery (CI/CD) pipelines to detect any regressions or issues as soon as they are introduced.
4. **Stability in Agile Projects**: As features evolve rapidly in sprints, APIs often remain stable, making them an ideal focus for automation testing. API tests provide confidence that the core system functions are intact, even as UI elements are developed and modified.
5. **Improved Test Coverage**: API testing increases the scope of test coverage by focusing on the core functionalities and edge cases that may not be easily testable via the UI. This is especially important for testing microservices, where different services need to communicate effectively.

Key Challenges and Solutions
1.   Challenge: Time Pressure to Develop and Test Within Short Cycles

One of the biggest challenges of **agile sprints** is the limited time available for both **development and testing**. Sprints typically last 1-2 weeks, during which the development team is expected to complete specific tasks, including writing code, performing unit tests, and validating features through integration and API tests. Given this tight timeframe, testers often face the challenge of **insufficient time** to fully test all aspects of an API.

- **Impact**: Short cycles can lead to **incomplete testing**, especially if bugs are found late in the sprint. This not only delays the sprint's deliverables but also increases the risk of introducing defects into production if testing is rushed or skipped entirely.

2.   Challenge: Rapid Changes in Features, Leading to Constantly Evolving APIs

Agile teams continuously add new features, enhance existing ones, or refactor code based on evolving business requirements. As a result, APIs are constantly changing during development. This means that automated tests need to be flexible enough to keep up with these frequent changes, or else they will quickly become outdated and require constant maintenance.

- **Impact**: Changes in the API structure (e.g., new endpoints, updated parameters) can easily break existing test scripts, leading to false positives or negatives. Testers may spend a significant amount of time **fixing and updating** their automation scripts instead of focusing on testing new features.

3.   Challenge: Ensuring API Tests are Scalable and Can Be Maintained as the API Evolves

As more features are added to the application, the number of **API tests** grows exponentially. Tests that worked in earlier iterations may become **harder to maintain** and manage as the codebase evolves. Furthermore, as more tests are added, execution time can increase significantly, which can slow down the feedback cycle, particularly if tests are not optimized for **parallel execution** or **automation**.

- **Impact**: As APIs evolve, failing to scale and maintain the tests properly can lead to **test bottlenecks**, delaying the CI/CD pipeline. If not managed correctly, API tests can become a burden rather than an asset, reducing the efficiency of testing efforts.

Solutions
1.   Prioritize Early and Frequent Testing Within the Sprint to Identify Issues Early

To tackle the challenge of **time pressure**, teams should adopt a practice of **early and continuous testing** throughout the sprint. Instead of waiting until the end of the sprint to test the API, testers should begin as soon as the API design and development start. By incorporating **test automation from day one**, teams can ensure that bugs are caught early in the development cycle when they are cheaper and easier to fix.

- **Strategy**: Implementing a "test early, test often" mindset helps distribute the testing effort over the entire sprint, reducing the burden on testers at the end. **Automated tests** can be integrated into the CI/CD pipeline, ensuring that tests are run every time a new build is deployed. This provides immediate feedback to developers, helping them to fix issues quickly.

2.   Use Mock Services or Stubs to Simulate External Services When They Are Not Yet Available

In agile sprints, external services or dependencies (like third-party APIs or internal microservices) may not be ready for testing when API tests need to be performed. This can slow down or block the testing process. To overcome this, testers can use **mock services** or **stubs** to simulate the behavior of external dependencies.

- **Strategy**: By using tools like **WireMock** or **Mockito**, testers can create a simulated environment where they can control the behavior of external services. This allows them to **test API endpoints** in isolation, even when the dependent services are not yet available. Using mocks ensures that testing continues without delays, enabling teams to complete their API testing within the sprint's timeframe.

3. Implement Automation to Ensure That API Tests Run Continuously and Provide Rapid Feedback to Developers

To address the scalability and maintenance challenge, teams should invest in building **robust automated API test suites** that can run as part of the **CI/CD pipeline**. Automating the API tests ensures that they are executed after every code commit or deployment, providing **rapid feedback** on the health of the system. By doing this, teams can keep pace with the frequent changes to the codebase in agile environments.

- **Strategy**: Use frameworks like **Rest Assured** or **Postman** for **API automation**. Automating API tests ensures that the core functionality of the application is constantly validated without requiring manual effort. Additionally, by incorporating features like **parallel execution** and **test retries**, teams can ensure that their tests are scalable and provide quick feedback. Investing in proper **test design patterns** and using tools like **Gauge** can help organize tests in a way that reduces maintenance overhead, even as the API evolves.

Furthermore, adopt **modular test designs** that allow for easy updates when API structures change. For instance, maintain **configurations for endpoints, paths, and payloads** separately, making it easier to modify tests when the API is updated. This will significantly reduce the time needed to maintain the tests and ensure they remain robust as the API evolves.

Practical Example: How These Strategies Work Together in a Sprint

Imagine a sprint where a new feature is being developed that requires changes to the API, such as adding a new endpoint for a user profile update. To ensure that this API is tested within the sprint:

- **Early Testing**: As soon as the API's basic structure is defined, testers begin writing **unit and integration tests** for the new endpoint using **Rest Assured**. Early testing helps detect issues in the API's logic before the UI or full feature is implemented.
- **Using Mocks:** If the backend service responsible for user authentication is not yet ready, testers set up a **mock service** to simulate user authentication. This allows them to test the new profile update endpoint in isolation without waiting for the entire authentication service to be completed.
- **Automation and Continuous Testing**: The API tests are added to the **CI/CD pipeline**. As developers push changes to the API, these automated tests run, verifying that the new endpoint works as expected and that existing APIs are not broken by the new changes. **Feedback is immediate**, and developers can fix any issues long before the sprint ends.

Sending a GET Request Using Rest Assured

Rest Assured is a powerful Java library that makes it easy to write readable, maintainable tests for RESTful APIs. When testing RESTful APIs, a GET request is one of the most common operations. The GET method is used to retrieve data from a server based on the request URL.

To send a **GET request** using Rest Assured, you need to:
1. Define the **endpoint** (URL) that you want to send the request to.
2. Optionally, specify any **headers**, **query parameters**, or **authentication details** if required by the API.
3. Execute the request and validate the **response** (typically JSON or XML format).

Example:

```java
import io.restassured.RestAssured;
import io.restassured.response.Response;

public class ApiTest {
    public static void main(String[] args) {
        // Define the base URI for the API
        RestAssured.baseURI = "https://api.example.com";

        // Send a GET request and store the response
        Response response = RestAssured
                          .given()
                          .get("/data");

        // Print the response body
        System.out.println(response.asString());
    }
}
```

In this example, the GET request retrieves data from the API, and the response is printed in the console. **Rest Assured** provides a fluent API, meaning you can chain methods together to specify more details about the request.

Key Considerations:
- Ensure the **URL is correct** and that the endpoint is functioning properly.
- Check the **status code** in the response to ensure the API call was successful (e.g., 200 OK for a successful request).

Sending a GET Request with Path Parameter and Query Parameter
In many cases, APIs use **path parameters** and **query parameters** to modify the data returned in a GET request. Path parameters are part of the URL itself, while query parameters are added to the URL as key-value pairs.
- **Path Parameter**: Used to specify a variable part of the URL. For example, an API to get user data might use a path like /users/{userId}, where userId is a path parameter.
- **Query Parameter**: Appended to the URL after a ? and used to filter or customize the results. For example, /users?sort=asc where sort=asc is a query parameter that sorts the users in ascending order.

  Example of GET with Path and Query Parameters:

```java
import io.restassured.RestAssured;
import io.restassured.response.Response;

public class ApiTest {
    public static void main(String[] args) {
        // Base URL
        RestAssured.baseURI = "https://api.example.com";

        // Sending GET request with path and query parameters
```

```java
Response response = RestAssured
                        .given()
                        .pathParam("userId", 101)  // Path Parameter
                        .queryParam("sort", "asc")  // Query Parameter
                        .get("/users/{userId}");


// Validate the status code and print the response
if (response.getStatusCode() == 200) {
    System.out.println(response.asString());
} else {
        System.out.println("Failed with Status Code: " + response.
getStatusCode());
        }
    }
}
```

In this example:
- The pathParam("userId", 101) method specifies the **path parameter** where userId is replaced by 101.
- The queryParam("sort", "asc") method adds a **query parameter** to sort the data in ascending order.
- The GET request fetches user data for user with ID 101, sorted by the specified query.
  Key Considerations:
- Ensure you understand the structure of the API you are testing.
- Validate **both path and query parameters** are correctly formatted to avoid errors in the request.

Understanding JSON Format and JSON Path

Most modern APIs return data in **JSON (JavaScript Object Notation)** format, which is lightweight and easy to parse. JSON is a key-value pair format where data is represented in a structured way, making it easier to work with in programming environments.

Example of JSON:
```json
{
   "id": 101,
   "name": "John Doe",
   "email": "john.doe@example.com",
   "roles": ["admin", "user"]
}
```
   In this JSON response:
- `id`, `name`, and `email` are **key-value pairs**.
- `roles` is an array of strings.

JSON Path is used to navigate through the JSON data to extract specific values. For instance, to get the user's name, you can use a JSON path like $.name, where $ represents the root of the JSON structure.

Example of JSON Path in Rest Assured:

```java
import io.restassured.RestAssured;
import io.restassured.response.Response;

public class ApiTest {
    public static void main(String[] args) {
        RestAssured.baseURI = "https://api.example.com";

        // Send GET request
        Response response = RestAssured.get("/users/101");

        // Extract the 'name' field from the JSON response
        String userName = response.jsonPath().getString("name");

        // Print the user's name
        System.out.println("User Name: " + userName);
    }
}
```

In this example, the **JSON Path** method `jsonPath().getString("name")` extracts the value of the name field from the JSON response.

Key Considerations:

- Learn to use JSON Path effectively to retrieve values from complex nested structures.
- Understand the JSON structure returned by the API and ensure that the correct keys are being accessed.

IMPORTANCE OF API TESTING

In today's software development landscape, especially with the rise of **agile** and **DevOps** methodologies, **API testing** has become a cornerstone of ensuring quality and stability in modern applications. APIs (Application Programming Interfaces) allow different services, applications, or microservices to interact seamlessly, acting as the glue between the backend and the frontend, or between internal and external systems. As businesses move towards **microservices architectures** and cloud-based solutions, testing at the API level is essential for verifying that individual components work together correctly, ensuring that the system functions as intended.

Why API Testing Is Essential?

1. **Early Detection of Defects**: APIs often handle critical business logic and expose the core functionality of an application. This means they can be tested at the **service level** before the front-end is fully developed. By testing APIs early in the development cycle, teams can identify bugs in the backend logic without having to wait for a full user interface. This not only speeds up the overall testing process but also **reduces the cost** of fixing defects. Bugs found in the service layer early on are much easier and cheaper to address than those found after full system integration.

2. **Faster Testing**: API tests are significantly faster than UI tests because they bypass the **graphical interface** and directly test the application logic. UI tests often involve interacting with multiple elements, which can slow down execution time, especially as the complexity of the interface grows. In contrast, API tests focus on the backend logic and can validate multiple endpoints quickly, providing **faster feedback** to

developers. This speed is particularly important in **continuous integration (CI)** pipelines where fast feedback loops are essential to keeping development cycles short and efficient.

3. **Increased Test Coverage**: Since APIs handle business-critical functions, data manipulation, and external service interactions, testing at the API level ensures that **complex scenarios** are validated. APIs expose various endpoints with different data parameters and responses, allowing testers to cover a wide range of test cases, including **edge cases** and **negative scenarios**. UI testing alone may not catch certain backend issues, such as data integrity problems or security vulnerabilities. Therefore, API testing ensures **thorough validation** of the application's core functionalities, leading to better overall test coverage.

4. **Independence from the User Interface: UI testing** can be brittle and time-consuming, often requiring frequent updates due to changes in the interface. APIs, on the other hand, tend to remain stable even when the UI undergoes significant modifications. This **stability** allows API tests to act as a **strong foundation for regression testing**. When the front-end is being redesigned or modified, API tests can still verify that the core functionality of the system works as expected. This independence allows development and testing to happen in parallel, improving the team's overall efficiency.

5. **Enhanced Security and Reliability**: APIs expose sensitive data and handle critical functions like **authentication**, **authorization**, and **data exchanges** between systems. By testing APIs, teams can identify potential **security vulnerabilities**, such as improper access control, data leaks, or weak encryption practices, long before they reach production. This ensures that APIs are **secure** and **reliable**, mitigating the risk of exposing sensitive information or encountering security breaches. Thorough API testing also helps ensure that the system can handle **unexpected inputs** and **malicious attacks** gracefully, making the software more robust and trustworthy

Key Challenges in API Testing

1. Challenge: Complexity of API Contracts

APIs often come with complex data models, extensive parameter lists, and intricate request/response structures. Each API endpoint may require specific inputs (e.g., headers, query parameters, body content) and return varying responses based on different conditions. Designing effective test cases for such diverse inputs can be challenging, especially when dealing with **dynamic data** or **complex data formats** like **JSON** or **XML**. Teams unfamiliar with the backend services may struggle to understand the API contracts fully, leading to incomplete or inaccurate test cases.

2. Challenge: Dependencies on External Services

Many APIs depend on **external services** such as third-party APIs, databases, or microservices. When these external systems are not available (due to outages, development delays, or maintenance), testing can be delayed, creating bottlenecks in the development cycle. This dependency on external services can make it difficult to test APIs in isolation, limiting test coverage and delaying feedback to developers.

3. Challenge: Frequent API Changes in Agile

In **agile environments**, where software development happens in short, iterative sprints, APIs are frequently updated to reflect new features or enhancements. These rapid changes can break existing automated tests, requiring frequent updates to the test scripts. For instance, a new version of the API may introduce new endpoints or modify existing ones, causing older tests to fail or become obsolete. This makes it challenging to maintain a stable and reliable set of API tests, especially when the development cycle is fast paced.

4. Challenge: Difficulty in Validating Complex Responses

APIs often return complex **JSON** or **XML** responses, which may contain deeply nested data structures, arrays, or dynamic values. Validating these responses accurately, especially when different scenarios return different response formats, can be challenging. Testers need to ensure that they not only check for the presence of data but also validate its accuracy, structure, and adherence to the API contract. This can become even more difficult when the API interacts with multiple services, each returning different parts of the response.

Solutions

Use of Tools and Frameworks for API Testing

- **API testing tools** like **Postman**, **Rest Assured**, and **SoapUI** provide powerful features to simplify the process of sending requests, verifying responses, and managing complex test cases. These tools allow testers to interact with APIs through an intuitive interface, reducing the complexity of building test cases manually. For example, **Postman** offers a user-friendly interface for sending requests, generating test scripts, and validating responses, while **Rest Assured** allows for automated testing in Java with a fluent API.
- These tools also offer **built-in support** for handling complex data formats (like JSON or XML), which makes it easier to validate responses. With **JSON path** or **XPath**, testers can extract and validate specific data points from within a response, simplifying the process of validating even the most complex responses.

Mock Services

- Mocking tools like **WireMock**, **Mockito**, or built-in features in API tools can simulate external services, allowing APIs to be tested in isolation without relying on external dependencies. Mocks replicate the behavior of external services, enabling testers to create specific scenarios (e.g., a service returning an error) without needing the actual service to be available.
- Using **mock services** ensures that tests can be run even when external systems are down or unavailable, allowing for uninterrupted testing during the development cycle. This also reduces the dependency on external services, enabling teams to test API interactions more comprehensively in various scenarios.

Automation and Continuous Testing

- Automating API tests ensures that they are **executed frequently**, often as part of a **CI/CD pipeline**. By incorporating API tests into the CI/CD pipeline, teams can run tests automatically after every build or deployment, providing rapid feedback to developers. This continuous testing approach ensures that any regressions or issues introduced by new API changes are detected early, reducing the risk of defects reaching production.
- Automation tools like **Rest Assured** or **Postman**'s **Newman** (for running Postman tests in CI/CD environments) enable the automation of API testing workflows, ensuring that tests are run consistently without manual intervention.

Versioning and Test Maintenance

- To avoid breaking existing tests when APIs are updated, it's essential to implement **version control** for both APIs and the corresponding test scripts. By maintaining multiple versions of an API, development teams can ensure that older versions remain functional while the new version is being tested and rolled out. This minimizes disruptions to the test suite and ensures **backward compatibility**.

- Keeping test scripts modular and reusable is key to reducing maintenance overhead. By separating common test logic from specific test cases, testers can quickly update or extend the tests when APIs change without needing to rewrite everything from scratch. This modular approach also makes the test suite easier to scale and maintain as the API grows and evolves.

TOOLS AND FRAMEWORKS FOR API TESTING

API testing has become a critical aspect of software development and quality assurance, especially in today's landscape, where applications rely heavily on **microservices, cloud-based services**, and **third-party integrations**. API testing tools and frameworks provide the means to **validate APIs**, ensuring their functionality, security, performance, and compliance with requirements. By using the right tools, teams can **automate** repetitive tasks, increase **test coverage**, and improve the **speed and reliability** of testing processes. Below is a detailed breakdown of the most popular and widely used **API testing tools** and **frameworks**, each suited to different aspects of API testing such as functional validation, automation, and performance analysis.

1. Postman

Postman is one of the most popular and user-friendly tools for **API testing**. It provides an intuitive interface that allows users to **build, send, and verify HTTP requests** for any API. Postman supports all standard HTTP methods, including **GET, POST, PUT, DELETE**, and others, making it versatile enough to test various API endpoints and operations.

Advantages:
- **Ease of Use**: Postman's user-friendly interface makes it accessible to both developers and testers, regardless of technical background. You can easily create and manage collections of API requests, making it ideal for **manual testing**.
- **Automation Capabilities**: Postman's built-in **JavaScript-based scripting** enables the automation of tests, assertions, and even workflows. Tests can be added at different levels (pre-request and post-request) to verify that the API response matches the expected results.
- **Collaboration Features**: Teams can collaborate effectively by sharing Postman **collections** and **environments** with team members, making it easy to maintain consistency across different environments (development, testing, production).
- **Built-In Assertions**: Postman includes built-in support for writing assertions to **validate responses** quickly, making it possible to check for status codes, response times, and JSON body structure in just a few clicks.
- **Newman**: Postman also provides a command-line companion tool called **Newman**, which allows tests to be integrated into CI/CD pipelines. This enables automated API testing in a continuous integration environment.

Best Suited For:
- Manual and exploratory API testing.
- Automating small to mid-sized API test suites.
- Teams looking for an easy-to-use tool with minimal setup for both individual and collaborative testing efforts.

2. Rest Assured

Rest Assured is a powerful **Java-based library** designed specifically for **automating REST API tests**. It simplifies the process of making HTTP requests and validating responses by providing a **fluent API** that is easy to read and write. **Rest Assured** is commonly used in projects that are written in Java and integrates seamlessly with popular Java-based test frameworks like **JUnit** and **TestNG**.

Advantages:

- **Fluent Interface**: Rest Assured's fluent interface allows developers and testers to write API tests in a way that is both **concise** and **readable**. This makes complex scenarios easy to implement, including multi-step API workflows.
- **Seamless Integration**: As a Java library, Rest Assured integrates naturally with Java-based build tools like **Maven** and **Gradle**. It also works well with popular test frameworks, including **JUnit** and **TestNG**, making it a great fit for Java development environments.
- **Support for Complex Validation**: Rest Assured has built-in support for validating **JSON** and **XML** responses using **JSONPath** and **XPath** respectively, which simplifies response validation for complex nested structures.
- **Authentication Support**: The tool supports various types of authentication, including **OAuth**, **Basic**, **Bearer tokens**, and **Digest authentication**, making it suitable for testing APIs that require different security mechanisms.

Best Suited For:

- Automated API testing within **Java projects**.
- Teams already using Java-based test frameworks like JUnit or TestNG.
- Complex test scenarios that require **chaining API calls** or handling **multi-step** workflows.

3. SoapUI

SoapUI is a comprehensive API testing tool built for both **REST** and **SOAP** web services. It offers an extensive set of features that go beyond functional testing, making it a strong candidate for **load testing**, **security testing**, and **data-driven testing**. **SoapUI** can be used by both technical and non-technical testers and is known for supporting complex testing scenarios, such as **message validation** for SOAP services.

Advantages:

- **Full Support for SOAP**: While many modern API testing tools focus on REST, SoapUI provides full support for **SOAP APIs**, including **WSDL-based** service testing, making it one of the few tools that can handle both REST and SOAP effectively.
- **Functional and Non-Functional Testing**: In addition to functional testing, SoapUI offers robust features for **load testing**, **security testing**, and **mocking services**. This makes it ideal for comprehensive API test coverage, from functional validation to stress testing.
- **Data-Driven Testing**: With SoapUI, testers can run data-driven tests using **parameterized inputs**, enabling them to cover a wide range of scenarios by feeding in multiple sets of data to API requests.
- **Groovy Scripting**: For advanced users, SoapUI provides support for **Groovy scripting**, which allows for extended test logic and custom assertions, giving testers more control over their test executions.

Best Suited For:

- Projects involving **SOAP APIs** in addition to REST APIs.
- Teams looking for an all-in-one solution that includes **functional, performance**, and **security testing**.
- Users with complex API testing needs that require advanced scripting and test customization.

4. JMeter

Primarily known as a **performance testing tool**, **JMeter** has gained popularity for its ability to handle **API testing**, especially for large-scale performance tests. It allows teams to simulate high loads on APIs to analyze their performance under stress. While JMeter is more focused on **load testing**, it can also be used for **functional API testing** in smaller projects.

Advantages:
- **Load Testing**: JMeter excels at **simulating concurrent users** or requests, making it ideal for load testing APIs. Teams can create test plans that simulate thousands of requests per second, helping them identify performance bottlenecks in their API architecture.
- **Extensive Protocol Support**: While JMeter is often used for HTTP-based APIs, it also supports a wide variety of protocols, including **FTP**, **TCP**, **JDBC**, and **WebSocket**, making it a versatile tool for testing various types of APIs.
- **Graphical Interface and Reports**: JMeter provides an intuitive graphical user interface for creating test plans, but it also includes detailed **performance reports** that show metrics like **response time**, **throughput**, and **error rate**.
- **Extensibility**: JMeter can be extended with various **plugins** and integrated into CI/CD pipelines, making it a flexible choice for teams looking to perform both **functional** and **non-functional testing** on their APIs.

Best Suited For:
- Teams focused on **performance** or **load testing** of APIs.
- Projects where **scalability** and **response time under high load** are critical metrics.
- API testing that requires support for multiple protocols beyond just HTTP.

5. Katalon Studio

Katalon Studio is an all-in-one test automation tool that supports testing across **APIs, web applications**, **mobile applications**, and **desktop applications**. It is particularly suited for teams looking for a user-friendly interface with powerful automation capabilities. Katalon Studio is built on top of **Selenium** and **Appium**, but it also provides built-in support for **API testing**.

Advantages:
- **Codeless Test Creation**: Katalon Studio provides a **codeless test creation** experience through its graphical interface, making it accessible for testers with little programming knowledge.
- **Integration with CI/CD**: It supports **integration with CI/CD pipelines**, allowing teams to execute API tests automatically as part of their continuous integration workflows.
- **Cross-Platform Testing**: Katalon Studio is a unified solution that supports testing across multiple platforms, including **web**, **mobile**, and **desktop**, making it ideal for end-to-end testing.
- **Comprehensive Reporting**: Katalon provides detailed reports for both functional and performance tests, helping teams track the overall health of their APIs and applications.

Best Suited For:
- Teams looking for a **codeless** or **low-code** automation tool.
- Comprehensive test automation across APIs, mobile, and web applications.
- Users who want an out-of-the-box solution with minimal configuration.

6. Karate

Karate is a relatively new but increasingly popular open-source framework specifically designed for **API testing**. Built on top of **Cucumber**, Karate allows testers to write **behavior-driven development (BDD)** style tests for APIs. One of its standout features is its ability to support both **functional testing** and **performance testing** within the same framework.

Advantages:

- **BDD-Style Syntax**: Karate uses a **Gherkin-based syntax**, making it accessible for testers familiar with **BDD** principles. This also makes tests more **readable** and **collaborative**, as they can be easily understood by non-technical team members.
- **Unified Functional and Performance Testing**: With Karate, teams can perform both **functional API testing** and **performance testing** using the same framework. This reduces the need for multiple tools and simplifies test maintenance.
- **Built-In Assertions and Reports**: Karate includes built-in support for validating API responses, with no need for external libraries to handle **JSON** or **XML** assertions. It also provides clear, **human-readable test reports**, improving transparency in test results.

Best Suited For:

- Teams adopting **BDD** principles.
- Organizations looking for a single framework that supports both **functional** and **performance** API testing.
- API testing that requires **collaborative** involvement from both technical and non-technical stakeholders.

7. Cypress

While **Cypress** is best known for its **end-to-end testing** capabilities for web applications, it also includes support for **API testing**. Cypress can be used to test REST APIs by making HTTP requests directly from within the test scripts, making it a good option for teams already using Cypress for UI testing.

Advantages:

- **Unified End-to-End and API Testing**: Cypress allows testers to combine both **UI tests** and **API tests** within the same testing framework, enabling end-to-end testing workflows that validate both the frontend and backend.
- **JavaScript-Based**: Since Cypress is built on JavaScript, it's a natural fit for developers and testers working in **JavaScript-based projects**. The syntax is straightforward and integrates seamlessly into modern JavaScript development workflows.
- **Fast Execution**: Cypress runs tests in the same environment as the browser, ensuring **fast and reliable execution** of both UI and API tests.

Best Suited For:

- Teams using **Cypress** for **end-to-end UI testing** and looking to expand into API testing.
- Developers and testers working in **JavaScript-heavy** environments.
- Testing scenarios where validating both the frontend and backend functionality is crucial.

8. Apigee

Apigee by Google is an **API management tool** that allows teams to design, secure, deploy, and manage APIs. Apigee also provides **API testing** capabilities, enabling teams to automate functional, load, and security testing. It is particularly useful in enterprise settings where managing large-scale API deployments is critical.

Advantages:
- **API Lifecycle Management**: Apigee provides end-to-end API management capabilities, including design, deployment, monitoring, and testing.
- **Security Testing**: Apigee excels at testing for **security vulnerabilities**, offering built-in tools for checking **authentication**, **authorization**, and **rate limiting**.
- **Monitoring and Analytics**: Apigee provides detailed **API analytics** and monitoring, helping teams track API performance and usage in real-time.

Best Suited For:
- Enterprise organizations that need **comprehensive API management** solutions.
- Teams that require both **API testing** and **monitoring** tools in a single platform.
- Large-scale API deployments with a focus on **security** and **performance**.

In a Nutshell

API testing is a critical aspect of software quality, and choosing the right tool can significantly improve the efficiency, accuracy, and scalability of testing efforts. Whether you're focused on **functional testing** with tools like **Postman** and **Rest Assured**, or looking for comprehensive solutions that include **performance** and **security testing**, there's a tool suited for your needs. By leveraging these tools and frameworks, teams can ensure their APIs are **reliable**, **secure**, and **performant**, which is essential in today's fast-paced development environments.

IMPLEMENTING API AUTOMATION WITH REST ASSURED

REST Assured is a powerful **Java-based** library designed specifically for testing **RESTful APIs**. Its simplicity and rich feature set make it ideal for teams looking to automate API testing efficiently, especially in **agile environments** where testing needs to be **fast** and **scalable**. REST Assured supports all HTTP methods-**GET, POST, PUT, PATCH, DELETE**, and more-allowing it to cover a wide range of API testing scenarios. It is particularly popular for teams working with **Java** who need seamless integration with **JUnit**, **TestNG**, and other testing frameworks.

REST Assured simplifies API automation by providing a **fluent interface**, which makes the code easy to write and maintain, allowing even complex test cases to be handled with minimal boilerplate code. Let's take a more detailed, granular look at why REST Assured is one of the most powerful API testing frameworks and how to implement it successfully .

Why Use REST Assured?

1. Simple, Fluent Syntax

REST Assured is known for its **fluent interface**, making the code much more readable and reducing the complexity typically associated with API testing. Instead of writing large blocks of code to handle HTTP requests, REST Assured allows you to chain methods that clearly express the intent of the test.

Example:

```
given()
    .baseUri("https://api.example.com")
    .header("Content-Type", "application/json")
.when()
    .get("/users/1")
.then()
    .statusCode(200)
    .body("name", equalTo("John Doe"))
    .body("email", equalTo("john.doe@example.com"));
```

In this code:
- **given()** sets up the preconditions for the request, like base URI and headers.
- **when()** specifies the HTTP method and endpoint.
- **then()** is used for validation (assertions) of the response. You can validate status codes, body contents, headers, etc.

The fluent interface helps you write concise tests without requiring excessive code, making it easier to maintain and scale your test suite as your API grows.

2. *Support for JSON, XML, and Other Data Formats*

REST Assured has **built-in support** for handling **JSON, XML,** and various other data formats. With **JSONPath** and **XMLPath,** testers can easily extract values from complex responses and validate them in a structured way. This makes it ideal for modern applications where APIs return nested JSON or XML structures.

Example (Handling a JSON response):

```
given()
    .baseUri("https://api.example.com")
.when()
    .get("/users/1")
.then()
    .statusCode(200)
    .body("address.street", equalTo("123 Main St"));
```

REST Assured supports deep traversal of JSON and XML responses, which is crucial when dealing with APIs that return complex, nested objects.

3. *Seamless Java Integration*

Since REST Assured is Java-based, it integrates seamlessly with **JUnit, TestNG,** and **Maven** or **Gradle** build tools. This makes it an ideal choice for teams already working in **Java environments.** You can easily integrate API tests into your existing test suites, execute them as part of **CI/CD pipelines,** and generate **reports** alongside other tests.

4. *Authentication Support*

REST Assured provides extensive support for various types of **authentications:**
- **Basic authentication.**
- **OAuth 1.0 and 2.0.**

- ○ **Bearer tokens.**
- ○ **Digest authentication.**

This ensures that APIs requiring authentication can be tested without needing additional libraries or workarounds.

Key Challenges in Implementing API Automation with REST Assured

Despite the strengths of REST Assured, there are several **challenges** teams may face when adopting the tool, especially if they are new to Java or test automation. Let's explore some of the key challenges and how to overcome them.

1. Challenge: Programming Knowledge

REST Assured is a **Java-based** tool, and as such, requires a **good understanding of Java** programming to write tests effectively. Manual testers or teams who are new to programming may find the learning curve steep, especially when writing complex test cases or handling **multi-step workflows** that involve **chaining API calls.**

Solutions

- ○ **Training and Resources**: To bridge the knowledge gap, invest in **training programs** and provide resources that help testers learn **Java** and REST Assured. There are **online tutorials, documentation, community forums**, and courses specifically tailored for API automation with REST Assured.
- ○ **Mentorship and Pair Programming**: Encourage **pair programming** sessions where experienced developers collaborate with testers, enabling them to learn **real-world API automation techniques.**
- ○ **Start Simple**: Gradually increase the complexity of test cases. Begin with **simple GET and POST requests** and slowly introduce more complex scenarios such as **handling dynamic data** or **chaining API calls.**

2. Challenge: Handling Dynamic Data

APIs often return **dynamic data**, such as **tokens, session IDs**, or **user-specific values**, which need to be **extracted and reused** in subsequent API requests. Managing this dynamic data across multiple test cases can be challenging, especially when dealing with multi-step workflows (e.g., **create user, get user details, update user**).

Solutions

- **Helper Methods**: Use **helper methods** to extract dynamic values (e.g., **tokens** or **IDs**) from responses and store them for later use. REST Assured allows you to extract response values using **JSONPath** or **XMLPath**, which can then be passed between requests.
- **Modular Test Design**: Structure your tests using **modular components**. For example, create separate methods for **authenticating users** or **extracting tokens** and reuse them across multiple tests. This will help in managing test complexity while making the test suite more maintainable.

Example (Handling dynamic tokens):

```
String token = given()
    .baseUri("https://api.example.com")
    .formParam("username", "testuser")
```

```
    .formParam("password", "password")
    .post("/auth/token")
    .jsonPath().getString("token");

given()
    .header("Authorization", "Bearer " + token)
    .get("/users/me")
.then()
    .statusCode(200);
```

In this example, the **token** is dynamically extracted from the response of the authentication request and reused for subsequent API calls.

3. Challenge: Test Maintenance

APIs are often evolving as new features are added or changes are made to existing endpoints, request parameters, or response structures. This results in test scripts breaking or needing updates, which can become time-consuming if the tests are not well-structured. Additionally, API tests can become brittle if they rely too heavily on specific values (hard-coded values), making them difficult to maintain.

Solutions

- **Utilize Modular Test Design**: Break down the test scripts into **reusable components**. For instance, instead of writing the same authentication or setup logic in every test, abstract those into reusable **helper methods** or **classes**. This not only makes tests more readable but also reduces maintenance effort when changes occur.
- **Parameterization**: Implement **data-driven testing** by parameterizing test data and separating it from the test logic. By storing input data in **external files** (e.g., JSON, CSV, or Excel files), you can easily update the test data without needing to modify the test logic.
- **Version Control for APIs**: Use **version control** for both the API itself and the test scripts. This ensures that older test scripts don't break when the API is updated, and testers can continue to run tests against older versions if needed.

Example (Parameterization with external data):

```
@DataProvider(name = "userData")
public Object[][] userData() {
    return new Object[][] {
        {"John", "Doe", "john.doe@example.com"},
        {"Jane", "Smith", "jane.smith@example.com"}
    };
}


@Test(dataProvider = "userData")
public void testCreateUser(String firstName, String lastName, String email) {
    given()
        .baseUri("https://api.example.com")
          .body("{ \"firstName\": \"" + firstName + "\", \"lastName\": \"" +
lastName + "\", \"email\": \"" + email + "\" }")
```

```
    .when()
        .post("/users")
    .then()
        .statusCode(201);
}
```

By using **data providers**, tests can run with different sets of data, making them more flexible and easier to maintain.

4. *Challenge: Version Control and Automated Pipelines*

In modern agile environments, integrating API automation into the **CI/CD pipelines** is crucial for continuous testing. However, this requires careful configuration to ensure that the tests are executed as part of the **build** and **deployment** pipelines. Additionally, managing changes to both API versions and test scripts can become complex if version control isn't properly maintained.

Solutions

- **Integrating with CI/CD**: Integrate REST Assured test cases into **Jenkins, GitLab CI**, or other CI/CD systems to ensure that tests run automatically after every build. This ensures that any issues introduced by new API changes are caught early.
- **Version Control and Branching**: Use version control systems like **Git** to manage both API and test versions. For APIs with multiple versions, ensure that you maintain separate branches for each version of the API and its associated tests. This avoids breaking older versions of the API and ensures that both old and new features are tested concurrently.
- **Continuous Reporting**: Set up automated **report generation** so that when tests run in the pipeline, detailed reports (e.g., **HTML reports, JUnit XML reports**) are automatically generated and sent to the team, providing insight into test results.

In a Nutshell

By implementing REST Assured effectively, teams can automate API testing in a way that is fast, scalable, and easy to maintain. Its **Java integration, support for various data formats**, and **fluent syntax** make it a powerful tool for API automation. However, overcoming challenges related to **programming knowledge, dynamic data handling**, and **test maintenance** is crucial to ensuring long-term success. With **proper training, modular test design**, and integration into **CI/CD pipelines**, REST Assured can be an invaluable part of your automation framework.

BUILDING API TEST AUTOMATION FRAMEWORK USING REST ASSURED

Building a comprehensive API test automation framework using **Rest Assured** involves more than just writing a few tests. It requires a well-organized structure that is maintainable, scalable, and can be easily integrated into **CI/CD pipelines**. This section will guide you through each step of setting up a **robust automation framework** using Rest Assured, from the initial project setup to advanced techniques like method chaining, configuration management, and generating detailed test reports. Each step is essential for ensuring that your API tests are reliable, reusable, and provide meaningful feedback.

Understanding Test Automation Framework and Project Setup

The first step in creating a reliable API testing framework is understanding the **test automation framework architecture**. A well-structured framework separates concerns, such as test data, configuration, and the actual test logic, making the framework easier to manage and scale over time.

Key Components of the Framework

1. **Test Layer**: Contains the test cases that will be executed, each corresponding to a different API endpoint or scenario.
2. **Application Layer (Business Logic Layer)**: Contains the logic for interacting with the API, making it reusable across multiple tests.
3. **Utility Layer**: Provides helper classes and methods, such as handling dynamic data, file management, or formatting requests.
4. **Configuration Layer**: Handles external configurations, such as **URLs**, **endpoints**, **API keys**, and **tokens**, allowing the framework to work in different environments (e.g., staging, production).

Project Setup

- Use a **Maven** or **Gradle** project for dependency management. This allows you to easily include required libraries like **Rest Assured**, **JUnit/TestNG**, **Extent Reports**, and **JSON libraries**.
- Organize your directory structure as follows:

```
src
 └── test            main
      └── java/com.yourcompany.framework
            ├── config      ➡  Configuration files (config.properties) directory
            ├── utilities   ➡  Utility classes like reading json, extracting tokens, etc.
            ├── clients     ➡  Test case classes (Test Layer) directory
            └── tests       ➡  Test cases for APIs
```

This modular organization ensures that changes in one component (e.g., the configuration) don't disrupt the entire framework.

Creating Automation Layer and Custom Rest Client

The **automation layer** is where the actual API interactions happen. Here, you create a **custom REST client** that abstracts the underlying details of API requests, making the test cases clean and easy to understand.

Creating a Custom Rest Client

The custom client encapsulates methods for sending HTTP requests like **GET**, **POST**, **PUT**, **PATCH**, and **DELETE**. This client serves as the reusable API interface that your tests will interact with.

```java
public class RestClient {

    // Method to send GET requests
    public Response getRequest(String endpoint) {
        return RestAssured.given()
                .baseUri(Config.getBaseUri())
                .header("Authorization", Config.getAuthToken())
                .when()
```

```java
                .get(endpoint);
    }

    // Method to send POST requests
    public Response postRequest(String endpoint, String body) {
        return RestAssured.given()
                .baseUri(Config.getBaseUri())
                .header("Content-Type", "application/json")
                .body(body)
                .when()
                .post(endpoint);
    }

    // Similarly, methods for PUT, DELETE, PATCH can be added
}
```

Advantages:
- **Reusability**: Instead of repeating the request logic in every test case, this layer encapsulates the details, making your tests more maintainable.
- **Customization**: You can customize how the client handles headers, cookies, authentication, or even error handling.

Writing Logic in the Application Layer
The **application layer** (or **business logic layer**) contains logic that corresponds to the specific API endpoints you are testing. This layer acts as a bridge between the custom REST client and the test cases, translating business requirements into actionable API requests.

Example:
```java
public class UserApi {

    private RestClient restClient = new RestClient();

    // Method to get a user by ID
    public Response getUserById(String userId) {
        String endpoint = "/users/" + userId;
        return restClient.getRequest(endpoint);
    }

    // Method to create a new user
    public Response createUser(String body) {
        return restClient.postRequest("/users", body);
    }
}
```

This layer ensures that the **business logic** is abstracted away from the test layer, making it easier to update the framework when the API structure changes.

Write First Test Case to Test GET HTTP Method in Test Layer

Now that you have the **application layer** set up, you can start writing your test cases. The **test layer** should contain only the actual test logic, such as verifying status codes, response times, and the data returned by the API.

Example:

```
public class UserApiTests {

    private UserApi userApi = new UserApi();

    @Test
    public void testGetUserById() {
        Response response = userApi.getUserById("123");
        response.then().statusCode(200);
        response.then().body("name", equalTo("John Doe"));
    }

}
```

In this test, the **userApi** class calls the **getUserById** method, and the response is validated to ensure the correct data is returned. The test is **simple** and **clean** because all the heavy lifting is handled by the **application layer** and **REST client**.

Adding Test Cases to Test POST, PUT, PATCH, and DELETE HTTP Methods

Once you've written your first **GET** test case, you can start adding tests for other HTTP methods like **POST**, **PUT**, **PATCH**, and **DELETE**. Each method serves a different function in REST APIs, and your framework should support them all.

Example (POST Request):

```
@Test
public void testCreateNewUser() {
    String userPayload = "{ \"name\": \"Jane Doe\", \"email\": \"jane.doe@
example.com\" }";
    Response response = userApi.createUser(userPayload);

    response.then().statusCode(201);
    response.then().body("id", notNullValue());
}
```

Example (PUT Request):

```
@Test
public void testUpdateUser() {
    String updatedPayload = "{ \"name\": \"Jane Smith\" }";
    Response response = userApi.updateUser("123", updatedPayload);

    response.then().statusCode(200);
    response.then().body("name", equalTo("Jane Smith"));
}
```

Adding tests for **all HTTP methods** ensures that the API's CRUD functionality (Create, Read, Update, Delete) is thoroughly tested.

Method Chaining – Testing an End-to-End Call Flow

In real-world scenarios, APIs don't exist in isolation. Often, you'll need to test an **end-to-end flow** that involves multiple API calls. **Method chaining** allows you to test a sequence of operations to verify that data is being passed and handled correctly through the system.

Example:
- **Create a new user**.
- **Retrieve the user** to verify the data was stored correctly.
- **Update the user**.
- **Delete the user** and ensure they no longer exist.

```java
@Test
public void testEndToEndUserFlow() {
    // 1. Create a new user
     String userPayload = "{ \"name\": \"John Doe\", \"email\": \"john.doe@
example.com\" }";
    Response createResponse = userApi.createUser(userPayload);
    String userId = createResponse.jsonPath().getString("id");

    // 2. Get the user
    Response getResponse = userApi.getUserById(userId);
    getResponse.then().statusCode(200);

    // 3. Update the user
    String updatedPayload = "{ \"name\": \"John Smith\" }";
    Response updateResponse = userApi.updateUser(userId, updatedPayload);
    updateResponse.then().statusCode(200);

    // 4. Delete the user
    Response deleteResponse = userApi.deleteUser(userId);
    deleteResponse.then().statusCode(204);
}
```

This method chaining test ensures that the API correctly handles each step in the user management lifecycle.

Optimizing Code

Optimizing your API automation framework is crucial for performance and maintainability. Some best practices include:
- **Reusable Components**: Use **helper classes** and **utility methods** to reduce code duplication.
- **Parallel Execution**: Enable **parallel test execution** to speed up the test runs, especially when dealing with large test suites.
- **Modular Design**: Keep test logic separate from API interaction logic. This allows for easy updates to test cases without affecting the underlying API client.

Reading Configuration from Config File

Instead of hardcoding values like **base URLs, API keys**, or **authentication tokens**, store them in a **config file** (e.g., properties or JSON file). This allows you to change configurations based on the environment (e.g., dev, staging, production) without modifying the test code.

Example (Config File):

```
base.uri=https://api.example.com
auth.token=Bearer abc123token
```

Example (Config Reader):

```java
public class Config {

    private static Properties properties;

    static {
        properties = new Properties();
        try (InputStream input = new FileInputStream("config.properties")) {
            properties.load(input);
        } catch (IOException ex) {
            ex.printStackTrace();
        }
    }

    public static String getBaseUri() {
        return properties.getProperty("base.uri");
    }

    public static String getAuthToken() {
        return properties.getProperty("auth.token");
    }
}
```

By externalizing the configuration, the framework becomes more flexible and easier to maintain across environments.

Utility to Generate HTML Reports Using Extent Reports

Extent Reports is a popular reporting library for **JUnit** or **TestNG** test results. It provides detailed, visually rich reports that can include screenshots, test steps, and even logs. This is valuable for stakeholders or team members who need to review the results without delving into raw test output.

Example (Setting Up Extent Reports):

```java
ExtentReports extent = new ExtentReports("extentReport.html", true);

@Test
public void testWithReporting() {
    ExtentTest test = extent.startTest("testGetUser");
```

```
    test.log(LogStatus.INFO, "Starting the GET User test");

    Response response = userApi.getUserById("123");
        test.log(LogStatus.PASS, "User  retrieved  successfully:  " + response.
asString());

    extent.endTest(test);
}
```

Generate HTML Report Using Extent Report

By generating a **detailed HTML report**, you can present a **clear picture** of test execution results, including:
- **Pass/Fail status**.
- **Test execution time**.
- **Details of assertions** and failures.
- **Screenshots** (if needed).

This enhances the **visibility of test results** across the team, especially during code reviews or **sprint retrospectives**.

Marking Test Status in Report

Marking the **test status** (pass, fail, skip) in the report is critical for identifying problematic areas quickly. **Extent Reports** allows you to capture not only the final test status but also detailed logs of each step.

```
if (response.getStatusCode() == 200) {
    test.log(LogStatus.PASS, "Test passed with status 200");
} else {
        test.log(LogStatus.FAIL,  "Test  failed  with  status:  " + response.
getStatusCode());
}
```

This granular logging ensures that even if a test fails, it's easy to pinpoint where the failure occurred.

In a Nutshell

By following these steps, you can create a well-structured, scalable, and maintainable **API test automation framework** using **Rest Assured**. This framework will enable your team to write clean, reusable tests, handle complex API workflows, and generate detailed reports, all while minimizing maintenance overhead. With this foundation, you can confidently test your APIs, ensuring that they are functional, performant, and secure across all environments.

Sending a POST Request

A **POST** request is used to send data to the server to **create a new resource**. It's one of the most used HTTP methods in REST APIs. When making a POST request, the data payload (the body of the request) is sent to the server, and the server typically responds with the newly created resource or a status code that indicates the success of the operation.

REST Assured makes it easy to send POST requests by allowing you to define the request body in various formats such as **String, Map,** or even **Java objects** (serialized into JSON/XML). Here we will discuss two common ways to send a POST request: using a **String** as the request payload and using a **Map** object for a more structured approach.

Sending a POST Request with Request Payload as String

Using a **String** to represent the body of a POST request is simple and allows for flexibility, especially when the payload is small or doesn't require much dynamic handling. The **String** is typically formatted as **JSON** or **XML**, depending on the API specifications.

Steps:
1. **Set Up the Base URI**: Define the base URI where the API is hosted.
2. **Create the Request Payload**: Prepare the data to be sent in the POST request body, often formatted as a **JSON String**.
3. **Define the Header**: Specify the content type in the header (usually application/json).
4. **Send the POST Request**: Use Rest Assured's fluent interface to send the POST request and capture the response.

Example (POST Request with JSON String):

```java
public class PostRequestExample {

    @Test
    public void sendPostRequestWithStringPayload() {
        // Define the request payload as a JSON string
        String payload = "{ \"name\": \"John Doe\", \"email\": \"john.doe@example.com\", \"age\": 30 }";

        // Send the POST request and capture the response
        Response response = given()
                            .baseUri("https://api.example.com")
                            .header("Content-Type", "application/json")
                            .body(payload)  // Attach the payload to the request
                        .when()
                            .post("/users")  // Endpoint for creating a new user
                        .then()
                            .statusCode(201)  // Verify that the status code is 201 (Created)
                            .extract().response();

        // Print the response
        System.out.println("Response Body: " + response.asString());
    }
}
```

Explanation:

- **Base URI**: The baseUri method defines the base URL of the API.
- **Request Body**: The `body()` method attaches the JSON string as the payload for the POST request.
- **Content-Type Header**: The header specifies the **Content-Type** as application/json to let the server know that it should expect JSON data.
- **Status Code Check**: The `statusCode(201)` assertion checks that the response indicates the resource was successfully created.

Advantages of Using String Payload:

- **Simplicity**: Ideal for small or static payloads that don't require complex dynamic data handling.
- **Quick Setup**: Easy to implement, especially for quick tests or simple API requests.

Sending a POST Request with Request Payload as Map Object

A more structured and flexible way to handle request payloads is to use a **Map**. With **Map objects**, you can dynamically construct the data to be sent in the request, allowing for easier management of large or complex payloads.

In REST Assured, a **Map** can automatically be converted to a **JSON object**, making it easier to represent hierarchical data without writing raw JSON strings.

Steps:

1. **Create a Map Object**: Populate the map with key-value pairs representing the fields in the JSON payload.
2. **Send the Request**: Use the `body()` method to pass the map as the request payload.
3. **Validate the Response**: Verify the status code and other details of the server response.

Example (POST Request with Map Payload):

```java
public class PostRequestWithMap {

    @Test
    public void sendPostRequestWithMapPayload() {
        // Create a map to represent the JSON payload
        Map<String, Object> payload = new HashMap<>();
        payload.put("name", "Jane Smith");
        payload.put("email", "jane.smith@example.com");
        payload.put("age", 28);

        // Send the POST request with the map as the body
        Response response = given()
                            .baseUri("https://api.example.com")
                            .header("Content-Type", "application/json")
                            .body(payload)  // REST Assured automatically
    converts the map to JSON
                            .when()
                            .post("/users")
                            .then()
                            .statusCode(201)
```

```java
                                    .extract().response();

        // Print the response
        System.out.println("Response Body: " + response.asString());
    }
}
```

Advantages of Using Map Payload:

- **Dynamic Data**: Using a Map makes it easier to add, remove, or modify fields dynamically, which is useful for testing scenarios that require different data sets.
- **Readability**: It is easier to read and manage complex payloads without needing to write large JSON strings manually.
- **Built-in Conversion**: REST Assured automatically converts the map to JSON, reducing the overhead of string formatting and parsing.
  #### When to Use String vs. Map Payload:
- **String Payload**: Best for simple or small requests, quick validation, or scenarios where the payload structure doesn't change.
- **Map Payload**: Ideal for tests where the payload needs to be dynamic or involves complex structures that are easier to manage programmatically.

Sending a PUT Request

A **PUT** request is used to **update an existing resource**. Unlike POST, which is typically used for creating resources, PUT requests replace the entire resource at the given URI with the data sent in the request body. PUT is idempotent, meaning multiple identical requests should have the same effect as a single request.

Steps:
1. **Identify the Resource**: Specify the resource (usually by ID) that needs to be updated.
2. **Prepare the Request Payload**: The payload should contain the updated values for the resource.
3. **Send the PUT Request**: Send the request to update the resource and verify the response.

Example:

```java
public class PutRequestExample {

    @Test
    public void sendPutRequest() {
        // Create a map for the updated user details
        Map<String, Object> updatedUser = new HashMap<>();
        updatedUser.put("name", "John Doe Updated");
        updatedUser.put("email", "john.updated@example.com");
        updatedUser.put("age", 35);

        // Send the PUT request to update the user
        Response response = given()
                            .baseUri("https://api.example.com")
                            .header("Content-Type", "application/json")
                            .body(updatedUser)
```

```
                          .when()
                             .put("/users/123")  // Update the user with ID
   123
                          .then()
                             .statusCode(200)
                             .extract().response();

        // Print the response
        System.out.println("Updated User Response: " + response.asString());
    }
}
```

Explanation:
- The PUT request in this example updates the user with the **ID 123**.
- The **map object** is used to pass the updated user information.
- The `statusCode(200)` ensures the update was successful.

Advantages of PUT:
- **Idempotency**: The same request can be sent multiple times without side effects, making it safe for retry logic in case of failures.
- **Comprehensive Updates**: PUT is ideal when updating most or all properties of a resource.

Sending a DELETE Request

The **DELETE** request is used to **remove a resource** from the server. When sending a DELETE request, the server typically responds with a **204 No Content** status if the deletion is successful or **404 Not Found** if the resource doesn't exist.

Steps:
1. **Identify the Resource**: Specify the resource to delete (usually by ID).
2. **Send the DELETE Request**: Verify the response to ensure the resource was deleted successfully.

Example:
```
    public class DeleteRequestExample {

        @Test
        public void sendDeleteRequest() {
            // Send the DELETE request to remove the user with ID 123
            Response response = given()
                                    .baseUri("https://api.example.com")
                                  .when()
                                     .delete("/users/123")  // Delete the user with
   ID 123
                                  .then()
                                     .statusCode(204)  // 204 indicates successful
   deletion
                                     .extract().response();
```

```
        // Print confirmation
      System.out.println("Delete Response Status: " + response.getStatusCode());
      }
   }
```

Explanation:
- The DELETE request removes the resource identified by the **/users/123** endpoint.
- The `statusCode(204)` asserts that the deletion was successful.

Advantages of DELETE:
- **Resource Cleanup**: DELETE requests are essential for cleaning up test data in API tests to avoid polluting the database.
- **Simple and Safe**: DELETE ensures that specific resources can be removed without side effects, as the action is idempotent sending the same DELETE request multiple times will have the same result.

In a Nutshell

In REST Assured, sending **POST**, **PUT**, and **DELETE** requests follows a similar pattern, making it easy to automate a wide variety of CRUD (Create, Read, Update, Delete) operations on RESTful APIs. By using **String** or **Map** objects as payloads, you can handle both static and dynamic data efficiently. Whether creating new resources, updating existing ones, or deleting unnecessary data, REST Assured offers the flexibility and ease needed to automate API testing in agile development environments.

INTEGRATING JMETER INTO REST ASSURED TESTS AND ITS ADVANTAGES

Apache JMeter and **Rest Assured** are two powerful tools in the domain of API testing, each offering distinct capabilities. **Rest Assured** is commonly used for functional API testing, allowing you to validate the correctness of API responses, while **JMeter** excels at **load testing**, simulating multiple concurrent users to test the performance and scalability of APIs. By integrating **JMeter** into **Rest Assured** tests, teams can expand their testing scope, covering both **functional** and **performance testing** in one unified flow.

Integrating **JMeter** with **Rest Assured** combines the strengths of both tools: **Rest Assured** for validating correctness and **JMeter** for assessing the system's performance under varying levels of load. This step-by-step guide explores how to integrate **JMeter** into Rest Assured-based test automation frameworks, the **advantages** of doing so, and the **key challenges** that come with it.

Advantages of Integrating JMeter into REST Assured Tests

1. **Unified Functional and Performance Testing:**

By integrating **JMeter** into **Rest Assured** tests, you can perform **functional validation** (correctness of API responses) and **load testing** (how the API performs under high traffic) in the same test flow. This ensures that your API performs well while still returning correct data even under stress.

2. **Seamless Transition:**

When integrated, **Rest Assured** handles the **functional API testing**, while **JMeter** can be used to simulate **real-world load conditions**. This ensures that after validating the API, you can directly simulate how it behaves when subjected to multiple concurrent requests.

3. **Early Detection of Performance Issues:**

Incorporating **JMeter** into **Rest Assured** tests allows you to catch performance bottlenecks early during the development cycle, especially during **continuous integration**. This proactive testing helps identify issues related to latency, response times, and API scaling before they become critical in production.

Step-by-Step Process for Integrating JMeter with REST Assured

Integrating **JMeter** into **Rest Assured** testing involves several steps. Below is a detailed, step-by-step guide to achieving this integration.

Pre-requisites
1. **JMeter Installed**: Download and install **Apache JMeter** from the official website. No installation is needed per se; you simply extract the files.
   o Official Website: **https://jmeter.apache.org/**
2. **Maven/Gradle Setup**: Ensure that your **Rest Assured** project is set up using **Maven** or **Gradle**, as this will simplify dependency management.
3. **JMeter Maven Plugin**: You'll need the **JMeter Maven plugin** to integrate JMeter into your test framework. This allows you to run JMeter tests alongside your Rest Assured tests.

Step 1: Setting Up JMeter in the Maven Project
You'll need to include the **JMeter Maven plugin** in your pom.xml file (if you're using Maven). This plugin will enable you to run JMeter scripts and generate performance test reports.

```xml
<plugin>
    <groupId>com.lazerycode.jmeter</groupId>
    <artifactId>jmeter-maven-plugin</artifactId>
    <version>3.1.0</version>
    <executions>
        <execution>
            <id>jmeter-tests</id>
            <goals>
                <goal>jmeter</goal>
            </goals>
        </execution>
    </executions>
</plugin>
```

This configuration ensures that JMeter test plans (JMX files) are executed during the Maven build process. Once this plugin is added to your project, you can run JMeter tests in parallel with your **Rest Assured** functional tests.

Step 2: Create a JMeter Test Plan (JMX File)
You need to create a **JMeter test plan** that defines how you want to simulate load on your API. A test plan is an XML file that can be created in JMeter's **GUI mode**. This file includes details like:
- **HTTP requests**: API endpoints to be tested.
- **Thread groups**: Define the number of users to simulate.
- **Assertions**: To validate the performance.
- **Listeners**: To gather and display performance metrics.

Steps in JMeter:

1. Open **JMeter** in GUI mode.
2. Create a **Thread Group**: This will define how many users you want to simulate and how many requests each user will send.
   - Example: Simulate 50 users sending 10 requests each to the API.
3. Add an **HTTP Request** sampler: This is where you specify the API endpoint (e.g., /users) and the request method (e.g., GET, POST).
4. Add **Assertions**: To validate the response status codes and body content.
5. Add **Listeners**: Such as "View Results Tree" and "Summary Report" to visualize test results (e.g., response times, errors).

   Save this **test plan** as a **.jmx** file (e.g., api_load_test.jmx).

Step 3: Link the JMeter Test Plan with REST Assured Tests

Once your JMeter test plan is ready, you need to link it to your **Rest Assured** tests. Here's how you can execute JMeter tests as part of your Maven build process.

In the pom.xml, define the location of the **.jmx** file created in JMeter:

```xml
<configuration>
    <testFilesIncluded>
        <testFile>src/test/jmeter/api_load_test.jmx</testFile>
    </testFilesIncluded>
    <resultsFileFormat>xml</resultsFileFormat>
</configuration>
```

With this configuration, the **JMeter test plan** will execute automatically when you run your Maven tests.

Step 4: Write REST Assured Functional Tests

Now, write your **Rest Assured** tests as usual. These tests will run first to validate the functionality of the APIs. If they pass, the **JMeter** performance tests will execute next.

Example Rest Assured Test:

```java
public class RestAssuredExample {

    @Test
    public void testGetUserDetails() {
        given()
            .baseUri("https://api.example.com")
            .when()
            .get("/users/1")
            .then()
            .statusCode(200)
            .body("name", equalTo("John Doe"));
    }
}
```

Step 5: Running Combined Tests

When you execute mvn clean test, both your **Rest Assured** and **JMeter** tests will run sequentially or in parallel. This enables you to:

- Validate that the **API works correctly** under normal conditions (Rest Assured tests).
- Assess the **performance and scalability** of the API under load (JMeter tests).

Step 6: Analyzing JMeter Reports

Once the JMeter tests are completed, you'll have a set of **performance reports** that show metrics like:

- **Response time distribution**.
- **Error percentage**.
- **Throughput**: Number of requests processed per second.
- **Latency**: Time taken to receive the first byte of the response.

These reports help assess how well the API handles real-world usage and whether it meets performance benchmarks.

Key Challenges in Integrating JMeter into REST Assured Tests

1.   Challenge: Complex Configuration

Integrating **JMeter** into an existing **Rest Assured** framework requires configuration changes in both the **Maven** setup and the project structure. Setting up the JMeter plugin correctly to ensure seamless execution with **Rest Assured** can be complex, especially for teams that are new to performance testing tools.

Solution

Follow **best practices** for Maven configuration and ensure that all dependencies are managed properly. Thoroughly test the integration with a simple JMeter test plan first, and incrementally scale up the complexity.

2.   Challenge: Resource Management During Load Testing

Running both **functional tests** and **load tests** simultaneously can lead to resource contention, especially on **local environments** or limited CI servers. Large-scale load tests might consume too many resources, affecting the functional test results.

Solution

Use **dedicated environments** for load testing, separating them from environments where functional tests are executed. Alternatively, you can run **functional tests first** and only execute **performance tests** after ensuring that the system is functionally correct.

3.   Challenge: Performance Data Validation

It can be difficult to **correlate functional testing results** with performance issues identified by JMeter. For example, JMeter might report response time degradation, but pinpointing whether this is due to functional issues or scalability problems can be difficult.

Solution

Use **log correlation** between JMeter and Rest Assured tests. Integrate **logging frameworks** like **Log4j** into your API tests to track request-response cycles, which can help in diagnosing performance issues by mapping them to specific functional failures.

4.   Challenge: Synchronizing JMeter and Rest Assured Tests

Synchronizing **JMeter load tests** and **Rest Assured** functional tests so they can run cohesively within the same pipeline can be difficult. JMeter tests may run for extended periods, leading to inconsistencies in the test pipeline.

Solution

Ensure that **test scheduling** is configured properly in your **CI/CD pipelines**. Run **JMeter** tests only after successful completion of **Rest Assured** functional tests. Alternatively, you can run smaller **performance smoke tests** before running full load tests.

Solutions Summary

1. **Use Modular Frameworks**: Separate **performance testing** and **functional testing** in your framework but run them sequentially in the same pipeline. This ensures that functional validation always precedes load testing without disrupting the flow.
2. **Leverage Cloud Resources**: If resource contention is an issue, consider running **JMeter tests in the cloud** (e.g., **AWS, Azure**). Cloud resources can simulate large user loads without affecting the local environment or CI/CD pipeline.
3. **Automate Report Analysis**: Integrate automated tools like **Grafana** or **InfluxDB** with **JMeter** to generate and visualize performance metrics automatically. This simplifies post-test analysis by showing performance trends and highlighting problem areas.

In a Nutshell

Integrating **JMeter** into your **Rest Assured** test framework provides a comprehensive solution that combines **functional testing** with **load testing**. This allows you to verify both the correctness and performance of your APIs in a single pipeline. By overcoming the challenges related to configuration, resource management, and test synchronization, teams can achieve more robust API testing and ensure their APIs are scalable, performant, and reliable.

EFFECTIVE API TESTING FOR IN-SPRINT AUTOMATION

In-sprint automation is crucial in agile development, where each sprint typically spans one to two weeks. Testing APIs effectively within such short timeframes requires a strategic approach that ensures quality without compromising speed. To achieve this, it's essential to incorporate **automated API testing** into the development pipeline, allowing teams to validate functionality, performance, and security as soon as features are developed.

This section provides an in-depth exploration of effective strategies for in-sprint API automation, detailing the **key challenges** of in-sprint automation and strategies to overcome them, while covering various testing types such as **positive, negative, boundary,** and **edge case testing**.

Key Strategies for Effective API Testing in In-Sprint Automation

1.   Test Early and Continuously

To maintain the pace of in-sprint automation, start testing as soon as development begins. This approach, often called **shift-left testing**, reduces the feedback loop, enabling quick detection and resolution of issues.

Types of Tests to Conduct Early:
- **Smoke Tests**: Run a minimal set of tests to ensure basic API endpoints are functional.
- **Contract Testing**: Verify that the API request and response structure (e.g., headers, parameters, JSON fields) match the expected format.

Example:

If a new POST endpoint is created to add a new user, you can run **smoke tests** to ensure it accepts the payload and returns a valid response code (e.g., 201 Created). Contract tests would then verify that all required fields are present in the response.

2. *Categorize and Prioritize Test Types (Positive, Negative, Boundary, Edge Cases)*

Different types of tests validate APIs under various conditions. Effective API testing involves comprehensive coverage using **positive tests, negative tests, boundary tests, and edge cases**.

Positive Testing:
- Verifies that the API works as expected with valid data.
- Ensures that the **happy path** scenarios produce the correct response.

Example: For an API that retrieves user details by ID, send a request with a valid user ID and check if the response includes correct user data.

Negative Testing:
- Validates the API's response to invalid data and scenarios.
- Helps ensure the API is resilient to incorrect or malicious inputs.

Example: For a POST /users API, send a request without a mandatory field (e.g., email) and verify that the API returns an appropriate error code (e.g., 400 Bad Request).

Boundary Testing:
- Ensures the API handles limits correctly, such as the minimum and maximum length of inputs.
- Verifies that endpoints can handle data at or near the edges of defined constraints.

Example: If the username length is constrained to 20 characters, test the API with usernames of 19, 20, and 21 characters to verify that it accepts valid inputs and rejects overly long ones.

Edge Case Testing:
- Tests the API with unexpected or extreme input values.
- Identifies how the API behaves with unusual inputs (e.g., special characters, large numbers, empty values).

Example: For a GET /transactions API, send a request for transactions on a leap day (February 29) to check how the API handles rare dates.

3. *Automate API Tests for Faster Feedback and Scalability*

To achieve in-sprint automation, API tests should be automated to ensure they are continuously executed throughout the sprint, reducing manual effort and providing faster feedback.

Automation Strategies:

- **Automated Test Suites**: Automate a suite of tests, including smoke, regression, and functional tests. Run these tests in parallel as part of the CI/CD pipeline.
- **Data-Driven Testing**: Use **parameterization** to create multiple test cases from a single test by feeding different input values. This approach allows efficient testing of various data points, such as boundary and edge cases.

Example:

For a POST /orders endpoint, you can use data-driven testing to automate scenarios with different product quantities, including zero, maximum quantity, and random values.

Tools for Automation:

- **Rest Assured**: For functional API testing, Rest Assured offers fluent syntax for writing automated tests in Java.
- **Postman and Newman**: Use Postman collections to group and organize tests, and execute them through the Newman CLI to run tests in CI/CD pipelines.
- **JMeter**: Integrate JMeter for performance testing in automated pipelines to measure response times and scalability.

4.   *Maintain Clear API Contracts and Use Contract Testing*

An API contract defines the expected structure, format, and requirements of an API request and response. Establishing clear contracts allows developers and testers to agree on a standard API behavior, reducing misunderstandings and ensuring consistency.

Contract Testing:

- Use contract testing tools, such as **Pact** or **Swagger**, to validate that API responses conform to the agreed structure.
- Automate contract tests to run at each build to catch mismatches early and ensure backward compatibility.

Example*:*

If the GET /products API is supposed to return id, name, and price, a contract test will validate that each field is present and has the correct data type (e.g., id as an integer, price as a decimal).

5.   *Mock External Dependencies for Isolation and Faster Testing*

In a microservices environment, APIs often depend on other services. Mocking external dependencies ensures that tests remain fast and isolated from issues in unrelated services.

Strategies for Mocking:

- **Use Mock Servers**: Tools like **WireMock** and **Mockito** simulate external API responses, allowing the team to focus on testing the target API without worrying about dependencies.
- **Create Stubs for Backend Systems**: Use stubs to simulate predictable responses from databases or services not available in the testing environment.

Example*:*

If the GET /orders API depends on a third-party shipping service, you can create a mock response for the shipping service, allowing you to test the API independently and reliably.

6. *Implement Continuous Integration (CI) with Automated API Testing*

Automated API tests should be part of the CI/CD pipeline to ensure they run with every build, enabling early feedback for developers on the API's functionality and performance.

Steps to Integrate with CI:
1. **Set Up the Pipeline**: Configure the CI pipeline to trigger API tests whenever new code is pushed to the repository.
2. **Run Automated Tests**: Add automated test scripts (e.g., JUnit, Rest Assured, Postman collections) to the CI configuration to ensure every build is validated.
3. **Generate and Publish Reports**: Use tools like **Extent Reports** or **Allure** to generate HTML reports that can be reviewed by the team.

Example:
After a developer pushes changes to the POST /users endpoint, the CI pipeline runs tests that verify the endpoint accepts new users and validates edge cases, such as missing fields or invalid emails.

7. *Incorporate Security Testing for API Robustness*

Security testing is essential to ensure that APIs are not vulnerable to threats like **SQL Injection, Cross-Site Scripting (XSS),** or **unauthorized access.**

Key Security Tests:
- **Authentication and Authorization**: Test if the API enforces valid authentication tokens and authorization checks for each endpoint.
- **Input Validation**: Check for SQL Injection, XSS, and other vulnerabilities by sending malicious data as input.
- **Rate Limiting**: Simulate a high volume of requests from a single user to test if the API enforces throttling limits.

Example:
For an API that manages sensitive user information, test for SQL Injection by inserting SQL commands as input. Check that the API responds with a 400 Bad Request or another error code rather than executing the command.

8. *Use Performance Testing to Evaluate Scalability and Stability*

Performance testing is crucial for assessing how well an API performs under expected and peak loads. It helps ensure that the API meets response time and scalability requirements.

Types of Performance Tests:
- **Load Testing**: Simulate the typical load to ensure the API performs well under expected traffic.
- **Stress Testing**: Simulate a higher-than-usual load to test the API's behavior under extreme conditions.
- **Spike Testing**: Simulate sudden surges in requests to evaluate if the API can handle traffic spikes without crashing.

Example:
For an e-commerce API, simulate a load of 500 requests per second on the POST /checkout endpoint to check for response time, throughput, and any latency issues that may arise during high traffic periods.

Key Challenges and Solutions in In-Sprint API Testing

Testing within the confines of a sprint cycle presents unique challenges due to time constraints, constantly evolving requirements, and dependency management. Below is a granular breakdown of common challenges in in-sprint API testing and detailed strategies to overcome them.

1. Challenge: Limited Time for Comprehensive Testing

In agile sprints, time is limited, often spanning just one to two weeks. Conducting comprehensive testing within such short periods can be challenging. Ensuring coverage across all API functionalities, edge cases, performance, and security in such a short window can be overwhelming.

Solutions: Prioritize and Plan Test Types Based on Criticality

- **Prioritize Critical Tests**: Focus on **smoke, functional, and contract testing** as these are crucial for validating the primary functionality and contract of the API. Smoke tests help verify that the main endpoints are functioning, functional tests ensure the API performs as intended, and contract tests validate the request and response structure.
- **Parallelize Performance and Security Testing**: Performance and security testing are important but can be deferred to parallel pipelines or even post-sprint. Running these tests in separate pipelines ensures that critical validations don't block the main pipeline while allowing extended tests to still be part of the CI/CD.
- **Modularize Test Suites**: Break down tests into modular suites that can run independently. For instance, critical functional tests can run with each code change, while less critical tests can run on a nightly basis.

Example:

Run smoke tests on every pull request, functional tests after every merge, and schedule performance and security tests nightly. This way, coverage is maximized without impacting development velocity.

2. Challenge: Handling Constantly Evolving APIs in Agile

In agile environments, APIs frequently change as new features are added, or existing ones are modified. Constant changes in endpoints, parameters, or response formats can lead to **test script failures** and **maintenance overhead**.

Solutions: Implement Contract Testing and Reusable, Flexible Test Scripts

- **Use Contract Testing Tools**: Tools like **Pact** or **Swagger** help automate contract testing. Contract testing ensures that as APIs evolve, the structure and types of requests and responses remain consistent or provide immediate feedback when changes occur. This approach helps detect API drift, reducing the likelihood of broken tests.
- **Parameterize Test Scripts**: Structure test scripts to **use parameters** instead of hardcoded values. Externalize parameters in files (e.g., JSON or YAML) so they can be updated without altering the core test scripts.
- **Modular and Reusable Scripts**: Create reusable components for common actions (e.g., authentication, payload generation) to avoid redundant updates when APIs evolve. By reusing common functions, testers only need to update in one place.

Example:

For a GET /users API, a contract test would validate that the response includes required fields like id, name, and email. If a developer accidentally removes a field or changes its data type, the contract test would fail immediately, alerting the team to potential integration issues.

3. Challenge: Dependencies on Unstable or Unavailable Services

APIs often depend on other services, such as third-party APIs or microservices. If these services are unavailable or unreliable, it can block testing, making it difficult to validate the API's behavior in isolation.

Solutions: Use Mocks and Stubs to Isolate Testing from Dependencies

- **Use Mock Servers**: Tools like **WireMock** or **MockServer** allow you to simulate the behavior of dependent services, ensuring that your tests can proceed even if the actual services are down. This helps you maintain **consistent test environments**.
- **Stub Responses for Reliability**: For internal dependencies (e.g., a database service), use stubs to provide pre-defined responses, allowing the API to be tested without relying on actual data sources or backend systems. This enables testing scenarios like successful requests, timeouts, or specific error responses.
- **Integration Tests for Real Services**: Maintain a separate suite of integration tests that interact with actual services, run less frequently to validate end-to-end workflows without affecting regular testing workflows.

Example:

If your API relies on a third-party payment service, set up a mock that returns pre-defined responses for successful payments, failed payments, or network errors. This allows you to test the API's handling of these scenarios without connecting to the live payment system.

4. Challenge: Managing Large Test Data for Boundary and Edge Case Testing

Testing for boundary values, edge cases, and various input scenarios can require a large amount of test data, making it difficult to manage within the sprint timeframe. Generating, updating, and maintaining this data manually can be time consuming and error prone.

Solutions: Adopt Data-Driven Testing and Parameterize Test Data

- **Use Data-Driven Testing**: Data-driven testing enables you to create multiple test cases by feeding different datasets into a single test. Parameterize the input values and store them in external files (e.g., CSV, JSON, Excel) to dynamically generate edge and boundary values.
- **Automate Test Data Generation**: Use tools or scripts to automatically generate test data for various scenarios. For example, generate random values within boundary limits (e.g., maximum string length) and include special characters for edge cases.
- **Separate Test Data from Test Logic**: Maintain test data in separate files or database tables, making it easy to update or extend datasets without modifying the test scripts. This approach improves scalability and allows testers to focus on adding new test cases.

Example:

For a POST /register endpoint, create a CSV file with test data covering valid email formats, invalid formats, maximum length, empty fields, and special characters. Use this file as input to test a wide range of scenarios without hardcoding data into the test scripts.

5. Challenge: Efficient Reporting and Analysis in CI/CD Pipelines

In a CI/CD environment, tests are run continuously, and it can be challenging to keep up with the volume of results. Without efficient reporting, analyzing failures and tracking test performance can become difficult, leading to delays in debugging and issue resolution.

Solutions: Use Reporting Tools and Integrate Notifications for Immediate Feedback

- **Detailed Reports with Tools**: Use reporting libraries like **Allure, Extent Reports**, or **JUnit XML** reports to provide comprehensive feedback on test results. These reports offer insights into pass/fail rates, response times, and can include screenshots or error logs for failed tests.
- **Real-Time Notifications**: Integrate CI/CD pipelines with communication tools (e.g., **Slack, Microsoft Teams**) to receive real-time notifications of test results. Set up alerts for critical test failures to allow team members to respond immediately.
- **Automated Trend Analysis**: Use dashboard tools like **Grafana** or **Jenkins Test Result Analyzer** to track trends in test performance, stability, and failure rates over time. This can help identify patterns in recurring issues, such as performance degradation or regression bugs.

Example:

Configure Allure Reports to automatically generate a detailed HTML report after each test run, summarizing test success rates, execution times, and detailed logs for each test case. Set up Slack notifications to alert the QA team when critical tests fail, enabling faster response and resolution.

In a Nutshell

Effective in-sprint API testing requires strategic planning and the use of diverse test types (positive, negative, boundary, edge, security, and performance) to ensure comprehensive coverage. By integrating automated tests into the CI/CD pipeline, leveraging contract testing, and isolating dependencies through mocks, teams can validate the functionality, performance, and security of APIs quickly and efficiently within each sprint. This approach enables early detection of issues, provides faster feedback, and ensures that APIs remain reliable and resilient in production.

API AUTOMATION SPRINT OBJECTIVES

In agile development, where speed and quality are paramount, **API testing** becomes a critical component of the software development lifecycle. API QA and automation in sprints aim to ensure that the services and integrations driving modern applications are functional, reliable, and scalable. Integrating **API QA** and **automation** with sprint objectives ensures that APIs are tested early and continuously, with a focus on delivering stable, high-quality services that meet the sprint's goals.

This in-depth analysis explores how **API QA**, **automation**, and **sprint objectives** align, the role of **API testing** in the agile process, and strategies to implement **effective API testing** within the constraints of agile sprints.

1.   API QA in Agile Sprints

Role of API QA in Agile Sprints

API QA in agile sprints involves continuously testing backend services, data flows, and integrations across the system. Unlike UI testing, API testing directly verifies the core logic and interactions between services, which is crucial for ensuring that the overall system functions as expected.

Key API QA Activities During Sprints

1. **API Test Planning**: At the start of each sprint, QA teams evaluate user stories and acceptance criteria to define **API test scenarios**. This includes identifying critical endpoints, validating business rules, and understanding data flows across services.

2. **Continuous API Testing**: API testing begins as soon as new endpoints are developed, ensuring that features are tested as they are implemented. **Unit testing**, **integration testing**, and **contract testing** are continuously executed to ensure the API behaves as expected.

3. **Regression Testing**: As more endpoints are added or modified, QA ensures that existing functionality is not affected. Automated **regression API tests** run regularly to catch issues caused by new features or changes.

Importance of API QA in Agile

- **Early Defect Detection**: Testing APIs early catches issues in backend services before they affect the UI, enabling faster resolution of bugs.
- **Independent of UI**: API testing can run in parallel to UI development, ensuring that services are functional and performant regardless of the state of the front-end.
- **System Integration**: APIs connect different components of the system; by continuously testing APIs, QA ensures that integrations work correctly across the application.

2. API Automation in Agile Sprints

Role of Automation in API Testing

API automation is fundamental for delivering reliable results in fast-paced agile environments. Automated API tests provide **rapid feedback**, ensuring that functionality, performance, and security are validated with every code change. In an agile sprint, where time is limited, automation increases **efficiency** and **coverage** without requiring manual effort for every test cycle.

Benefits of API Automation in Sprints

- **Faster Feedback Loop**: Automated API tests can run immediately after a developer commits code, providing fast feedback on the correctness of the API, including status codes, response times, and data integrity.
- **Continuous Integration (CI)**: API automation integrates seamlessly with **CI/CD pipelines**, triggering tests as soon as code is pushed. This guarantees that APIs are continuously tested in real-time, reducing the likelihood of introducing bugs into production.
- **Reusability and Scalability**: Automated API tests are reusable across different environments (e.g., dev, staging, production) and can be scaled to handle larger test suites as the project grows. They can also be configured to test multiple data sets, ensuring broad coverage.
- **Comprehensive Testing**: API automation enables various types of tests, including:
  - **Functional Testing**: Validating if the API returns the correct data and behaves as expected.
  - **Integration Testing**: Ensuring that different services or modules interact correctly.
  - **Contract Testing**: Verifying that APIs adhere to agreed-upon contracts (e.g., correct request/ response format).
  - **Security Testing**: Automating checks for vulnerabilities such as authentication failures, SQL injection, and improper data handling.
  - **Performance and Load Testing**: Simulating concurrent user requests to assess API performance under load.

Common API Automation Tools

1. **Rest Assured**: Widely used for automating functional and integration API tests in Java environments.
2. **Postman + Newman**: Allows teams to create and automate API collections with Postman and run them in CI environments using Newman.

3. **JMeter**: Primarily for performance testing, JMeter simulates heavy loads on APIs.
4. **SoapUI**: Popular for testing both REST and SOAP web services, supporting functional, security, and load testing.

Challenges with API Automation in Sprints

1. **Time Constraints**: Automating tests within the short time frame of a sprint can be challenging, especially when new features are being developed rapidly.
2. **Test Maintenance**: As APIs evolve, automated test scripts may need regular updates to keep up with changes in endpoints, parameters, and responses.
3. **Integration with Tools**: API automation tools need to be well-integrated with other tools in the tech stack, such as CI pipelines and code repositories.

3. API Sprints in Agile Development

Sprint Overview from an API Perspective

In the context of API development, a **sprint** is a short, focused effort to deliver working API functionality in incremental stages. Each sprint typically aims to deliver fully functional API endpoints that meet the sprint's acceptance criteria.

Sprint Process for API Development:

1. **Sprint Planning**: In each sprint, the team breaks down the API features (endpoints, business rules, integrations) that need to be delivered. QA collaborates closely with developers to identify **testable scenarios** early on.
2. **API Development and Testing**: As developers build the API endpoints, QA continuously runs automated tests to validate responses, error handling, and edge cases. Testing happens in parallel with development to prevent bottlenecks.
3. **Sprint Review and Retrospective**: At the end of each sprint, the team reviews the API functionality delivered and identifies any quality issues or improvements for the next sprint.

Challenges in API Sprints:

- **Tight Timeframes**: Sprints usually last 1-2 weeks, making it difficult to cover all edge cases and scenarios in that time.
- **Concurrent Development**: APIs often evolve during a sprint as new requirements emerge, which can disrupt test planning.
- **Complex Integrations**: APIs are part of a larger system, meaning they often have dependencies on other services, making testing more complex.

4. Objectives of API QA and Automation in Agile Sprints

1. Deliver High-Quality, Stable APIs Within Sprint Cycles

The primary objective of API QA and automation in sprints is to deliver fully functional and stable APIs within the time constraints of a sprint. Automated testing ensures that all features are validated and regression tests are continuously run.

How to Achieve This:

- **Automation of Critical API Tests**: Automate the testing of key API endpoints (e.g., user authentication, data retrieval) to ensure that every code change is validated immediately.

- **Continuous Feedback Loops**: Integrate API tests with CI pipelines to ensure feedback on API changes is delivered to developers in real-time. Failures should trigger notifications for immediate action.

2. *Early Detection of API Defects and Bugs*

The sooner defects are identified, the easier they are to fix. By integrating API testing into the sprint cycle, bugs are caught early before they affect the larger system or cause delays in the sprint.

How to Achieve This:

- **Shift-Left API Testing**: Involve QA in sprint planning to identify test scenarios for each API endpoint and automate as much as possible from the start.
- **Test Automation at Every Build**: Use tools like **Rest Assured** or **Postman** to run tests against every build. This ensures that developers are alerted to issues as soon as possible.

3. *Maintain API Regression Stability*

Regression testing is essential to ensure that changes to APIs don't break existing functionality. Automated regression tests need to run continuously to validate that both new and old API features work as expected.

How to Achieve This:

- **Automate Regression Test Suites**: Ensure that all critical API endpoints are covered by automated regression tests. These tests should be modular, easy to maintain, and scalable across multiple environments.
- **Run Regression Tests in CI Pipelines**: Integrate regression tests into the CI/CD pipeline to catch regressions as soon as new changes are made to the codebase.

4. *Increase Sprint Velocity with Automation Without Sacrificing API Quality*

A key objective in agile is to **increase sprint velocity** (i.e., the number of tasks completed during a sprint) while maintaining high quality. API automation plays a critical role by reducing manual effort and ensuring that tests can run quickly and continuously.

How to Achieve This:

- **Focus Automation on Key API Endpoints**: Prioritize automating tests for high-risk, high-value API endpoints that are frequently used or changed. This allows teams to focus manual testing on complex, exploratory scenarios.
- **Parallel API Test Execution**: Use parallelization techniques to run multiple API tests concurrently, speeding up test execution time and allowing more coverage within the sprint.

5. *Align API QA Objectives with Business Goals*

API testing must align with the overall business objectives. Every API endpoint being developed or modified should directly contribute to business needs, whether that's improving performance, scalability, or delivering new features.

How to Achieve This:

- **Collaboration with Product Owners**: QA should work closely with product owners and stakeholders to understand how API functionalities impact the user experience or system performance. This ensures that test cases are aligned with business requirements.

- **Track and Report API Quality Metrics**: Measure API performance (e.g., response times, error rates) and report these metrics to the broader team to demonstrate how testing efforts are contributing to business success.

In a Nutshell

Integrating **API QA**, **automation**, and **sprint objectives** is essential for ensuring that API development is fast, efficient, and high-quality in agile environments. By leveraging **automation**, teams can speed up testing, increase coverage, and provide continuous feedback throughout the sprint cycle. Effective API QA enables early defect detection, stable API regressions, and alignment with business goals, ensuring that teams can deliver fully functional, shippable API increments without compromising on quality or velocity.

The key to success is focusing on **continuous integration**, **automating high-priority tests**, and ensuring that **API testing is flexible** enough to adapt to evolving requirements and business needs, making the process both scalable and sustainable in fast-paced agile environments.

COMPREHENSIVE API TEST STRATEGY FOR IN-SPRINT AUTOMATION

An effective **API Test Strategy for in-sprint automation** must cover various testing scenarios, including **functional**, **non-functional**, **security**, and **performance testing**, to ensure high-quality API delivery within the constraints of a sprint. In agile development, in-sprint API automation plays a critical role in achieving faster feedback, reducing manual efforts, and ensuring the quality of the services that drive modern applications.

Below is a comprehensive API test strategy tailored for **in-sprint automation**, outlining the key testing types, coverage scenarios, and examples.

Objectives of the API Test Strategy

The primary objectives of this strategy are:

- **Early Detection of Bugs**: Identify functional, security, and performance issues early in the sprint to reduce the cost of fixing defects.
- **Continuous Integration**: Ensure automated API tests are integrated into the **CI/CD pipeline**, providing rapid feedback on the status of API development.
- **Comprehensive Test Coverage**: Ensure that all critical aspects of the API (functional, edge cases, security, performance, etc.) are validated.
- **Maintainability**: Create modular, reusable, and maintainable test cases that evolve with the API as the project progresses.

API Test Strategy Components

1. Functional Testing

Functional testing ensures that the API meets the business requirements by validating its behavior against specified inputs and expected outputs. This type of testing should cover:

- **Happy Path Scenarios**: Validate that the API works as expected with valid input data.
- **Negative Testing**: Ensure the API behaves appropriately when receiving invalid input data.
- **Boundary and Edge Case Testing**: Test how the API handles data at the boundary limits of what it is designed to process.

Functional Test Types:

1. **Positive Testing**:
   - **Scenario**: Validate that a POST /users endpoint successfully creates a new user with valid input.
   - **Example**:

```
@Test
public void createUser_withValidInput_shouldReturn201() {
    String userPayload = "{ \"name\": \"John Doe\", \"email\": \"john.doe@
example.com\", \"age\": 30 }";

    given()
        .header("Content-Type", "application/json")
        .body(userPayload)
    .when()
        .post("/users")
    .then()
        .statusCode(201)
        .body("id", notNullValue())
        .body("name", equalTo("John Doe"));
}
```

2. **Negative Testing**:
   - **Scenario**: Validate that the POST /users endpoint returns a 400 Bad Request error when the email is missing.
   - **Example**:

```
@Test
public void createUser_withMissingEmail_shouldReturn400() {
    String invalidPayload = "{ \"name\": \"John Doe\", \"age\": 30 }";

    given()
        .header("Content-Type", "application/json")
        .body(invalidPayload)
    .when()
        .post("/users")
    .then()
        .statusCode(400);
}
```

3. **Boundary Testing**:
   - **Scenario**: Validate that the POST /users endpoint accepts a name of maximum length (e.g., 50 characters) but rejects longer names.
   - **Example**:

```
@Test
public void createUser_withMaxLengthName_shouldSucceed() {
    String maxLengthName = "a".repeat(50);
    String userPayload = "{ \"name\": \"" + maxLengthName + "\", \"email\":
\"john.doe@example.com\", \"age\": 30 }";
```

```java
    given()
        .header("Content-Type", "application/json")
        .body(userPayload)
    .when()
        .post("/users")
    .then()
        .statusCode(201);
}


@Test
public void createUser_withExceedingNameLength_shouldReturn400() {
    String exceedingName = "a".repeat(51);
    String invalidPayload = "{ \"name\": \"" + exceedingName + "\", \"email\":
\"john.doe@example.com\", \"age\": 30 }";

    given()
        .header("Content-Type", "application/json")
        .body(invalidPayload)
    .when()
        .post("/users")
    .then()
        .statusCode(400);
}
```

4. **Edge Case Testing**:
    ○ **Scenario**: Validate that the GET /transactions API returns valid responses for edge dates like leap years or unusual date formats.
    ○ **Example**:
```java
@Test
public void getTransactions_withLeapDay_shouldReturnValidTransactions() {
    given()
        .header("Authorization", "Bearer token")
    .when()
        .get("/transactions?date=2024-02-29")
    .then()
        .statusCode(200)
        .body("transactions.size()", greaterThan(0));
}
```

Tools for Functional Testing:

- **Rest Assured** (Java)
- **Postman** (for manually testing and automating via collections)
- **JUnit/TestNG** for running tests

2. Integration Testing

Integration testing verifies that different services or systems communicate effectively through the API. It tests whether the API correctly interacts with external databases, other microservices, or third-party services.

Scenario:

- **Scenario**: Validate that the POST /orders API correctly interacts with the payment service and the inventory service.
- **Example**:

```
@Test
public void createOrder_shouldSuccessfullyProcessPaymentAndReduceInventory() {
        String orderPayload = "{ \"userId\": \"123\", \"productId\": \"456\",
\"quantity\": 1, \"paymentInfo\": { \"cardNumber\": \"4111111111111111\" } }";

    given()
        .header("Content-Type", "application/json")
        .body(orderPayload)
    .when()
        .post("/orders")
    .then()
        .statusCode(200)
        .body("orderStatus", equalTo("Confirmed"))
        .body("paymentStatus", equalTo("Success"))
        .body("inventoryStatus", equalTo("Updated"));
}
```

Tools for Integration Testing:

- **Rest Assured**
- **WireMock** for mocking dependent services
- **MockServer** for creating mock APIs to simulate third-party services

3. Contract Testing

Contract testing ensures that an API conforms to a defined contract (e.g., OpenAPI, Swagger). It verifies that the API's request and response structure are consistent, even as the API evolves.

Scenario:

- **Scenario**: Validate that the GET /users/{id} API conforms to the defined contract (JSON structure, response fields, types).

Example Using Pact:

```
@Pact(consumer = "UserService", provider = "UserAPI")
public RequestResponsePact createPact(PactDslWithProvider builder) {
    return builder
        .given("User with ID 123 exists")
        .uponReceiving("A request for user details")
        .path("/users/123")
```

```
        .method("GET")
        .willRespondWith()
        .status(200)
        .body("{ \"id\": \"123\", \"name\": \"John Doe\", \"email\": \"john.
doe@example.com\" }")
        .toPact();
}


@Test
@PactTestFor(pactMethod = "createPact")
public void runContractTest(MockServer mockServer) {
    given()
        .baseUri(mockServer.getUrl())
    .when()
        .get("/users/123")
    .then()
        .statusCode(200)
        .body("id", equalTo("123"))
        .body("name", equalTo("John Doe"))
        .body("email", equalTo("john.doe@example.com"));
}
```

Tools for Contract Testing:
- **Pact** for contract testing between consumer and provider.
- **Swagger/OpenAPI** for API documentation and testing.

4. *Performance and Load Testing*

Performance testing ensures that the API can handle expected and unexpected load, providing insights into response times, scalability, and potential bottlenecks.

Performance Testing Types:
1. **Load Testing**: Tests how the API performs under expected traffic.
2. **Stress Testing**: Identifies how the API behaves under excessive traffic.
3. **Spike Testing**: Simulates traffic spikes to assess API stability.

Scenario:
- **Scenario**: Validate that the GET /products API can handle 1,000 concurrent users without performance degradation.
- **Example Using JMeter**:
1. Set up a JMeter test plan.
2. Define a **Thread Group** to simulate 1,000 concurrent users.
3. Add an **HTTP Request** for the GET /products API.
4. Use **Listeners** to analyze response times and throughput.

Tools for Performance Testing:
- **JMeter** for load, stress, and performance testing.
- **Gatling** for performance testing.
- **BlazeMeter** for cloud-based load testing.

5. Security Testing

Security testing ensures that the API is protected against vulnerabilities such as **SQL injection**, **XSS attacks**, or **unauthorized access**. Security testing is crucial, especially when APIs deal with sensitive data (e.g., user information, payments).

Scenario:
- **Scenario**: Validate that the POST /login API enforces proper authorization and rejects invalid credentials.

Example:
```
@Test
public void login_withInvalidCredentials_shouldReturn401() {
        String loginPayload = "{ \"username\": \"wrong_user\", \"password\":
\"wrong_pass\" }";

    given()
        .header("Content-Type", "application/json")
        .body(loginPayload)
    .when()
        .post("/login")
    .then()
        .statusCode(401);
}
```

Tools for Security Testing:
- **OWASP ZAP** for automated security scanning.
- **Burp Suite** for manual and automated security testing.

6. Regression Testing

Regression testing ensures that new changes or features don't break existing API functionality. Automating regression tests ensures coverage of all critical functionality throughout sprints.

Scenario:
- **Scenario**: Validate that new changes to the POST /orders API do not affect the existing GET /orders/ {id} API functionality.

Example:
```
@Test
public void getOrder_withExistingOrder_shouldReturnOrderDetails() {
    given()
        .header("Authorization", "Bearer token")
    .when()
```

```
        .get("/orders/123")
    .then()
        .statusCode(200)
        .body("orderId", equalTo("123"))
        .body("orderStatus", equalTo("Confirmed"));
}
```

Tools for Regression Testing:

- **Rest Assured**
- **JUnit/TestNG** with CI/CD integration for automatic regression testing.

3.   Continuous Integration (CI) and Reporting

CI Integration: Automate API tests to run within the **CI/CD pipeline** after every build. This ensures immediate feedback and faster resolution of issues.

Tools for CI Integration:

- **Jenkins**: Automate and schedule API tests using tools like **Rest Assured** and **Postman**.
- **GitLab CI**: Integrate API tests to trigger upon code push or merge requests.

  Reporting: Use reporting tools like **Allure** or **Extent Reports** to generate detailed reports after each test execution. Automated notifications should be sent to teams to quickly address failures.

In a Nutshell

An effective **API Test Strategy for in-sprint automation** must encompass comprehensive **functional, integration, contract, performance, security**, and **regression testing**. By automating these tests and integrating them into the **CI/CD pipeline**, teams can ensure that APIs are tested continuously and comprehensively, ensuring high quality and rapid feedback. This approach reduces manual effort, accelerates defect detection, and ensures that each API meets performance, security, and functional requirements within the sprint's constraints.

## CHAPTER 6

SOURCE CONTROL AND AUTOMATION IN AGILE DEVELOPMENT

In Agile software development, delivering features swiftly without compromising quality is essential. This balance hinges on streamlined source control, automated testing, and robust CI/CD pipelines. This chapter delves into practical applications of Git, Docker, Jenkins, GitHub Actions, and continuous feedback mechanisms, with real-world examples and code snippets to showcase how these tools support Agile workflows. By integrating these practices, teams can improve efficiency, maintain high standards, and enable rapid, reliable delivery throughout development cycles.

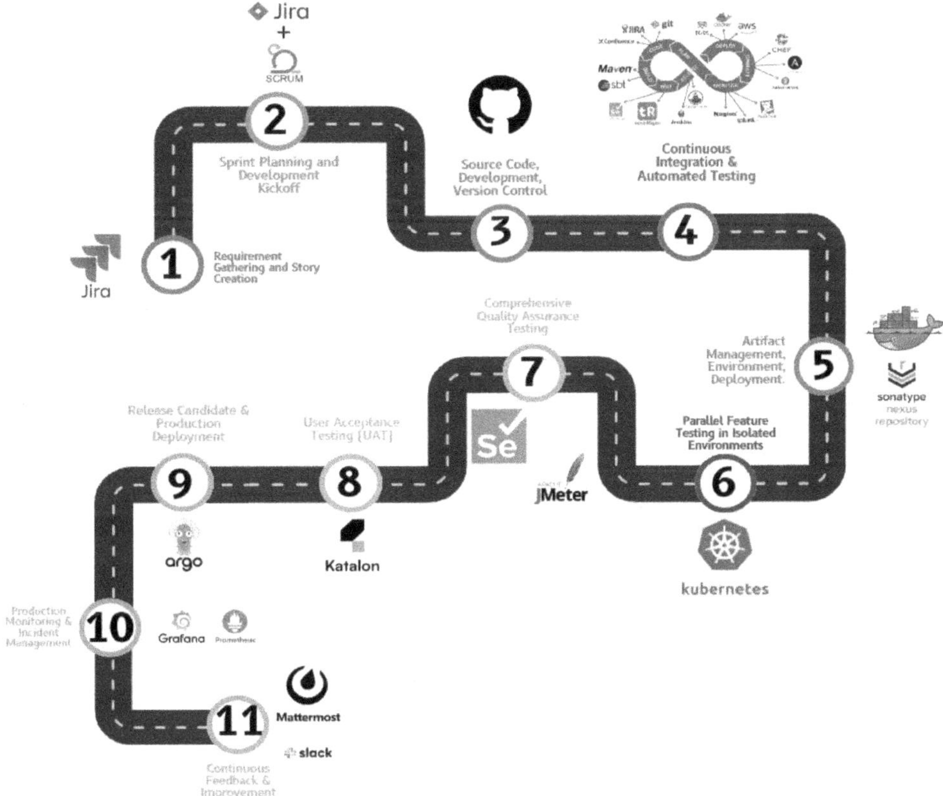

SOURCE CONTROL MANAGEMENT WITH GIT

Efficient source control management (SCM) is essential in Agile environments, where teams frequently collaborate and update code. Git is a distributed version control system that excels in Agile projects, enabling multiple contributors to work in parallel without disrupting each other's progress. It keeps a complete history of all changes, allowing for easy rollbacks, smooth integration, and effective conflict resolution. In this section, we'll discuss why Git is a vital tool in Agile workflows and examine key concepts like branching, merging, and CI/CD integration to streamline and enhance collaboration.

Why Git is Essential

Git's distributed architecture allows each team member to have a full local copy of the repository, which includes the entire project history. This setup is advantageous in Agile environments for several reasons:

- Collaboration and Independence: Developers can work offline and make changes without impacting the central repository, which allows for parallel work without dependencies.
- Change History and Accountability: Git's complete change history ensures that every modification is recorded, making it easy to track who made specific changes and why. This transparency fosters accountability, especially in large, multi-developer projects.
- Safe Experimentation: Developers can create isolated branches to test features or bug fixes, and once verified, they can merge these changes into the main branch without affecting others.

For instance, if a recent code update inadvertently breaks a set of Selenium tests, Git's rollback capabilities allow the team to quickly revert to a stable version while investigating the issue separately. This functionality preserves workflow continuity, a critical aspect in Agile sprints.

Key Git Concepts for Agile Development

To make the most of Git in Agile, it's essential to understand its core concepts, particularly branching, merging, and CI/CD integration.

Branching and Merging

Branching in Git allows developers to work on features, bug fixes, or testing in isolated environments. This process is central to Agile development, where continuous changes are the norm. With branching, developers can create a dedicated branch for a specific feature, such as feature/discount-tests, and work on it independently.

- **Example Scenario:** Suppose you're developing automated tests for a new "discount code" feature. By creating a branch (feature/discount-tests), you can write, test, and refine your code independently of the main codebase.
- **Feature Branching Workflow:** Once testing and validation are complete, you can merge the branch back into the main branch, preserving stability. This approach ensures that any experimental or in-progress code does not interfere with the main production-ready code.
- **Managing Conflicts:** In cases where multiple developers have modified similar parts of the code, Git provides tools for conflict resolution. Developers can review conflicting lines, decide which version to keep, and complete the merge without affecting the rest of the codebase.

Best Practices for Branching and Merging

- **Use Descriptive Branch Names:** Naming conventions like feature/discount-tests or bugfix/user-login clarify the branch purpose, making it easy for team members to understand the branch's function.
- **Small, Frequent Commits:** Commit small changes frequently, with descriptive messages. This practice allows for easier reviews, quick rollbacks, and improved traceability.
- **Regular Merging:** Sync branches with the main branch regularly to reduce the risk of conflicts, especially in Agile sprints where the codebase changes rapidly.

CI/CD Integration with Git

Continuous Integration and Continuous Deployment (CI/CD) pipelines are essential in Agile development, as they automate testing, building, and deployment, providing immediate feedback on code quality and functionality. Git seamlessly integrates with CI/CD systems, automating tests and deployments as soon as code changes are pushed.

- **Automated Testing on Push:** In a typical CI/CD setup, automated tests run whenever a developer pushes code to a shared branch, such as the main branch. This integration ensures that any potential issues are detected early, allowing developers to fix them promptly.
- **Immediate Feedback:** When a test fails, the CI/CD system notifies the developer instantly, helping prevent unstable code from progressing further. This feedback loop is invaluable in Agile sprints, where frequent changes require constant testing and verification.
- **Reducing Manual Intervention:** With Git integrated into CI/CD, processes like testing, building, and deployment can occur without manual intervention. This automation frees up developers to focus on feature development and bug fixes.

Example CI/CD Workflow:

- A developer pushes changes to the feature/discount-tests branch.
- The CI/CD system detects the push and triggers automated tests, such as unit tests, integration tests, and Selenium tests.
- If all tests pass, the developer receives a confirmation, indicating the code is ready for merging.
- If tests fail, the CI/CD system immediately notifies the developer with details of the failure, allowing for a quick fix and retesting.

Best Practices for Git and CI/CD Integration

- **Automate Early and Often:** Integrate automated testing and deployment as early in the sprint as possible. This ensures that every code change undergoes quality checks from the start.
- **Use Pull Requests for Code Review:** Before merging to main, create a pull request. This step enables code review, which is critical for maintaining code quality, particularly in Agile workflows with high volumes of changes.
- **Tag Stable Versions:** Use Git tags to mark stable versions of the codebase. In case of major issues, tags provide clear points for reverting to a known good state.

Example: Using Git for Agile CI/CD

Suppose your Agile team is implementing a "discount code" feature, which involves multiple developers working on front-end changes, backend integration, and automated tests. Here's how Git's branching, merging, and CI/CD integration streamline the workflow:

1. **Create Feature Branches:** Each developer creates their own branch, e.g., feature/discount-UI, feature/discount-backend, and feature/discount-tests, isolating work on different aspects of the feature.
2. **Independent Development:** Developers work independently within their branches, committing frequently and describing changes clearly.
3. **Automated Testing on Push:** Each branch is linked to the CI/CD pipeline, which automatically runs tests each time code is pushed. Developers get immediate feedback if their changes cause test failures.
4. **Code Review and Merging:** Once individual work is complete and all tests pass, developers open pull requests. Team members review these requests for code quality and adherence to standards before merging them into a dev branch.

5. **Integration Testing:** The CI/CD pipeline runs a final suite of tests on the dev branch to confirm that all parts work together as expected. If successful, the code is merged into the main branch for deployment.

This structured approach using Git, combined with CI/CD, reduces the risk of errors, enables fast feedback, and ensures that code quality remains high throughout the sprint.

In a Nutshell

Git is indispensable in Agile development due to its robust SCM capabilities and its seamless integration with CI/CD systems. Its branching and merging functionality, combined with automated testing and deployment, provides a structured yet flexible framework that aligns with the iterative nature of Agile sprints. By adopting Git and implementing best practices for branching, merging, and CI/CD, Agile teams can boost productivity, enhance collaboration, and maintain high code quality throughout their development cycles.

Using Git for Automation Projects: Basic Commands and Eclipse Integration

For Agile teams involved in automation projects, using Git effectively streamlines collaboration, code management, and deployment. Git's commands for cloning, committing, and pushing changes form the foundation for daily development tasks, while IDE integrations like Eclipse simplify the workflow further by allowing Git operations directly within the development environment. This section details essential Git commands for automation projects and offers a step-by-step guide to implementing Git in Eclipse, from setup to conflict resolution.

Basic Git Commands for Automation Projects

When working on automation projects, especially those involving frequent updates and multiple contributors, having a strong grasp of core Git commands is critical. Here are key Git commands for setting up, updating, and managing codebases in a collaborative environment.

1. ### Cloning a Repository
   - **Command:** `git clone https://github.com/your-repo.git`
   - **Purpose:** `git clone` is used to create a local copy of a remote repository, bringing the entire codebase, including history, branches, and files, to your local machine. This command is essential for getting started on a project.
   - **Example:** For an automation project, you might clone a repository that contains both test scripts and configuration files needed for testing across multiple environments.

2. ### Checking the Status of Your Working Directory
   - **Command:** `git status`
   - **Purpose:** `git status` provides an overview of changes in your working directory, including files that are staged, modified, or untracked. It's a crucial command to run before making commits, as it helps ensure that only intended changes are included.
   - **Example:** After modifying test scripts or adding new ones, run git status to verify that your changes are ready for staging.

3. ### Staging Changes for Commit
   - **Command:** `git add .` *or* `git add [filename-1]…[filename-n]`
   - **Purpose:** Staging changes with `git add` prepares them for the next commit. The . argument stages all changes, while specifying filenames allows for selective staging.

- o **Example:** In automation projects, it's common to stage only relevant test files or configuration updates while excluding temporary files or logs.

4. *Committing Changes with a Descriptive Message*
- o **Command:** `git commit -m "Add automated tests for discount codes"`
- o **Purpose:** Committing in Git saves a snapshot of the staged changes. Including a descriptive message is essential for tracking purposes, as it provides context for the changes.
- o **Best Practice:** Use clear, concise commit messages like `"Add automated tests for discount codes"` to improve traceability, especially useful in Agile sprints with frequent updates.

5. *Pushing Changes to the Remote Repository*
- o **Command:** `git push`
- o **Purpose:** `git push` sends committed changes to the remote repository, making them available to the rest of the team. This step is essential for collaboration, allowing team members to access the latest updates.
- o **Example:** After testing locally, you might push a set of validated scripts to the main repository, enabling CI/CD systems to run them on the shared environment.

These commands form the backbone of source control in automation projects, providing a reliable workflow for adding, tracking, and sharing code changes.

Implementing Git in Eclipse and Using the Command Line

For developers who prefer an integrated development environment, Eclipse offers Git integration through its Git plugin. Using Git within Eclipse allows for seamless management of code and version control without switching to the command line, which is especially beneficial in Agile teams where efficient workflows are key.

1. *Setting Up Git in Eclipse*

Before using Git in Eclipse, ensure the Git plugin is installed. The plugin can be downloaded directly from the Eclipse Marketplace.

- o **Install the Git Plugin:** From the Eclipse Marketplace, search for "EGit" (Eclipse's Git plugin) and install it. This plugin enables developers to perform Git operations within Eclipse, streamlining the workflow.
- o **Configuring Git in Eclipse:** After installation, configure Git settings such as user name and email by navigating to Preferences > Team > Git. This configuration ensures that commits are correctly attributed.

2. *Cloning a Repository in Eclipse*

With the Git plugin installed, you can clone a repository directly from within Eclipse.

- o **Clone Repository:** Select File > Import > Git > Projects from Git > Clone URI. Enter the repository URL, choose the desired branches, and complete the import process. The repository is now available as a project within Eclipse.
- o **Working Locally:** You now have a local version of the project. This setup allows you to write, test, and debug automation scripts (e.g., Selenium tests) within the IDE before pushing updates to the main repository.

3. *Committing and Pushing Changes in Eclipse*

Once changes are made and tested, Eclipse's Git interface simplifies the process of staging, committing, and pushing updates.

- ○ **Staging Changes:** In the Eclipse Git perspective, select the files you've modified. Right-click and choose Add to Index to stage changes.
- ○ **Committing Changes:** Right-click the project, select Commit, and enter a descriptive message. This interface allows you to review staged changes before finalizing the commit.
- ○ **Pushing to Remote:** After committing, choose Commit and Push to update the remote repository. This step ensures that your changes are available to the team and integrated into any CI/CD workflows.

Scenario: Resolving Conflicts with Command-Line Git

Occasionally, merge conflicts arise, particularly in Agile projects where multiple developers contribute frequently. While Eclipse provides some conflict resolution tools, the command line offers greater control and flexibility for complex conflicts.

- **Example:** Suppose two developers modify the same Selenium test script. When one developer tries to merge their branch, Git detects conflicting changes and prevents the merge.
- **Steps to Resolve via Command Line:**
1. Run `git pull` to fetch the latest changes.
2. Identify conflicting files by running `git status`.
3. Open the conflicting files, and look for sections marked with `<<<<<<` and `>>>>>>`, which indicate conflicting code blocks.
4. Choose the correct version for each conflict, save the changes, and mark the file as resolved by staging it with git add `[filename]`.
5. Complete the merge with `git commit`, and push the changes to update the remote repository.

The command line provides precise control over each conflict, allowing developers to make intentional decisions about which changes to keep. This approach ensures clean merges and minimizes disruption to the main codebase.

Docker Integration for Test Automation

In Agile development, testing environments must be consistent to ensure accurate and reliable test results. Docker has become a valuable tool for achieving this consistency, especially in automation projects involving Selenium. Docker allows developers to package tests and their dependencies in isolated containers, so they run identically across different environments, which is particularly beneficial when tests behave differently on local machines versus CI servers due to environmental discrepancies.

This section explores why Docker is essential for Selenium test automation, explains how to set up and run tests in a Dockerized environment, and addresses common challenges teams may face.

Why Use Docker for Selenium Tests?

Docker is a containerization tool that packages applications, along with all necessary libraries, dependencies, and environment configurations, into portable containers. In the context of Selenium testing, Docker offers several advantages:

- **Environment Consistency:** By packaging the testing environment into containers, Docker ensures that tests run the same way regardless of the host environment. This consistency eliminates common issues where tests pass on a developer's machine but fail in CI/CD environments.

- **Browser and Driver Compatibility:** Selenium tests often require specific versions of browsers and drivers. Docker allows you to specify exact versions, ensuring compatibility and reducing discrepancies across different machines.
- **Parallel Test Execution:** Docker enables the creation of a Selenium Grid, where multiple containers run different browser instances concurrently, allowing teams to execute tests across various browsers and devices in parallel. This is crucial for large test suites, as it accelerates test execution time and feedback.
- **Scenario:** Imagine your team needs to test a web application on both Chrome and Firefox to ensure cross-browser compatibility. With Docker-Compose, you can set up a Selenium Grid that simultaneously runs tests across Chrome and Firefox instances, delivering consistent results across different environments.

Understanding Docker and Docker-Compose for Selenium Test Execution

Docker itself is a powerful tool, but Docker-Compose extends its functionality by enabling developers to manage multi-container applications with a single configuration file. In Selenium automation, Docker-Compose is particularly useful for setting up and managing a Selenium Grid with multiple browser nodes.

Docker Basics for Selenium:
- ○ **Docker Images:** An image is a snapshot of an environment, including the operating system, software, and dependencies. Selenium provides official Docker images for running different browser instances (e.g., Chrome and Firefox), which simplifies setting up environments tailored for testing.
- ○ **Docker Containers:** Containers are instances of Docker images that run as isolated environments. When running Selenium tests, containers serve as individual, reproducible test environments.

Docker-Compose for Multi-Container Management:
- ○ **Definition File:** Docker-Compose uses a docker-compose.yml file to define and configure multiple containers. For a Selenium Grid setup, this file specifies details for the Selenium Hub (the central coordinator for test sessions) and browser nodes (e.g., Chrome and Firefox).
- ○ **Scalability:** Docker-Compose allows you to scale the number of containers dynamically, meaning you can adjust the number of Chrome or Firefox nodes as needed. This flexibility is essential for handling large test suites or scaling down to conserve resources.

Setting Up a Selenium Grid with Docker-Compose

A Selenium Grid allows multiple tests to run in parallel across various browsers, which is invaluable for Agile teams aiming for rapid feedback. The Selenium Grid has two main components:
- **Selenium Hub:** A centralized server that manages test sessions and coordinates requests to browser nodes.
- **Browser Nodes:** Containers that run specific browser instances (e.g., Chrome or Firefox) where tests are executed.

Below is a basic docker-compose.yml configuration file to set up a Selenium Grid with one Chrome and one Firefox node (yaml).

```yaml
version: '3'
services:
  selenium-hub:
    image: selenium/hub
    ports:
      - "4444:4444" # Hub for managing test sessions
```

```yaml
  chrome:
    image: selenium/node-chrome
    depends_on:
      - selenium-hub
    environment:
      - HUB_HOST=selenium-hub
  firefox:
    image: selenium/node-firefox
    depends_on:
      - selenium-hub
    environment:
      - HUB_HOST=selenium-hub
```

Explanation:

- **selenium-hub:** This container acts as the central hub that routes test requests to available nodes. It is exposed on port `4444`, which can be accessed by test scripts.
- **chrome and firefox Nodes:** Each browser container (node) connects to the hub, allowing the hub to assign tests to these nodes based on the availability of Chrome and Firefox instances.
- **Starting the Selenium Grid:** To start the grid, navigate to the directory containing the docker-compose. yml file and run:

```
docker-compose up -d
```

This command initiates the hub and browser containers in detached mode (`-d`), allowing you to run tests without keeping the terminal window open. Once started, the Selenium Grid is accessible at `http://localhost:4444/wd/hub`, which can be used as the endpoint for your Selenium WebDriver scripts.

Scaling Selenium Nodes with Docker-Compose

In some scenarios, such as running large test suites, you may need more than one instance of each browser to run tests faster. Docker-Compose allows you to scale up (or down) the number of browser containers on demand, which is beneficial for Agile sprints that require fast feedback.

Scaling Up Chrome and Firefox Nodes

```
docker-compose up -d --scale chrome=3 --scale firefox=3
```

This command scales the grid to three Chrome and three Firefox nodes, increasing test capacity and reducing test execution time.

- **Scaling Down:** To reduce resource usage, you can scale down the number of browser nodes by specifying a lower value for each browser type, freeing up system resources.

Configuring Selenium Code to Run on Docker Containers

Once the Selenium Grid is running, your Selenium scripts need to be configured to connect to the Dockerized grid endpoint rather than the local browser driver.

1. **Specify the Remote WebDriver URL:** Point your WebDriver to the Selenium Hub URL (`http://localhost:4444/wd/hub`), which will route test commands to available nodes.
2. **Example Code:**

```java
import org.openqa.selenium.WebDriver;
import org.openqa.selenium.chrome.ChromeOptions;
```

```java
import org.openqa.selenium.remote.RemoteWebDriver;

import java.net.MalformedURLException;
import java.net.URL;

public class SeleniumDockerTest {
    public static void main(String[] args) {
        try {
            // Configure ChromeOptions
            ChromeOptions chromeOptions = new ChromeOptions();

            // Set up the Remote WebDriver to connect to the Selenium Hub
WebDriver driver = new RemoteWebDriver(new URL("http://localhost:4444/wd/hub"),
chromeOptions);

            // Run test actions
            driver.get("http://example.com");

            // Print the page title
            System.out.println("Page title is: " + driver.getTitle());

            // Close the browser
            driver.quit();

        } catch (MalformedURLException e) {
            e.printStackTrace();
        }
    }
}
```

Explanation
- **ChromeOptions**: Used to set up options for the Chrome browser.
- **RemoteWebDriver**: Configured with the Selenium Hub URL (`http://localhost:4444/wd/hub`) to enable remote execution on the Dockerized Selenium Grid.
- **driver.getTitle()**: Prints the title of the loaded page.
- **driver.quit()**: Closes the WebDriver session and releases resources.

This setup allows the test script to connect to the Selenium Hub, which distributes test execution across the available browser nodes (Chrome, Firefox, etc.).

Executing Tests in Parallel on Docker Containers
Parallel execution is essential for Agile teams that need to run large test suites efficiently. By running tests in parallel across multiple containers, Docker significantly reduces the time required for complete test runs.
1. **Test Suite Parallelization:** Many test frameworks, such as TestNG (Java) or Pytest (Python), support parallel test execution out of the box. Combined with a scaled Selenium Grid, this setup ensures rapid execution of test cases across different browsers and environments.

2. **Setting Up Parallel Execution:**

    For example, with TestNG, specify parallel test execution in the XML configuration file:

```
<suite name="Parallel Test Suite" parallel="tests" thread-count="4">
  <test name="Test Chrome">
    <!-- Test configurations for Chrome -->
  </test>
  <test name="Test Firefox">
    <!-- Test configurations for Firefox -->
  </test>
</suite>
```

3. **Results Collection:** Parallel execution can complicate test result collection, but most CI/CD systems (like Jenkins) are equipped to handle this. They aggregate test results, providing a complete overview of execution and failures.

Key Challenges and Solutions

1. *Challenge: Browser Version Compatibility*

Different CI/CD environments may have mismatched browser versions, leading to test failures.

Solution

Using Docker images with specific versions of browsers and drivers ensures compatibility. Select Docker images with the required versions for your tests to maintain consistency.

2. *Challenge: Resource Management*

Running multiple Docker containers can consume significant memory and CPU resources, which may affect system performance.

Solution

Monitor container resource usage using Docker commands like docker stats or tools like Prometheus. Scale down containers when not in use and run docker-compose down after test execution to free up resources.

3. *Challenge: Container Orchestration and Cleanup*

Containers left running after test execution can consume resources and lead to conflicts.

Solution

Always run docker-compose down after completing tests. For scheduled CI/CD jobs, add cleanup commands to ensure containers are removed automatically after test completion.

4. *Network Stability*

Remote connections to the Selenium Grid can face network interruptions, causing test failures.

Solution

Configure retry logic in tests to handle intermittent network issues. Additionally, consider using Docker networks to isolate the Selenium Grid containers from external network disruptions.

Practical Tip

To avoid resource drain, always run `docker-compose down` after your tests complete. This command stops and removes all containers defined in your `docker-compose.yml`, freeing up system resources and ensuring a clean environment for the next test run.

In a Nutshell Docker and Docker-Compose provide powerful tools for creating stable, reproducible environments in Selenium test automation. By enabling a consistent setup across development and CI environments, Docker helps Agile teams achieve faster, more reliable testing processes that align with the needs of rapid development cycles.

GitHub Actions Automation: Setting Up and Extending CI/CD Pipelines

GitHub Actions is a CI/CD platform that allows teams to automate testing, building, and deployment workflows directly from their GitHub repositories. This integration is especially useful for Agile teams focused on continuous integration and fast feedback, as it allows for workflows that run on every push, pull request, or branch merge. GitHub Actions provides the flexibility to automate nearly any task within the software lifecycle, from code linting to deployment, helping maintain high code quality and reducing manual intervention.

This section will cover how to set up a CI/CD pipeline with GitHub Actions, extend workflows with additional steps for quality checks, and leverage existing workflows from the GitHub Marketplace for common programming languages.

Setting Up a Basic CI/CD Pipeline with GitHub Actions for Java-Based Selenium Projects

For Java projects, especially those involving Selenium for test automation, GitHub Actions can automate key stages such as building, testing, code quality checks, and conditional deployment. This automation is crucial in Agile environments where testing and feedback need to be continuous. Below is a detailed guide on setting up a CI/CD pipeline for a Java-based Selenium project, along with steps to enhance code quality and security through linting and dependency management.

Step 1: Create a Workflow File
To start, you'll need to create a new workflow file in your repository:
- If not already present, create a `.github/workflows` directory in your repository.
- Inside this directory, create a YAML file named, for example, `java-selenium-ci.yml`.

Step 2: Define Triggering Events
Specify the events that will trigger this workflow. For most CI/CD workflows in Agile development, it's beneficial to run tests on both push and pull_request events to catch issues early.

```
name: Java Selenium CI/CD Pipeline
on: [push, pull_request]
```

This configuration triggers the workflow whenever code is pushed to the repository or when a pull request is opened, enabling early detection of issues before merging.

Step 3: Define Jobs
Jobs are individual tasks that can run in sequence or parallel. For Java projects, a typical CI/CD workflow includes setting up the Java environment, building the project, running tests, and performing additional checks for code quality.

```yaml
jobs:
  build:
    runs-on: ubuntu-latest
    steps:
      - name: Check out the repository
        uses: actions/checkout@v2

      - name: Set up Java
        uses: actions/setup-java@v2
        with:
          java-version: '11'  # Specify Java version, e.g., 11 or 17

      - name: Cache Maven dependencies
        uses: actions/cache@v2
        with:
          path: ~/.m2/repository
          key: ${{ runner.os }}-maven-${{ hashFiles('**/pom.xml') }}
          restore-keys: |
            ${{ runner.os }}-maven-

      - name: Build with Maven
        run: mvn -B clean install

      - name: Run Selenium Tests
        run: mvn test
```

Explanation of Workflow Steps

1. **Check Out the Code**: The `actions/checkout@v2` action clones the repository, making the code available for the build process.
2. **Set Up Java**: The `actions/setup-java@v2` action installs the specified Java version (e.g., Java 11), ensuring compatibility with the project's requirements.
3. **Cache Maven Dependencies**: Caching Maven dependencies speeds up builds by reusing dependencies from previous runs. This step only downloads dependencies if the pom.xml file changes.
4. **Build with Maven**: This step compiles the Java project and builds it using `mvn clean install`.
5. **Run Selenium Tests**: Executes the Selenium test suite with `mvn test`. If tests pass, the workflow continues; if tests fail, the workflow stops, and feedback is provided.

Scenario: Ensuring Tests Pass Before Merging

In an Agile workflow, it's essential to validate that all tests pass before merging code into main branches. GitHub Actions supports this through automated checks on pull requests:

1. **Pull Request Workflow**: The configuration in on: [push, pull_request] ensures that the workflow runs on every new pull request, helping catch issues early.
2. **Review and Approval**: Once the tests pass, the code can be reviewed by team members to ensure quality before merging.

3. **Automated Checks**: GitHub visually displays workflow statuses (pass or fail) on pull requests, making it easy to see if code is ready. If any tests fail, GitHub Actions provides detailed logs for troubleshooting.

Extending the Workflow with Additional Steps for Quality Assurance

Beyond basic testing, additional checks like linting and security audits improve code quality and maintainability, especially in collaborative Agile teams.

Adding Code Quality Checks with SpotBugs

SpotBugs is a static analysis tool for Java that helps detect potential bugs and code smells. Integrating SpotBugs into the workflow ensures high code quality by identifying issues early.

```
- name: Run SpotBugs
  run: mvn spotbugs:check
```

Explanation:

- **SpotBugs**: This step runs SpotBugs as part of the Maven build, flagging issues like null pointer dereferences or redundant code. SpotBugs can halt the workflow if critical issues are found, ensuring only high-quality code moves forward.

Adding Dependency Management and Security Checks with OWASP Dependency-Check

For Java projects, dependency vulnerabilities are a critical concern. OWASP Dependency-Check identifies known vulnerabilities in project dependencies, reducing the risk of security issues in production.

```
- name: Run Dependency Check
  run: mvn org.owasp:dependency-check-maven:check
```

Explanation:

- **OWASP Dependency-Check**: This step performs a security audit of dependencies, generating a report of any known vulnerabilities. If vulnerabilities are found, they can be reviewed and resolved before merging, enhancing project security.

Conditional Deployment

Once testing, linting, and security checks pass, you can add a deployment step that triggers only on the main branch. This ensures that only fully tested and reviewed code is deployed to production.

```
- name: Deploy to Production
  if: github.ref == 'refs/heads/main' && success()
  run: ./deploy-script.sh
```

Explanation:

- **Conditional Deployment**: This step deploys code only if all previous checks pass and the workflow is running on the main branch. It protects production environments from unstable or unreviewed code.

Example Workflow File for Java-Based Selenium Project

Below is a complete GitHub Actions workflow for a Java Selenium project that includes building, testing, linting, and security checks, with conditional deployment:

```
name: Java Selenium CI/CD Pipeline

on: [push, pull_request]
```

```yaml
jobs:
  build:
    runs-on: ubuntu-latest
    steps:
      - name: Check out the repository
        uses: actions/checkout@v2

      - name: Set up Java
        uses: actions/setup-java@v2
        with:
          java-version: '11'

      - name: Cache Maven dependencies
        uses: actions/cache@v2
        with:
          path: ~/.m2/repository
          key: ${{ runner.os }}-maven-${{ hashFiles('**/pom.xml') }}
          restore-keys: |
            ${{ runner.os }}-maven-

      - name: Build with Maven
        run: mvn -B clean install

      - name: Run Selenium Tests
        run: mvn test

      - name: Run SpotBugs
        run: mvn spotbugs:check

      - name: Run Dependency Check
        run: mvn org.owasp:dependency-check-maven:check

      - name: Deploy to Production
        if: github.ref == 'refs/heads/main' && success()
        run: ./deploy-script.sh
```

Workflow Breakdown

1. **Check Out the Repository**: Clones the repository for access to code.
2. **Set Up Java**: Installs Java 11 for compatibility with the Java Selenium project.
3. **Cache Maven Dependencies**: Saves time by caching dependencies, improving workflow efficiency.
4. **Build with Maven**: Compiles and builds the Java project.
5. **Run Selenium Tests**: Executes Selenium tests to ensure all UI functionalities work as expected.
6. **Run SpotBugs**: Performs static code analysis to catch potential bugs.
7. **Run Dependency Check**: Audits dependencies for known vulnerabilities, enhancing security.

8. **Deploy to Production**: Deploys only if the workflow passes on the main branch, protecting production from unreviewed code.

Additional Tips for Java-Based CI/CD with GitHub Actions

1. **Parallel Jobs for Faster Execution**: Run code quality checks (SpotBugs) and dependency checks (OWASP) as separate jobs that execute in parallel to speed up the workflow.
2. **Environment-Specific Variables**: Store sensitive information, such as API keys or database credentials, in GitHub Secrets, and reference them in your workflow.
3. **Custom Notifications**: Use slack or email notifications to alert teams on workflow completion or failures, ensuring prompt feedback in Agile environments.
4. **Test Coverage Reports**: Integrate tools like JaCoCo for test coverage and add a step to generate coverage reports, allowing the team to track and improve code coverage.

Challenges in Setting Up a CI/CD Pipeline with GitHub Actions for Java-Based Selenium **Projects and Solutions**

Implementing a CI/CD pipeline for Java-based Selenium projects using GitHub Actions can significantly enhance productivity and code quality, but it may come with its own set of challenges. Here are common obstacles teams might encounter, along with strategies to address them effectively.

1. Challenge: Long Build and Test Execution Times

Java-based projects with Selenium tests can have lengthy build and test times, especially if the project is large or tests require multiple browsers. This can lead to slower feedback loops and affect productivity, particularly in fast-paced Agile sprints.

Solutions

- **Use Caching**: Cache Maven dependencies to avoid downloading them in each workflow run, which can reduce execution time considerably.
-

```
- name: Cache Maven dependencies
  uses: actions/cache@v2
  with:

    path: ~/.m2/repository

    key: ${{ runner.os }}-maven-${{ hashFiles('**/pom.xml') }}
    restore-keys: |
      ${{ runner.os }}-maven-
```

- **Parallelize Tests**: Use GitHub Actions' matrix builds or parallel jobs to split tests across multiple environments, such as different browsers or OS versions. For example, Selenium tests for Chrome and Firefox can be run concurrently.
- **Selective Testing**: Run only the tests related to modified files by leveraging GitHub Actions filters and scripts to detect changes, which helps avoid running the entire test suite unnecessarily.

2. Challenge: Intermittent Test Failures Due to Selenium and WebDriver Instability

Selenium tests can sometimes fail intermittently due to WebDriver timeouts, slow network responses, or inconsistent element loading times. These issues can lead to false negatives, reducing confidence in the test results.

Solutions

- **Use Explicit Waits**: Replace implicit waits in Selenium scripts with explicit waits, which wait for specific elements to be ready. This approach is more reliable and minimizes false negatives.

```
WebDriverWait wait = new WebDriverWait(driver, Duration.ofSeconds(10));
WebElement element = wait.until(ExpectedConditions.
visibilityOfElementLocated(By.id("example")));
```

- **Implement Retry Logic**: Wrap flaky test cases in retry logic to re-run them a limited number of times if they fail. This approach can be implemented at the framework level with JUnit's @Retry annotation or custom code to detect and retry failures.
- **Use Headless Browsers**: Running tests in headless mode (without a UI) can reduce test execution time and network instability, especially for CI environments that don't require UI interactions.

3. Challenge: Difficulty in Debugging Workflow Failures

Debugging failures in GitHub Actions workflows can be challenging, especially when workflows involve multiple steps, external dependencies, or occur on remote environments that are not immediately accessible.

Solutions

- **Enable Step Debugging**: Set the ACTIONS_STEP_DEBUG secret to true to obtain verbose logs. Detailed logs provide more information for troubleshooting, helping to pinpoint issues in each workflow step.
- **Use Self-Hosted Runners for Local Testing**: Run workflows locally or with self-hosted GitHub Actions runners, which allows for better access and control. Use a tool like act, a CLI tool that enables running GitHub Actions locally for faster debugging.
- **Persist Artifacts for Debugging**: Save logs, screenshots, or reports as artifacts that can be downloaded and reviewed post-execution. For example, save Selenium screenshots on test failure for visual debugging:
-
```
- name: Upload Test Artifacts
  if: failure()
  uses: actions/upload-artifact@v2
  with:

    name: selenium-screenshots

    path: path/to/screenshots
```

4. Challenge: Dependency Management and Security Vulnerabilities

Java projects often depend on multiple libraries, some of which may have vulnerabilities or become outdated. Regularly managing and updating these dependencies can be complex and time-consuming.

Solutions

- **Automated Dependency Checks**: Use OWASP Dependency-Check in the GitHub Actions workflow to scan for known vulnerabilities in project dependencies. This ensures that potential security risks are flagged and mitigated before deployment.
-
```
- name: Run Dependency Check
  run: mvn org.owasp:dependency-check-maven:check
```
- **Dependabot Integration**: Enable GitHub Dependabot to automatically monitor dependencies and create pull requests when new versions are available. Dependabot keeps dependencies up-to-date, reducing the likelihood of vulnerabilities.

- **Audit Dependency Versions**: Use Maven Enforcer Plugin to enforce dependency versions and avoid conflicts or outdated versions. Add the plugin to the project's pom.xml and specify version rules.

5. Challenge: Handling Secrets and Sensitive Information Securely

CI/CD pipelines often require access to sensitive information, such as API keys, credentials, or database URLs. Mismanagement of these secrets can lead to security risks if they are exposed.

Solutions

- **Store Secrets in GitHub Secrets**: Use GitHub's encrypted secrets management to store sensitive information. This ensures that sensitive data is kept secure and accessed only by authorized workflows.

```
- name: Access API Key
  env:

    API_KEY: ${{ secrets.API_KEY }}

  run: echo "Using API Key"
```

- **Restrict Access by Environment**: Configure secrets specifically for production, staging, or development environments to avoid accidental exposure of production secrets in non-production workflows.
- **Rotate Secrets Regularly**: Implement a policy for regular rotation of secrets, especially for critical keys. Update the secrets in GitHub and inform relevant team members about the rotation policy.

6. Challenge: Inconsistent Browser and WebDriver Versions

In Selenium projects, compatibility between WebDriver and browser versions is crucial. Mismatched versions can lead to failures in CI/CD pipelines and inconsistent test results.

Solutions

- **Use Selenium Docker Images**: Use prebuilt Selenium Docker images that bundle specific browser and WebDriver versions, ensuring compatibility and reducing setup time. Specify the image versions in the Docker configuration file.

```
services:

  selenium:

    image: selenium/standalone-chrome:latest
    ports:
      - 4444:4444
```

- **Pin Browser and Driver Versions**: In environments where Docker isn't used, explicitly set browser and driver versions. Use tools like WebDriverManager, which automatically synchronizes driver versions with installed browsers.

```
WebDriverManager.chromedriver().setup();
WebDriver driver = new ChromeDriver();
```

7. Challenge: Managing Resource Constraints on GitHub's Free Tier

For projects on GitHub's free plan, there are limitations on the number of concurrent jobs and total usage minutes, which can slow down or interrupt workflows for large or resource-intensive projects.

Solutions

- **Optimize Workflow Triggers**: Use GitHub Actions filters to run workflows only on necessary events, such as changes to specific directories or files. This can save CI/CD minutes by avoiding redundant workflow executions.

```
on:

  push:

    paths:

      - 'src/**'

      - 'tests/**'
```

- **Use Self-Hosted Runners**: Self-hosted runners allow for unlimited workflow execution time without affecting GitHub's usage quotas. They provide greater control and are cost-effective for resource-intensive projects.
- **Cache Dependencies and Artifacts**: Reuse dependencies and test artifacts by caching them between runs. This approach reduces time and resource usage, as dependencies don't need to be re-downloaded for each workflow.

8. Challenge: Integrating Parallel Workflows and Conditional Deployments

Configuring conditional workflows and parallel jobs for Agile pipelines can become complex, especially for projects that need multi-environment testing or staged deployment.

Solutions

- **Use Job Dependencies**: Define dependencies between jobs to create conditional workflows. For example, deployment jobs can depend on successful completion of build and test jobs.

```
jobs:

  build:

    runs-on: ubuntu-latest
    steps: [ ... ]
  deploy:

    needs: build

    runs-on: ubuntu-latest
    if: github.ref == 'refs/heads/main' && success()
    steps: [ ... ]
```

- **Define Conditional Deployments by Branch**: Only allow deployment jobs to run on specific branches (e.g., main or release). This reduces the risk of unintentional deployments and ensures only stable code is deployed.
- **Use Matrix Builds for Parallel Testing**: Set up matrix builds to run tests across different environments simultaneously. This configuration allows the team to test on multiple browser/OS configurations without slowing down the workflow.

In a Nutshell

Setting up a robust CI/CD pipeline for Java-based Selenium projects on GitHub Actions requires attention to potential challenges like execution time, test stability, dependency management, and security. By leveraging caching, parallelization, conditional workflows, and best practices for handling secrets, teams can build efficient, scalable pipelines. These strategies ensure the CI/CD pipeline supports the rapid iteration cycles of Agile development, delivering timely feedback, maintaining high code quality, and reducing risks in deployment.

Jenkins Integration: Scheduling Selenium Tests for Automated Testing

Jenkins is a powerful CI/CD tool that supports scheduling and automating tasks, making it ideal for running Selenium tests regularly. Automated test scheduling helps Agile teams maintain application stability by ensuring that regressions or issues are caught early, especially in large-scale projects where changes are frequent. By setting up Jenkins to run Selenium tests on a schedule, teams can ensure continuous quality assurance even outside of active development cycles.

This section covers the process of setting up a Jenkins job to automate Selenium test execution with a scheduled pipeline, including steps for setting up a Selenium Grid with Docker, managing code retrieval, and handling test execution and cleanup. Additionally, we address common challenges and offer solutions to overcome them.

Understanding CI/CD and Setting Up a Jenkins Job

A Jenkins job enables the automation of repetitive tasks, such as building, testing, and deploying code. With Jenkins, these tasks can be orchestrated to run in sequence, providing reliable results and reducing manual intervention. Here's how to set up and configure Jenkins for scheduled Selenium testing:

1. **Install Jenkins**: Ensure Jenkins is installed and accessible. You can install it on a local machine or set it up on a dedicated server.
2. **Install Required Plugins**: Install the following plugins:
   - **Git Plugin**: Enables Jenkins to pull code directly from Git repositories.
   - **Pipeline Plugin**: Allows Jenkins to define and run declarative pipelines, which makes managing complex jobs easier.
   - **Docker Plugin**: Required if using Docker for containerized environments, such as setting up Selenium Grids.
3. **Set Up Jenkins Job**: In Jenkins, create a new pipeline job, naming it appropriately (e.g., "Scheduled Selenium Tests"). Set the job to run as a pipeline and configure it to use a Jenkinsfile, where you define the CI/CD pipeline stages.

Creating a Jenkins Pipeline for Automated Testing with Scheduling

Using a Jenkinsfile, you can define an end-to-end pipeline for scheduled Selenium testing. This file contains configuration for scheduling, pulling code, setting up the Selenium Grid, executing tests, and cleaning up the environment.

Here's an example Jenkinsfile configuration:

groovy

```
pipeline {
    agent any
    triggers {
```

```groovy
        cron('H 0 * * *') // Schedule the job to run every day at midnight (H
uses hash value of the job name for better system load management and assigns
a value between 0-59 to the minute)
    }
    stages {
        stage('Checkout Code') {
            steps {
                git url: 'https://github.com/your-repo.git' // Pull the latest
code from Git repository
            }
        }
        stage('Setup Selenium Grid') {
            steps {
                sh 'docker-compose up -d' // Launch Selenium Grid with Docker-
Compose
            }
        }
        stage('Run Selenium Tests') {
            steps {
                sh 'mvn clean test' // Execute Selenium tests using Maven
            }
        }
        stage('Tear Down Selenium Grid') {
            steps {
                sh 'docker-compose down' // Stop and remove Docker containers
to free resources
            }
        }
    }
}
```

Explanation of Pipeline Stages

1. **Checkout Code**: The git command pulls the latest code from the specified Git repository, ensuring that the tests run on the latest version of the codebase.
2. **Setup Selenium Grid**: This stage uses Docker-Compose to start a Selenium Grid environment. The grid configuration, specified in the `docker-compose.yml` file, typically includes a hub container and browser nodes (e.g., Chrome, Firefox). This setup allows tests to run in a stable, controlled environment.
3. **Run Selenium Tests**: Maven commands (`mvn clean test`) are used to execute the test suite. TestNG tests, defined in the project, run on the configured Selenium Grid, allowing parallel execution across different browsers if needed.
4. **Tear Down Selenium Grid**: After test execution, this stage stops and removes Docker containers using docker-compose down. This step ensures that resources are freed and prevents containers from being left running, which could consume unnecessary resources.

Scheduling Selenium TestNG Tests with Jenkins CI/CD Tool

Using the cron syntax in Jenkins, you can set up recurring schedules for the job. In the example above, `cron('H 0 * * *')` schedules the job to run at midnight every day. This automation provides several benefits:

- **Regular Regression Testing**: Scheduled tests catch regressions early, ensuring that new code doesn't break existing functionality.
- **Reduced Manual Intervention**: With scheduling, tests run consistently without requiring manual initiation, improving reliability in detecting issues.
- **Time-Saving for Teams**: Running tests off-peak hours (e.g., nightly) allows developers to start each day with up-to-date test results, accelerating debugging and issue resolution.

Running Selenium Tests via Command Line and Jenkins

For flexibility, you can run Selenium tests through both the command line and Jenkins:

1. **Running Tests from the Command Line**:
   - Use `mvn clean test` to execute tests locally. This command is useful for local debugging or validation before pushing changes to Git.
   - If using Docker, run docker-compose up to set up the Selenium Grid and docker-compose down to stop it after tests.
2. **Running Tests in Jenkins**:
   - Jenkins automates the entire pipeline using the Jenkinsfile. Once configured, Jenkins pulls the latest code, sets up the environment, executes tests, and cleans up, providing results without manual input.
   - Jenkins logs every step, enabling you to monitor pipeline stages and troubleshoot issues when tests fail.

Key Challenges and Solutions

Implementing a CI/CD pipeline in Jenkins for Selenium testing comes with a few common challenges. Here's a breakdown of these issues and methods to overcome them.

1. Challenge: Long Test Execution Times

Large test suites or high numbers of test cases can lead to long execution times, delaying feedback and increasing resource usage.

Solutions

- **Parallel Test Execution**: Use TestNG's parallel execution settings to run tests concurrently across different browser nodes in the Selenium Grid. Modify the testng.xml configuration to enable parallel testing.
- **Selective Test Execution**: Only run specific tests if changes are limited to a certain module or functionality. Configure the Jenkins pipeline to pass specific test classes or methods to `mvn test` command based on code changes.
- **Distributed Testing**: For very large test suites, consider using multiple Jenkins agents to distribute testing. Each agent can run a subset of tests, aggregating results for a complete overview.

2. Challenge: Intermittent Test Failures Due to Browser or Network Issues

Selenium tests can sometimes fail due to flaky test behavior, network issues, or timing problems, leading to unreliable results and reduced trust in the pipeline.

Solutions

- **Implement Explicit Waits**: Avoid using implicit waits in Selenium tests; instead, apply explicit waits to handle dynamic elements that may take time to load.
- **Retry Mechanism**: Use TestNG's `@Retry` or similar retry mechanisms for flaky tests. Retries reduce false failures due to network glitches or transient issues.
- **Headless Mode for Consistency**: Running tests in headless mode can eliminate UI rendering differences and stabilize test behavior in CI environments.

3. Challenge: Managing Environment Setup and Clean-up

Setting up and tearing down a Selenium Grid with Docker can lead to resource overhead, and leaving containers running accidentally can consume server resources.

Solutions

- **Automate Clean-up**: Use docker-compose down in the pipeline to stop and remove containers immediately after test execution. Additionally, set resource limits in Docker to prevent containers from overconsuming resources.
- **Use Jenkins Post-Build Actions**: Use Jenkins pipeline's post block to add clean-up commands that run after every build, regardless of success or failure. This ensures that clean-up happens even if tests fail.

```
post {
    always {
        sh 'docker-compose down'
    }
}
```

4. Challenge: Difficulty in Debugging Failures

Debugging issues in Jenkins can be challenging, especially when logs are extensive or when failures occur in containerized environments.

Solutions

- **Enable Detailed Logging**: Add detailed logging in Selenium scripts to capture element states, URLs, and other test parameters. This information aids in understanding why tests fail in certain environments.
- **Persist Test Artifacts**: Save screenshots, logs, and HTML dumps as artifacts in Jenkins. Use the `archiveArtifacts` step in the Jenkins pipeline to retain these resources, allowing for post-execution analysis.

```
archiveArtifacts artifacts: 'path/to/screenshots/*'
```

- **Use Remote Debugging**: Set up remote debugging on Selenium nodes to troubleshoot complex issues interactively. This approach can be helpful for inspecting browser state in cases of failure.

5. Challenge: Managing Browser and WebDriver Compatibility

Mismatched browser and WebDriver versions can lead to test failures, especially when Selenium or WebDriver updates.

Solutions

- **Pin Specific Versions**: Define specific versions of browsers and WebDrivers in the Docker configuration. For example, use selenium/standalone-chrome:latest to ensure Chrome and its driver remain synchronized.

- **Use WebDriverManager**: For local testing environments or non-Docker setups, use WebDriverManager to automatically manage compatible WebDriver versions.

```
WebDriverManager.chromedriver().setup();
WebDriver driver = new ChromeDriver();
```

- **Regular Version Validation**: Schedule periodic checks or tests to validate that browsers and WebDrivers are compatible with the current tests.

6. Challenge: Resource Constraints on Jenkins Server

Running resource-intensive jobs on a single Jenkins server can cause system overload, resulting in slow pipeline execution and potential instability.

Solutions

- **Distributed Build Environment**: Set up multiple Jenkins agents on separate machines or containers, allowing the workload to be distributed. This setup reduces strain on any single server and improves pipeline efficiency.
- **Resource Allocation and Limits**: Limit the resources Docker containers can use by setting CPU and memory limits in the `docker-compose.yml` file. This prevents containers from consuming excessive resources on the Jenkins server.

```
services:

  selenium-hub:

    image: selenium/hub
    deploy:

      resources:

        limits:

          cpus: "0.5"

          memory: "512M"
```

In a Nutshell

Setting up a Jenkins CI/CD pipeline for scheduling Selenium tests enables Agile teams to continuously verify application stability, catch regressions early, and ensure consistent quality. By leveraging Jenkins' capabilities for automated scheduling, Dockerized Selenium Grids, and a robust pipeline, teams can build a reliable testing environment that supports continuous integration and deployment.

Addressing challenges such as long execution times, flaky tests, debugging complexities, and resource management further enhances the CI/CD pipeline's stability and efficiency. Implementing the solutions outlined above provides a sustainable approach to maintaining high-quality software with minimal manual intervention, enabling Agile teams to focus on new features and improvements.

Continuous Integration in Agile Sprints: Challenges and Solutions

In Agile development, continuous integration (CI) is a cornerstone practice that supports rapid iterations by ensuring code quality and application stability as new changes are introduced. As Agile teams often work in short sprints with multiple developers contributing daily, CI helps detect conflicts, errors, and integration issues early. CI in Agile sprints emphasizes in-sprint automation, where automated builds and tests provide immediate feedback to developers, allowing them to make fast, informed adjustments.

However, the Agile approach to CI brings specific challenges, such as handling frequent code changes, managing lengthy test suites, and optimizing testing speed without sacrificing thoroughness. This section explores these challenges in detail and provides solutions using parallel testing, critical path testing, and Jenkins pipeline configuration to optimize CI for Agile sprints.

Key Challenges in Continuous Integration for Agile Sprints

1. Challenge: Frequent Code Changes

- In Agile sprints, development cycles are short, and code changes are frequent, often multiple times a day. With numerous developers working on different parts of the codebase, the risk of code conflicts, integration issues, or broken features increases.
- Rapidly evolving code can lead to errors that might not be immediately apparent, creating a bottleneck if unresolved issues accumulate.

2. Challenge: Lengthy Test Suites

- Comprehensive test suites are essential to ensure application stability, but running the entire suite with every change is time-consuming and resource-intensive.
- Lengthy test execution times can disrupt the development flow, delaying feedback for developers and slowing down the sprint's overall pace.
- Especially in Agile environments where iterations are short and decisions need to be made swiftly, lengthy test suites can hinder progress.

Solutions to Address CI Challenges in Agile Sprints

To overcome these challenges, Agile teams can implement parallel test execution, critical path testing, and efficient pipeline management. These practices speed up testing, reduce bottlenecks, and provide critical feedback without sacrificing test coverage or code quality.

1. Parallel Test Execution

Parallel test execution allows teams to divide the test suite into smaller groups and run these tests concurrently, effectively reducing overall testing time and improving the speed of feedback. By distributing tests across multiple stages or resources, CI pipelines can complete testing faster without compromising on thoroughness.

Implementing Parallel Test Execution in Jenkins Pipeline

In a Jenkins pipeline, you can configure parallel stages to split test execution into different categories, such as UI and API tests. This setup allows tests to run simultaneously, maximizing resource utilization.

```
pipeline {
  agent any
  stages {
      stage('Parallel Tests') {
          parallel {
              stage('UI Tests') {
                  steps {
                      sh 'mvn test -Dgroup=ui' // Run UI-specific tests
                  }
              }
              stage('API Tests') {
```

```
            steps {
                sh 'mvn test -Dgroup=api' // Run API-specific tests
            }
        }
    }
  }
}
```

Explanation:

- **Parallel Stages**: The parallel block enables UI Tests and API Tests to run at the same time, reducing the overall test execution time.
- **Test Categorization**: Tests are categorized into UI and API groups, each handling specific types of tests. This division allows faster execution and makes it easier to identify issues within specific parts of the application.

Benefits in Agile Sprints

- **Immediate Feedback**: Faster test execution means that developers receive feedback sooner, enabling them to address issues within the same sprint.
- **Improved Resource Efficiency**: Parallel testing uses Jenkins agents more effectively, reducing idle time and maximizing throughput.

2. Critical Path Testing

In Agile sprints, where development moves quickly, not all tests need to run with every commit. Critical path testing allows teams to prioritize essential tests that validate core functionalities on every commit while reserving full regression tests for scheduled runs. This approach accelerates CI without compromising on critical coverage.

Key Steps in Critical Path Testing

1. **Identify Critical Tests**: Determine which tests cover the most important application functionality (e.g., login, checkout, payment). These tests should run on every code commit to ensure core features remain stable.
2. **Schedule Full Regression Runs**: Run full regression tests at specific times, such as nightly or at the end of a sprint. This setup ensures thorough testing while reducing the need for every test to run on each commit.

Implementing Critical Path Testing in Jenkins

In Jenkins, you can configure separate test stages or jobs to handle critical tests and full regression tests. Using pipeline conditions, Jenkins can trigger specific stages based on branch, time, or other criteria.

```
pipeline {
  agent any
  stages {
      stage('Critical Tests') {
          steps {
              sh 'mvn test -Dgroup=critical' // Run essential tests only
```

```
                }
            }
        stage('Full Regression Tests') {
            when {
                branch 'main' // Run on main branch or scheduled time
            }
            steps {
                sh 'mvn test' // Run all tests in the suite
            }
        }
    }
}
```

Explanation:

- **Conditional Execution**: The when directive ensures that full regression tests only run on the main branch or at scheduled times, saving time on feature branches.
- **Critical vs. Full Testing**: Separating critical tests from the full suite allows critical tests to run quickly and frequently, while the full suite runs less often but ensures comprehensive coverage.

Benefits in Agile Sprints

- **Reduced Cycle Time**: By limiting tests on every commit to critical tests, developers receive feedback more quickly, avoiding delays from non-essential tests.
- **Efficient Resource Use**: Running the full suite less frequently conserves resources and avoids redundant testing of unaffected code areas.

3.   Implementing Parallel and Critical Path Testing in Jenkins Pipeline

Combining parallel execution with critical path testing can optimize CI pipelines in Agile sprints by reducing execution time and prioritizing key tests. Here's an example Jenkins pipeline configuration that uses both techniques:

```
pipeline {
  agent any
  stages {
      stage('Parallel Tests') {
          parallel {
              stage('Critical UI Tests') {
                  steps {
                      sh 'mvn test -Dgroup=ui -Dgroup=critical' // Run critical
UI tests only
                  }
              }
              stage('Critical API Tests') {
                  steps {
                      sh 'mvn test -Dgroup=api -Dgroup=critical' // Run critical
API tests only
                  }
```

```
                }
            }
        }
        stage('Full Regression') {
            when {
                branch 'main'
            }
            steps {
                sh 'mvn test' // Run full regression suite on main branch or
scheduled time
            }
        }
    }
}
```

Explanation:

- **Critical Path in Parallel**: Critical UI and API tests are executed in parallel, providing immediate feedback on core functionalities without waiting for the entire suite.
- **Full Regression Trigger**: The full regression suite runs only on the main branch, saving time and resources during active development on feature branches.

Benefits for In-Sprint Automation

- **Faster Feedback for Developers**: Developers get feedback faster on critical features, allowing them to address issues within the sprint.
- **Balanced Resource Consumption**: Running the full regression only on main reduces resource strain during active development, optimizing CI for Agile needs.

Key Challenges and Solutions in Continuous Integration for Agile Sprints

Despite the benefits, implementing continuous integration in Agile sprints presents some unique challenges. Here's an overview of these challenges and how they can be effectively addressed.

1. Challenge: Managing Frequent Code Changes and Merge Conflicts

In Agile sprints, code is updated frequently, and multiple developers work on the same codebase. This can lead to conflicts or broken builds when changes are integrated.

Solutions

- **Feature Branches and Pull Requests**: Encourage the use of feature branches and pull requests for isolated development. Merge code only when feature-specific tests pass to avoid introducing unstable code.
- **Automated Merge Testing**: Use Jenkins or GitHub Actions to automatically test code on every pull request, preventing issues from being merged into the main branch.
- **Regular Rebase and Sync**: Encourage developers to rebase their branches with the latest main branch frequently to catch conflicts early.

2. Challenge: Long Execution Times Due to Large Test Suites

Running all tests on every change can slow down development, making it difficult to maintain rapid feedback cycles within short Agile sprints.

Solutions

- **Parallel Testing**: Use parallel execution to split tests across multiple stages, reducing overall run time. Configure Jenkins agents to handle different categories of tests (e.g., UI, API) concurrently.
- **Critical Path Testing**: Limit tests to critical functionalities for regular commits, and run full regression tests on scheduled times. This approach prioritizes essential tests, ensuring rapid feedback for high-impact areas.

3. Challenge: High Resource Consumption and Cost in CI/CD

Continuous testing and parallel execution can be resource-intensive, which might lead to high infrastructure costs and system strain, especially when managing multiple test environments.

Solutions

- **Optimized Scheduling**: Run full regression tests during off-peak hours (e.g., nightly), and limit tests on each commit to critical ones.
- **On-Demand Infrastructure**: Use cloud-based Jenkins agents that can scale up or down based on demand, reducing resource costs for non-essential tests.
- **Resource Constraints on Containers**: In Dockerized environments, apply resource limits to containers running Selenium or other resource-heavy tests to avoid overloading.

4. Challenge: Dealing with Flaky Tests and Inconsistent Results

Flaky tests—tests that sometimes pass and sometimes fail due to non-deterministic reasons—can erode confidence in CI results and slow down the Agile workflow.

Solutions

- **Root Cause Analysis for Flakiness**: Regularly analyze and refactor flaky tests, isolating causes like network issues, race conditions, or slow responses from third-party services.
- **Retry Logic for Critical Tests**: Implement retry mechanisms for critical tests, allowing tests to re-run up to a specified number of times before marking them as failed.
- **Headless Browser Mode for Stability**: Run Selenium tests in headless mode to reduce variability and improve test consistency.

In a Nutshell

Continuous integration in Agile sprints is essential for maintaining code quality, stability, and rapid feedback. By implementing parallel testing, critical path testing, and efficient pipeline management in Jenkins, Agile teams can optimize their CI pipelines to support in-sprint automation without overwhelming resources. Addressing challenges such as frequent code changes, long execution times, resource constraints, and flaky tests ensures a smooth, reliable CI process that aligns with Agile goals, enabling teams to deliver high-quality software efficiently.

Continuous Feedback Integration in CI/CD Pipelines for Agile Sprints

Continuous feedback is essential in Agile environments, particularly during in-sprint automation, where developers need immediate insights into their code's performance and stability. A well-designed CI/CD pipeline with real-time feedback mechanisms allows teams to identify and resolve issues as they arise, ensuring that development remains smooth and productive. Integrating notifications, monitoring, and performance analysis into CI/CD workflows with tools like Slack, Prometheus, Grafana, and New Relic can significantly improve Agile sprints by providing detailed insights and helping teams respond swiftly to changes in application behavior.

This section explains the importance of continuous feedback in Agile workflows, outlines how to set up real-time notifications and monitoring, and explores strategies for overcoming common challenges. In addition to Jenkins configuration for Slack notifications, we'll also delve into using Prometheus, Grafana, and New Relic for comprehensive monitoring of CI/CD performance.

Enhancing CI/CD with Continuous Feedback in Agile Sprints

Continuous feedback within CI/CD pipelines enables developers to be promptly notified about build or test failures, helping them address issues before they escalate. In Agile sprints, where speed and adaptability are paramount, integrating continuous feedback into CI/CD pipelines helps teams meet sprint goals, align with quality standards, and accelerate issue resolution.

Example Jenkins Pipeline for Continuous Feedback with Slack Notifications

Here's a sample Jenkins pipeline that sends Slack notifications upon build success or failure:

```
pipeline {
  agent any
  stages {
      stage('Build and Test') {
          steps {
              sh 'mvn clean install' // Build the project and run tests
          }
      }
  }
  post {
      success {
          slackSend(color: 'good', message: "Build Succeeded: ${env.JOB_NAME}
#${env.BUILD_NUMBER}") // Notify on success
      }
      failure {
          slackSend(color: 'danger', message: "Build Failed: ${env.JOB_NAME}
#${env.BUILD_NUMBER}") // Notify on failure
      }
  }
}
```

Explanation:

- **Build and Test Stage**: Executes `mvn clean install`, which cleans the project, and then compiles the code, runs tests, and builds the project.
- **Post-Build Notifications**:
  - **Success Notification**: A Slack message with a green indicator is sent upon build success, keeping the team informed.

○ **Failure Notification**: If the build fails, a red notification is sent, prompting developers to address the issue promptly.

Benefits for In-Sprint Automation

- **Immediate Awareness**: Real-time Slack notifications ensure that the team is instantly aware of build statuses, allowing for quick action if issues arise.
- **Transparency**: By sharing build results openly, all team members can track progress and align efforts to resolve any blockers.

Monitoring CI/CD Pipeline Performance with Prometheus, Grafana, and New Relic

Beyond immediate feedback, performance monitoring tools provide visibility into the CI/CD pipeline's efficiency and stability. Using tools like Prometheus, Grafana, and New Relic, teams can monitor test execution times, build performance, and resource usage, allowing them to address bottlenecks and improve efficiency.

Prometheus: Real-Time Metric Collection

Prometheus is an open-source monitoring tool that collects metrics from various sources, storing them in a time-series database for real-time analysis. It's especially useful for tracking CI/CD metrics in Jenkins, such as test execution time, job completion rates, and resource consumption.

Steps to Integrate Prometheus with Jenkins

1. **Install the Prometheus Plugin in Jenkins**:
   ○ Install the Jenkins Prometheus Metrics Plugin, which exposes Jenkins metrics at an endpoint that Prometheus can scrape.
2. **Configure Prometheus to Scrape Jenkins Metrics**:
   ○ Add the Jenkins endpoint to Prometheus's configuration file (prometheus.yml) to enable data collection (yaml):

```yaml
scrape_configs:

  - job_name: 'jenkins'

    metrics_path: '/prometheus'
    static_configs:
      - targets: ['<jenkins-url>:<port>']
```

3. **Define CI/CD Metrics**:
   ○ Use Prometheus to track critical CI/CD metrics, such as:
     - **Build Duration**: Measures the average time it takes for builds to complete.
     - **Test Execution Time**: Monitors how long it takes to execute tests.
     - **Success and Failure Rates**: Tracks the number of successful and failed builds over time.

Benefits of Prometheus in Agile Sprints

- **Real-Time Alerts**: Prometheus can trigger alerts if builds take longer than expected or if failure rates exceed a threshold, enabling proactive troubleshooting.
- **Granular Insights**: Prometheus offers detailed metrics, allowing teams to drill down into specific performance aspects, such as test duration, for optimization.

Grafana: Visualizing CI/CD Metrics

Grafana is a visualization tool that works with Prometheus to create dashboards, enabling teams to see real-time metrics briefly. By connecting Grafana to Prometheus, teams can build dashboards that display trends in CI/CD performance, such as build times, error rates, and resource usage.

Steps to Integrate Grafana with Prometheus

1. **Install Grafana**: Set up Grafana either locally or in the cloud, depending on your infrastructure.
2. **Connect Prometheus as a Data Source**:
   - In Grafana, add Prometheus as a data source by entering the Prometheus server URL.
3. **Create CI/CD Dashboards**:
   - Use Grafana's dashboard features to create visualizations, such as:
     - **Build Duration Dashboard**: Displays trends in average build duration, helping teams identify slowdowns.
     - **Failure Rate Trends**: Shows the ratio of failed builds to successful ones, indicating code stability.
     - **Resource Usage**: Visualizes CPU and memory consumption during builds, providing insight into infrastructure usage.

Benefits of Grafana in Agile Sprints

- **Visual Feedback**: Dashboards provide immediate visual feedback on pipeline performance, making it easy for teams to spot and address anomalies.
- **Performance Trend Analysis**: Over time, Grafana's historical views help teams identify patterns, such as increasing build durations, and optimize pipeline performance.

New Relic: Comprehensive Application and Pipeline Monitoring

New Relic provides end-to-end monitoring for applications and infrastructure, offering more advanced insights into CI/CD pipeline performance. By integrating New Relic with Jenkins, teams can monitor not only CI/CD metrics but also the performance of applications being tested, identifying performance regressions early in the development cycle.

Steps to Integrate New Relic with Jenkins

1. **Install New Relic Agents**:
   - Install New Relic agents on Jenkins servers or containers to monitor build and test environments.
2. **Set Up Custom CI/CD Monitoring**:
   - Use New Relic's custom events and logging to capture Jenkins build metrics and visualize them alongside application performance metrics.
3. **Define Alert Conditions**:
   - Configure alert conditions for build duration, error rates, or unusual resource spikes during CI/CD processes.

Benefits of New Relic in Agile Sprints

- **End-to-End Visibility**: New Relic monitors both the CI/CD pipeline and the application under test, allowing teams to detect performance regressions directly linked to recent code changes.
- **Detailed Performance Analysis**: New Relic's advanced analytics, such as transaction tracing and infrastructure monitoring, provide deeper insights, enabling teams to correlate build performance with application metrics.

Implementing Continuous Feedback for In-Sprint Automation

For Agile sprints, immediate feedback is critical to enable quick response times and minimize disruptions. Here's how continuous feedback can be effectively implemented with Slack notifications, Prometheus, Grafana, and New Relic:

1. **Real-Time Notifications for Builds and Tests**:
   - **Slack**: Notifications on build success or failure allow developers to stay informed and respond quickly. Slack provides the immediacy needed to support Agile workflows.
2. **Automated Code Quality Feedback**:
   - Integrate static analysis tools (e.g., SonarQube) and security checks (e.g., OWASP Dependency-Check) within the CI/CD pipeline, with results posted to Slack or emailed to the team.
3. **Real-Time Performance Monitoring**:
   - **Prometheus and Grafana** provide monitoring and visualization for Jenkins metrics, allowing teams to track CI/CD performance in real-time and spot trends.
   - **New Relic** extends monitoring to include application and infrastructure metrics, offering a broader perspective on how code changes impact application performance.

Key Challenges in Continuous Feedback Integration and Solutions

While continuous feedback integration offers numerous advantages, Agile teams may face several challenges. Here's how to address common obstacles in Agile CI/CD workflows.

1.   *Challenge: Excessive Notifications Leading to Alert Fatigue*

Excessive notifications for every build or test can lead to alert fatigue, where developers may overlook critical alerts due to the high volume.

Solutions

- **Threshold-Based Notifications**: Configure notifications to trigger only when specific conditions are met, such as failed builds or high resource consumption. For example, only notify when the build fails, reducing the number of non-critical alerts.
- **Channel Customization**: Use separate channels for different notifications (e.g., #ci-build-status for general builds and #ci-alerts for failures). This allows team members to monitor only the channels that are most relevant to them.
- **Periodic Summary Alerts**: Send summary notifications at the end of each day or sprint, providing a concise overview of CI/CD performance and any significant issues.

2.   *Challenge: Delayed Feedback Due to Long Execution Times*

Lengthy builds or test executions delay feedback, slowing down sprint velocity and responsiveness.

Solutions

- **Parallel Testing**: Use parallel execution to split tests across multiple agents, reducing build time.
- **Critical Path Testing**: Prioritize running essential tests for each commit and reserve the full regression suite for scheduled or nightly builds.
- **Incremental Builds**: Configure Jenkins to perform incremental builds, where only modified components are tested, speeding up the feedback loop.

3.   *Challenge: Effectively Analyzing Performance Data from Multiple Sources*

With tools like Prometheus, Grafana, and New Relic collecting data, it can be challenging to manage and derive actionable insights from various metrics.

Solutions

- **Define Core Metrics**: Identify essential metrics for Agile goals, such as build success rate, average test duration, and resource usage. Focus on metrics that directly impact sprint goals.
- **Unified Dashboards**: Use Grafana to combine metrics from Prometheus and New Relic into unified dashboards. Centralized visualization reduces the need to switch between tools, simplifying analysis.
- **Automated Reports**: Set up automated reports that compile key metrics at the end of each sprint. Summarized reports help teams reflect on CI/CD efficiency and identify areas for improvement.

4. Challenge: Ensuring Reliable Integrations and Dependency Management

Continuous feedback relies on external integrations, which can be prone to downtime or compatibility issues, affecting feedback consistency.

Solutions

- **Failover Notification Systems**: Set up alternative notification channels (e.g., email) that can serve as a fallback if Slack is unavailable, ensuring critical alerts still reach the team.
- **Redundant Monitoring**: Use multiple monitoring tools to cross-reference metrics (e.g., Prometheus for CI/CD and New Relic for application monitoring), ensuring consistent performance data.
- **Health Checks**: Schedule periodic health checks for external integrations to verify connectivity with Slack, Prometheus, Grafana, and New Relic. Alerts can be configured to notify when integration issues are detected, enabling quick resolution.

In a Nutshell

Integrating continuous feedback into CI/CD pipelines with Slack, Prometheus, Grafana, and New Relic helps Agile teams improve response times, maintain code quality, and streamline sprint processes. With real-time notifications, comprehensive monitoring, and data visualization, teams can track performance trends, optimize pipelines, and support rapid iterations.

- **CI/CD Pipelines for Agile Sprints**: Continuous feedback ensures developers receive instant updates on code quality, aligning with Agile's emphasis on adaptability and responsiveness. This is particularly valuable for in-sprint automation, where the goal is to respond to issues within the sprint.
- **Long-Term Optimization**: Continuous feedback enables iterative improvement of CI/CD processes. By gradually refining pipelines, monitoring performance, and automating key tasks, teams can achieve efficient and resilient CI/CD workflows that complement Agile objectives.

By integrating a balanced feedback loop that includes notifications, monitoring, and performance analysis, CI/CD pipelines can serve as powerful tools to support Agile development, helping teams meet sprint objectives efficiently while maintaining high standards for software quality.

CASE STUDIES

CASE STUDY 1: BUILDING AN INTEGRATED AUTOMATION FRAMEWORK FOR A FINANCIAL SERVICES PLATFORM

Scenario

A major financial services provider needed to deliver new features on an online banking platform while ensuring strict security, compliance, and reliability standards. The platform supported key financial operations, including user transactions, balance inquiries, fund transfers, and bill payments. Due to the sensitive nature of the data and the high volume of daily transactions, the organization faced stringent regulatory requirements, making robust, consistent testing a critical component of every release. The goal was to establish an in-sprint automation strategy that would integrate seamlessly within Agile sprints, maintain high standards of data protection, and meet compliance mandates.

Strategy and Setup

To tackle these needs, the organization adopted a multi-layered approach to testing that incorporated front-end, back-end, and database validation, with a strong focus on in-sprint automation for quick feedback and streamlined feature releases.

Multi-Layered Automation Framework

A comprehensive, multi-layered automation framework was developed to cover all facets of the application, including UI, API, and database. This structure allowed tests to run concurrently, validating the application from end to end.

1. ***UI Layer:***
   - **Tool Selection**: Selenium and TestNG were chosen for their compatibility with the financial services provider's technology stack and for their strong support for web-based test automation.
   - **Core Workflows**: The UI layer covered crucial workflows, including user login, fund transfers, transaction history viewing, and profile management.
   - **Framework Structure**: Using the Page Object Model (POM) approach, the UI tests were organized into reusable components, encapsulating UI elements and actions. This made the codebase modular, reducing duplication and enhancing maintainability.
   - **Accessibility and Cross-Browser Testing**: In addition to functional testing, the framework included accessibility tests to comply with industry standards, as well as cross-browser tests to ensure a consistent user experience across different platforms.

2. *API Layer:*
   - **Tool Selection**: REST Assured was chosen for API testing due to its robust capabilities for verifying RESTful services.
   - **Scope of API Testing**: Tests focused on core financial APIs, including those for transaction processing, data validation, and error handling. Tests covered API response times, data accuracy, and edge cases, such as invalid requests and rate limits.
   - **Security and Data Integrity**: API tests were designed to include security checks, ensuring data encryption and secure data transfer between services.

3. *Database Layer:*
   - **Tool Selection**: JDBC was used to run SQL queries for database validation.
   - **Data Validation**: Tests ensured that data entered through the UI and API layers was accurately reflected in the database. For example, a successful transaction in the UI was verified in the database to ensure consistency.
   - **Transaction Integrity**: Database tests validated transaction rollbacks in case of failures, ensuring that no partial transactions affected the financial records.

CI/CD Pipeline Using Jenkins and Docker

To facilitate continuous testing and deployment, a CI/CD pipeline was configured using Jenkins and Docker.

1. *Pipeline Structure:*
   - **Modular Pipelines**: Jenkins pipelines were segmented into distinct stages: UI testing, API testing, and database testing. This modular structure allowed each layer to run independently or in parallel, improving pipeline efficiency.
   - **Triggering Mechanism**: The pipeline was set to trigger automatically on every code commit, ensuring that new changes were tested as they were integrated. Nightly runs performed full regression tests, covering all application aspects.

2. *Parallel Test Execution:*
   - **Dockerized Test Environments**: Docker containers were used to replicate production-like environments for testing. Each pipeline stage had its dedicated Docker environment, ensuring consistency across UI, API, and database tests.
   - **Resource Efficiency**: Running tests in parallel across Docker containers allowed the team to reduce the total test execution time, enabling in-sprint feedback without interrupting the development workflow.

3. *Integration with Git for Version Control:*
   - **Branch-Specific Pipelines**: The team used feature branches for each development task, with Jenkins configured to run the relevant tests on every commit. Only stable branches (e.g., main) triggered full regression tests, while feature branches ran focused tests, maintaining high performance.

Continuous Feedback Using Prometheus, Grafana, and New Relic

To support Agile sprints, continuous feedback was integrated into the pipeline using monitoring and alerting tools. This provided visibility into CI/CD performance and allowed the team to track key metrics.

1. *Prometheus:*
   - **Real-Time Metric Collection**: Prometheus collected metrics from Jenkins on build duration, test execution times, and failure rates. Alerts were set for long-running builds or frequent test failures, allowing the team to identify and address bottlenecks.
   - **Customized Alerts**: Alerts were configured to notify the development team via Slack and email, ensuring they were promptly informed of any disruptions in the CI/CD pipeline.

2. *Grafana:*
   - **Dashboard Visualization**: Grafana was used to visualize Prometheus metrics in real time, displaying dashboards for build stability, test pass/fail rates, and performance trends.
   - **Stakeholder Access**: Grafana dashboards were accessible to stakeholders, including QA managers and project leads, providing a visual summary of the test and build pipeline performance.

3. *New Relic:*
   - **Performance Monitoring**: New Relic Application Performance Monitoring (APM) tracked the application's behavior in test environments, identifying potential performance issues under simulated user loads.
   - **Proactive Issue Detection**: New Relic alerts were configured to monitor memory usage, response times, and error rates. If issues arose during testing, they could be addressed within the sprint, preventing performance bottlenecks in production.

Key Challenges and Solutions

In this case study, the financial services provider encountered several specific challenges that were critical to address for successful in-sprint automation. Below, each challenge is paired with the tailored solution that helped overcome it.

1. *Challenge: Maintaining Test Data Consistency*

Financial data tests require fresh, consistent data for each cycle. However, repeatedly resetting sensitive data in a compliant manner was difficult due to privacy regulations.

Solutions: Automated Data Provisioning

- **Scripted Data Generation**: Custom scripts generated anonymized test data that met regulatory standards, ensuring compliance and consistency.
- **Environment Reset**: Docker containers were automatically reset after each test cycle, providing clean, isolated environments and maintaining data integrity across test runs.

2. *Challenge: Reducing Test Execution Time*

Running the entire regression suite during each sprint slowed down the feedback loop, conflicting with the Agile goal of rapid iteration.

Solutions: Critical Path Testing

- **Prioritization Strategy**: Critical transaction flows and high-impact areas were tested on every commit, providing targeted coverage for key functionalities.
- **Nightly Full Regression**: Full regression tests were scheduled to run nightly, ensuring comprehensive test coverage without blocking development workflows during active sprint hours.

3. Challenge: Ensuring Security Compliance

Testing environments that handle financial data needed to adhere to strict regulatory standards, including data protection, encryption, and access control.

Solutions: Containerized Environments with Docker

- **Environment Isolation**: Docker containers created isolated, production-like environments, meeting security and compliance requirements without impacting other test environments.
- **Consistent Test Environments**: Containers replicated the production environment closely, allowing tests to be run in a secure, compliant setup that minimized the risk of data breaches or regulatory violations.

4. Challenge: Accelerating Feedback Loop for Developers

Developers needed near-instant feedback on builds to reduce rework and align with Agile sprint timelines. Traditional testing cycles created delays.

Solutions: Parallel Testing and Slack Notifications

- **Parallel Execution**: Jenkins was configured to run UI, API, and database tests in parallel across Docker containers, reducing the time needed to complete test cycles.
- **Real-Time Notifications**: Slack notifications were integrated to alert developers immediately on build status changes, ensuring timely action on issues and fostering a responsive development workflow.

5. Challenge: Maintaining Visibility and Transparency for Stakeholders

Project stakeholders needed real-time insights into test coverage, performance metrics, and CI/CD health to track project progress effectively and support decision-making.

Solutions: Continuous Feedback with Prometheus, Grafana, and New Relic

- **Real-Time Metrics via Prometheus**: Prometheus tracked metrics such as build duration and test success/failure rates, setting thresholds to alert the team on anomalies.
- **Visual Dashboards with Grafana**: Grafana dashboards provided visual representations of test progress, coverage, and pipeline stability, accessible to both development and stakeholder teams.
- **New Relic for Application Monitoring**: New Relic tracked application performance under test loads, identifying potential bottlenecks that could affect production and allowing preemptive optimization.

Outcomes

1. **Accelerated Feedback:**
    - Parallel testing, combined with automated Slack notifications, enabled developers to receive build feedback within minutes. This instant feedback loop reduced rework and enabled quicker decision-making within the sprint.

2. **Reduced Regression Time:**
    - By leveraging automation, the team reduced regression testing time by 60%, allowing more complex features to be integrated within the sprint timeline without delay.

3. **Enhanced Stability and Transparency:**
    - Continuous feedback via Prometheus and Grafana dashboards allowed proactive monitoring of test health, ensuring that build stability was maintained consistently. Stakeholders had real-time access to test progress and coverage, building trust and transparency.

End-to-End Solution and Sprint Workflow Integration

To integrate this framework seamlessly into Agile sprints, the solution incorporated stakeholder feedback and real-time demos:

1. ***End-to-End Workflow***
   - **User Story Preparation**: During sprint planning, user stories included clear acceptance criteria and defined automation requirements. Testers and developers collaborated to ensure alignment on test coverage for each feature.
   - **Test Automation as Part of Definition of Done (DoD)**: The Definition of Done included automation as a mandatory criterion, ensuring that every feature completed during the sprint was tested automatically.
   - **Demo and Stakeholder Feedback**: During sprint reviews, stakeholders viewed automated test results and were presented with visual dashboards in Grafana, illustrating test coverage and pass rates.

2. ***Collaboration with Product Owners***
   - **Acceptance Criteria Validation**: Product Owners validated the acceptance criteria with the test team, ensuring test cases met business requirements and provided a real-world perspective on functionality.
   - **Stakeholder Access to CI/CD Metrics**: Grafana dashboards gave stakeholders access to test progress, failure trends, and stability, allowing them to identify areas of concern.

3. ***Release Planning:***
   - **Continuous Release Readiness**: With automated testing integrated into the CI/CD pipeline, the team maintained a constant state of release readiness. Only builds that met all automated testing criteria and passed quality gates were promoted to production.
   - **Automated Reporting**: New Relic and Grafana automatically generated reports at the end of each sprint, capturing key metrics that informed release decisions and sprint retrospectives.

Key Takeaways

This case study highlights the benefits of implementing a multi-layered automation framework, parallelized testing, and continuous feedback to meet the demands of Agile sprints in a high-stakes financial environment. By integrating robust, automated testing and real-time feedback within sprints, the financial services provider could maintain product quality and compliance, reduce time-to-market for new features, and continuously enhance user trust and satisfaction.

CASE STUDY 2: STREAMLINED IN-SPRINT AUTOMATION FOR A GLOBAL E-COMMERCE PLATFORM

Scenario

A global e-commerce company needed an efficient in-sprint automation framework to support the rapid release of new features, such as improved payment gateways, dynamic inventory management, and optimized order processing. With high traffic volumes, frequent deployments, and a need to maintain a seamless user experience, the company faced the challenge of implementing robust in-sprint automation within its Agile framework. Automation had to cover critical functional, non-functional, and performance tests, while providing timely feedback for continuous improvement.

Strategy and Setup

To achieve these goals, the e-commerce company implemented a hybrid automation framework and integrated continuous feedback mechanisms to streamline development, testing, and release processes within sprints.

Hybrid Automation Framework

The team created a hybrid framework that combined functional, non-functional, and performance testing. This approach provided comprehensive coverage of the platform's core features and performance, from front-end to back-end.

1. *Functional Testing Layer*
   - **Tool Selection**: Selenium and Cucumber were chosen for functional testing, allowing test scripts to be written in natural language, which facilitated communication with non-technical stakeholders.
   - **Core Workflows**: Tests covered critical workflows, such as product search, checkout, and payment processing, ensuring that the main user journeys functioned as expected.
   - **Cross-Browser and Device Testing**: To ensure consistency across platforms, the functional tests included compatibility checks for different browsers (e.g., Chrome, Firefox, Safari) and devices (e.g., mobile, tablet).

2. *Non-Functional Testing Layer*
   - **Load and Performance Testing**: JMeter was integrated to simulate high traffic volumes, ensuring the platform could handle peak load without degradation.
   - **Security Testing**: Automated scans using OWASP ZAP identified security vulnerabilities in the e-commerce application, ensuring compliance with data protection standards.
   - **Accessibility Testing**: Tests were added to validate WCAG accessibility standards, enhancing usability for all customers, including those with disabilities.

3. *API Testing Layer*
   - **Tool Selection**: Postman and REST Assured were used to automate tests for key APIs, covering functionalities like inventory updates, order processing, and user account management.
   - **Data Validation and Response Time Checks**: API tests included data validation and latency measurements, ensuring that APIs met response time thresholds critical for a smooth user experience.

CI/CD Pipeline Using GitHub Actions

The company opted for GitHub Actions as the CI/CD pipeline due to its native integration with GitHub, scalability, and flexibility for automating build, test, and deployment processes.

1. *Conditional Workflows*
   - **Build Verification Tests (BVTs)**: BVTs were configured to run automatically on every code commit, verifying essential workflows like checkout and payment. This allowed for immediate detection of issues that could affect critical user journeys.
   - **Selective Regression**: Full regression tests were scheduled nightly, covering the entire codebase to ensure stability while keeping in-sprint execution times short.

2. *Automated Code Quality Checks*
   - **Linting and Static Analysis**: Pre-built workflows from the GitHub Actions Marketplace were added to perform code linting and static analysis, detecting code quality issues and enforcing best practices.
   - **Security Scans**: Security checks were automated to scan dependencies for vulnerabilities, identifying risks in third-party libraries used in the platform.

3. *Parallel Execution*
   - **Functional and Performance Tests**: GitHub Actions was configured to run functional and performance tests in parallel, reducing overall test execution time and ensuring that critical issues were detected early in the development process.

Continuous Feedback and Monitoring with Prometheus, Grafana, and New Relic

For a global platform handling millions of users, monitoring tools were essential to ensure that performance and functionality met customer expectations. The company implemented continuous feedback using Prometheus, Grafana, and New Relic for comprehensive CI/CD monitoring and insights into application health.

1. *Prometheus*
   - **Real-Time Metrics Collection**: Prometheus collected metrics on build duration, test execution time, and resource usage, providing real-time insights into CI/CD performance.
   - **Alerting for Anomalies**: Thresholds were defined for key metrics (e.g., build time, error rates), and alerts were sent to the team when these limits were breached, allowing for immediate action.

2. *Grafana*
   - **Dashboard Visualization**: Grafana dashboards displayed real-time and historical trends, including build success rates, failure patterns, and performance statistics. These dashboards were accessible to both technical and non-technical stakeholders for full transparency.
   - **Stakeholder Insights**: Grafana's visualizations helped stakeholders monitor the health of the CI/CD pipeline and supported data-driven decisions regarding feature releases.

3. *New Relic*
   - **Application Monitoring**: New Relic APM provided end-to-end visibility into the platform's performance under test conditions, allowing the team to track application behavior, memory usage, and response times.

- ○ **Proactive Issue Detection**: New Relic alerted the team when application performance deviated from expected baselines, allowing developers to address potential production issues preemptively.

Key Challenges and Solutions

1.   Challenge: Handling High Traffic Volumes

Testing had to account for peak traffic conditions to ensure platform stability and responsiveness during high demand periods.

Solutions: Load and Performance Testing with JMeter

- **Realistic Traffic Simulation**: JMeter was configured to simulate high-traffic conditions, allowing the team to test performance under peak loads.
- **Performance Baselines and Alerts**: New Relic was used to establish performance baselines. Alerts were triggered if response times exceeded these baselines, helping the team identify bottlenecks early in the sprint.

2.   Challenge: Managing Dependency on External APIs

The platform relied on third-party APIs for critical functions like payment processing, shipping calculations, and inventory updates, introducing potential dependencies that could slow down testing.

Solutions: Mock Services for External APIs

- **API Mocking with Postman**: Mock services were created in Postman to simulate third-party APIs, allowing tests to run reliably without waiting on actual API responses.
- **Consistent API Response Testing**: These mocks were configured to mimic real API behavior, providing predictable responses that allowed for uninterrupted testing and better control over test outcomes.

3.   Challenge: Avoiding Alert Fatigue Among Developers

With many notifications being triggered during builds and tests, developers were becoming overwhelmed, which led to desensitization to alerts.

Solutions: Targeted Notifications with GitHub Actions

- **Critical-Only Notifications**: GitHub Actions was configured to send notifications only on critical events, such as test failures, major performance deviations, or security vulnerabilities.
- **Aggregated Summary Alerts**: At the end of each day, a summary of test results and CI/CD metrics was automatically sent to the team, allowing them to review key insights without being overwhelmed by real-time alerts.

4.   Challenge: Maintaining Data Consistency Across Tests

Test data was subject to frequent updates, creating the risk of data contamination and inconsistencies between test runs, especially in shared environments.

Solutions: Automated Data Provisioning and Environment Reset

- **Dynamic Test Data Creation**: Scripts were created to generate or refresh test data automatically, providing clean datasets for each test cycle.
- **Environment Reset Using Docker**: Docker containers were reset to their initial state at the end of each test run, ensuring a consistent environment and avoiding issues with outdated or corrupted data.

5. Challenge: Ensuring Cross-Browser and Device Compatibility

With a diverse user base, the platform had to be tested across various browsers and devices to ensure consistent functionality and performance.

Solutions: Cross-Browser Testing with Selenium Grid

- **Selenium Grid Setup**: Selenium Grid was configured to run parallel tests across multiple browsers and devices, ensuring compatibility and reducing execution time.
- **BrowserStack Integration for Mobile Testing**: BrowserStack was integrated to handle mobile device compatibility, covering different OS versions and screen sizes to replicate real user environments.

Outcomes

1. **Accelerated Feedback:**
   - Parallel test execution and real-time notifications enabled developers to receive rapid feedback on code changes, reducing the average time from code commit to feedback by 45%. This quick turnaround empowered teams to make adjustments within the sprint, maintaining Agile velocity.

2. **Enhanced Platform Stability:**
   - Regular performance testing using JMeter, coupled with New Relic monitoring, helped the team proactively address performance issues. This led to a 30% reduction in performance-related incidents, ensuring the platform remained responsive even during peak usage times.

3. **Improved Transparency and Collaboration:**
   - Grafana dashboards provided stakeholders with easy access to real-time CI/CD insights. Visualizations of build success rates, test coverage, and performance metrics fostered transparency, improving communication between development, QA, and business teams.

4. **Release Readiness with Continuous Monitoring:**
   - By continuously monitoring application performance and reliability through New Relic, the team maintained a state of release readiness. Only builds that passed all automated tests and met performance baselines were promoted to production, reducing the risk of post-release issues.

End-to-End Solution and Sprint Workflow Integration

This comprehensive approach was designed to integrate seamlessly with Agile sprints, providing continuous feedback and supporting efficient, high-quality releases:

1. *Planning and Preparation*
   - **User Stories with Automation Criteria**: During sprint planning, each user story included automation requirements. Developers and testers collaborated to identify automation priorities, ensuring that key scenarios were covered within the sprint.

- o **Definition of Done (DoD):** The DoD included automation testing for each feature, so a story could only be closed if its associated automated tests passed.

2. ***In-Sprint Execution***
- o **BVTs on Code Commits:** GitHub Actions automatically ran BVTs on each commit, giving developers immediate feedback on critical functionality. This kept the sprint on track and minimized last-minute bug fixes.
- o **Stakeholder Collaboration:** Stakeholders reviewed real-time dashboards in Grafana and participated in sprint reviews, allowing them to monitor progress and provide feedback on application performance.

3. ***Sprint Review and Release***
- o **Demo and Continuous Feedback:** During sprint demos, test results and performance metrics from Grafana dashboards were presented, giving stakeholders a clear view of progress and application stability.
- o **Automated Reporting:** At the end of each sprint, New Relic generated automated reports on application performance, uptime, and stability, which informed release readiness decisions.

Key Takeaways

By addressing the specific needs of a high-traffic e-commerce platform, the team was able to design an in-sprint automation strategy that supported rapid feature delivery without sacrificing quality. With effective test coverage, continuous feedback, and proactive monitoring, the company improved both development velocity and platform reliability, enabling a seamless user experience for customers worldwide.

CASE STUDY 3: AUTOMATING LEGACY SYSTEM TESTING FOR A HEALTHCARE PROVIDER

Scenario

A healthcare provider operating an older, legacy system faced the challenge of modernizing their testing approach to support Agile sprints. The system handled critical patient data and healthcare operations, including patient records, scheduling, billing, and reporting. With regulatory compliance requirements (such as HIPAA) and the complexity of the legacy codebase, implementing in-sprint automation was essential for enabling faster releases and improving quality. However, this had to be done without disrupting ongoing development efforts or compromising data privacy.

Strategy and Setup

To support Agile sprints, the healthcare provider adopted a multi-layered testing framework designed to incrementally automate the legacy system. The automation focused on UI, API, and database testing layers, each of which played a critical role in providing reliable feedback while maintaining compliance standards.

Custom Test Automation Framework

A custom framework was developed to handle the unique challenges of legacy code, combining Selenium, TestNG, REST Assured, and JDBC for comprehensive test coverage. This framework was built to work with the legacy system's structure while gradually increasing automation coverage in line with the sprint timelines.

1. *UI Layer*
   - **Tool Selection**: Selenium and TestNG were chosen to automate the legacy system's front end, allowing the team to cover key patient workflows, including login, record management, and report generation.
   - **Page Object Model (POM)**: The POM pattern was implemented to make the tests more modular and maintainable, given the legacy system's complex UI.
   - **Cross-Browser Testing**: Compatibility across different browsers was tested to accommodate the system's user base, which included various healthcare professionals accessing the system through different setups.

2. *API Layer*
   - **Tool Selection**: REST Assured was used to automate API testing, which was essential for validating data exchanges between healthcare services (e.g., billing, scheduling, and patient data retrieval).
   - **Data Accuracy and Validation**: API tests verified data accuracy and integrity, ensuring that each service maintained patient data consistency across the system.
   - **Security and Compliance Checks**: Automated tests ensured compliance with healthcare regulations by verifying data encryption and secure data handling in all API communications.

3. *Database Layer*
   - **Tool Selection**: JDBC was used to create SQL scripts that validated data stored in the database against expected outcomes from UI and API layers.
   - **Data Validation**: Database checks ensured that patient records, appointment schedules, and billing information were stored accurately and consistently in the database.
   - **Transaction Integrity**: Database tests verified that transactions (e.g., updates to patient records) were completed successfully and rolled back if errors occurred, maintaining data integrity and compliance with regulatory standards.

CI/CD Pipeline Using Jenkins and Docker

To support Agile workflows, a CI/CD pipeline was created using Jenkins for automated builds and Docker for consistent, isolated testing environments. This allowed testing to be seamlessly integrated into the development process, even with the complexities of the legacy system.

1. *Pipeline Structure*
   - **Modular Jenkins Pipelines**: The CI/CD pipeline was modular, with separate stages for UI, API, and database testing, making it easier to troubleshoot issues within each layer.
   - **Triggered on Code Commits**: The pipeline was set to run tests on each code commit to the main branch, ensuring that any code changes were validated immediately. Full regression tests were configured to run nightly to minimize impact on sprint timelines.

2. *Dockerized Test Environments*
   - **Legacy Environment Replication**: Docker containers were set up to mirror the legacy production environment, ensuring that tests were executed in environments that closely resembled production.
   - **Isolated Test Runs**: Each Jenkins build ran in a separate Docker container, allowing isolated, consistent test environments free from interference between tests.

3. Data Security and Compliance

- ○ **Data Anonymization Scripts**: Automated scripts anonymized patient data before tests, ensuring that test environments complied with data protection regulations (e.g., HIPAA).
- ○ **Automated Environment Reset**: At the end of each test cycle, containers were reset to their original state, providing a clean, compliant environment for the next test cycle.

Continuous Feedback with Prometheus, Grafana, and New Relic

Continuous monitoring was crucial for tracking the performance and stability of the legacy system, especially with the addition of new features. Prometheus, Grafana, and New Relic were used to provide feedback throughout the CI/CD pipeline.

1. Prometheus

- ○ **Real-Time Metrics Collection**: Prometheus collected data on build duration, test execution times, and resource usage, allowing the team to monitor the impact of automation on system performance.
- ○ **Compliance Monitoring**: Alerts were configured to track compliance issues, such as test durations exceeding specified limits, which could indicate inefficiencies or risks.

2. Grafana

- ○ **Dashboard Creation for Real-Time Monitoring**: Grafana dashboards displayed test results, pass/fail trends, and compliance status in real time. This visibility helped the team ensure adherence to regulatory requirements and maintain consistent test quality.
- ○ **Stakeholder Access**: Grafana dashboards were shared with compliance officers and project managers, providing transparency and enabling stakeholders to stay informed about testing outcomes.

3. New Relic

- ○ **Application Performance Monitoring (APM)**: New Relic APM tracked application performance metrics under test, identifying performance bottlenecks in the legacy system that could impact users.
- ○ **Proactive Issue ReSolutions**: By monitoring response times, memory usage, and error rates, New Relic helped the team proactively address potential issues that could affect system reliability and compliance.

Key Challenges and Solutions

1. Challenge: Handling Large Data Volumes in Tests

The legacy system involved complex data dependencies, with large volumes of patient and transaction data, making it difficult to set up fresh test environments and ensure data consistency.

Solutions: Automated Data Provisioning and Environment Reset

- **Automated Data Generation**: Scripts were created to automatically provision and anonymize test data, enabling fresh data for each test cycle without compromising compliance.
- **Dockerized Environment Reset**: Docker containers were reset after each test cycle, ensuring a clean environment and avoiding data contamination across test runs.

2.   Challenge: Ensuring Compliance with Health Regulations

Given the sensitivity of patient data, testing environments had to meet strict compliance standards, including HIPAA regulations for data privacy and security.

Solutions: Data Anonymization and Secure Containers

- **Automated Data Anonymization**: Data anonymization scripts ensured that test data was compliant with privacy regulations, allowing the use of real-world scenarios without exposing sensitive information.
- **Secure Docker Containers**: Test environments were containerized with secure configurations that isolated data, ensuring no unauthorized access to patient information and maintaining compliance with HIPAA standards.

3.   Challenge: Stabilizing Flaky Tests in a Legacy Environment

Initial automated tests were prone to failure due to the unpredictable nature of the legacy system, including inconsistent UI behaviors and dependencies on outdated libraries.

Solutions: Retry Logic and Stability Enhancements

- **Retry Mechanisms**: Retry logic was implemented in UI and API tests to handle intermittent failures, allowing tests to rerun automatically if they failed on the first attempt.
- **Cleanup Scripts for Environment Stability**: Scripts were developed to reset application states between tests, minimizing flaky test behavior and ensuring consistency across test runs.

4.   Challenge: Gradually Increasing Test Coverage Without Slowing Down Sprints

The legacy system had minimal test coverage initially, and adding automated tests incrementally risked slowing down sprint timelines.

Solutions: Incremental Coverage Expansion with Priority Focus

- **Critical Path Testing First**: High-priority workflows, such as patient record updates and appointment scheduling, were automated first to provide immediate value and mitigate high-risk areas.
- **Progressive Coverage Expansion**: Additional tests were added gradually, based on risk assessment, ensuring that the testing framework expanded without overwhelming the sprint workflow.

5.   Challenge: Maintaining Visibility and Transparency with Compliance Teams

Compliance teams needed real-time visibility into test results and system health to ensure adherence to regulatory requirements and data security standards.

Solutions: Continuous Feedback and Dashboard Access

- **Prometheus and Grafana Dashboards**: Real-time dashboards provided compliance teams with insight into testing progress, pass/fail rates, and any compliance-related alerts.
- **Automated Compliance Reports**: Reports generated at the end of each sprint summarized test outcomes and compliance status, helping compliance officers track adherence to regulatory standards and document test history.

Outcomes

1. **Accelerated Feedback Loop for Developers*:***
   - The automation framework provided real-time feedback via Jenkins and Slack notifications, allowing developers to receive immediate insights on build status and test results. This reduced the time required to detect and fix issues, aligning well with Agile sprint goals.

2. **Improved Data Compliance and Security*:***
   - Automated data anonymization and secure Docker containers ensured compliance with data privacy regulations, allowing the healthcare provider to use production-like data without risking sensitive information.

3. **Enhanced Test Stability and Reduced Flakiness*:***
   - The retry logic, cleanup scripts, and Dockerized environments stabilized previously flaky tests. This stability improved confidence in test results, reduced debugging time, and minimized false positives.

4. **Incremental Increase in Test Coverage*:***
   - By prioritizing critical path tests, the team achieved immediate test coverage in high-risk areas while gradually expanding to cover the full system. This incremental approach allowed for increased test coverage without slowing down the sprint workflow.

5. **Stakeholder and Compliance Engagement*:***
   - The use of Grafana and Prometheus for real-time dashboards empowered compliance teams and stakeholders with visibility into test performance, compliance status, and system health. This transparency facilitated collaboration and ensured that all teams had access to critical insights for informed decision-making.

End-to-End Solution and Sprint Workflow Integration

To integrate in-sprint automation with Agile processes, the solution incorporated compliance requirements, stakeholder feedback, and continuous monitoring throughout each sprint.

1. ***Sprint Planning and Story Preparation***
   - **User Stories with Automation Criteria**: Each user story included detailed acceptance criteria that outlined automation requirements. Testers and developers collaborated to identify the most critical features for automation.
   - **Definition of Done (DoD) with Compliance**: The Definition of Done included automated testing and data compliance, ensuring that each feature met regulatory standards before being marked as complete.

2. ***In-Sprint Execution and Continuous Feedback***
   - **Build Verification Tests (BVTs)**: Automated BVTs were configured to run on each code commit, focusing on critical workflows to provide immediate feedback on essential functionalities.
   - **Stakeholder Reviews with Grafana Dashboards**: Compliance officers and project managers reviewed Grafana dashboards during sprint reviews to monitor progress and validate compliance adherence.

3. *Release Readiness and Compliance Reporting*
   - **Automated Compliance Reports**: New Relic and Prometheus generated end-of-sprint reports summarizing test results, compliance status, and performance metrics. These reports provided documentation for compliance audits and release decisions.
   - **Final Release Checks**: Only builds that passed all automated tests, met performance baselines, and adhered to compliance standards were approved for release to production.

Key Takeaways

This case study demonstrates how a healthcare provider effectively modernized its testing approach for a legacy system, enabling in-sprint automation that met Agile and regulatory needs. By implementing a custom framework, prioritizing critical tests, and continuously monitoring compliance, the healthcare provider achieved rapid feedback, improved data security, and enhanced collaboration with stakeholders. These practices resulted in a more efficient release cycle, improved product quality, and alignment with stringent healthcare regulations.

CASE STUDY 4: LEVERAGING GITHUB ACTIONS FOR IN-SPRINT BUILD VERIFICATION TESTS (BVTS) FOR A TECHNOLOGY STARTUP

Scenario

A technology startup developing a SaaS platform faced the challenge of maintaining rapid iteration cycles while ensuring software stability. The platform, designed for a large user base, required new features and updates to be deployed frequently without compromising performance or reliability. The startup's development team needed an efficient, in-sprint automation strategy to run build verification tests (BVTs) on every code commit, ensuring that only stable builds progressed to later stages of testing and deployment. GitHub Actions was chosen as the CI/CD platform due to its native integration with GitHub, ease of use, and support for automated workflows.

Strategy and Setup

To support the Agile framework, the team implemented an automation strategy focused on build verification tests (BVTs) within each sprint. The goal was to catch issues early, streamline feedback for developers, and ensure code quality without interrupting the rapid pace of development.

Automated Build Verification Test (BVT) Framework

The team created a lean BVT framework that prioritized essential test coverage and minimized execution time. This framework was designed to validate critical functionality, data integrity, and performance metrics on every code commit, ensuring a stable foundation for further development.

1. *BVT Scope and Structure*
   - **Functional Tests**: Key user workflows were covered by functional tests to verify essential actions, including login, data retrieval, and settings configurations.
   - **API Verification**: API tests were designed to validate core service responses, response times, and data accuracy, especially in high-use areas like account management and data analytics.
   - **Critical Path Testing**: Only the most essential tests were included in the BVTs, focusing on high-impact areas to reduce execution time while maximizing coverage.

2. ***Workflow Automation Using GitHub Actions***
    o **Modular Workflow Configuration**: GitHub Actions was set up with modular workflows that allowed the team to run specific tests based on the type of code change (e.g., BVTs on every commit, full regression testing nightly).
    o **Parallel Execution**: Tests were configured to run in parallel across multiple virtual environments, reducing test time and providing feedback in minutes.
    o **Triggered by Code Events**: The BVTs were set to trigger on every pull request and commit to the main branch, providing early feedback to developers.

3. ***Selective Regression Testing***
    o **Full Regression Tests on a Schedule**: While BVTs provided immediate feedback on core functionality, full regression tests were run nightly to ensure comprehensive test coverage without delaying active development within the sprint.
    o **Targeted Test Execution**: Specific tests related to the areas of recent changes were run in addition to BVTs, allowing for focused testing without unnecessary overhead.

CI/CD Pipeline and GitHub Actions Integration

The startup leveraged GitHub Actions to create a streamlined CI/CD pipeline that automated builds, BVTs, and deployments, while keeping code quality high.

1. ***Pipeline Structure***
    o **Build and Test Workflow**: The CI/CD pipeline included a dedicated workflow for building the application and running BVTs. Only if BVTs passed did the workflow proceed to deploy or trigger additional tests.
    o **Conditional Deployment**: Deployment to staging environments was conditional on the success of BVTs, ensuring only stable builds were pushed forward.

2. ***Automated Quality Checks and Static Analysis***
    o **Code Linting and Security Scans**: GitHub Actions workflows integrated pre-built static analysis and security checks, identifying code quality issues and potential vulnerabilities early in the development cycle.
    o **Dependency Checks**: GitHub Dependabot was configured to monitor and update dependencies, ensuring that any security patches were promptly applied to the codebase.

3. ***Parallel Testing Setup***
    o **Concurrent Test Execution**: GitHub Actions was configured to run functional and API tests in parallel across virtual environments, reducing total test execution time and ensuring that BVTs provided rapid feedback.

Continuous Feedback with Prometheus, Grafana, and New Relic

To support in-sprint automation and maintain platform reliability, the team implemented real-time monitoring tools to provide continuous feedback on application performance and CI/CD pipeline health.

1. ***Prometheus for CI/CD Monitoring***
    o **Pipeline Performance Metrics**: Prometheus collected data on build times, test pass/fail rates, and error counts, providing insights into the efficiency of the CI/CD pipeline.

- **Alerting for Anomalies**: Alerts were set to trigger if specific thresholds, such as extended test duration or high error rates, were exceeded. Alerts were routed to the development team for immediate action.

2. Grafana for Visual Dashboards
- **CI/CD Health Visualization**: Grafana dashboards visualized Prometheus metrics, displaying build success rates, test completion times, and error trends over time. This visibility allowed the team to spot patterns and optimize the CI/CD process.
- **Stakeholder Access**: Grafana dashboards provided stakeholders with real-time insights into build quality and CI/CD performance, improving transparency and fostering a data-driven decision-making culture.

3. New Relic for Application Performance
- **APM Integration for Performance Monitoring**: New Relic tracked application performance during BVTs, monitoring response times, memory usage, and error rates, which allowed the team to proactively detect and address issues.
- **Proactive Performance Alerts**: New Relic alerts were configured to notify the team of significant performance degradations or resource bottlenecks, enabling timely intervention and preventing issues from reaching production.

Key Challenges and Solutions

1. Challenge: Slow Feedback on Code Commits
Long feedback cycles on code commits were causing delays, as developers often had to wait for test results before moving forward.

Solutions: Parallel Execution and Modular BVTs
- **Concurrent Testing**: Tests were configured to run concurrently in GitHub Actions, allowing functional and API tests to execute simultaneously and significantly reducing overall feedback time.
- **Lean BVTs**: By focusing only on high-impact tests, the BVT suite was kept lean and quick, providing immediate feedback on critical functionality without overloading the pipeline.

2. Challenge: Managing Multiple Pipelines Efficiently
The startup needed to manage multiple pipelines for different branches and types of tests without creating bottlenecks.

Solutions: Conditional Workflows in GitHub Actions
- **Branch-Based Triggering**: Workflows were configured to trigger selectively based on branch type, with BVTs running on feature branches and full regression tests on the main branch and staging.
- **Environment-Specific Pipelines**: Separate workflows for development, staging, and production ensured that each pipeline was optimized for its respective environment, minimizing resource usage and avoiding unnecessary delays.

3. Challenge: Avoiding Bottlenecks in CI/CD During Peak Development
During peak development times, high volumes of automation tasks led to queuing, which delayed feedback and affected productivity.

Solutions: Targeted Workflow Scheduling and Priority-Based Execution

- **Workflow Scheduling**: Non-critical tests, such as full regression and performance tests, were scheduled to run during off-peak hours, while BVTs remained prioritized for real-time feedback.
- **Priority-Based Execution**: Tests critical to in-sprint goals, such as those validating recent code changes, were prioritized to ensure they ran immediately upon code commits, minimizing queue times and improving responsiveness.

4.   Challenge: Managing Dependencies and Third-Party Integrations

The application relied on third-party integrations, which could impact test results and CI/CD stability if those services were unavailable.

Solutions: Mocking External Services and Dependency Management

- **API Mocks in Postman**: Mock services were created to simulate third-party API responses, allowing tests to run reliably even if external services were down or experiencing delays.
- **Dependabot for Dependency Updates**: GitHub Dependabot was configured to monitor dependencies and automatically apply security updates, ensuring that the codebase remained secure without manual intervention.

5.   Challenge: Alert Fatigue from Overwhelming Notifications

Developers were experiencing alert fatigue due to frequent notifications from the CI/CD pipeline, leading to desensitization to important alerts.

Solutions: Selective Notifications and Aggregated Summaries

- **Critical Alerts Only**: Notifications were configured to trigger only on critical events, such as failed builds, failed BVTs, or major performance deviations. Non-critical alerts were suppressed to reduce noise.
- **Daily Summary Reports**: Automated daily reports summarized key metrics, including test pass rates, build stability, and any compliance concerns, allowing developers to review CI/CD health immediately without constant interruptions.

Outcomes

1.   Accelerated Feedback for Developers:
- Lean BVTs and parallel execution significantly reduced feedback time, with developers receiving test results in under 10 minutes per commit. This faster feedback loop enabled the team to quickly iterate and resolve issues within the sprint.

2.   Enhanced Platform Stability:
- The combination of critical path testing in BVTs and nightly full regressions ensured that only stable builds progressed, reducing the frequency of integration issues. Performance monitoring in New Relic further safeguarded platform stability by proactively detecting potential bottlenecks.

3.   Efficient Resource Management:
- Conditional workflows and off-peak test scheduling prevented resource bottlenecks during peak development times, optimizing CI/CD performance and ensuring timely feedback for high-priority tasks.

4. **Improved Transparency and Collaboration:**
   - Grafana dashboards made CI/CD metrics accessible to both developers and stakeholders, fostering transparency and data-driven decisions. Real-time insights into build stability and test coverage facilitated informed decision-making during sprint reviews and planning.

5. **Reliable Deployment Pipeline:**
   - GitHub Actions workflows provided a dependable, automated pipeline that maintained high code quality across environments. Only builds that passed automated BVTs and compliance checks were promoted to staging or production, reducing deployment risks.

End-to-End Solution and Sprint Workflow Integration

The in-sprint automation strategy was integrated directly into the Agile sprint workflow, supporting both rapid feedback and collaborative decision-making.

1. *Sprint Planning with Test Automation Criteria*
   - **User Story Preparation**: During sprint planning, automation criteria were defined for each user story. Developers and testers collaborated to identify critical BVTs required for feature validation, ensuring automation was included as part of the Definition of Done (DoD).
   - **Automation Ownership**: Testers and developers worked together to create BVTs for new features, with ownership clearly defined to streamline test updates and ensure alignment with sprint goals.

2. *In-Sprint Execution and Real-Time Feedback*
   - **BVT Execution on Commits**: Automated BVTs ran on each code commit, giving developers immediate feedback on stability. This continuous validation process allowed for timely course corrections within the sprint, maintaining Agile velocity.
   - **Stakeholder Visibility via Dashboards**: Stakeholders, including product managers and QA leads, reviewed test results and pipeline metrics in Grafana during sprint reviews, ensuring transparency and aligning team efforts with project goals.

3. *Release Readiness and Compliance Reporting*
   - **Automated Release Reporting**: New Relic and Prometheus generated end-of-sprint reports, summarizing test results, build stability, and application performance. This provided stakeholders with clear release readiness insights, allowing them to make informed deployment decisions.
   - **Final Approval Criteria**: Only builds that passed all BVTs and met performance benchmarks were considered for production deployment, reinforcing quality and minimizing the risk of post-release issues.

Key Takeaways

This case study illustrates how a technology startup successfully leveraged GitHub Actions for in-sprint automation, ensuring fast, reliable feedback on build quality and application performance. By focusing on lean, targeted BVTs, implementing continuous monitoring, and optimizing resource usage, the startup created a CI/CD pipeline that supported rapid iteration and stable releases. This in-sprint automation strategy enabled the team to scale efficiently, meet sprint goals, and maintain high product quality in a fast-paced development environment.

Top of Form

CONCLUSION: ACHIEVING MASTERY IN IN-SPRINT AUTOMATION FOR AGILE TESTING

As we conclude *In-Sprint Automation Mastery: Elevate Your Agile Testing Game*, it's clear that effective Agile testing goes beyond just executing automated scripts. It involves a strategic approach to integrating automation practices directly within each sprint, ensuring that every code change is validated and aligned with Agile's goal of continuous, high-quality delivery. This book provides a comprehensive roadmap-from foundational concepts to advanced strategies-for teams aiming to leverage in-sprint automation to improve efficiency, enhance collaboration, and reduce time-to-market.

RECAP OF KEY TAKEAWAYS

The journey through this book has been structured to cover every critical component of in-sprint automation. Here's a recap of the key lessons that can guide your team toward sustainable Agile testing practices.

1.   Understanding Agile and the Role of In-Sprint Automation

Agile is a framework rooted in flexibility, rapid feedback, and close collaboration. In-sprint automation reinforces these principles by ensuring that automated tests are part of every sprint, enabling teams to validate new code and features in real time. Automating within sprints not only accelerates feedback loops but also empowers teams to release reliable, tested code continuously.

2.   Establishing Core Agile Testing Principles

Agile testing isn't just about faster testing; it's about smart testing. Establishing principles such as defining clear user stories, setting achievable sprint goals, and cultivating a collaborative team culture forms the backbone of successful in-sprint automation. By embedding automation into Agile testing principles—like the Definition of Done (DoD) and continuous feedback—teams can maintain quality while staying aligned with project objectives.

3.   Building a Comprehensive Automation Framework

Developing a strong automation framework is essential for executing reliable and reusable tests that align with sprint objectives. From UI and API tests to database and security testing, frameworks like Selenium, TestNG, REST Assured, and more provide teams with the tools to validate every layer of the application. A well-structured automation framework with clear layers (such as application, testing, and configuration layers) improves modularity, scalability, and maintainability, making it easy to adapt to evolving requirements.

4. Leveraging TDD and BDD for Effective Test Coverage

Test-Driven Development (TDD) and Behavior-Driven Development (BDD) are invaluable practices for creating testable code that aligns with both technical and business requirements. TDD promotes code that is robust and easily validated, while BDD bridges the gap between business stakeholders and technical teams. By adopting TDD and BDD, teams ensure that automation is not just technical but meaningful, capturing real-world requirements directly in test scripts.

5. Implementing and Optimizing CI/CD Pipelines in Agile Sprints

A CI/CD pipeline is the lifeline of in-sprint automation. Tools like Jenkins, GitHub Actions, and Docker enable teams to automate build, test, and deployment processes, turning code into validated, deployable artifacts with each commit. By prioritizing critical path testing within the pipeline and scheduling full regression tests during off-hours, teams can optimize pipeline efficiency, maximize feedback speed, and maintain stability across rapid deployments.

6. Harnessing Continuous Feedback for Rapid Iteration

Real-time feedback is a cornerstone of Agile testing. Monitoring tools like Prometheus, Grafana, and New Relic provide immediate insights into CI/CD health and application performance, helping teams catch issues early and resolve them before they impact production. Continuous feedback, in the form of alerts, dashboards, and reports, allows developers, testers, and stakeholders to make informed, data-driven decisions in real time, reinforcing a culture of proactive quality management.

7. Adapting to Common Challenges with Targeted Solutions

Throughout the book, we discussed practical solutions to common challenges in in-sprint automation—whether handling large test data, integrating automation in legacy systems, managing test flakiness, or preventing alert fatigue. By implementing these targeted solutions, teams can adapt their automation practices to meet specific project needs, regardless of the complexity or unique demands of the environment.

ENCOURAGEMENT FOR CONTINUOUS LEARNING AND IMPROVEMENT

In-sprint automation is not a one-time achievement; it is a journey of continuous learning, experimentation, and refinement. As you integrate the practices outlined in this book, keep in mind that the field of Agile testing is always evolving. Staying at the forefront requires a commitment to continuous improvement, not only in technical practices but in team collaboration, tool evaluation, and process optimization.

To make the most of your in-sprint automation journey, consider these ongoing practices:

Embrace New Tools and Technologies

The landscape of test automation, CI/CD, and monitoring is constantly evolving. As new tools emerge, consider how they could enhance or streamline your automation processes. Whether it's exploring AI-driven test optimization, new CI/CD orchestration tools, or advanced monitoring solutions, being open to innovation will keep your automation practices efficient and effective.

Foster a Culture of Collaboration and Cross-Functional Communication

In-sprint automation is most successful when the entire team shares responsibility for quality. Encourage open lines of communication between developers, testers, and product owners to ensure alignment on goals, requirements, and test coverage. A collaborative culture strengthens the feedback loop, enabling faster issue resolution and fostering a shared sense of ownership over product quality.

Regularly Review and Refine Automation Processes

Just as Agile encourages continuous improvement in software, the automation framework itself should be continuously refined. Conduct retrospectives focused on automation performance, CI/CD efficiency, and test coverage, and look for areas to optimize. Small improvements over time can lead to significant gains in productivity and reliability, keeping your automation practices aligned with sprint goals.

Engage with the Testing Community for Inspiration and Insight

The automation and Agile testing communities are rich sources of knowledge, innovation, and practical advice. Attend conferences, participate in webinars, and engage in online forums to stay connected with industry trends. Learning from the experiences of others can inspire new approaches and provide solutions to challenges unique to your projects.

Commit to Documentation and Knowledge Sharing

Comprehensive documentation of automation practices, CI/CD configurations, and testing frameworks is essential for scalability and maintainability. Create a knowledge-sharing culture by documenting key learnings, successes, and improvements. This not only aids onboarding new team members but also ensures consistency as the team scales.

LOOKING AHEAD

In-sprint automation is a powerful enabler of Agile excellence. By embedding automation within the sprint structure, teams can ensure quality at every stage of the development lifecycle, reduce the risk of regressions, and meet the fast-paced demands of modern software delivery. This book has equipped you with the strategies, frameworks, and best practices to build an automation process that not only supports but enhances Agile workflows.

As you move forward, remember that in-sprint automation mastery is about blending technical expertise with a strategic mindset. Balancing the technical depth of testing with the collaborative, iterative spirit of Agile will help you deliver reliable software that meets both business and user needs. We hope this book has provided you with the insights, tools, and confidence to integrate in-sprint automation effectively, supporting your team's journey toward continuous improvement and Agile success.

APPENDIX A: LIST OF TOOLS AND RESOURCES

This appendix compiles a comprehensive list of tools across various categories essential for achieving effective in-sprint automation. Each tool and framework is chosen for its proven value in Agile testing and continuous integration, addressing key needs like automation, CI/CD, collaboration, and monitoring.

1. VERSION CONTROL SYSTEMS

Git Git is a distributed version control system widely used for tracking code changes and facilitating collaboration among development teams. In Agile environments, Git is crucial for managing branch workflows, enabling parallel development, and integrating with CI/CD pipelines.

- **Key Features**: Branching and merging, reversion capabilities, history tracking, and multi-environment support.
- **Best Practices:** Use feature branches and pull requests for code integration; set up automated triggers for builds and tests upon commit.
- **Popular Platforms**:
  - **GitHub**: Provides Git repository hosting with built-in CI/CD (GitHub Actions) and extensive project management tools for Agile teams.
  - **GitLab**: An all-in-one DevOps platform with robust CI/CD capabilities and integrated project tracking.
  - **Bitbucket**: Known for its integration with Jira and other Atlassian tools, offering Git repository hosting and CI/CD via Bitbucket Pipelines.

2. CONTINUUS INTEGRATION AND CONTINUOUS DEPLOYMENT (CI/CD) TOOLS

Jenkins Jenkins is a leading open-source automation server that enables teams to automate testing, build, and deployment processes. Its vast plugin ecosystem supports various integrations and customization options, making it a flexible choice for complex CI/CD pipelines.

- **Key Features**: Pipeline as code (Jenkinsfile), plugin ecosystem, parallel test execution, and extensive customization.
- **Best Practices:** Use Jenkins declarative pipelines for modular builds, automate test execution for build verification, and leverage Docker for consistent test environments.
- **Use Case**: Running scheduled tests, build verification, continuous integration, and staging deployments.
  GitHub Actions GitHub Actions provides native CI/CD within GitHub, allowing for event-driven workflows directly connected to repository actions (e.g., push, pull request).
- **Key Features**: GitHub-native CI/CD, GitHub Marketplace for pre-built actions, and parallel workflow capabilities.
- **Best Practices:** Integrate linting, security checks, and unit tests on commits; use Marketplace actions to streamline setup.

- **Use Case**: Automating test and build pipelines, continuous deployment, code quality checks, and compliance automation.

GitLab CI GitLab CI is integrated into GitLab and offers a seamless CI/CD experience with DevOps functionality, from code commit to deployment.
- **Key Features**: Containerized builds, integrated DevOps, built-in security scans, and custom runners.
- **Best Practices:** Use Auto DevOps for streamlined pipeline setup, configure runners for parallel execution, and monitor build efficiency.
- **Use Case**: Full DevOps lifecycle automation, combining CI/CD with Agile project tracking.

3. TEST AUTOMATION FRAMEWORKS

Selenium Selenium is a powerful tool for automating web applications, allowing teams to write tests in various languages and run them across different browsers. It is often integrated with other frameworks like TestNG and Cucumber for full-stack testing.
- **Key Features**: Cross-browser testing, remote execution via Selenium Grid, and integration with popular frameworks.
- **Best Practices:** Implement the Page Object Model (POM) to organize UI tests for better maintainability; use Selenium Grid for parallel execution.
- **Use Case**: Cross-browser UI testing of key workflows, including login, search, and checkout flows.

TestNG TestNG is a Java-based testing framework designed for flexibility in creating and managing test cases. It supports parallel execution, data-driven testing, and dependency management.
- **Key Features**: Annotations for defining test structure, grouping for related tests, and custom report generation.
- **Best Practices**: Leverage TestNG's XML configuration for suite execution, set up parallel tests for faster feedback, and use dependency injections for reusability.
- **Use Case**: Structuring complex test suites, running regression tests, and integrating with CI/CD pipelines for fast feedback.

Cucumber Cucumber enables Behavior-Driven Development (BDD) through human-readable Gherkin syntax, allowing test scenarios to align closely with business requirements.
- **Key Features**: Gherkin syntax for plain language test steps, support for multiple programming languages, and integration with Selenium for UI testing.
- **Best Practices:** Collaborate with stakeholders to define acceptance criteria in Gherkin; use tags to organize tests for targeted execution.
- **Use Case**: Testing feature acceptance criteria, aligning automation with business goals, and fostering collaboration between technical and non-technical teams.

4. API TESTING TOOLS

Postman Postman simplifies API testing by providing a user-friendly interface for crafting HTTP requests and organizing them in collections for automated execution.
- **Key Features**: API request building, automated workflows, test assertions, and documentation support.
- **Best Practices:** Organize tests using collections, use Postman Environments for managing configurations, and integrate Postman in CI/CD for automated API validation.
- **Use Case**: API endpoint testing, verifying responses, data validation, and error handling.

REST Assured REST Assured is a Java library for API automation, commonly used to validate REST services in a CI/CD context.
- **Key Features**: DSL for HTTP requests, JSON and XML validation support, and integration with TestNG for structured test reporting.
- **Best Practices:** Use REST Assured to validate API response data, set up environment configurations to run tests across different stages, and integrate with CI/CD for continuous API validation.
- **Use Case**: End-to-end validation of CRUD operations, API response times, and error handling in backend services.

5. PERFORMANCE TESTING TOOLS

JMeter Apache JMeter is an open-source tool designed to simulate heavy user traffic and test the performance and scalability of web applications.
- **Key Features**: Load testing, integration with CI/CD, distributed testing capabilities.
- **Best Practices:** Set up test scenarios for various user loads, schedule JMeter tests to run during nightly builds, and integrate with monitoring tools for performance insights.
- **Use Case**: Simulating concurrent user traffic to test application limits, detecting bottlenecks, and validating SLAs.

New Relic New Relic is an application performance monitoring (APM) tool that provides insights into the health and performance of applications, tracking metrics like response times, throughput, and error rates.
- **Key Features**: APM, real-time alerting, data analytics, and anomaly detection.
- **Best Practices:** Configure alerts based on response time thresholds, integrate with CI/CD to catch performance issues early, and leverage APM data for identifying and resolving bottlenecks.
- **Use Case**: Monitoring app health in real-time, ensuring performance SLAs are met, and analyzing historical data for proactive improvements.

6. MONITORING AND ALERTING TOOLS

Prometheus Prometheus is a time-series database and monitoring tool often used for tracking CI/CD metrics, system health, and application performance.
- **Key Features**: Time-series data storage, powerful querying language (PromQL), and integration with Grafana for visualization.
- **Best Practices:** Set up Prometheus to track key CI/CD metrics (e.g., build duration, error rates); use alerts to notify on critical issues during tests.
- **Use Case**: Monitoring test performance and CI/CD reliability, alerting teams to anomalies, and enabling data-driven optimization.

Grafana Grafana is a visualization platform that integrates with Prometheus and other data sources to create customizable dashboards for monitoring and analysis.
- **Key Features**: Real-time visualizations, customizable dashboards, and alerting based on thresholds.
- **Best Practices:** Build dashboards for different stakeholder needs (e.g., team-specific, project-wide) and configure alerts to highlight deviations in test and build performance.
- **Use Case**: Visualizing test coverage, build success rates, and historical CI/CD trends to identify performance bottlenecks.

7. COLLABORATION AND PROJECT MANAGEMENT TOOLS

Jira Jira is a project management tool designed for Agile workflows, supporting sprint planning, backlog management, and task tracking.
- **Key Features**: Kanban and Scrum boards, issue tracking, customizable workflows, and integration with CI/CD tools.
- **Best Practices:** Use Jira's issue linking to associate user stories with CI/CD events, track test failures, and prioritize sprint backlogs based on testing feedback.
- **Use Case**: Managing sprints, tracking feature development, and ensuring tasks meet the Definition of Done.
    Slack Slack is a messaging platform that supports real-time communication and integrates with various automation and CI/CD tools.
- **Key Features**: Real-time messaging, notification channels, integration with CI/CD pipelines and monitoring tools.
- **Best Practices:** Set up Slack channels for build alerts, test results, and code commits, facilitating immediate feedback and collaboration.
- **Use Case**: Notifying teams on build and test outcomes, facilitating quick discussions, and supporting remote Agile teams.

8. DOCUMENTATION AND KNOWLEDGE MANAGEMENT TOOLS

Confluence Confluence is a knowledge-sharing platform by Atlassian that supports documentation, collaboration, and Agile team management.
- **Key Features**: Collaborative document editing, integration with Jira, and version control for tracking document changes.
- **Best Practices:** Document test strategies, CI/CD setups, and automation frameworks; use it as a central repository for guidelines and best practices.
- **Use Case**: Creating and sharing test strategies, maintaining release notes, and documenting automation frameworks.

GitHub Wikis GitHub Wikis provide a simple, version-controlled space within GitHub repositories for project documentation.
- **Key Features**: Markdown support, version control, and ease of access within GitHub.
- **Best Practices:** Use GitHub Wikis for repository-specific documentation, link to related files, and create troubleshooting guides for team reference.
- **Use Case**: Creating project documentation directly tied to code repositories, including setup instructions, guidelines, and troubleshooting steps.

ADDITIONAL RESOURCES

The following additional resources are practical, hands-on tools and platforms that provide further support and enrichment for in-sprint automation practices. Unlike formal references and reading materials, these resources offer interactive environments, templates, libraries, and community forums where teams can explore, test, and enhance their automation workflows.

1. Template Repositories and Example Workflows

GitHub Actions Workflow Templates

GitHub offers a variety of pre-configured workflow templates in its Marketplace. These templates cover CI/CD automation, code scanning, testing, deployment, and more, enabling teams to get started with GitHub Actions quickly.

- **Key Templates**: CI/CD for Node.js, Python, Java, Rust, and custom workflows.
- **Best Use**: Use these templates as a base for configuring workflows that match your project requirements, saving time on manual setup.

Jenkins Pipeline Library

The Jenkins Pipeline Library provides reusable scripts and configurations that teams can integrate into their Jenkins pipelines. It includes common configurations for building, testing, deploying, and monitoring.

- **Best Use**: Use these templates to standardize your CI/CD pipeline across projects, promoting consistency and best practices.

Selenium Example Repositories

Selenium's official GitHub includes example repositories demonstrating browser automation in multiple languages (e.g., Java, Python, C#).

- **Best Use**: Use these as a starting point for building UI test suites or customizing them to fit your test framework.

2. Automation and CI/CD Testing Sandboxes

BrowserStack Live

BrowserStack provides a cloud-based sandbox where you can test web applications across real browsers and devices, allowing you to evaluate cross-browser compatibility for your UI tests.

- **Best Use**: Use this platform to validate your UI tests across various devices and browsers, ensuring cross-platform reliability.

Docker Playground

 Docker Playground offers an interactive environment for testing Docker containers, networks, and volumes without installing Docker locally.

- **Best Use**: Use Docker Playground to test container configurations and compose files before integrating Docker into your CI/CD pipeline.

Postman API Playground

Postman's API Playground provides an environment for testing and experimenting with APIs. It includes ready-to-use public APIs for testing automation workflows.

- **Best Use**: Practice writing API tests, organize collections, and simulate common API scenarios to validate response behaviors and error handling.

3. CI/CD Best Practice Repositories and Frameworks

CircleCI Configurations Repository

CircleCI's GitHub repository offers example configurations and pipelines, designed to showcase best practices in CI/CD and automation. Configurations include workflows for deployment, testing, and environment provisioning.

- **Best Use**: Use these configurations to create efficient, scalable CI/CD pipelines that support Agile testing requirements.

GitLab CI/CD Example Pipelines

GitLab's example repositories offer CI/CD pipeline templates for various use cases, including automated testing, deployment to Kubernetes, and setting up continuous delivery workflows.

- **Best Use**: Reference these templates to build GitLab CI/CD pipelines for different languages and frameworks, promoting efficient pipeline setup.

BDD Framework Examples with Cucumber

Cucumber provides example BDD (Behavior-Driven Development) frameworks and repositories, which demonstrate best practices for creating Gherkin-based scenarios and step definitions.

- **Best Use**: Reference these examples to structure BDD tests that align with Agile user stories and acceptance criteria, making tests accessible to non-technical stakeholders.

4. Automation Communities and Open-Source Contributions

Ministry of Testing

Ministry of Testing is an online community dedicated to software testing, offering resources, events, and forums for automation testers. It includes Q&A sections, articles, and tutorials on emerging testing practices.

- **Best Use**: Use this community for expert insights, troubleshooting support, and staying up to date with the latest testing trends.

Stack Overflow

Stack Overflow is a go-to platform for technical problem-solving, offering community-driven answers on a wide range of CI/CD, automation, and coding issues.

- **Best Use**: Post specific automation questions or explore common troubleshooting threads to resolve challenges with your CI/CD setups.

GitHub Discussions and Issues

GitHub Discussions and Issues are invaluable for interacting directly with the contributors of tools and frameworks like Selenium, TestNG, and GitHub Actions.

- **Best Use**: Engage with the community to ask questions, report issues, and contribute to feature requests, helping you stay connected with the development and improvement of key tools.

DevOps and Testing Conferences (e.g., DevOps World, SeleniumConf)

Conferences such as DevOps World and SeleniumConf provide both online and in-person events featuring talks, hands-on sessions, and workshops.

- **Best Use**: Attend these conferences to gain insights from industry leaders, expand your skills, and connect with other professionals focused on DevOps and test automation.

5. CI/CD Monitoring and Testing Utilities

Prometheus Operator for Kubernetes

Prometheus Operator simplifies Prometheus deployments within Kubernetes clusters, automating monitoring setup and resource management.

- **Best Use**: Use this tool to monitor CI/CD pipeline metrics in Kubernetes environments, enabling efficient resource scaling and performance tracking.

Grafana Labs Dashboards

Grafana Labs provides a collection of pre-configured dashboards for monitoring CI/CD performance, tracking system metrics, and analyzing test coverage.

- **Best Use**: Use these dashboards as templates to monitor critical CI/CD and testing metrics in real time, providing immediate insights to development teams.

Allure Reporting for TestNG and Junit

Allure is a flexible reporting tool compatible with TestNG and JUnit, designed for creating comprehensive visual reports of test results.

- **Best Use**: Integrate Allure with your automation framework to generate interactive, detailed test reports that enhance transparency and support issue tracking.

Dependabot for GitHub

Dependabot is a GitHub-integrated tool for automatically monitoring and updating project dependencies to ensure the latest security patches and stable releases.

- **Best Use**: Configure Dependabot to automatically update dependencies, minimizing risks associated with outdated libraries and improving project security.

6. Hands-On Labs and Practice Projects

Test Automation University

Test Automation University provides free courses and hands-on labs on various automation tools, including Selenium, REST Assured, Cypress, and TestNG.

- **Best Use**: Take courses to build hands-on experience with automation frameworks, especially in areas like UI, API, and performance testing.

Katalon Academy

Katalon Academy offers interactive courses and tutorials on test automation with Katalon Studio, covering fundamentals to advanced practices.

- **Best Use**: Use Katalon Academy to gain a structured understanding of automation, particularly if you're using Katalon Studio for UI or API testing.

Code Kata Platforms (e.g., CodeWars, HackerRank)

Code Kata platforms such as CodeWars and HackerRank offer challenges that strengthen coding skills essential for automation.

- **Best Use**: Practice problem-solving skills and coding fundamentals that are directly applicable to writing robust automation scripts.

7. Public Cloud Resources for Testing

AWS Free Tier

AWS offers a free tier that includes EC2, RDS, and S3 instances, which can be used to test infrastructure automation, database integration, and cloud-based CI/CD pipelines.

- **Best Use**: Use the AWS free tier to prototype infrastructure as code, practice deploying applications, and validate automated tests in a scalable environment.

Google Cloud Free Tier

Google Cloud provides a free tier with access to compute, storage, and Kubernetes resources, allowing teams to experiment with cloud-based test environments.

- **Best Use**: Leverage Google Cloud to test Kubernetes deployments, execute cloud-based performance tests, or build CI/CD pipelines for cloud-hosted applications.

Microsoft Azure DevTest Labs

Azure DevTest Labs allow for creating isolated test environments with configurable VMs, simplifying environment management for CI/CD pipelines.

- **Best Use**: Use DevTest Labs to configure staging environments, validate CI/CD processes, and optimize test resource allocation without impacting production.

SUMMARY

These resources, platforms, and communities provide Agile teams with hands-on support for building, maintaining, and optimizing in-sprint automation workflows. By leveraging these resources, teams can stay informed on best practices, troubleshoot issues efficiently, and continuously improve their CI/CD and automation strategies. Each resource complements the foundational concepts discussed in this book, enabling readers to build upon their automation knowledge in a practical, scalable way.

Bottom of Form

APPENDIX B: SAMPLE TEST AUTOMATION PROJECTS

The sample test automation repository has test automation projects for automating in-sprint/functional/ regression tests for the Web and API Application using BDD (Behavioral Driven Development) and TDD (Test Driven Development).

The tests are built using different technologies such as **Gherkin**, **JAVA**, **Cucumber BDD**, **TestNG**, **Karate DSL**, **Selenium WebDriver 4**, **REST Assured** and **Maven**.

Test Automation Projects
- **WebAutomation-BDD**
- **WebAutomation-TDD**
- **ApiAutomation-RestAssured-BDD**
- **ApiAutomation-KarateDSL**

Github Repository: https://github.com/insprintautomation/TestAutomationProjects.git

PROJECT 1: WEBAUTOMATION BDD

This test automation project is for automating in-sprint/functional/regression tests for the **saucedemo** Web Application using **Behavioral Driven Development (BDD)** framework. The tests are built using **Gherkin**, **JAVA**, **Selenium WebDriver 4**, **Cucumber BDD**, **TestNG** and **Maven**. Framework uses **Page Object Model (POM)** using Page Factory.

Prerequisites
- **JDK 11+** to run Java-based tests
- **Maven** for dependency management and running tests
- **Allure** for starting allure reports
- **IDE** IntelliJ or other

Clone the Repository
```
git clone https://github.com/insprintautomation/TestAutomationProjects.git
cd TestAutomationProjects/WebAutomation-BDD
```

Install Dependencies
Make sure `Maven` is installed on your machine. Then, run the following command to install all the dependencies: `mvn clean install -DskipTests`

Project Structure

```
WebAutomation-BDD
        | pom.xml
        ├── src
        |   ├── main
        |   |   ├── java
        |   |   |   ├── com.web.automation.pageobjects
        |   |   |   |   ├── CartPage.java
        |   |   |   |   ├── CheckoutPage.java
        |   |   |   |   ├── InventoryPage.java
        |   |   |   |   └── LoginPage.java
        |   |   |   └── com.web.automation.utils
        |   |   |       ├── CommonUtil.java
        |   |   |       ├── Constants.java
        |   |   |       ├── CSVDataUtil.java
        |   |   |       └── DriverManager.java
        |   |   └── resources
        |   |       └── extent.properties
        |   └── test
        |       ├── java
        |       |   └── com.saucedemo.bdd.automation.test
        |       |       ├── DataConstants.java
        |       |       ├── PageObjects.java
        |       |       ├── runner
        |       |       |   ├── TestNGRunner.java
        |       |       |   └── TestNGRunnerReRunFailed.java
        |       |       └── stepdefinitions
        |       |           ├── BaseSetup.java
        |       |           ├── CartSteps.java
        |       |           ├── CheckoutSteps.java
        |       |           ├── InventorySteps.java
        |       |           └── LoginSteps.java
        |       └── resources
        |           ├── data
        |           |   └── accounts.csv
        |           ├── features
        |           |   ├── login.feature
        |           |   └── productOrder.feature
        |           └── config.properties
        ├── reports
        |   ├── allure-results
        |   ├── cucumber
        |   ├── extent
        |   └── screenshots
        └── README.md
```

Configuration

Create a `src/main/resources/extent.properties` file to configure the extent report.

```
basefolder.name= reports/extent/ExtentReport
basefolder.datetimepattern = MMM-d_HH-mm-ss
extent.reporter.spark.start=true
extent.reporter.spark.out=index.html
screenshot.dir=reports/screenshots
screenshot.rel.path=../screenshots/
```

Create a `src/test/resources/config.properties` file to configure the browser, device lab, environment, timeouts and other configs.

```
# All values can be over witten by command ex: -Dbrowser=safari
# execution environment and device config
browser = chrome
headless = false
testLab = local
labUrl=
# test environment config
environment = test
test.url = https://www.saucedemo.com/
# test accounts config
accountsCSV = src/test/resources/data/accounts.csv
# timeout config
implicit.wait = 10
explicit.wait = 30
pageload.wait = 20
script.wait = 5

screenshot.file = reports/screenshot/screenshot-%s.png
```

Framework Utils

DriverManager: DriverManager.java has reusable methods to create driver instance for all types of browsers, create capabilities/driver options, stop driver, load url and take screenshots.

CSVDataUtil: CSVDataUtil.java has methods to load CSV accounts file and get account data based on account type provided.

CommonUtil: CommonUtil.java has methods to load properties file and get value from command line arguments or properties file, and other utility methods.

Constants: Constants.java has BrowserType enum and other constants.

Page Objects

Page Object Model (POM) is a design pattern used to create object-oriented classes that serve as an interface to the web page. A Page Object class is a model that represents a page in your application and encapsulates all the interactions with the page elements (e.g., buttons, forms, fields) on that page.

The PageFactory class is part of the Selenium WebDriver library and helps in implementing the Page Object Model (POM) design pattern, making your code more maintainable and readable. For the `Saucedemo` web application, below page object classes are created using Page Factory and contains web elements and methods to interact with those elements.

Login Page:

```java
public class LoginPage {
    // page factory
    @FindBy(id = "user-name")
    private WebElement userNameBox;

    @FindBy(css = "#password")
    private WebElement passwordBox;

    @FindBy(name = "login-button")
    private WebElement loginBtn;

    @FindBy(css = "[data-test='error'")
    private WebElement error;

    // login using username and email provided
    public void login(String userName, String password) {
        userNameBox.sendKeys(userName);
        passwordBox.sendKeys(password);
        loginBtn.click();
    }

    // validates error message displayed in login page for invalid login
    public void checkError(String expectedError) {
        String actualError = error.getText();
        assertTrue(actualError.contains(expectedError),
          "Check error displayed in login: '%s' has '%s'".formatted(actualError,
expectedError));
    }
}
```

Inventory Page:

```java
public class InventoryPage {
    @FindBy(css = ".title")
    private WebElement title;

    @FindBy(css = "a.shopping_cart_link")
    private WebElement cartLink;

    // dynamic locator - creates locator at runtime based on product name
    provided
```

```java
    private WebElement addToCartBtn(String productName) {
                    return   getDriver().findElement(By.name("add-to-cart-%s".
formatted(productName)));
    }

    public void checkTitle(String expectedTitle) {
        assertEquals(title.getText(), expectedTitle);
    }

    // Adds list of products to cart and navigates to cart page
    public void addProductsToCart(String[] products) {
        for (String product : products) {
            addToCartBtn(product.trim()).click();
        }
        cartLink.click();
    }
}
```

Cart Page:

```java
public class CartPage {
    @FindBy(id = "checkout")
    private WebElement checkoutBtn;

    public void continueToCheckout() {
        checkoutBtn.click();
    }
}
```

Checkout Page:

```java
public class CheckoutPage {
    @FindBy(id = "first-name")
    private WebElement firstName;

    @FindBy(css = "input[data-test='lastName']")
    private WebElement lastName;

    @FindBy(xpath = "//input[@data-test='postalCode']")
    private WebElement zipCode;

    @FindBy(className = "submit-button")
    private WebElement continueBtn;

    @FindBy(name = "finish")
    private WebElement finishBtn;
```

```java
@FindBy(className = "title")
private WebElement title;

@FindBy(css = "[data-test='pony-express']")
private WebElement completeImg;

@FindBy(className = "complete-header")
private WebElement completeHeader;

@FindBy(className = "complete-text")
private WebElement completeDesc;

// enters customer info and navigates to review page
public void enterCustomerInfo(Map<String, String> data) {
    firstName.sendKeys(data.get("firstName"));
    lastName.sendKeys(data.get("lastName"));
    zipCode.sendKeys(data.get("zipCode"));
    continueBtn.click();
}

public void submitOrder() {
    finishBtn.click();
}

// validates the order confirmation page
public void checkOrderConfirmation() {
    assertEquals(title.getText(), "Checkout: Complete!");
    assertEquals(completeImg.getAttribute("alt"), "Pony Express");
    assertEquals(completeHeader.getText(), "Thank you for your order!");
    assertEquals(completeDesc.getText(), "Your order has been dispatched,
and will arrive just as fast as the pony can get there!");
    }
}
```

PageObject Initialization: PageFactory.initElements(driver, this) initializes the elements annotated with @FindBy based on the provided driver instance. It binds the elements to the corresponding web elements on the page.

```java
public class PageObjects {
    public PageObjects() {
        initializePageObjects();
    }

    public LoginPage loginPage;
    protected InventoryPage inventoryPage;
    protected CartPage cartPage;
    protected CheckoutPage checkoutPage;
```

```
    public void initializePageObjects() {
            loginPage = PageFactory.initElements(DriverManager.getDriver(),
LoginPage.class);;
            inventoryPage = PageFactory.initElements(DriverManager.getDriver(),
InventoryPage.class);
        cartPage = PageFactory.initElements(DriverManager.getDriver(), CartPage.
class);
            checkoutPage = PageFactory.initElements(DriverManager.getDriver(),
CheckoutPage.class);
    }
  }
```

BDD Tests

Below is the test scripts for testing `login` and `product order` features in `Saucedemo` web application using `Cucumber BDD` approach.

Feature File:

login.feature: Validates the login functionality of Saucedemo web application. Positive and negative scenarios with data driven testing is implemented.

```
  @login @regression @smoke
  Feature: Login
    As a customer, I should be able to successfully login with valid credentials,
and see error for invalid credentials.

    Background:
      Given I am in login page

    @smoke @positive
    Scenario Outline: Login Successfully as <accountType> user
      When I login as a <accountType> user
      Then I should see inventory page
      @good
      Examples:
        | accountType |
        | standard    |
        | visual      |
      @bad
      Examples:
        | accountType |
        | problem     |
        | performance |
        | error       |

    @negative
    Scenario Outline: Login as <accountType> user and check the error message
```

```gherkin
When I login as a <accountType> user
Then I should see '<error>' message
Examples:
  | accountType   | error                                 |
  | locked        | Sorry, this user has been locked out  |
  | empty         | Username is required                  |
  | passwordEmpty | Password is required                  |
  | invalid       | Username and password do not match any user |
```

productOrder.feature: Validates product ordering flow for Saucedemo web application. Data driven testing is implemented to place order for different products data.

```gherkin
@order @regression @smoke
Feature: Product Order
  As a customer, I should be able to browse products, add products to cart and
place order successfully.

  Background:
    Given I am in login page

  @smoke @positive
  Scenario Outline: Successfully place order for product(s) - <products>
    Given I login as a <accountType> user
    When I add '<products>' products to cart
    And I proceed to checkout
    And I enter customer information
    And I review & submit the order
    Then I should see order confirmation
    @good
    Examples:
      | accountType | products                                   |
      | standard    | sauce-labs-backpack                        |
      | visual      | sauce-labs-bike-light, sauce-labs-bolt-t-shirt |
```

Step Definitions:

`LoginSteps.java` has step definitions for the Login page operations.

```java
package com.saucedemo.bdd.automation.test.stepdefinitions;

public class LoginSteps extends PageObjects {
    @Given("I am in login page")
    public void loginPage() {
        DriverManager.loadUrl();
    }

    @When("I login as a {} user")
    public void loginAsAUser(String userType) {
        Map<String, String> account = getAccount(userType);
        loginPage.login(account.get("userName"), account.get("password"));
    }
```

```java
@Then("I should see {string} message")
public void iShouldSeeMessage(String expectedError) {
    loginPage.checkError(expectedError);
}
}
```

`InventorySteps.java` **has step definitions for the Inventory page operations.**

```java
public class InventorySteps extends PageObjects {
    @Then("I should see inventory page")
    public void checkInventoryPage() {
        inventoryPage.checkTitle(DataConstants.PRODUCTS);
    }

    @When("I add {string} products to cart")
    public void iAddProductsToCart(String product) {
        String[] products = product.split(",");
        inventoryPage.addProductsToCart(products);
    }
}
```

`CartSteps.java` **has step definitions for the Cart page operations.**

```java
public class CartSteps extends PageObjects {
    @And("I proceed to checkout")
    public void proceedToCheckout() {
        cartPage.continueToCheckout();
    }
}
```

`CheckoutSteps.java` **has step definitions for the Checkout page operations.**

```java
public class CheckoutSteps extends PageObjects {
    @And("I enter customer information")
    public void enterCustomerInfo() {
        checkoutPage.enterCustomerInfo(DataConstants.custInfoData);
    }

    @And("I review & submit the order")
    public void iReviewSubmitTheOrder() {
        checkoutPage.submitOrder();
    }

    @Then("I should see order confirmation")
    public void iShouldSeeOrderConfirmation() {
        checkoutPage.checkOrderConfirmation();
        DriverManager.getScreenshot();
    }
}
```

BaseSetup:

`BaseSetup.java` has the common code for setup and tear down. Methods can use cucumber or testng/junit annotations. Below code uses annotation from cucumber, `@BeforeAll` to load the properties and csv accounts file. `@Before` to initialize the driver instance for each test. `@After` to stop the driver instance for each test.

```java
public class BaseSetup extends PageObjects {

    private final DriverManager driverManager;

    public BaseSetup(DriverManager driverManager) {
        this.driverManager = driverManager;
    }

    @BeforeAll
    public static void suiteSetup() {
        loadProperties("src/test/resources/config.properties");
        String accountsCSV = getProperty("accountsCSV");
        loadAccounts(accountsCSV);
    }

    @Before
    public void beforeScenario(Scenario scenario) {
        driverManager.initializeDriver();
    }

    @After
    public void afterScenario(Scenario scenario) {
        driverManager.stopDriver();
    }

    @AfterAll
    public static void suiteTearDown() {}
}
```

Test Runner:

Test Runner class can be created using TestNG or JUnit. Below is the example code for running tests using TestNG.

```java
package com.saucedemo.bdd.automation.test.runner;

@CucumberOptions(
        features = "classpath:features",
        glue = "com.saucedemo.bdd.automation.test.stepdefinitions",
        tags = "@smoke",
        monochrome = true,
        dryRun = false,
```

```
        plugin = {"html:reports/cucumber/cucumber.html",
               "json:reports/cucumber/cucumber.json",
          "com.aventstack.extentreports.cucumber.adapter.ExtentCucumberAdapter:",
               "io.qameta.allure.cucumber7jvm.AllureCucumber7Jvm",
               "rerun:reports/cucumber/failed_scenarios.txt",
               "pretty"},
        publish = true
)
public class TestNGRunner extends AbstractTestNGCucumberTests {
    @DataProvider(parallel = true)
    public Object[][] scenarios() {
        return super.scenarios();
    }
}
```

Test Runner to run failed scenarios from previous execution.

```
package com.saucedemo.bdd.automation.test.runner;


import io.cucumber.testng.AbstractTestNGCucumberTests;
import io.cucumber.testng.CucumberOptions;
import org.testng.annotations.DataProvider;


@CucumberOptions(
        features = "@reports/cucumber/failed_scenarios.txt",
        glue = "com.saucedemo.bdd.automation.test.stepdefinitions",
        monochrome = true,
        plugin = {"html:reports/cucumber/cucumber.html",
        "json:reports/cucumber/cucumber.json",
      "com.aventstack.extentreports.cucumber.adapter.ExtentCucumberAdapter:",
        "pretty"}
)
public class TestNGRunnerReRunFailed extends AbstractTestNGCucumberTests {
    @DataProvider(parallel = false)
    public Object[][] scenarios() {
        return super.scenarios();
    }
}
```

CSV Test Data

CSV data file is used to store test accounts. Other columns can be added based on the requirement. `CSVDataUtil.java` has methods to read and get values from CSV file.

```
accountType,userName,password,environment
standard,standard_user,secret_sauce,all
visual,visual_user,secret_sauce,test
locked,locked_out_user,secret_sauce,test
```

Running BDD Tests

Add build step in pom.xml to run tests using `maven-surefire-plugin`.

```xml
<build>
    <plugins>
        <plugin>
            <groupId>org.apache.maven.plugins</groupId>
            <artifactId>maven-surefire-plugin</artifactId>
            <version>3.1.2</version>
            <configuration>
                <testFailureIgnore>false</testFailureIgnore>
                <systemPropertyVariables>
                    <allure.results.directory>
                        ${project.basedir}/reports/allure-results
                    </allure.results.directory>
                </systemPropertyVariables>
                <argLine>
                            -javaagent:"${settings.localRepository}/org/aspectj/
aspectjweaver/${aspectj.version}/aspectjweaver-${aspectj.version}.jar"
                </argLine>
            </configuration>
            <dependencies>
                <dependency>
                    <groupId>org.aspectj</groupId>
                    <artifactId>aspectjweaver</artifactId>
                    <version>${aspectj.version}</version>
                </dependency>
            </dependencies>
        </plugin>
    </plugins>
</build>
```

CommandLine:

Change to directory `WebAutomation-BDD`.

To execute all tests, run maven command `mvn clean test`.

To filter specific group of `Cucumber BDD` tests and execute, run maven command `mvn clean test -Dcucumber.filter.tags="@order" -Denvironment=test`.

To run `Cucumber BDD` tests using parallel threads, run maven command `mvn clean test -Ddataproviderthreadcount=5`.

Run/Debug configurations in IntelliJ:

Create run/debug configurations in IntelliJ using menu navigation `Run -> Edit Configurations -> Add New Configurations`

Using `Maven` configuration, Select `Maven` from the run/debug configurations window. Name the configuration, enter command `clean test -Dcucumber.filter.tags="@order" -Denvironment=test` in Run input box, select `WebAutomation-BDD` module and Apply.

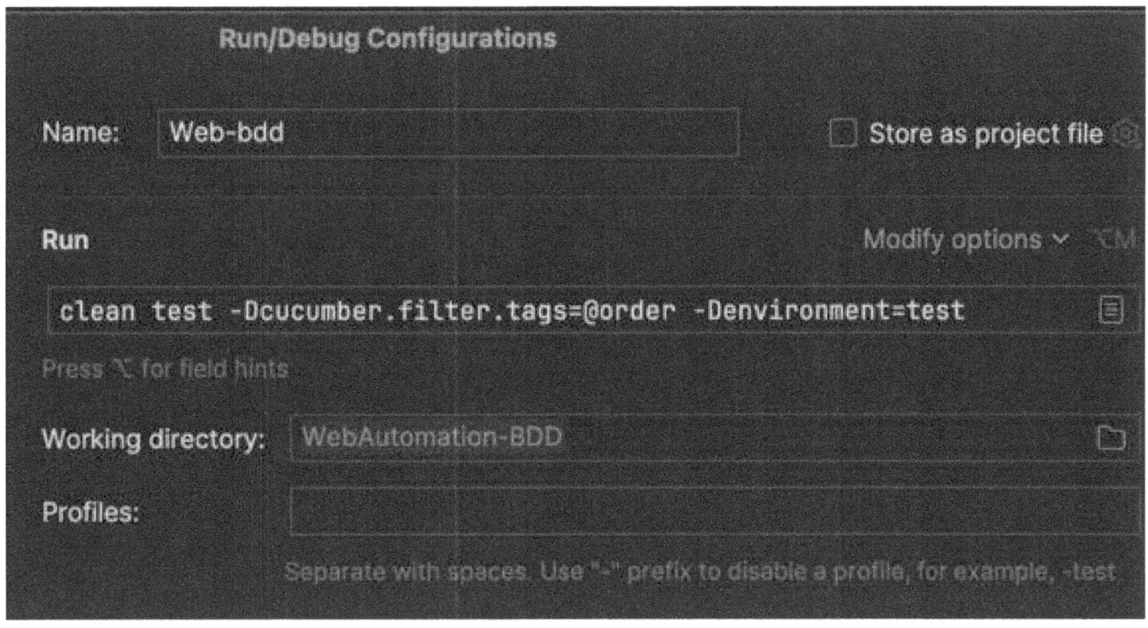

Using TestNG configuration, Select TestNG from the run/debug configurations window. Name the configuration, select WebAutomation-BDD module and TestNGRunner.java class and click Apply.

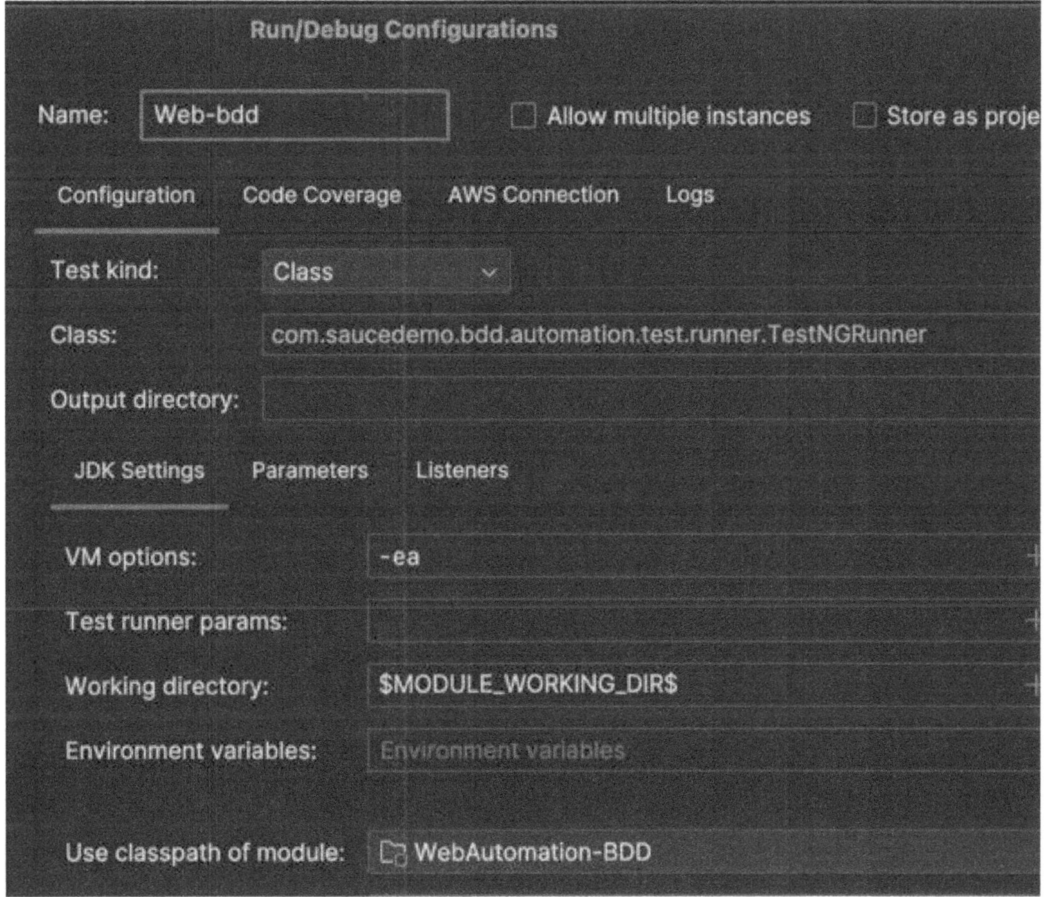

To Run/Debug configuration, select the saved configuration and click Play or Debug button.

```
Run Console Output:
```

Reports

After the test execution, allure, cucumber and extent reports will be generated in `reports` directory.

Allure Report:

Start the allure report using command line `allure serve` from the `reports` directory.

```
Allure Report Overview
```

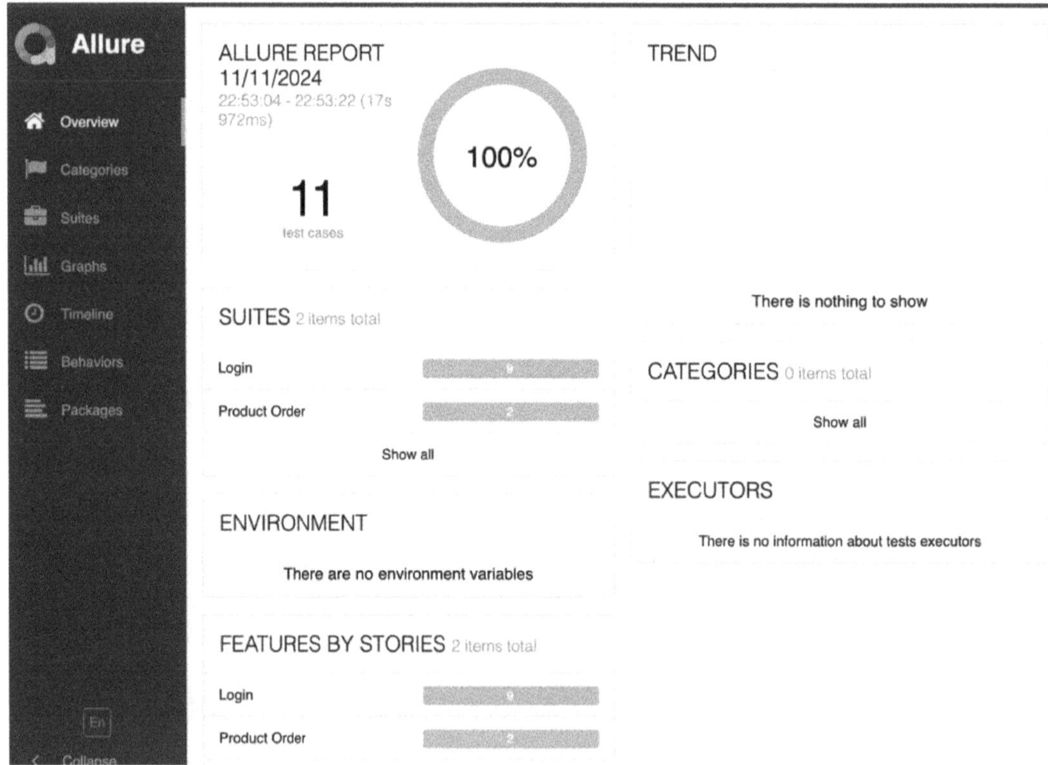

Allure Report Behaviors

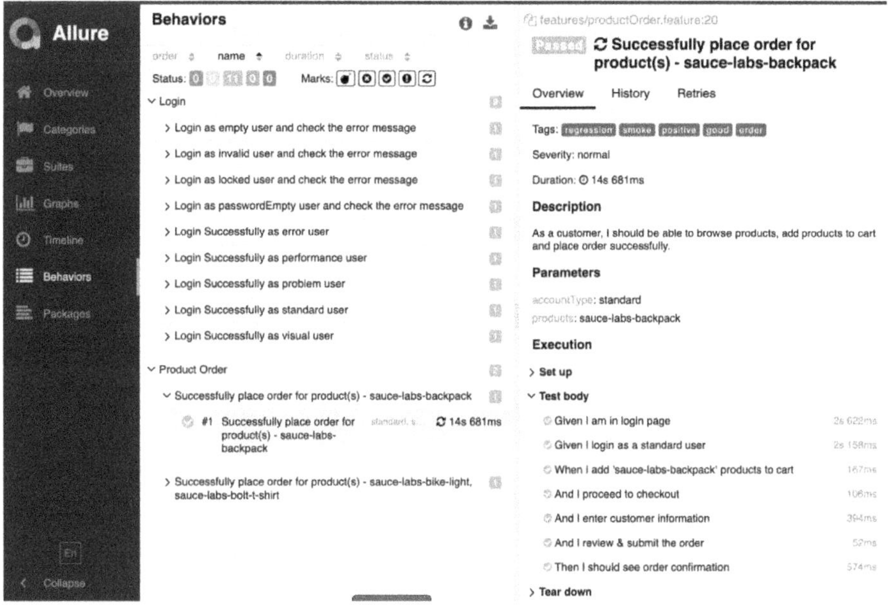

Extent Report: Open `reports/extent/index.html` in browser.

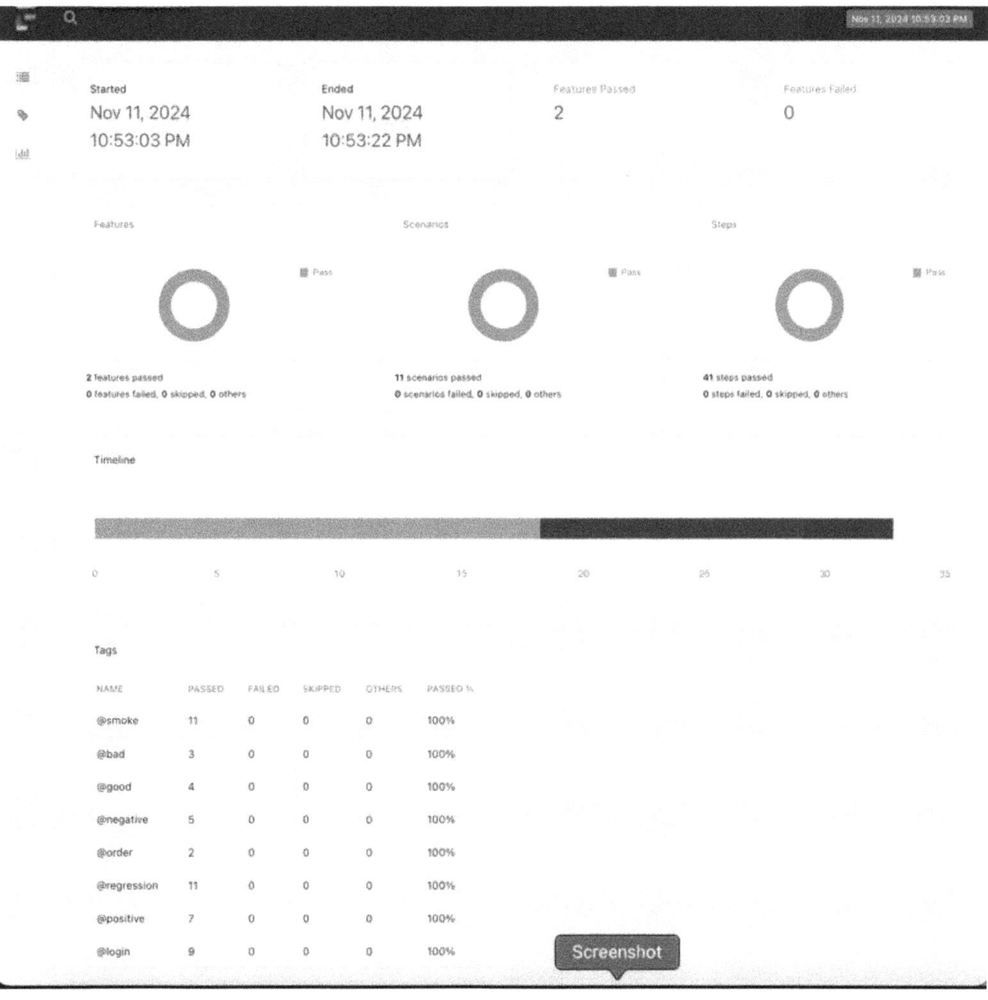

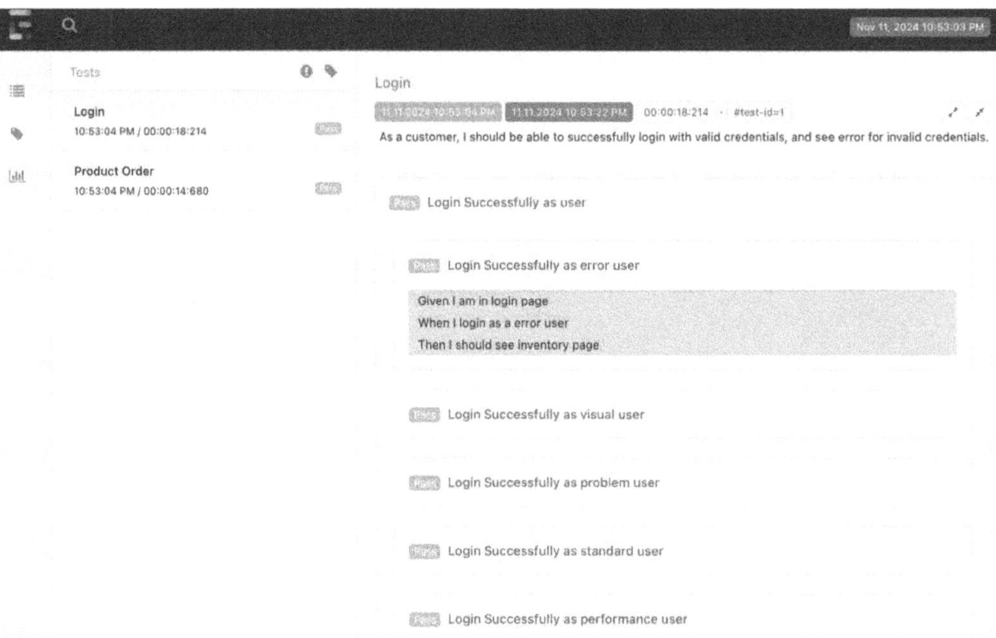

Cucumber Report: Open `reports/cucumber/cucumber.html` in browser.

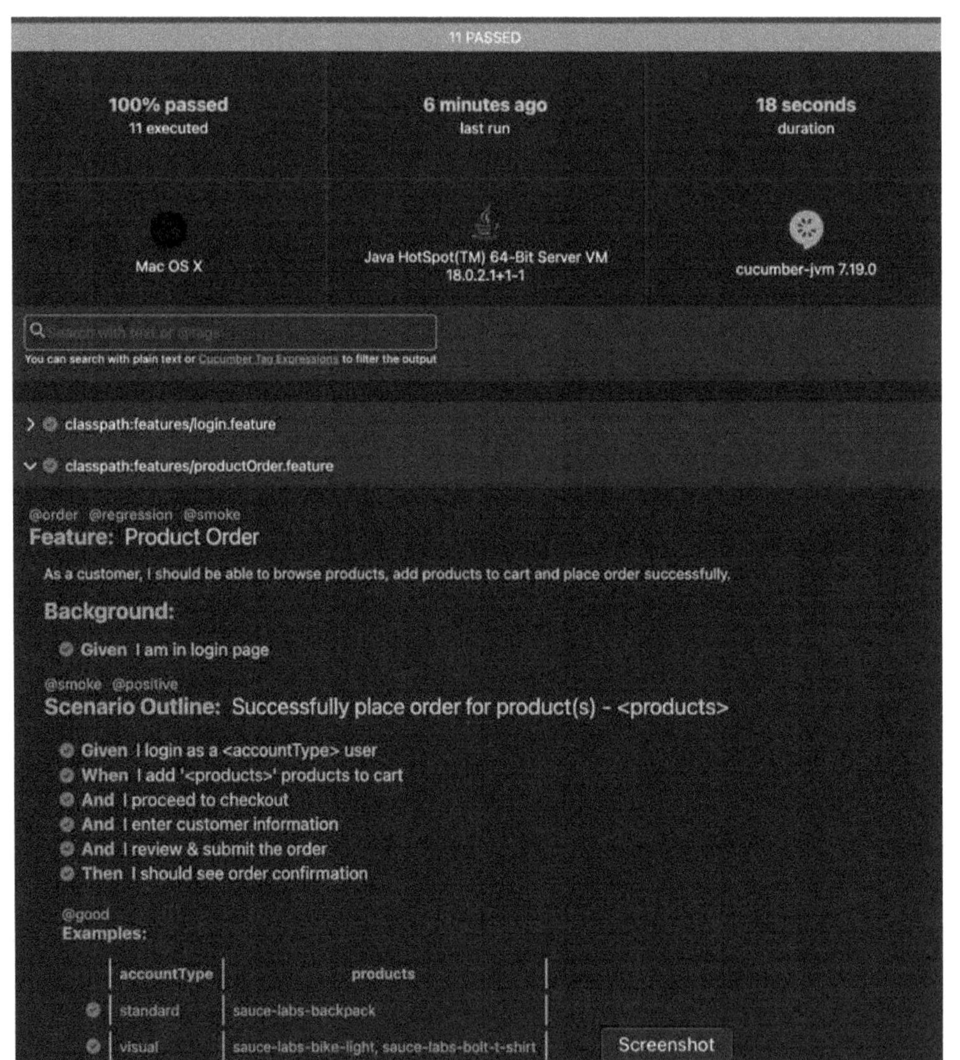

Screenshot: See screenshot images in reports/screenshots

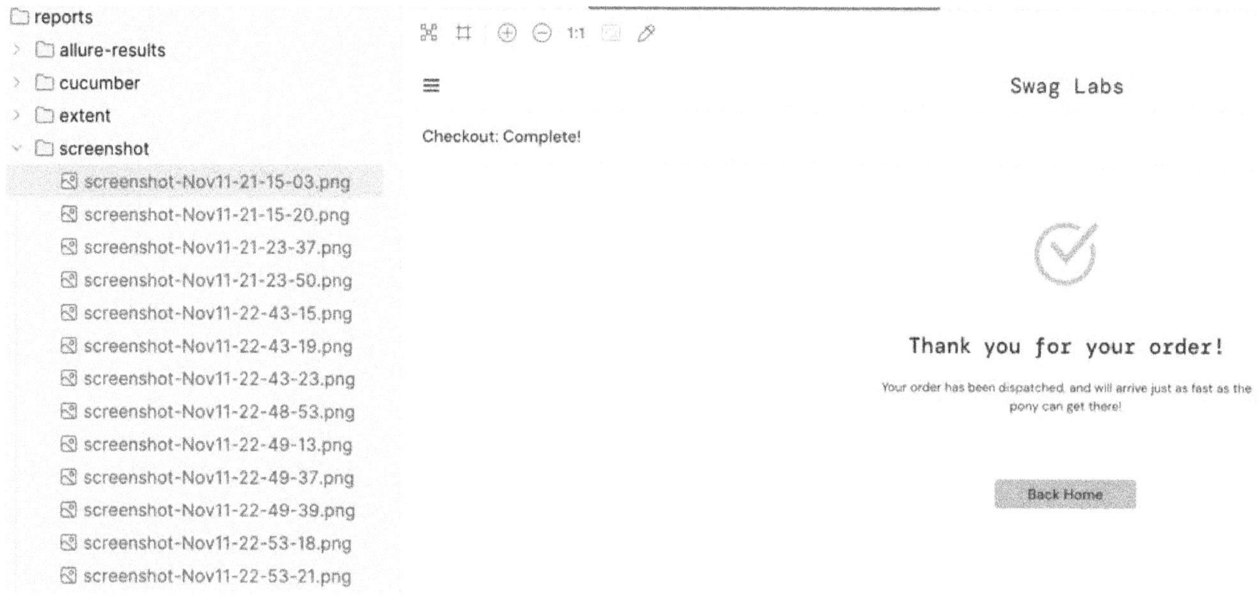

Prerequisites

- **JDK 11+** to run Java-based tests
- **Maven** for dependency management and running tests
- **Allure** for starting allure reports
- **IDE** Intellij or other

Clone the Repository

```
git clone https://github.com/insprintautomation/TestAutomationProjects.git
cd TestAutomationProjects/WebAutomation-TDD
```

Install Dependencies

Make sure `Maven` is installed on your machine. Then, run the following command to install all the dependencies: `mvn clean install -DskipTests`

PROJECT 2: WEBAUTOMATION TDD

This test automation project is for automating in-sprint/functional/regression tests for the **saucedemo** Web Application using **Test Driven Development (TDD)** framework. The tests are built using **JAVA**, **Selenium WebDriver 4**, **TestNG** and **Maven**. Framework uses **Page Object Model (POM)**.

Project Structure

```
WebAutomation-TDD
        | pom.xml
        ├── src
        |   ├── main
        |   |   └── java
        |   |       ├── com.web.automation.pageobjects
        |   |       |   ├── CartPage.java
        |   |       |   ├── CheckoutPage.java
        |   |       |   ├── InventoryPage.java
        |   |       |   └── LoginPage.java
        |   |       └── com.web.automation.utils
        |   |           ├── dataprovider
        |   |           |   ├── JsonDataProvider.java
        |   |           |   └── model
        |   |           |       ├── CustomerInfo.java
        |   |           |       └── TestData.json
        |   |           ├── CommonUtil.java
        |   |           ├── Constants.java
        |   |           ├── CSVDataUtil.java
        |   |           ├── DriverManager.java
        |   |           └── WebUtil.java
        |   └── test
        |       ├── java
        |       |   └── com.saucedemo.tdd.automation
        |       |       ├── DataConstants.java
        |       |       ├── PageObjects.java
        |       |       └── test
        |       |           ├── BaseSetup.java
        |       |           ├── LoginTest.java
        |       |           └── ProductOrder.java
        |       └── resources
        |           ├── data
        |           |   ├── accounts.csv
        |           |   ├── loginTest.json
        |           |   └── productOrderTest.json
        |           └── config.properties
        ├── reports
        |   ├── allure-results
        |   ├── extent
        |   └── screenshots
        └── README.md
```

Configuration

Create a `src/test/resources/config.properties` file to configure the browser, device lab, environment, timeouts and other configs.

```
# All values can be overwritten by command ex: -Dbrowser=safari
# execution environment and device config
browser = chrome
headless = false
testLab = local
labUrl=
# test environment config
environment = test
test.url = https://www.saucedemo.com/
# test accounts config
accountsCSV = src/test/resources/data/accounts.csv
# timeout config
implicit.wait = 10
explicit.wait = 30
pageload.wait = 20
script.wait = 5

screenshot.file = reports/screenshot/screenshot-%s.png
```

Framework Utils

DriverManager: DriverManager.java has reusable methods to create driver instance for all types of browsers, create capabilities/driver options, stop driver, load url and take screenshots.

CSVDataUtil: CSVDataUtil.java has methods to load CSV accounts file and get account data based on account type provided.

CommonUtil: CommonUtil.java has methods to load properties file and get value from command line arguments or properties file, and other utility methods.

Constants: Constants.java has BrowserType enum and other constants.

WebUtil: has reusable wrapper methods on top of Selenium to perform operations on Web Application.

```java
public class WebUtil extends DriverManager {

    public WebElement getElement(By locator) {
        return getDriver().findElement(locator);
    }

    @Step("Type value '{value}' in element '{element}'")
    public void typeValue(By element, String value) {
        getElement(element).sendKeys(value);
    }
```

```java
@Step("Click on element '{element}'")
public void click(By element) {
    getElement(element).click();
}


@Step("Get text value of element '{element}'")
public String getText(By element) {
    return getElement(element).getText();
}


@Step("Get '{attribute}' attribute value of element '{element}'")
public String getValue(By element, String attribute) {
    return getElement(element).getAttribute(attribute);
}

}
```

Data Provider: In TestNG, a DataProvider is a powerful feature that allows you to run a test method multiple times with different sets of data. It is useful when you want to run the same test with different inputs to validate various conditions.

Below `JsonDataProvider.java` has the code to handle JSON data for TestNG tests using DataProvider.

```java
public class JsonDataProvider {

    /**
     * Data Provider gets data from JSON based on Test executed. Test will be
executed for no of data sets available.
     *
     * @param testContext (ITestNGMethod) testng ITestNGMethod has various
methods to get current test method executed
     * @return data list iterator
     */
    @DataProvider(name = Constants.JSON_DATA_PROVIDER, parallel = true)
    public Iterator<Object[]> jsonDataProvider(ITestNGMethod testContext)
throws IOException {
        String testName = testContext.getMethodName();
        String jsonFileName = testContext.getRealClass().getSimpleName();
        File jsonFile = new File(String.format(Constants.JSON_DATA_FILE,
jsonFileName));
        List<TestData> jsonDataList = getJsonDataArray(jsonFile, testName);
        if (jsonDataList.isEmpty()) {
            jsonDataList = getJsonDataArray(jsonFile, testName);
        }
        Collection<Object[]> dataList = new ArrayList<>();
        for (TestData jsonData : jsonDataList) {
            dataList.add(new Object[]{jsonData});
        }
        return dataList.iterator();
    }
```

```java
    /**
     * Reads JSON file content and returns the value for key as a List of
TestData object's. Used for JSON Array data.
     * Test data can be excluded using 'excludeTest' parameter.
     *
     * @param jsonFile JSON file
     * @param key       to get a specific JSONObject from JSON file
     * @throws IOException when file not found or unable to get data
     */
    private List<TestData> getJsonDataArray(File jsonFile, String key) throws
IOException {
        Map<String, Object> jsonData = CommonUtil.readJsonFile(jsonFile);
        List<Map<String, Object>> dataList = (List<Map<String, Object>>)
jsonData.get(key);
        if (Objects.isNull(dataList)) {
            log.info(String.format("Data not exists for key '%s' in file %s.",
key, jsonFile));
            return Collections.emptyList();
        }
        List<TestData> testDataList = new ArrayList<>();
    ObjectMapper objectMapper = new ObjectMapper().configure(SerializationFeature.
FAIL_ON_EMPTY_BEANS, false);
        dataList.forEach(data -> {
            // integrates accounts.csv
            if (data.containsKey(Constants.ACCOUNT_TYPE)) {
                Map<String, String> accountData = CSVDataUtil.getAccount(data.
get(Constants.ACCOUNT_TYPE).toString());
                if (!accountData.isEmpty()) {
                    data.putAll(accountData);
                }
            }
            testDataList.add(objectMapper.convertValue(data, TestData.class));
        });
        return testDataList;
    }
}
```

TestData Model: Below is the TestData model class to parse JSON data and use it in Test scripts. Additional model classes and fields can be based on the requirement.

```java
package com.web.automation.utils.dataprovider.model;

import lombok.Getter;
import lombok.Setter;
import lombok.ToString;

@Getter @Setter @ToString
public class TestData {
```

```java
    private String accountType;
    private String userName;
    private String password;
    private String environment;
    private String error;
    private List<String> products;
    private CustomerInfo customerInfo;
}
```

Page Objects

Page Object Model (POM) is a design pattern used to create object-oriented classes that serve as an interface to the web page. A Page Object class is a model that represents a page in your application and encapsulates all the interactions with the page elements (e.g., buttons, forms, fields) on that page. For the `Saucedemo` web application, below page object classes are created using Page Object Model and contains web elements and methods to interact with those elements.

Login Page:

```java
public class LoginPage extends WebUtil {

    private final By userNameBox = By.id("user-name");

    private final By passwordBox = By.cssSelector("#password");

    private final By loginBtn = By.name("login-button");

    private final By error = By.cssSelector("[data-test='error'");

    // login using username and email provided
    @Step("Login as '{data.accountType}' user")
    public void login(TestData data) {
        typeValue(userNameBox, data.getUserName());
        typeValue(passwordBox, data.getPassword());
        click(loginBtn);
    }

    // validates error message displayed in login page for invalid login
    @Step("Check login page shows error '{expectedError}'")
    public void checkError(String expectedError) {
        String actualError = getText(error);
        assertTrue(actualError.contains(expectedError),
            "Check error displayed in login: '%s' has '%s'".formatted(actualError,
expectedError));
    }
}
```

Inventory Page:

```java
public class InventoryPage extends WebUtil {

    private By title = By.cssSelector(".title");

    private By cartLink = By.cssSelector("a.shopping_cart_link");

    // dynamic locator - creates locator at runtime based on product name
provided
    private WebElement addToCartBtn(String productName) {
        return  getDriver().findElement(By.name("add-to-cart-%s".
formatted(productName)));
    }

    @Step("Check value inventory page title is '{expectedTitle}'")
    public void checkTitle(String expectedTitle) {
        assertEquals(getText(title), expectedTitle);
    }

    @Step("Add '{products}' to Cart")
    public void addProductsToCart(List<String> products) {
        for (String product : products) {
            addToCartBtn(product.trim()).click();
        }
        click(cartLink);
    }
}
```

Cart Page:

```java
public class CartPage extends WebUtil {

    private final By checkoutBtn = By.id("checkout");

    @Step("Continue to Checkout Page")
    public void continueToCheckout() {
        click(checkoutBtn);
    }
}
```

Checkout Page:

```java
public class CheckoutPage extends WebUtil {

    private final By firstName = By.id("first-name");

    private final By lastName = By.cssSelector("input[data-test='lastName']");
```

```java
    private final By zipCode = By.xpath("//input[@data-test='postalCode']");

    private final By continueBtn = By.className("submit-button");

    private final By finishBtn = By.name("finish");

    private final By title = By.className("title");

    private final By completeImg = By.cssSelector("[data-test='pony-express']");

    private final By completeHeader = By.className("complete-header");

    private final By completeDesc = By.className("complete-text");

    @Step("Enter Customer Information in Checkout page")
    public void enterCustomerInfo(CustomerInfo data) {
        typeValue(firstName, data.getFirstName());
        typeValue(lastName, data.getLastName());
        typeValue(zipCode, data.getZipCode());
        click(continueBtn);
    }

    @Step("Submit Order")
    public void submitOrder() {
        click(finishBtn);
    }

    @Step("Check Order Confirmation page")
    public void checkOrderConfirmation() {
        assertEquals(getText(title), "Checkout: Complete!");
        assertEquals(getValue(completeImg, "alt"), "Pony Express");
        assertEquals(getText(completeHeader), "Thank you for your order!");
        assertEquals(getText(completeDesc), "Your order has been dispatched,
and will arrive just as fast as the pony can get there!");
        getScreenshot();
    }
}
```

PageObject Initialization: `PageObjects.java` has the page object class initialization.

```java
public class PageObjects {
    protected LoginPage loginPage = new LoginPage();
    protected InventoryPage inventoryPage = new InventoryPage();
    protected CartPage cartPage = new CartPage();
    protected CheckoutPage checkoutPage = new CheckoutPage();


}
```

Test Data

CSV Data: CSV data file in `src\test\resources\data.accounts.csv` is used to store test accounts. Other columns can be added based on the requirement. `CSVDataUtil.java` has methods to read and get values from CSV file. It can be integrated with JsonDataProvider using JSON data file.

```
accountType,userName,password,environment
standard,standard_user,secret_sauce,all
visual,visual_user,secret_sauce,test
locked,locked_out_user,secret_sauce,test
```

JSON Data: JSON data file in `src\test\resources\` is used to store test data required for TestNG tests. JSON data file is organized based on the Test Class and Method names. `JsonDataProvider.Json` class read the JSON data file based on the Test executed.

Below is the `LoginTest.json` JSON data file for Tests in `LoginTest.java` class. For example, TestNG executes `loginSuccessTest` method for the number of accountType's provided in the JSON file.

```json
{
  "loginSuccessTest": [
    {
      "accountType": "standard"
    },
    {
      "accountType": "visual"
    },
    {
      "accountType": "problem"
    },
    {
      "accountType": "performance"
    },
    {
      "accountType": "error"
    }
  ],

  "loginFailureTest": [
    {
      "accountType": "locked",
      "error": "Sorry, this user has been locked out"
    },
    {
      "accountType": "empty",
      "error": "Username is required"
    },
    {
      "accountType": "passwordEmpty",
      "error": "Password is required"
```

```
        },
        {
          "accountType": "invalid",
          "error": "Username and password do not match any user"
        }
      ]
    }
```

ProctOrder.json

```
    {
      "productOrderTest": [
        {
          "accountType": "standard",
          "products": ["sauce-labs-backpack"],
          "customerInfo": {
            "firstName": "test",
            "lastName": "test",
            "zipCode": "19000"
          }
        },
        {
          "accountType": "visual",
          "products": ["sauce-labs-bike-light", "sauce-labs-bolt-t-shirt"],
          "customerInfo": {
            "firstName": "test1",
            "lastName": "test1",
            "zipCode": "18000"
          }
        }
      ]
    }
```

TestNG Tests

Below is the test scripts for testing `login` and `product order` features in `Saucedemo` web application using `TestNG TDD` approach.

Login Test: Validates the login functionality of Saucedemo web application. Positive and negative scenarios with data driven testing is implemented.

```java
package com.saucedemo.tdd.automation.test;

import com.saucedemo.tdd.automation.DataConstants;
import com.web.automation.utils.dataprovider.JsonDataProvider;
import com.web.automation.utils.dataprovider.model.TestData;
import io.qameta.allure.Feature;
import org.testng.annotations.Test;
```

```java
public class LoginTest extends BaseSetup {

    @Test(groups = {DataConstants.SMOKE, DataConstants.REGRESSION, DataConstants.
    LOGIN},
            dataProvider = JSON_DATA_PROVIDER, dataProviderClass = JsonDataProvider.
    class)
        @Feature(DataConstants.LOGIN)
        public void loginSuccessTest(TestData data) {
            loginPage.login(data);
            inventoryPage.checkTitle(DataConstants.PRODUCTS);
        }


    @Test(groups = {DataConstants.SMOKE, DataConstants.REGRESSION, DataConstants.
LOGIN},
            dataProvider = JSON_DATA_PROVIDER, dataProviderClass = JsonDataProvider.
class)
        @Feature(DataConstants.LOGIN)
        public void loginFailureTest(TestData data) {
            loginPage.login(data);
            loginPage.checkError(data.getError());
        }
    }
```

ProductOrder Test: Validates product ordering flow for Saucedemo web application. Data driven testing is implemented to place order for different product's data.

```java
package com.saucedemo.tdd.automation.test;

import com.web.automation.utils.dataprovider.JsonDataProvider;
import com.web.automation.utils.dataprovider.model.TestData;
import io.qameta.allure.Feature;
import org.testng.annotations.Test;

import static com.saucedemo.tdd.automation.DataConstants.*;
import static com.web.automation.utils.Constants.JSON_DATA_PROVIDER;

public class ProductOrderTest extends BaseSetup {

    @Test(groups = {SMOKE, REGRESSION, LOGIN},
        dataProvider = JSON_DATA_PROVIDER, dataProviderClass = JsonDataProvider.
class)
        @Feature(PRODUCT_ORDER)
        public void productOrderTest(TestData data) {
            loginPage.login(data);
            inventoryPage.addProductsToCart(data.getProducts());
            cartPage.continueToCheckout();
            checkoutPage.enterCustomerInfo(data.getCustomerInfo());
```

```java
        checkoutPage.submitOrder();
        checkoutPage.checkOrderConfirmation();
    }
}
```

BaseSetup: `BaseSetup.java` has the common code for setup and tear down. Method uses testng annotations. Below code uses annotation from TestNG, `@BeforeSuite` to load the properties, csv accounts file and initialize Extent report. `@BeforeMethod` to initialize the driver instance, load test url and create test in Extent report for each test. `@AfterMethod` to stop the driver instance for each test. `@AfterSuite` to stop the Extent report.

```java
package com.saucedemo.tdd.automation.test;

import com.aventstack.extentreports.ExtentReports;
import com.aventstack.extentreports.reporter.ExtentSparkReporter;
import com.saucedemo.tdd.automation.PageObjects;
import com.web.automation.utils.DriverManager;
import org.testng.ITestContext;
import org.testng.ITestResult;
import org.testng.annotations.AfterMethod;
import org.testng.annotations.AfterSuite;
import org.testng.annotations.BeforeMethod;
import org.testng.annotations.BeforeSuite;

import static com.web.automation.utils.CSVDataUtil.loadAccounts;
import static com.web.automation.utils.CommonUtil.getProperty;
import static com.web.automation.utils.CommonUtil.loadProperties;
import static com.web.automation.utils.DriverManager.loadUrl;

public class BaseSetup extends PageObjects {

    private final DriverManager driverManager;
    private static ExtentReports extentReport;

    public BaseSetup() {
        driverManager = new DriverManager();
    }

    @BeforeSuite
    public static void suiteSetup() {
        extentReport = new ExtentReports();
      ExtentSparkReporter extentSparkReport = new ExtentSparkReporter("reports/
extent/extentReport.html");
        extentReport.attachReporter(extentSparkReport);
        loadProperties("src/test/resources/config.properties");
        String accountsCSV = getProperty("accountsCSV");
        loadAccounts(accountsCSV);
    }
```

```java
@BeforeMethod
public void beforeMethod(ITestContext testContext) {
    extentReport.createTest(testContext.getName());
    driverManager.initializeDriver();
    loadUrl();
}


@AfterMethod
public void afterMethod(ITestResult result) {
    driverManager.stopDriver();
}


@AfterSuite
public static void suiteTearDown() {
    extentReport.flush();
}
}
```

Running TestNG Tests

Add build step in pom.xml to run tests using `maven-surefire-plugin`.

```xml
<build>
    <plugins>
        <plugin>
            <groupId>org.apache.maven.plugins</groupId>
            <artifactId>maven-surefire-plugin</artifactId>
            <version>3.1.2</version>
            <configuration>
                <systemPropertyVariables>
                  <allure.results.directory>${project.basedir}/reports/allure-results</allure.results.directory>
                </systemPropertyVariables>
                <argLine>
                        -javaagent:${settings.localRepository}/org/aspectj/aspectjweaver/${aspectj.version}/aspectjweaver-${aspectj.version}.jar
                </argLine>
                <includes>
                        <include>**/com.saucedemo.tdd.automation.test/*.java</include>
                </includes>
            </configuration>
            <dependencies>
                <dependency>
                    <groupId>org.aspectj</groupId>
                    <artifactId>aspectjweaver</artifactId>
                    <version>${aspectj.version}</version>
```

```
            </dependency>
          </dependencies>
        </plugin>
      </plugins>
    </build>
```

CommandLine:

Change to directory `WebAutomation-TDD`.

To execute all tests, run maven command `mvn clean test`.

To filter specific group of `TestNG` tests and execute, run maven command `mvn clean test -Dgroups=order -Denvironment=test`.

To run `TestNG` tests using parallel threads, run maven command `mvn clean test -Dparallel=methods -Dthreadcount=5 -Ddataproviderthreadcount=2`.

`Run Console Output:`

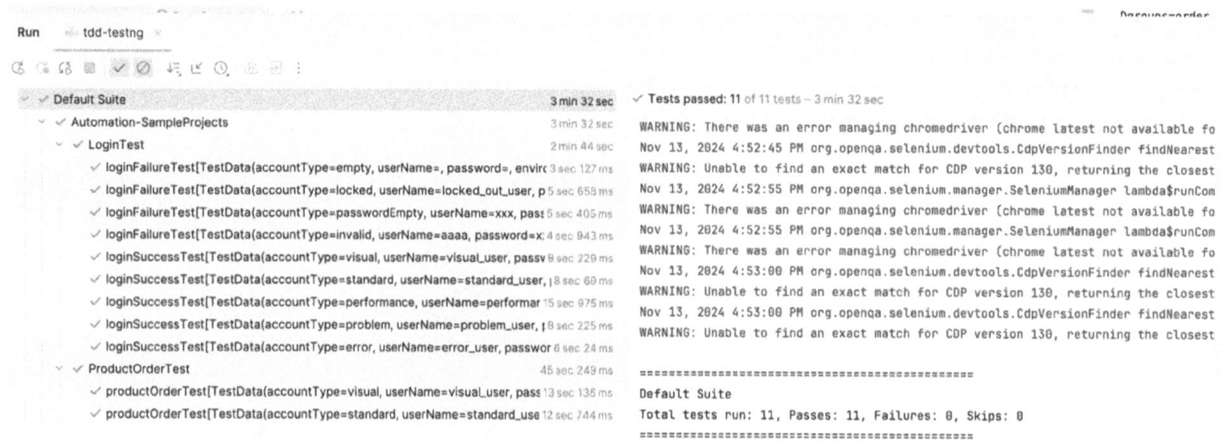

Reports

After the test execution, allure and extent reports will be generated in `reports` directory.

Allure Report:

Start the allure report using command line `allure serve` from the `reports` directory.

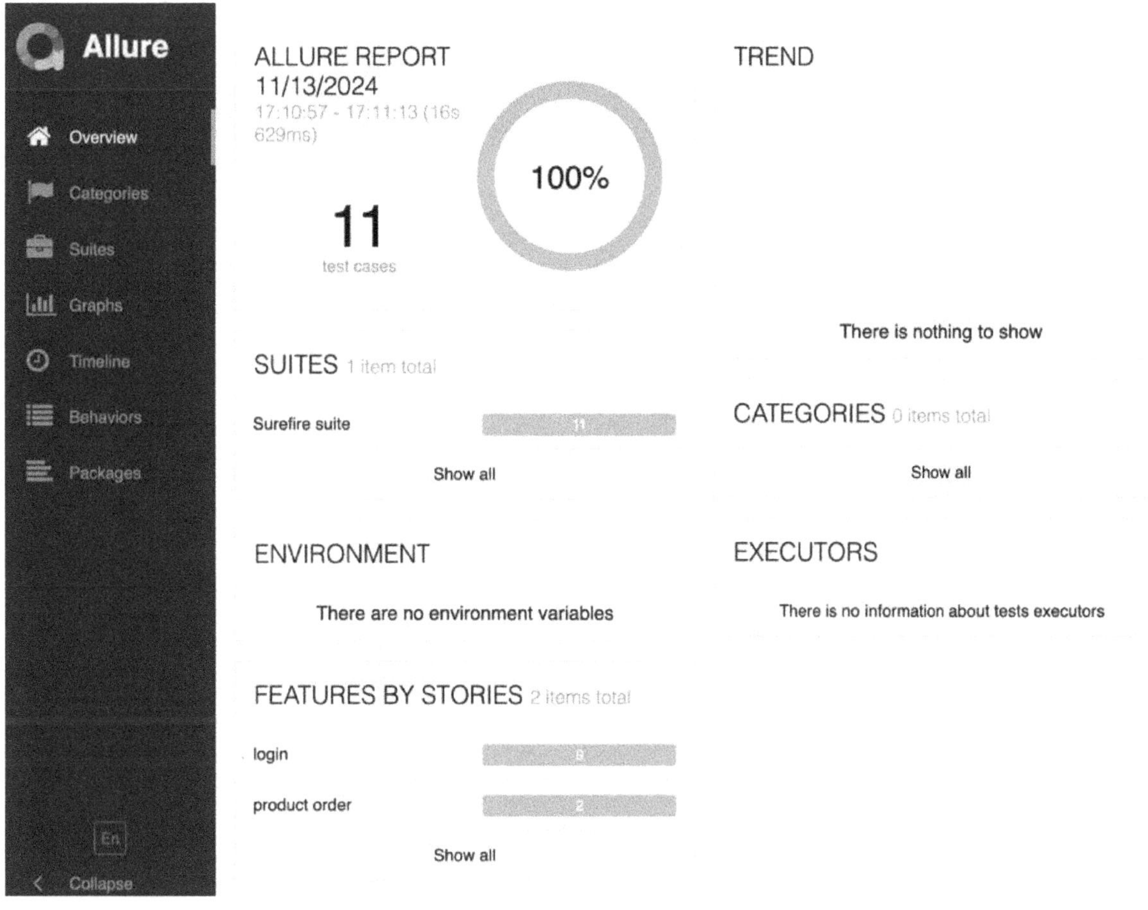

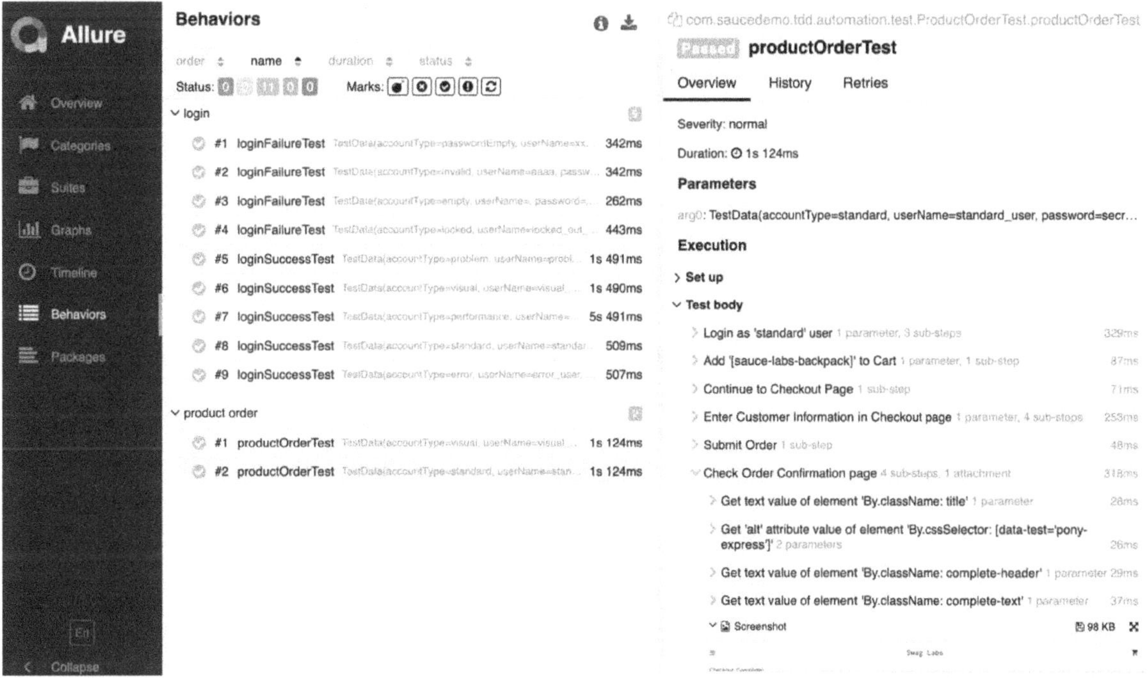

Extent Report: Open `reports/extent/extentReport.html` in browser.

Screenshot: See screenshot images in reports/screenshots

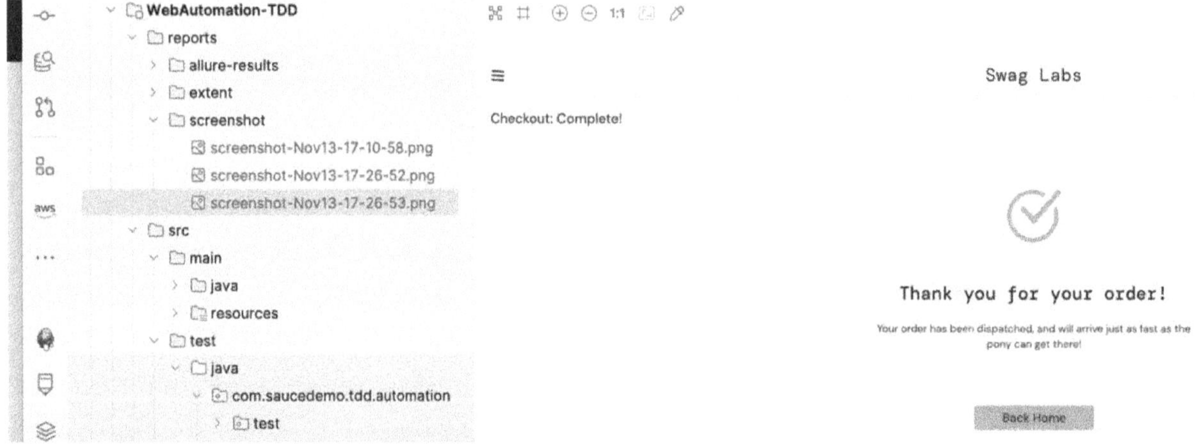

PROJECT 3: API AUTOMATION-RESTASSURED-BDD

This test automation project is for automating in-sprint/functional/regression tests for **PetStore** API Application using BDD and TDD. The tests are built using **Gherkin**, **JAVA**, **RestAssured**, **Cucumber BDD**, **TestNG** and **Maven**. Framework utility methods are developed on top of RestAssured. Common steps required for API automation are automated as part of the framework, this enables code re-usability, faster script development, easy maintenance and apt for in-sprint automation.

Prerequisites

- **JDK 11+** to run Java-based tests

- **Maven** for dependency management and running tests
- **Allure** for starting allure reports
- **IDE** Intellij or other

Clone the Repository

```
git clone https://github.com/insprintautomation/TestAutomationProjects.git
cd Automation-SampleProjects/ApiAutomation-RestAssured-BDD
```

Install Dependencies

Make sure `Maven` is installed on your machine. Then, run the following command to install all the dependencies: `mvn clean install -DskipTests`

Project Structure

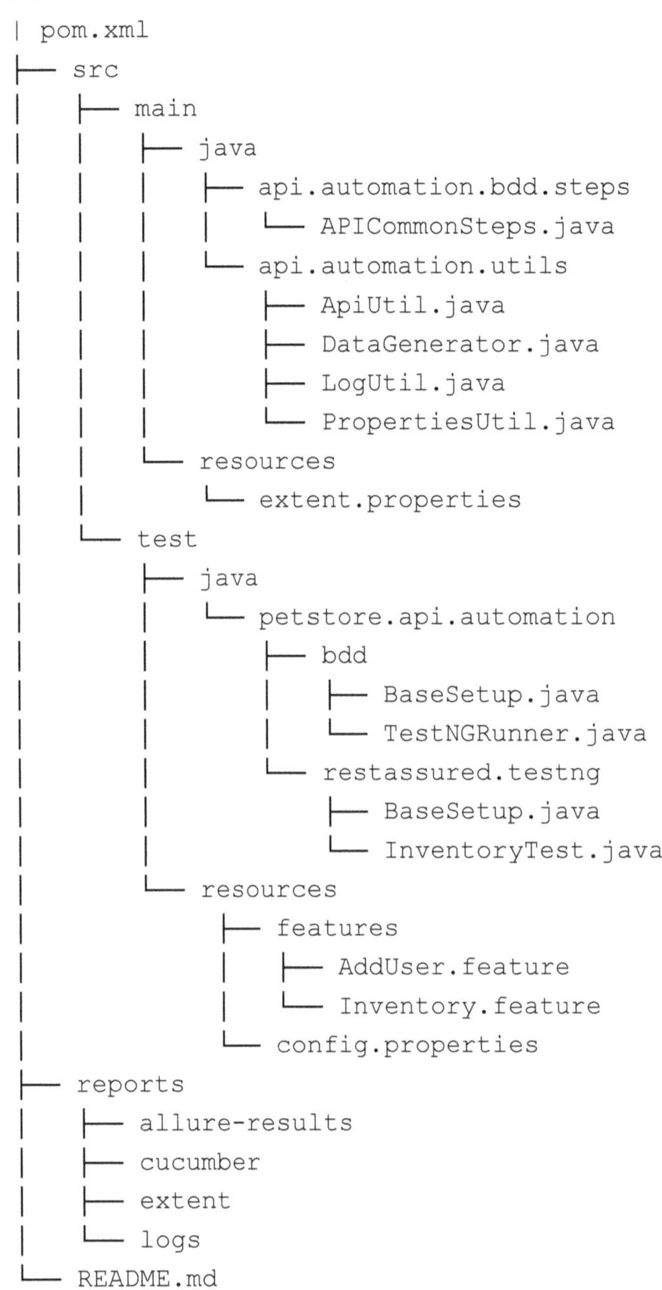

```
ApiAutomation-RestAssured-BDD
        | pom.xml
        ├── src
        |   ├── main
        |   |   ├── java
        |   |   |   ├── api.automation.bdd.steps
        |   |   |   |   └── APICommonSteps.java
        |   |   |   └── api.automation.utils
        |   |   |       ├── ApiUtil.java
        |   |   |       ├── DataGenerator.java
        |   |   |       ├── LogUtil.java
        |   |   |       └── PropertiesUtil.java
        |   |   └── resources
        |   |       └── extent.properties
        |   └── test
        |       ├── java
        |       |   └── petstore.api.automation
        |       |       ├── bdd
        |       |       |   ├── BaseSetup.java
        |       |       |   └── TestNGRunner.java
        |       |       └── restassured.testng
        |       |           ├── BaseSetup.java
        |       |           └── InventoryTest.java
        |       └── resources
        |           ├── features
        |           |   ├── AddUser.feature
        |           |   └── Inventory.feature
        |           └── config.properties
        ├── reports
        |   ├── allure-results
        |   ├── cucumber
        |   ├── extent
        |   └── logs
        └── README.md
```

Configuration

Create a `src\main\resources\extent.properties` file to configure the extent report.

```
basefolder.name= reports/extent/ExtentReport
basefolder.datetimepattern = MMM-d_HH-mm-ss
extent.reporter.spark.start=true
extent.reporter.spark.out=index.html
```

Create a `src\test\resources\config.properties` file to configure the environment, API baseurl and report flags.

```
environment=prod
# report and log config
```

```
consoleLogs=false
cucumberLogs=false
allureLogs=true
logFile=true
attachLogs=false
# api base url
prod.api.url=https://petstore.swagger.io/
test.api.url=
# api base path
inventory=v2/store/inventory
user=v2/user
```

Framework Utils

ApiUtil: ApiUtil.java has common reusable wrapper methods using RestAssured to create API request and perform response validations.

LogUtil: LogUtil.java has methods to create log files and adds step details in cucumber and allure report based on the config flags.

PropertiesUtil: PropertiesUtil.java has methods to load properties file and get value from command line arguments or properties file.

DataGenerator: `DataGenerator.java` uses Faker library to get random test data required to construct the request JSON for User account creation.

```java
package helpers;

import com.github.javafaker.Faker;
import net.minidev.json.JSONObject;
import java.security.SecureRandom;

public class DataGenerator {
        private static final String CHARACTERS =
"ABCDEFGHIJKLMNOPQRSTUVWXYZabcdefghijklmnopqrstuvwxyz0123456789!@#$%^&*()-_=+";
    private static final int PASSWORD_LENGTH = 8;

    public static String getUserRequestJson() {
        Faker faker = new Faker();
        JSONObject json = new JSONObject();
        json.put("id", faker.number().randomNumber());
        json.put("username", faker.name().username());
        json.put("firstName", faker.name().firstName());
        json.put("lastName", faker.name().lastName());
        json.put("email", faker.internet().emailAddress());
        json.put("password", getRandomPassword());
        json.put("phone", faker.phoneNumber().cellPhone());
        json.put("userStatus", 0);
```

```java
            return json.toString();
    }

    private static String getRandomPassword() {
        SecureRandom random = new SecureRandom();
        StringBuilder password = new StringBuilder(PASSWORD_LENGTH);
        for (int i = 0; i < PASSWORD_LENGTH; i++) {
            int index = random.nextInt(CHARACTERS.length());
            password.append(CHARACTERS.charAt(index));
        }
        return password.toString();
    }
}
```

BDD Tests

Below is the test scripts for testing inventory and user endpoints in `Petstore` API using `Cucumber BDD` approach.

Feature File:

Inventory.feature: Performs a `GET` request on endpoint `v2/store/inventory` and validates the response.

```gherkin
@smoke @inventory
Feature: Get Inventory

  Background: Define URL
    Given I set baseurl for inventory service

  @in-sprint @story-test123
  Scenario: Get Inventory details
    When I submit GET request
    Then I see response status 200
    And I see response matches for fields
      | sold      | [>=]1 |
      | pending   | [>=]0 |
      | available | [>=]0 |
```

User.feature: Performs a `POST` request on endpoint `v2/user` and validates the response. Uses a custom DataGenerators JAVA class to get test data using Faker and generates request body.

```gherkin
@smoke @addUser
Feature: Add User

  Background: Define URL
    Given I set baseurl for user service

  @in-sprint @story-test123
  Scenario: Add User successfully
    Given I set request JSON from getUserRequestJson
```

```
When I submit POST request
Then I see response status 200
And I see response matches for fields
  | code    | 200      |
  | type    | [string] |
  | message | [string] |
```

Step Definitions:

`APICommonSteps.java` has step definitions for the most common steps required for api automation. It uses `ApiUtil.java` methods to perform API operations.

```java
package com.api.automation.bdd.steps;

import com.api.automation.utils.LogUtil;
import com.api.automation.utils.ApiUtil;
import com.api.automation.utils.DataGenerator;
import io.cucumber.datatable.DataTable;
import io.cucumber.java.en.And;
import io.cucumber.java.en.Given;
import io.cucumber.java.en.Then;
import io.cucumber.java.en.When;
import lombok.extern.slf4j.Slf4j;
import java.lang.reflect.InvocationTargetException;
import java.lang.reflect.Method;
import java.util.HashMap;
import java.util.Map;
import java.util.Objects;

@Slf4j
public class APICommonSteps {

    private ApiUtil apiUtil;

    @Given("I set baseurl for {} service")
    public void setBaseurl(String apiName) {
        apiUtil = new ApiUtil();
      LogUtil.logStep("Given I set baseurl for %s service".formatted(apiName));
        apiUtil.setBaseUrl(apiName); }

    @And("I set {} parameters")
    public void setParameters(String parameterType, DataTable params) {
        LogUtil.logStep("Given I set %s parameters".formatted(parameterType));
        Map<String, String> inputParams = Objects.isNull(params)
                ? new HashMap<>()
                : new HashMap<>(params.asMap());
        apiUtil.setParams(parameterType, new HashMap<>(inputParams));
    }
```

```java
@And("I set headers")
public void setHeaders(DataTable headers) {
    LogUtil.logStep("Given I set headers %s".formatted(headers));
    apiUtil.setHeaders(new HashMap<>(headers.asMap()));
}

@When("I submit {} request")
public void submitRequest(String method) {
    LogUtil.logStep("When I submit %s request".formatted(method));
    apiUtil.submitRequest(method);
}

@Then("I see response status {}")
public void verifyResponseStatus(Integer statusCode) {
    LogUtil.logStep("Then I see response status %s".formatted(statusCode));
    apiUtil.verifyResponseStatus(statusCode);
}

@Then("I see response matches for fields")
public void verifyResponseBody(DataTable data) {
    LogUtil.logStep("Then I see matches for fields %s".formatted(data));
    apiUtil.verifyResponseBody(data.asMap());
}

@Then("I see response header value matches for headers")
public void verifyResponseHeaders(DataTable data) {
    LogUtil.logStep("Then I see response header value matches for headers %s".formatted(data));
    apiUtil.verifyResponseHeaders(new HashMap<>(data.asMap()));
}

@Then("I check all {} items")
public void verifyResponseBodyAllItems(String jsonPath, DataTable data) {
    LogUtil.logStep("Then I check all %s items %s".formatted(jsonPath, data));
    apiUtil.verifyResponseAllItems(jsonPath, new HashMap<>(data.asMap()));
}

@Then("I save {} as {} from response")
public void saveResponse(String jsonPath, String name) {
    LogUtil.logStep("Then I save %s as %s from response".formatted(jsonPath, name));
    apiUtil.saveResponse(jsonPath, name, false);
}

@Then("I get random {} from response & save as {}")
```

```java
    public void saveResponseRandom(String jsonPath, String name) {
        LogUtil.logStep("Then I get random %s from response & save as %s".
formatted(jsonPath, name));
        apiUtil.saveResponse(jsonPath, name, true);
    }


    @Then("I see response matches json schema {}")
    public void verifyJsonSchema(String fileName) {
        LogUtil.logStep("Then I see response matches json schema %s".
formatted(fileName));
        apiUtil.verifyJsonSchema(fileName);
    }


    @And("I set request JSON string")
    public void setRequestBodyAsString(String requestBody) {
        LogUtil.logStep("Given I set request JSON string %n %s".
formatted(requestBody));
        apiUtil.setRequestJson(requestBody);
    }


    @Given("I set request JSON from {}")
    public void setRequestBody(String requestJsonMethod) {
        LogUtil.logStep("Given I set request JSON from %s".
formatted(requestJsonMethod));
        try {
          Method dataMethod = DataGenerator.class.getMethod(requestJsonMethod);
            Object requestJson = dataMethod.invoke(new DataGenerator());
            setRequestBodyAsString(String.valueOf(requestJson));
            } catch (NoSuchMethodException | IllegalAccessException |
InvocationTargetException e) {
            throw new RuntimeException(e);
        }
    }


    @And("I set {} as {}")
    public void setValue(String name, String value) {
        LogUtil.logStep("Given I set %s as %s".formatted(name, value));
        apiUtil.saveValue(name, value);
    }
}
```

BaseSetup:

`BaseSetup.java` has the common code for setup and tear down. Methods can use cucumber or testng/junit annotations. Below example code uses `@BeforeAll` annotation from cucumber to load the properties file.

```java
package com.petstore.api.automation.bdd;

import com.api.automation.utils.PropertiesUtil;
import io.cucumber.java.BeforeAll;

public class BaseSetup {

    @BeforeAll
    public static void beforeAll() {
        PropertiesUtil.loadProperties("config.properties");
    }
}
```

Test Runner:

Test Runner class can be created using TestNG or JUnit. Below is the example code for running tests using TestNG.

```java
package com.petstore.api.automation.bdd;

import io.cucumber.testng.AbstractTestNGCucumberTests;
import io.cucumber.testng.CucumberOptions;
import org.testng.annotations.DataProvider;

@CucumberOptions(
        features = "classpath:features",
         glue = {"com.api.automation.bdd.steps", "com.petstore.api.automation.
bdd"},
        tags = "@smoke",
        monochrome = true,
        dryRun = false,
        plugin = {"html:reports/cucumber/cucumber.html",
                "json:reports/cucumber/cucumber.json",
        "com.aventstack.extentreports.cucumber.adapter.ExtentCucumberAdapter:",
                "io.qameta.allure.cucumber7jvm.AllureCucumber7Jvm",
                "rerun:reports/cucumber/failed_scenarios.txt",
                "pretty"},
        publish = true
)
public class TestNGRunner extends AbstractTestNGCucumberTests {
```

```
    @DataProvider(parallel = true)
    public Object[][] scenarios() {
        return super.scenarios();
    }
}
```

TestNG Tests

Approach 1: Using RestAssured methods

Below are the scripts for testing add user endpoint `v2/user` for petstore API using RestAssured and TestNG.

```java
package com.petstore.api.automation.restassured.testng;

import com.api.automation.utils.DataGenerator;
import com.api.automation.utils.PropertiesUtil;
import io.restassured.RestAssured;
import org.testng.annotations.Test;
import static org.hamcrest.CoreMatchers.equalTo;
import static org.hamcrest.CoreMatchers.not;
import static org.hamcrest.Matchers.empty;

public class UserTest extends BaseSetup {
    //  Using RestAssured directly
    @Test
    public void userTest() {
        String requestBody = DataGenerator.getUserRequestJson();
        String baseUri = PropertiesUtil.getProperty("prod.api.url");
        RestAssured.given()
                .log().all()
                .baseUri(baseUri)
                .header("Content-Type", "application/json")
                .body(requestBody)
                .when()
                .post("v2/user")
                .then()
                .log().all()
                .statusCode(200)
                .body("code", equalTo(200))
                .body("type", not(empty()))
                .body("message", not(empty()));
    }
}
```

Approach 2: Using ApiUtil methods Below is the scripts for testing add inventory endpoint `v2/store/inventory` for petstore API using `ApiUtil.java`. ApiUtil has wrapper methods for API operations which uses RestAssured.

```java
package com.petstore.api.automation.restassured.testng;
```

```java
import com.api.automation.utils.ApiUtil;
import org.testng.annotations.Test;
import static io.restassured.http.Method.GET;

public class InventoryTest extends BaseSetup {
    //  Using ApiUtil wrapper methods which uses RestAssured
    @Test
    public void inventoryTest() {
        ApiUtil apiUtil = new ApiUtil();
        apiUtil.setBaseUrl("inventory");
        apiUtil.submitRequest(GET.name());
        apiUtil.verifyResponseStatus(200);
        apiUtil.verifyResponseBody("sold", "[>=]1");
        apiUtil.verifyResponseBody("pending", "[>=]0");
    }
}
```

Running BDD Tests

Add build step in pom.xml to run tests using `maven-surefire-plugin`.

```xml
<build>
    <plugins>
        <plugin>
            <groupId>org.apache.maven.plugins</groupId>
            <artifactId>maven-surefire-plugin</artifactId>
            <version>3.1.2</version>
            <configuration>
                <testFailureIgnore>false</testFailureIgnore>
                <systemPropertyVariables>
                    <allure.results.directory>
                        ${project.basedir}/reports/allure-results
                    </allure.results.directory>
                </systemPropertyVariables>
                <argLine>
                        -javaagent:"${settings.localRepository}/org/aspectj/
aspectjweaver/${aspectj.version}/aspectjweaver-${aspectj.version}.jar"
                </argLine>
            </configuration>
            <dependencies>
                <dependency>
                    <groupId>org.aspectj</groupId>
                    <artifactId>aspectjweaver</artifactId>
                    <version>${aspectj.version}</version>
                </dependency>
            </dependencies>
        </plugin>
    </plugins>
</build>
```

CommandLine:

Change to directory `ApiAutomation-RestAssured-BDD`.

To execute all tests, run maven command `mvn clean test`.

To filter specific group of `Cucumber BDD` tests and execute, run maven command `mvn clean test -Dcucumber.filter.tags="@inventory" -Denvironment=prod`.

To run `Cucumber BDD` tests using parallel threads, run maven command `mvn clean test -Ddataproviderthreadcount=5`.

Running TestNG Tests

Add build profile step in pom.xml to run tests using `maven-surefire-plugin`.

```xml
<profiles>
    <profile>
        <id>testng</id>
        <build>
            <plugins>
                <plugin>
                    <groupId>org.apache.maven.plugins</groupId>
                    <artifactId>maven-surefire-plugin</artifactId>
                    <version>3.1.2</version>
                    <configuration>
                        <systemPropertyVariables>
                         <allure.results.directory>${project.basedir}/reports/
testng/allure-results</allure.results.directory>
                        </systemPropertyVariables>
                        <argLine>
                            -javaagent:${settings.localRepository}/org/aspectj/
aspectjweaver/${aspectj.version}/aspectjweaver-${aspectj.version}.jar
                        </argLine>
                        <includes>
                            <include>**/com.petstore.api.automation.restassured.
testng/*.java</include>
                        </includes>
                    </configuration>
                    <dependencies>
                        <dependency>
                            <groupId>org.aspectj</groupId>
                            <artifactId>aspectjweaver</artifactId>
                            <version>${aspectj.version}</version>
                        </dependency>
                    </dependencies>
                </plugin>
            </plugins>
        </build>
    </profile>
</profiles>
```

CommandLine:

Change to directory `ApiAutomation-RestAssured-BDD`.

To execute all tests, run maven command `mvn clean test -Ptestng`.

To filter specific group of `TestNG` tests and execute, run maven command `mvn clean test -Ptestng -Dgroups="inventory" -Denvironment=prod`.

To run `TestNG` tests in parallel, run maven command `mvn clean test -Ptestng -Dgroups="inventory" -Dthreadcount=5`.

Reports

After the test execution, allure, cucumber and extent reports will be generated in `reports` directory.

Allure Report: Start the allure report using command line `allure serve` from the `reports` directory.

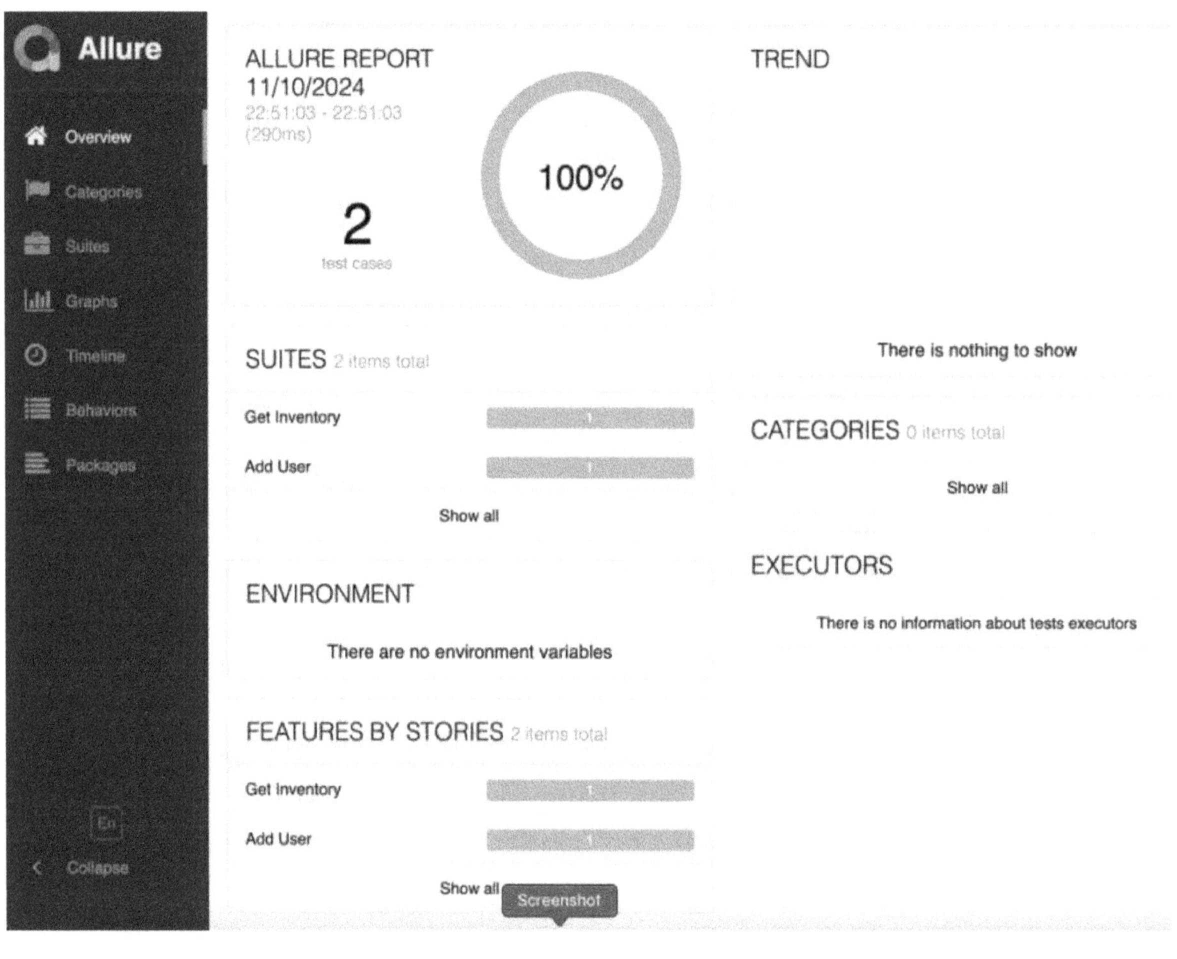

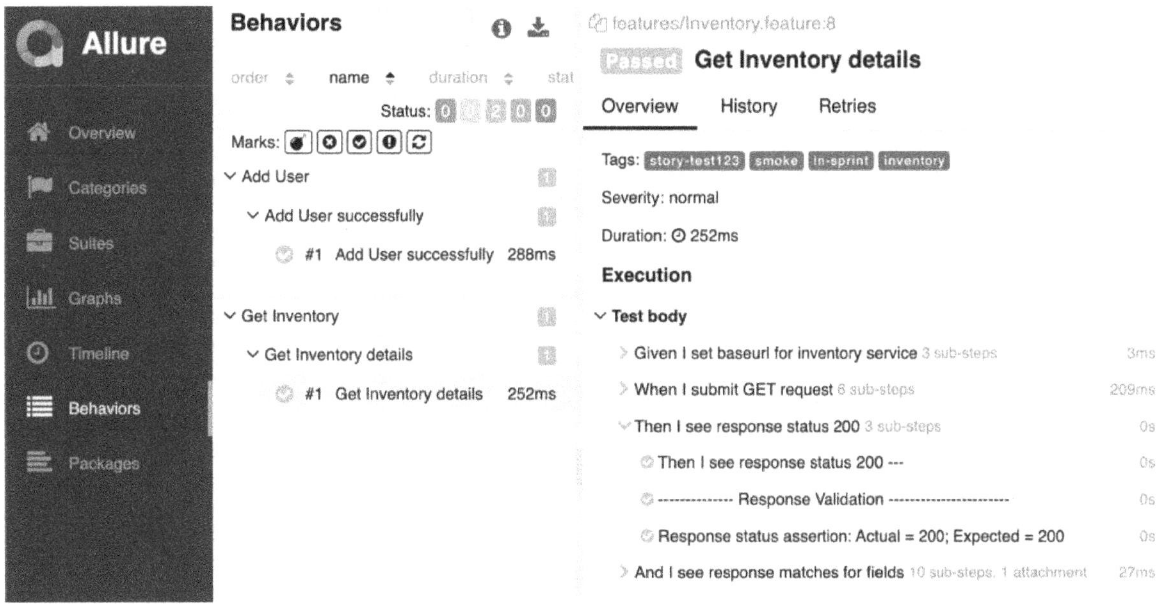

Cucumber Report: Open reports/cucumber/cucumber.html in browser.

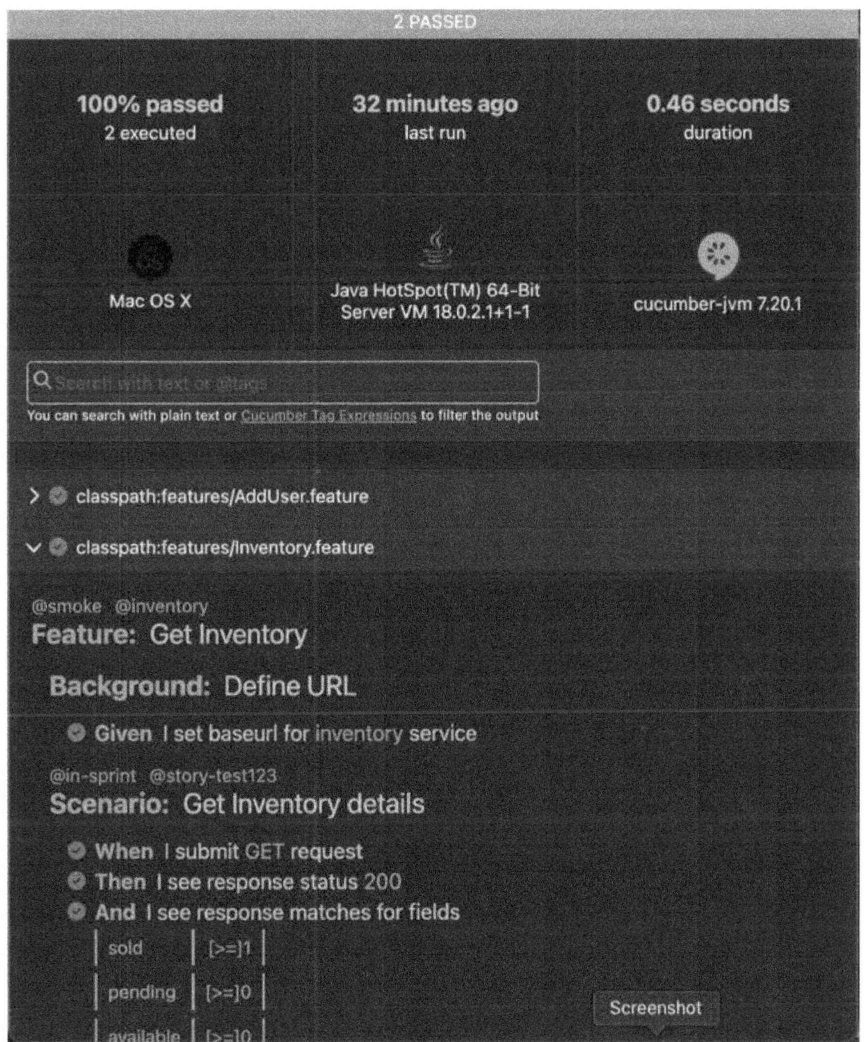

Extent Report: Open reports/extent/index.html in browser.

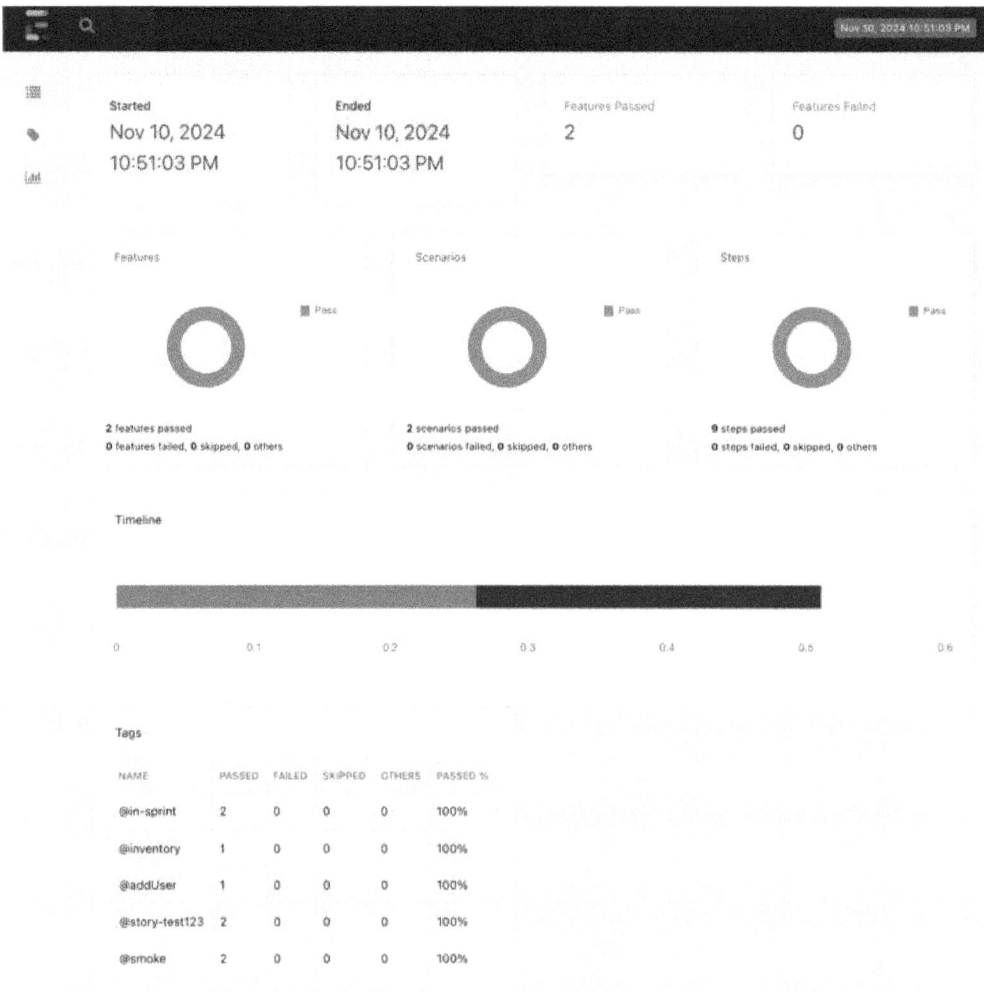

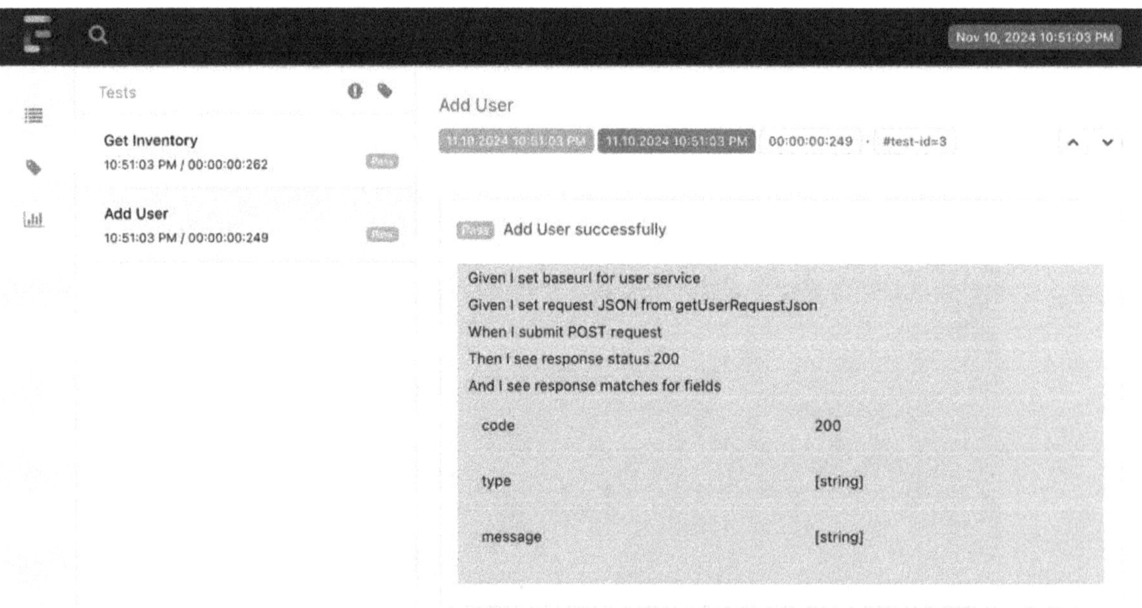

Logs: Open reports/logs/logs.txt file.

```
INFO : ------------- Creating Request ------------------------
INFO : API Request URL: https://petstore.swagger.io/v2/store/inventory
INFO : Request URI: https://petstore.swagger.io/v2/store/inventory
INFO : Submitting GET request
Request method: GET
Request URI:       https://petstore.swagger.io/v2/store/inventory
Proxy:             <none>
Request params:  <none>
Query params:    <none>
Form params:     <none>
Path params:     <none>
Headers:           Accept=*/*
Cookies:           <none>
Multiparts:        <none>
Body:              <none>
INFO : ------------- Response ----------------------------
INFO : {
    "sold": 49,
    "The Best Dog of World": 1,
    "string": 70,
    "unavailable": 4,
    "pending": 29,
```

PROJECT 4: API AUTOMATION-KARATEDSL

This test automation project for automating in-sprint/functional/regression tests for the **PetStore** API Application using BDD (Behavioural Driven Development). The tests are built using **Gherkin**, **JAVA**, **Karate DSL**, **JUnit** and **Maven**.

Karate DSL is a popular open-source framework for API testing that is built on top of **Cucumber**. It allows you to write tests in a simple, readable domain-specific language (DSL) with minimal setup. Karate integrates both API testing and UI testing in one framework, offering powerful features like performance testing, mocking, and data-driven testing.

Prerequisites

- **JDK 11+** to run Java-based tests
- **Maven** for dependency management and running tests
- **IDE** Intellij or other

Clone the Repository

```
git clone https://github.com/insprintautomation/TestAutomationProjects.git
cd Automation-SampleProjects/ApiAutomation-KarateDSL
```

Install Dependencies

Make sure `Maven` is installed on your machine. Then, run the following command to install all the dependencies: `mvn clean install -DskipTests`

Project Structure

```
ApiAutomation-KarateDSL
        | pom.xml
        ├── src
        |    └── test
        |         └── java
        |              ├── helpers
        |              |    ├── DataGenerator.java
        |              |    └── Login.feature
        |              ├── petstore
        |              |    ├── PetstoreTest.java
        |              |    └── features
        |              |         ├── AddUser.feature
        |              |         └── Inventory.feature
        |              ├── logback-test.xml
        |              └── karate-config.js
        └── README.md
```

Karate Configuration

Create a `karate-config.js` file and configure the environment, API baseurl and base steps.

```javascript
function fn() {
  var env = karate.env; // get system property 'karate.env'
  karate.log('karate.env system property was:', env);
  if (!env) {
    env = 'dev';
  }
  var config = {
    apiUrl: 'https://petstore.swagger.io/'
  }
  let sessionId = karate.callSingle('classpath:helpers/Login.feature', config).
sessionId
//  karate.configure('headers', {Authorization: 'Token ' + accessToken})
  return config;
}
```

Create a `JUnit` **Test runner class** `PetstoreTest.java`.

```java
package petstore;

import com.intuit.karate.Results;
import com.intuit.karate.Runner;
import org.junit.jupiter.api.Test;
import static org.junit.jupiter.api.Assertions.assertEquals;
```

```java
public class PetstoreTest {
    @Test
    void testParallel() {
        Results results = Runner.path("classpath:petstore")
                .outputCucumberJson(true)
                .parallel(5);
        assertEquals(0, results.getFailCount(), results.getErrorMessages());
    }
}
```

BDD Tests

Below is the test scripts for testing inventory and user feature/endpoints in Petstore API. Refer Karate documentation for the step's usage.

Inventory.feature: Performs a GET request on endpoint `v2/store/inventory` and validates the response.

```gherkin
@smoke @regression @inventory
Feature: Get Inventory

  Background: Define URL
    Given url apiUrl


  @in-sprint @story-test123
  Scenario: Get Inventory details
    Given path 'v2/store/inventory'
    When method Get
    Then status 200
    And assert response.sold >= 1
    And assert response.pending >= 0
    And assert response.available >= 0
```

User.feature: Performs a POST request on endpoint `v2/user` and validates the response. Uses a custom DataGenerators JAVA class to get test data using Faker and generates request body.

```gherkin
@smoke @regression @addUser
Feature: Add User

  Background: Define URL
    * def dataGenerator = Java.type('helpers.DataGenerator')
    Given url apiUrl


  @story-test123 @in-sprint
  Scenario: Add User successfully
    Given path 'v2/user'
```

```
* def requestJson = dataGenerator.getUserRequestJson()
And request requestJson
When method Post
Then status 200
And match response.code == 200
And match response == {"code":200,"type":"#string","message":'#string'}
```

Data Generator

`DataGenerator.java` uses Faker library to get random test data required to construct the request JSON for User account creation.

```java
package helpers;

import com.github.javafaker.Faker;
import net.minidev.json.JSONObject;
import java.security.SecureRandom;

public class DataGenerator {
  private static final String CHARACTERS =
"ABCDEFGHIJKLMNOPQRSTUVWXYZabcdefghijklmnopqrstuvwxyz0123456789!@#$%^&*()-_=+";
  private static final int PASSWORD_LENGTH = 8;

  public static JSONObject getUserRequestJson() {
    Faker faker = new Faker();
    JSONObject json = new JSONObject();
    json.put("id", faker.number().randomNumber());
    json.put("username", faker.name().username());
    json.put("firstName", faker.name().firstName());
    json.put("lastName", faker.name().lastName());
    json.put("email", faker.internet().emailAddress());
    json.put("password", getRandomPassword());
    json.put("phone", faker.phoneNumber().cellPhone());
    json.put("userStatus", 0);
    return json;
  }


  private static String getRandomPassword() {
    SecureRandom random = new SecureRandom();
    StringBuilder password = new StringBuilder(PASSWORD_LENGTH);
    for (int i = 0; i < PASSWORD_LENGTH; i++) {
      int index = random.nextInt(CHARACTERS.length());
      password.append(CHARACTERS.charAt(index));
    }
    return password.toString();
  }
}
```

Running Tests

Add build step in pom.xml to run tests using `maven-surefire-plugin`.

```xml
<build>
    <testResources>
        <testResource>
            <directory>src/test/java</directory>
            <excludes>
                <exclude>**/*.java</exclude>
            </excludes>
        </testResource>
    </testResources>
    <plugins>
        <plugin>
            <groupId>org.apache.maven.plugins</groupId>
            <artifactId>maven-surefire-plugin</artifactId>
            <version>${maven.surefire.version}</version>
            <configuration>
                <argLine>-Dfile.encoding=UTF-8</argLine>
            </configuration>
        </plugin>
    </plugins>
</build>
```

CommandLine:

Change to directory `ApiAutomation-KarateDSL`.

To execute all tests, run maven command `mvn clean test`.

To filter specific group of tests and execute, run maven command `mvn test -Dkarate.options="--tags @inventory"`.

Reports

After the test execution, Karate reports will be generated in `target\karate-reports` directory. Open `karate-summary.html` in browser.

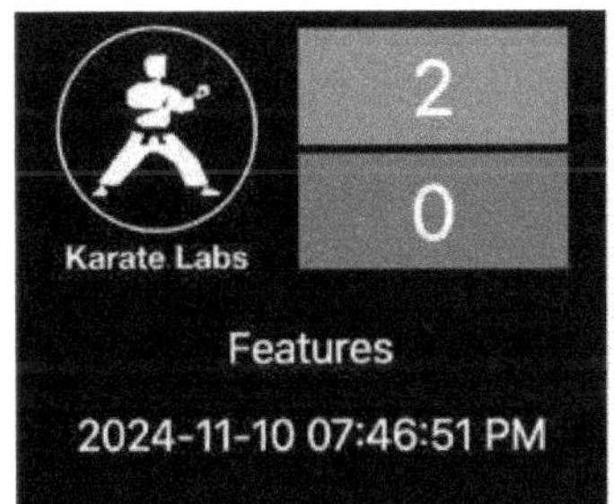

Tags | Timeline					
Feature	**Title**	**Passed**	**Failed**	**Scenarios**	**Time (ms)**
petstore/features/AddUser.feature	Add User	1	0	1	637
petstore/features/Inventory.feature	Get Inventory	1	0	1	236

To see the tests and steps details for a feature, click on the feature file link.

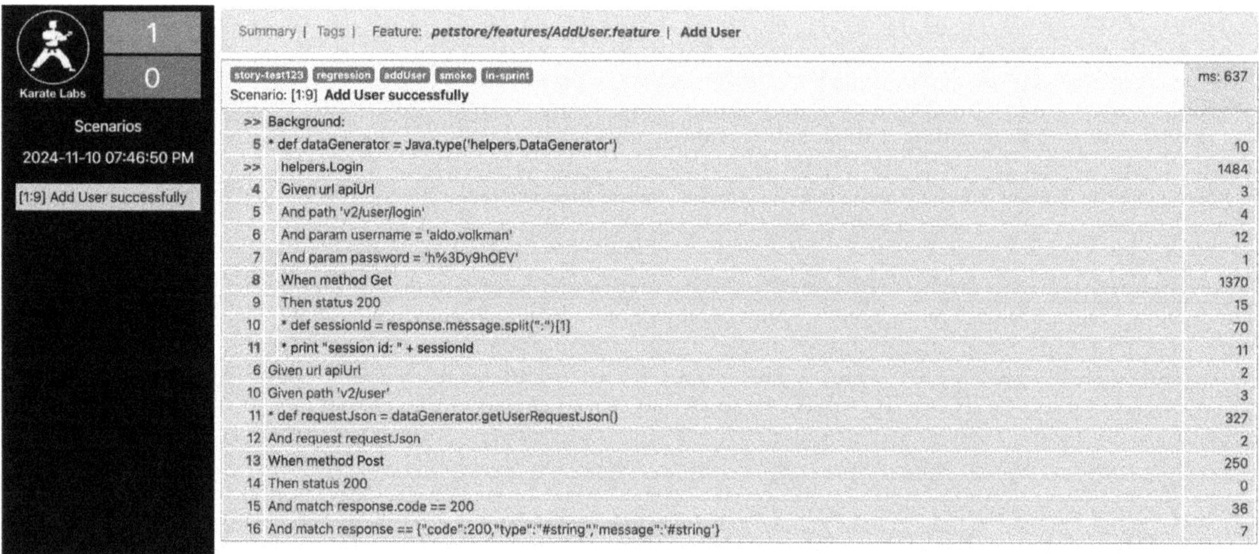

To see the logs, click on the steps having links.

APPENDIX C: GLOSSARY OF TERMS

This detailed glossary provides definitions and explanations of essential terms in Agile testing, in-sprint automation, and CI/CD. Each entry offers conceptual context to help readers deepen their understanding of practices, tools, and strategies within Agile environments.

A

Acceptance Criteria
- **Definition**: Conditions a user story must meet to be considered complete, typically defining functional and non-functional requirements.
- **Context**: Serves as the foundation for creating automated tests and is essential for user acceptance testing to verify that features align with stakeholder expectations.

Acceptance Testing
- **Definition**: Testing conducted to verify if the system meets business requirements and user expectations.
- **Context**: Often performed by end users or clients, acceptance testing helps validate that the product is ready for release.

Activity Diagram
- **Definition**: A visual representation of a process flow, showing sequential activities and decision points.
- **Context**: Helps teams understand workflows and identify potential issues in system operations.

Affinity Estimation
- **Definition**: A technique for categorizing user stories by relative size and complexity, promoting rapid estimation.
- **Context**: Helps Agile teams quickly assess effort for each story, fostering alignment on task complexity.

Agile Coach
- **Definition**: A mentor who supports Agile adoption, facilitating practices and helping teams improve processes.
- **Context**: The coach fosters team collaboration, continuous improvement, and alignment with Agile principles.

Agile Manifesto
- **Definition**: A declaration of values and principles advocating flexibility, collaboration, and customer satisfaction in software development.
- **Context**: Guides Agile methodologies and emphasizes iterative development and adaptability to change.

Agile Methodology
- **Definition**: An iterative approach to software development that prioritizes flexibility, frequent feedback, and incremental delivery.
- **Context**: Encourages collaborative, adaptive planning to meet evolving user needs.

Agile Release Train (ART)
- **Definition**: A collection of Agile teams working towards a common goal within SAFe, delivering value incrementally through Program Increments (PIs).
- **Context**: Used in large-scale Agile environments to align multiple teams on shared objectives.

Automated Regression Suite
- **Definition**: A suite of automated tests that ensure new changes don't negatively affect existing functionality.
- **Context**: Essential in Agile for maintaining software stability as new features are added.

Automation Tool
- **Definition**: Software used to automate testing tasks, such as Selenium for UI testing or Appium for mobile.
- **Context**: Reduces manual testing, accelerating feedback and enhancing test coverage within Agile sprints.

B

Backlog Grooming
- **Definition**: The process of refining the product backlog to ensure items are clearly defined, estimated, and prioritized.
- **Context**: Ensures backlog items are prepared for upcoming sprints, allowing the team to start work without delays.

Behavior-Driven Development (BDD)
- **Definition**: An Agile development practice that involves defining requirements as executable examples in plain language.
- **Context**: BDD fosters collaboration between business and technical teams, using tools like Cucumber to create understandable test scenarios.

Behavioral Test
- **Definition**: A test type that verifies the behavior of a system under different conditions.
- **Context**: Behavioral tests validate user expectations and usability, ensuring a satisfactory user experience.

Burndown Chart
- **Definition**: A visual tool that shows the remaining work versus time in a sprint or project.
- **Context**: Tracks progress, helping teams gauge if they are on pace to meet sprint goals.

Burnup Chart
- **Definition**: A chart showing completed work against the total planned work over time.
- **Context**: Helps teams visualize progress and manage scope changes.

C

Cadence
- **Definition**: The predictable rhythm of Agile events, like sprint planning and reviews.
- **Context**: Establishes a structured flow for Agile processes, promoting consistency.

Cohesion
- **Definition**: A design principle referring to the alignment of functionalities within a module.
- **Context**: High cohesion makes code easier to maintain and enhances modularity in test automation.

Code Coverage
- **Definition**: A metric indicating the percentage of code executed by tests.
- **Context**: Used to identify untested paths and enhance test thoroughness within CI/CD.

Code Review
- **Definition**: An examination of source code by other developers to catch issues and improve quality.
- **Context**: Improves code quality, ensures adherence to standards, and fosters knowledge sharing.

Continuous Deployment (CD)
- **Definition**: Automatically deploying code to production after passing all automated tests.
- **Context**: Helps Agile teams deliver new functionality continuously, ensuring software is always releasable.

Continuous Integration (CI)
- **Definition**: The practice of merging code changes frequently, with automated tests validating each change.
- **Context**: Ensures that new code integrates smoothly, catching issues early and enabling rapid feedback.

Cumulative Flow Diagram (CFD)
- **Definition**: A Kanban-based visualization that shows the state of tasks (e.g., to-do, in progress, done) over time.
- **Context**: Tracks bottlenecks and provides a high-level view of project progress.

Cross-Browser Testing
- **Definition**: Testing a web application across different browsers to ensure consistent functionality.
- **Context**: Ensures a consistent user experience and identifies browser-specific issues in UI tests.

Cross-Platform Testing
- **Definition**: Verifying that an application performs consistently across different OS and devices.
- **Context**: Ensures applications meet requirements on platforms like Windows, iOS, and Android.

D

Daily Stand-up
- **Definition**: A short, daily meeting where team members discuss progress, plans, and blockers.
- **Context**: Promotes transparency, quick issue resolution, and team alignment.

Definition of Done (DoD)
- **Definition**: A shared checklist specifying when a user story or task is complete.
- **Context**: Ensures consistency in meeting quality standards and project requirements.

DevOps
- **Definition**: A set of practices bridging software development and IT operations to improve software quality and release frequency.
- **Context**: Emphasizes CI/CD, infrastructure automation, and collaboration for streamlined delivery.

Dynamic Testing
- **Definition**: Testing that involves executing the software to validate its functionality.
- **Context**: Includes functional, regression, and performance testing to identify runtime issues.

E

Exploratory Testing
- **Definition**: A manual testing approach where testers actively explore the application to discover defects without predefined scripts.
- **Context**: Allows testers to use intuition and creativity, often revealing complex, unexpected issues.

Extreme Programming (XP)
- **Definition**: An Agile methodology focused on technical excellence and frequent releases, emphasizing practices like pair programming and TDD.
- **Context**: Improves software quality through disciplined engineering practices and collaborative planning.

F

Feature Toggle
- **Definition**: A technique for enabling or disabling features via configuration without deploying new code.
- **Context**: Allows for safe feature rollouts, A/B testing, and controlled experimentation in Agile environments.

Functional Testing
- **Definition**: Verifying that the software meets functional requirements by focusing on application features.
- **Context**: Ensures that key features, such as login and checkout, work as intended.

H

Hardening Sprint
- **Definition**: A sprint dedicated to fixing bugs, improving performance, and stabilizing the product before release.
- **Context**: Commonly used for final polish and quality assurance before deployment.

I

Impediment
- **Definition**: An obstacle that blocks progress toward sprint goals.
- **Context**: The Scrum Master works to remove impediments, enabling the team to maintain productivity.

Increment
- **Definition**: A potentially shippable product version that includes all completed backlog items from a sprint.
- **Context**: Each increment builds on the previous, delivering continuous value to users.

Incremental Development
- **Definition**: Building functionality in small, usable parts that are delivered incrementally.
- **Context**: Enables frequent releases and accommodates user feedback.

In-Sprint Automation
- **Definition**: Developing automated tests within the same sprint as the feature, ensuring immediate test coverage.
- **Context**: Reduces testing bottlenecks and ensures that new features are validated and ready for release by sprint end.

Integration Testing
- **Definition**: Testing combined modules to ensure they function together as expected.
- **Context**: Validates module interfaces and catches integration issues early in development.

Invest Criteria
- **Definition**: A checklist for well-written user stories: Independent, Negotiable, Valuable, Estimable, Small, and Testable.
- **Context**: Ensures stories are actionable and clear, making planning and estimation more accurate.

Iteration
- **Definition**: A short development cycle within Agile, typically one to four weeks, focused on completing a set of user stories.
- **Context**: Provides regular opportunities for feedback and continuous progress.

Iteration Goal
- **Definition**: The objectives set for a specific iteration, providing focus and clarity on expected outcomes.
- **Context**: Helps align the team on priorities and purpose.

K

Kaizen
- **Definition**: A Japanese term for "continuous improvement."
- **Context**: Encourages ongoing enhancements in processes, products, and team dynamics in Agile.

Kanban
- **Definition**: An Agile methodology that emphasizes visualizing work and limiting WIP to improve flow.
- **Context**: Used to balance workload and reduce bottlenecks through continuous task management.

L

Large Solution Level
- **Definition**: A SAFe level managing complex systems across multiple Agile Release Trains.
- **Context**: Focuses on delivering coordinated, large-scale solutions that require cross-team alignment.

Lean Portfolio Management (LPM)
- **Definition**: A SAFe practice focused on aligning projects and resources to organizational goals.
- **Context**: Ensures strategic alignment and efficient resource allocation across Agile projects.

M

Minimum Marketable Feature (MMF)
- **Definition**: The smallest feature that can deliver value to users.
- **Context**: Helps prioritize development efforts to achieve quick feedback and early value delivery.

Minimum Viable Product (MVP)
- **Definition**: A functional, minimal product version released to validate market demand.
- **Context**: Provides rapid feedback, allowing teams to iterate based on user responses.

MoSCoW Prioritization
- **Definition**: A method for categorizing requirements into Must Have, Should Have, Could Have, and Won't Have.
- **Context**: Assists teams in focusing on critical features first.

N

Non-Functional Requirements (NFRs)
- **Definition**: Requirements specifying system attributes like performance, security, and scalability.
- **Context**: Ensures the system meets user expectations beyond functionality.

P

Pair Programming
- **Definition**: A practice where two developers work together, with one writing code and the other reviewing.
- **Context**: Increases code quality, fosters knowledge sharing, and reduces errors.

Parking Lot Chart
- **Definition**: A tool for tracking issues or features that need to be addressed later.
- **Context**: Keeps track of deferred items without distracting from current priorities.

Persona Mapping
- **Definition**: Creating user personas to represent different segments of the product's audience.
- **Context**: Guides design and development by focusing on specific user needs and goals.

Planning Poker
- **Definition**: An Agile estimation technique where team members use cards with numbers to estimate the effort required for user stories.
- **Context**: Facilitates consensus by having team members reveal their estimates simultaneously, helping identify varying perspectives and reach an agreement on effort.

Product Backlog
- **Definition**: A prioritized list of features, enhancements, and fixes that represent the work required to achieve the product vision.
- **Context**: Managed by the Product Owner, the backlog is continuously refined to reflect changing priorities, helping guide sprint planning.

Product Increment
- **Definition**: The cumulative result of all completed work during a sprint, forming a potentially shippable version of the product.
- **Context**: Ensures that each increment builds upon previous work, aligning with Agile's goal of delivering continuous, incremental value.

Product Owner
- **Definition**: The individual responsible for maximizing the value of the product and managing the product backlog.
- **Context**: Acts as the voice of the customer, ensuring that the team works on the highest-priority items to deliver business value.

Program Increment (PI) Planning
- **Definition**: A SAFe event where teams plan their work for the next Program Increment (usually a set of 5-10 iterations).
- **Context**: Aligns all teams within an Agile Release Train, ensuring consistent objectives and priorities for upcoming iterations.

Q

Quality Assurance (QA)
- **Definition**: A set of activities designed to ensure software quality by improving the development process and identifying defects early.
- **Context**: QA includes testing, code reviews, and adherence to coding standards to maintain high-quality releases.

R

Refactoring
- **Definition**: The process of restructuring existing code without changing its external behavior, improving readability, and reducing complexity.
- **Context**: Helps maintain clean, manageable code, making it easier to test, extend, and automate.

Regression Testing
- **Definition**: Testing that verifies recent changes do not negatively impact existing functionality.
- **Context**: Often automated within CI/CD pipelines to provide continuous assurance that code changes don't introduce regressions.

Release Burnup
- **Definition**: A chart that shows progress towards a release goal by tracking completed work over time.
- **Context**: Helps teams and stakeholders visualize remaining work and scope changes.

Release Train Engineer (RTE)
- **Definition**: A facilitator in SAFe responsible for ensuring smooth operations within an Agile Release Train.
- **Context**: The RTE coordinates events, facilitates cross-team collaboration, and helps remove roadblocks to maintain momentum.

Requirement Traceability Matrix (RTM)
- **Definition**: A document that maps requirements to test cases, ensuring comprehensive test coverage.
- **Context**: Verifies that all requirements are met in the final product, often essential for regulatory compliance.

Risk-Based Testing
- **Definition**: A testing approach that prioritizes testing activities based on the risk and potential impact of defects.
- **Context**: Ensures critical areas receive more testing, optimizing resources and mitigating high-risk issues.

Risk Register
- **Definition**: A document used to track project risks, their potential impact, mitigation plans, and ownership.
- **Context**: Essential in project management to proactively manage and address risks.

S

Scaled Agile Framework (SAFe)
- **Definition**: A framework for scaling Agile practices across large organizations, aligning multiple teams on shared goals.
- **Context**: Supports enterprise-level Agile transformation, enabling Agile principles to be applied at scale.

Scope Creep
- **Definition**: The gradual expansion of a project's scope beyond its original objectives, often leading to delays and cost overruns.
- **Context**: Agile practices like backlog refinement help manage scope creep by prioritizing requirements and limiting changes during sprints.

Scrum Board
- **Definition**: A visual tool used to track the status of tasks and user stories in a sprint.
- **Context**: Facilitates team transparency, allowing everyone to see task progress, identify bottlenecks, and stay aligned on sprint goals.

Scrum Master
- **Definition**: A servant leader responsible for facilitating Scrum ceremonies and ensuring the team follows Scrum principles.
- **Context**: The Scrum Master removes impediments and coaches the team in Agile practices to enhance productivity and collaboration.

Self-Organizing Team
- **Definition**: An Agile team that autonomously decides how best to accomplish tasks without outside direction.
- **Context**: Self-organizing teams take ownership of their work, fostering accountability and empowering team members to make decisions.

Servant Leadership
- **Definition**: A leadership philosophy that focuses on empowering and supporting the team rather than directing it.
- **Context**: Servant leaders prioritize team needs, creating an environment where team members can succeed.

Specification by Example (SBE)
- **Definition**: Using concrete examples to clarify requirements and guide development.
- **Context**: Helps bridge the gap between business and technical teams, ensuring shared understanding and alignment.

Spike
- **Definition**: A time-boxed research activity aimed at reducing risk or uncertainty in user stories or tasks.
- **Context**: Often used to explore technical challenges and gather information before committing to a particular approach.

Sprint

- **Definition**: A time-boxed period, usually lasting 1-4 weeks, during which a team completes a set of tasks.
- **Context**: Sprints enable Agile teams to deliver incremental improvements and gather regular feedback.

Sprint Backlog

- **Definition**: A list of tasks or user stories that the development team commits to completing within a sprint.
- **Context**: Derived from the product backlog, the sprint backlog represents the team's work for the iteration.

Sprint Planning

- **Definition**: A meeting at the beginning of each sprint where the team selects items from the backlog to work on.
- **Context**: Ensures alignment on sprint goals and clarifies the scope of work for the sprint.

Sprint Retrospective

- **Definition**: A meeting held at the end of each sprint for the team to reflect on what went well and what can be improved.
- **Context**: Promotes continuous improvement, enabling the team to enhance processes and productivity over time.

Sprint Review

- **Definition**: A meeting where the team presents completed work to stakeholders, gathering feedback for the next iteration.
- **Context**: Helps ensure alignment with business goals and allows stakeholders to provide input on the team's progress.

Story Decomposition

- **Definition**: Breaking down larger user stories into smaller, manageable tasks.
- **Context**: Simplifies estimation, execution, and planning, helping teams work more efficiently.

Story Mapping

- **Definition**: A technique for visualizing and prioritizing user stories along the customer journey.
- **Context**: Helps teams identify key features and prioritize development according to user needs.

Story Point

- **Definition**: A unit of measure for estimating the effort needed to complete a user story.
- **Context**: Facilitates planning by providing a relative measure of complexity, risk, and effort.

Swarming

- **Definition**: A practice where team members collectively work on a high-priority task until it is complete.
- **Context**: Accelerates progress on critical items and fosters collaboration.

Sustainable Pace
- **Definition**: Maintaining a consistent, productive work rate that avoids burnout.
- **Context**: Encourages work-life balance and long-term productivity.

System Demo
- **Definition**: A demonstration of the combined work of all Agile teams in a program increment, typically held at the end of each iteration.
- **Context**: Provides stakeholders with visibility into progress and alignment across teams.

T

Team Velocity
- **Definition**: A measure of the average amount of work a team completes in a sprint, typically in story points.
- **Context**: Helps teams forecast capacity and set realistic sprint goals.

Technical Debt
- **Definition**: The accumulated cost of taking shortcuts in code quality to meet short-term goals.
- **Context**: In Agile, reducing technical debt is important to maintain software quality and prevent future challenges.

Test Case
- **Definition**: A set of conditions and steps used to verify that a specific feature or functionality works as expected.
- **Context**: Essential for ensuring software meets functional requirements and user expectations.

Test Coverage
- **Definition**: A metric that indicates the extent to which code is covered by tests.
- **Context**: High test coverage helps identify untested paths, ensuring software reliability.

Test-Driven Development (TDD)
- **Definition**: A development practice in which tests are written before the code, guiding the feature's implementation.
- **Context**: TDD ensures that functionality is tested from the start, supporting a test-first approach in Agile.

Test Pyramid
- **Definition**: A model that advocates for more low-level unit tests than high-level end-to-end tests.
- **Context**: Balances test types for optimal feedback speed, reliability, and cost-effectiveness.

Theme
- **Definition**: A collection of related user stories that contribute to a common goal.
- **Context**: Helps organize and prioritize features, aligning them with business objectives.

Three Amigos

- **Definition**: A collaboration technique where a developer, tester, and product owner discuss a user story's acceptance criteria.
- **Context**: Ensures a shared understanding of requirements, improving story clarity and alignment.

Timeboxing

- **Definition**: Setting a fixed time limit for an activity, after which it must end, regardless of completion.
- **Context**: Encourages focus and prioritization, helping teams avoid spending excessive time on any one task.

Tracer Bullet

- **Definition**: An approach where a simple, working version of a solution is implemented to explore the problem space.
- **Context**: Helps teams validate assumptions and refine requirements early in development.

U

User Acceptance Testing (UAT)

- **Definition**: Testing performed by end users to confirm if the software meets their needs and is ready for release.
- **Context**: Ensures the product aligns with user expectations before deployment.

User Persona

- **Definition**: A fictional character representing a segment of the target audience.
- **Context**: Helps the team understand user goals and pain points, informing design and development.

User Story

- **Definition**: A brief, user-centered description of a feature or functionality.
- **Context**: Guides development, providing context on what to build and why.

V

Value Stream Mapping

- **Definition**: A method to map all steps involved in delivering value to the customer.
- **Context**: Identifies inefficiencies, helping teams streamline processes.

Velocity

- **Definition**: A measure of the work a team can complete in a sprint, used for capacity planning.
- **Context**: Helps set realistic sprint goals based on past performance.

Vertical Slice

- **Definition**: A user story that includes work across all layers of an application, from UI to database.
- **Context**: Ensures end-to-end functionality is tested and demonstrated within a sprint.

W

Walkthrough
- **Definition**: A review session where a developer presents their work to the team for feedback.
- **Context**: Helps identify improvements and confirm alignment with requirements.

Waterfall Model
- **Definition**: A linear development model where all phases are completed sequentially.
- **Context**: Contrasts with Agile, often resulting in late discovery of defects and slower iterations.

Wireframe
- **Definition**: A visual representation of a UI's layout, focusing on structure and user flow.
- **Context**: Used in early design to map out user experience before development.

Work in Progress (WIP)
- **Definition**: Tasks currently in progress.
- **Context**: Limiting WIP reduces multitasking and enhances focus.

Work Item
- **Definition**: Any tracked piece of work, such as a user story, task, or bug.
- **Context**: Essential for Agile tracking and prioritizing efforts.

X

XP Practices
- **Definition**: Best practices from Extreme Programming, including pair programming and TDD.
- **Context**: XP practices enhance quality and foster team collaboration.

Z

Zero Defects
- **Definition**: An approach aiming to deliver defect-free code.
- **Context**: Emphasizes quality at every stage, prioritizing rigorous testing and high standards.

APPENDIX D: REFERENCES AND FURTHER READING

BOOKS

1. **"Agile Testing: A Practical Guide for Testers and Agile Teams"** by Lisa Crispin and Janet Gregory
   - Covers Agile testing concepts, including automation, continuous integration, and testing practices that align with Agile methodologies and in-sprint workflows.

2. **"Continuous Delivery: Reliable Software Releases through Build, Test, and Deployment Automation"** by Jez Humble and David Farley
   - A deep dive into CI/CD practices, emphasizing automation and deployment techniques that support Agile and in-sprint processes.

3. **"The Scaled Agile Framework (SAFe) Distilled: A Practical Guide to Scaling Agile in the Enterprise"** by Richard Knaster and Dean Leffingwell
   - Discusses the application of SAFe in large organizations, covering practices like Agile Release Trains, PI planning, and automation across teams, which are key to scaling in-sprint testing.

4. **"Leading SAFe® 5.0"** by Dean Leffingwell
   - Provides an in-depth look at implementing SAFe, including strategies for integrating in-sprint testing and automation across PI planning and iterations.

5. **"Test-Driven Development: By Example"** by Kent Beck
   - A must-read for TDD practitioners, offering practical insights into building tests alongside development, which is critical for successful in-sprint automation.

6. **"Cloud Native DevOps with Kubernetes"** by Justin Garrison and Kris Nova
   - A guide to cloud-native DevOps, CI/CD, and in-sprint automation practices using Kubernetes in cloud environments, relevant for Agile teams working with containerized setups.

ARTICLES AND RESEARCH PAPERS

1. **"Agile Software Development with SAFe"** by Dean Leffingwell
   - Explores SAFe practices, including Agile Release Trains and integrated automation for consistent testing across sprints and program increments.

2. **"Scaling Agile @ Spotify"**
   - Spotify's unique approach to Agile scaling, including how they integrate CI/CD and in-sprint automation practices to support multi-team environments.

3. **"Accelerate: State of DevOps Report"** by Google Cloud
   - An annual report that explores DevOps practices, focusing on CI/CD and in-sprint automation, based on research from high-performing software teams.

4. **"The Agile Manifesto"**
   - A foundational document for Agile principles, emphasizing values like adaptability and collaboration that guide Agile and in-sprint automation practices.

WEBSITES AND ONLINE RESOURCES

1. **Scaled Agile Framework (SAFe) – Official Site - www.scaledagileframework.com**
   - Offers comprehensive resources on SAFe, Agile Release Trains, and PI planning, with insights into implementing in-sprint automation at scale.

2. **AWS DevOps and CI/CD Resources - https://aws.amazon.com/devops/**
   - Provides guides for building CI/CD pipelines and supporting in-sprint automation through AWS services like CodePipeline and CodeBuild.

3. **Microsoft Azure DevOps Documentation - https://azure.microsoft.com/en-us/services/devops/**
   - Covers Azure DevOps services for version control, CI/CD, and automation tools that enhance Agile workflows and in-sprint testing.

4. **Google Cloud DevOps Solutions** - https://cloud.google.com/solutions/devops
   - CI/CD and testing tools for Agile and in-sprint automation, with support for Kubernetes and Google's cloud-native DevOps suite.

5. **BrowserStack - www.browserstack.com**
   - A cross-browser testing platform that provides access to real devices and browsers for automated testing, supporting in-sprint UI testing on a wide range of platforms.

6. **LambdaTest - www.lambdatest.com**
   - Offers automated cross-browser testing on a cloud-based platform, allowing in-sprint testing across multiple devices and browsers for rapid feedback.

7. **Jenkins Documentation - www.jenkins.io/doc**
   - Jenkins resources for setting up CI/CD pipelines, supporting in-sprint automation and workflow integration.

8. **Selenium Documentation - www.selenium.dev/documentation**
   - The official Selenium documentation for setting up and executing cross-browser UI tests within in-sprint workflows.

TOOLS AND FRAMEWORKS

1. **Selenium Grid**
   - Supports parallel execution of tests across different browsers and environments, a key enabler for rapid in-sprint automation and cross-browser compatibility.

2. **JUnit & TestNG**
   - Java-based testing frameworks widely used for TDD and BDD in CI/CD pipelines, facilitating in-sprint testing through integration with Jenkins and other CI tools.

3. **Docker**
   - A containerization platform for creating consistent test environments, enabling parallel testing and in-sprint deployment testing for Agile teams.

4. **Allure Reports**
   - A reporting tool that integrates with various test frameworks to produce detailed reports, aiding in-sprint test transparency and feedback during sprint reviews.

5. **AWS CodePipeline and CodeBuild**
   - AWS tools for automating CI/CD, which allow Agile teams to integrate in-sprint testing and deployment on a scalable cloud platform.

6. **Azure Pipelines**
   - A part of Azure DevOps that offers multi-platform CI/CD, supporting Agile teams with robust cloud-based in-sprint automation capabilities.

7. **Prometheus and Grafana**
   - Monitoring and visualization tools that track real-time metrics on CI/CD and in-sprint pipeline performance, providing critical feedback for iterative improvement.

8. **Google Cloud Build**
   - CI/CD tool for building, testing, and deploying applications on Google Cloud, ideal for in-sprint automation in Kubernetes environments.

ONLINE COURSES

1. **Coursera: "Agile Development Specialization" by the University of Virginia**
   - A series of courses that cover Agile fundamentals, SAFe, and CI/CD automation, with a focus on incorporating automation within sprints.

2. **AWS Certified DevOps Engineer – Professional** (Available on AWS Training)
   - Focuses on DevOps automation practices, CI/CD, and in-sprint automation on AWS, covering tools like CodePipeline and CodeBuild.

3. **Microsoft Azure DevOps Engineer Expert Certification**
   - Certification that covers Azure DevOps and CI/CD, essential for Agile teams adopting cloud-based, in-sprint automation workflows.

4. **Pluralsight: "Test Automation Foundations"**
   o Introduces test automation strategies and tools for Agile workflows, including in-sprint UI testing with cross-browser tools like BrowserStack and LambdaTest.

SUMMARY

These resources provide a robust foundation for understanding Agile testing, SAFe, CI/CD, and cross-browser testing. Including tools like BrowserStack and LambdaTest, this appendix equips readers with insights into cloud-based testing and automation, which are crucial for achieving reliable, scalable, and rapid feedback in Agile sprints.